A BRIEF
HISTORY OF
AMERICAN
CULTURE

ALSO BY ROBERT M. CRUNDEN

The Mind and Art of Albert Jay Nock

A Hero In Spite of Himself: Brand Whitlock In Art, Politics and War

From Self to Society, 1919–1941

Editor, *The Superfluous Men: Conservative Critics of American Culture,*
1900–1945

Ministers of Reform: The Progressives' Achievement in American Civilization,
1889–1920

Editor, *Traffic of Ideas Between India and America*

American Salons: Encounters with European Modernism, 1885–1917

A BRIEF
HISTORY OF
AMERICAN
CULTURE

Robert M. Crunden

NORTH CASTLE BOOKS

Armonk, New York
London, England

First paperback edition, 1996
Published in the United States by M. E. Sharpe, Inc.

Copyright © 1994 by Paragon House Publishers
Reprinted by special arrangement with Paragon House Publishers

Library of Congress Cataloging-in-Publication Data

Crunden, Robert Morse.
A brief history of American culture / Robert M. Crunden.
p.   cm.
"A North castle book."
Originally published: Helsinki : SHS, 1990.
Includes bibliographical references and index.
ISBN 1-56324-865-4 (pbk.)
1. United States—Civilization.
I. Title.
E169.1.C8358   1996
306'.0973—dc20
96-3536
CIP
Printed in the United States of America

The paper used in this publication meets the minimum requirements of
American National Standard for Information Sciences—
Permanence of Paper for Printed Library Materials,
ANSI Z 39.48-1984.

∞

EB (p)   10   9   8   7   6   5   4   3   2

North Castle Books
An imprint of M. E. Sharpe, Inc.

For Evelyn Anne Crunden and Rebecca Jane Crunden

Contents

PART IV
A National Culture, 1901–1941

PART V
A Cosmopolitan Culture, 1941–present

Preface

Culture can be a fighting word. For some it will always refer to the Victorian ideal of Matthew Arnold, of the best that has been thought and said in a given environment. More recent writers have rejected this view as literary and elitist and stressed a more anthropological notion of the complex behavior patterns of all people. I am not comfortable with either view, for neither seems to me to reflect what casual usage usually implies, especially casual usage outside the environment under analysis.

Several recent books have addressed the question without really settling anything. I would prefer to opt out of this kind of debate entirely, since in practice it too often reflects contemporary political concerns of the analysts without telling readers what they want to know. I define culture as creative achievements at any level: classical music as well as commercial innovation, much-admired novels as well as intricate thrillers. A cultural history is thus a record of the conditions that produced all kinds of innovation and of the behavior of individuals as they responded to those conditions.

The thesis this book argues is that American culture is essentially a peculiar mixture of Christianity, capitalism, and democracy, *in that order*. In terms of cultural influence, the dominant group of early settlers was puritan; so forceful were their personalities that they overpowered other influences, ranging from American Indians to Spanish missionaries. The practice of capitalism emerged under the domination of puritan religious values, and business long had religious sanction in ways that few European countries could or wanted to duplicate. Democratic practice emerged slowly, and in many ways democratic theory emerged from that practice. Few paid much formal attention to these processes as they evolved until the Revolution, during the 1770s and 1780s, forced everyone to rethink all aspects of American culture.

Among other accomplishments, the Civil War (1861–1865) fastened Northern religious, economic, and political ideas on a nation in no sense unanimous in accepting them. Such topics as "the Protestant ethic," "the American character," "social Darwinism," and so on usually derive from this threefold heritage. Competitive groups, whether Southern cavalier, Southwestern Spanish, California

Oriental, or European immigrant, have often challenged this dominant culture, but they have had to do so from the position of outsider. No one at the time questioned which cultural values predominated, even though many questioned their validity or beneficence. Since World War II things have become noticeably different, and historians have become much more careful in phraseology and capacity for generalization. But it needs stressing that while many peoples and values now constitute American democracy, the institutional framework for that democracy was set long ago, when the dominant cultural forces were at least outwardly more homogeneous.

The book also has a chronological organization that interacts with the thematic. It has five parts; although the dating is only approximate, the discussion often ranges outside the announced boundaries, and the emphasis may at first glance seem odd. The first part, from the beginnings to 1815, is the period of local culture. Settlements depended chiefly on England, not on each other; the indigenous activity that did occur developed from local adaptations of imported ideas, and intracontinental communications were poor. The American Revolution and its aftermath did much to forge a sense of national unity at the very top, but few people were aware of themselves as anything more than citizens of Newport or Charleston on a daily basis. The local communities of greatest creativity were Boston, from 1630 until the revolutionary turmoil of the 1770s; Philadelphia, from the beginning of the Age of Franklin around 1740 until the ascension of President Jefferson in 1801; and Virginia, that collection of localities without a center but symbolized by the Virginia dynasty in the White House from the inauguration of George Washington through the Peace of Ghent, with a dull afterglow of influence lingering into the 1820s with the Monroe administration.

The country was a sectional culture from 1815 until the inauguration of Theodore Roosevelt in 1901. It is the subject of two parts, one on the period when the North was distinct from the South and West, and a second one that examines in more detail the aspects of Northern culture which became national. The fighting of the second war against England and the events leading up to the first Missouri Compromise brought a new generation to prominence. Henry Clay, Daniel Webster, and John C. Calhoun clearly represented sections rather than cities, and in time the sections became identified with the acceptance or rejection of the institution of slavery. The key question became: Would Northern capitalism and individualism conquer the opening West, or would slavery, with all its economic, religious, and moral consequences, dominate? Whoever won would effectively control the country and the culture. The North won, and its efforts at reconstruction kept the South subordinate until 1877; economically, it remained subordinate for generations. Social Darwinism, pragmatism, the Gospel of Wealth, and so on are thus sectional concepts that became "American" because the North won the war.

Theodore Roosevelt was the first president to have been too young to have the war shape his consciousness. Both Northern and Southern by parentage, he was viscerally American in outlook and so were his successors; in this case the presidents were emblematic of the larger consensus. Thus from 1901 until American entry into World War II in 1941 was the period of national culture. A provincial country could finally take itself for granted and seek some place for itself in the community of nations. Major artists like Frank Lloyd Wright and Charles Ives matured within the Protestant tradition, while artists from other backgrounds also emerged: Eugene O'Neill from Roman Catholicism, Gertrude Stein from Judaism. Black jazz musicians became role models for both black and white Americans, and by the end of the period a few jazz bands were actually integrated, even if audiences frequently remained segregated. The upper echelons of the New Deal clearly demonstrated that so-called minority groups, gathered together, were becoming the majority. Jews sat on the Supreme Court, a Roman Catholic ran the majority political party, and a black rose to a high if token position in the army. The country was clearly moving even if it had a long way to go toward full integration.

The Second World War so thoroughly speeded this process up that it seems accurate to call the period since 1941 that of a cosmopolitan culture. Blacks and Japanese-Americans suffered greatly during the 1940s, but as time went on the nation felt increasingly guilty about its behavior to both races, and the advances in civil rights during the 1950s and 1960s were a clear expression of a determination that the time had come to live up to the nation's professed ideals. People of all ethnic backgrounds began to glorify their roots rather than to evade them. A Roman Catholic became president, a black sat on the Supreme Court, and Jews in economics and literature won Nobel Prizes. At the top, if not always at the local country club, anything seemed possible. In addition to this meritocratic environment, talented foreigners in significant numbers arrived during the Nazi era, and many stayed. Their arrival ended any sense that America was inferior, and the results of their labors were crucial to American achievement from the teaching of art history to the development of the hydrogen bomb. Foreign policy assumed unprecedented importance, and in time was directed by Americans with names like Kissinger and Brzezinski. Americans read the morning paper and worried about Berlin, Nicaragua, and Tiananman Square; they came home from work to see their favorite television personalities comment on the Cuban missile crisis, the oil situation in Riyadh, or the war in Vietnam. The whole world had come to America, and Americans seemed determined to investigate that world personally as well as politically. This all represented a vast change from the early seventeenth century.

Acknowledgments

This book has evolved over a number of years, in several countries. It began as a series of lectures given in Helsinki in 1976 and repeated in Tampere, Finland. On subsequent terms spent teaching abroad, at the University of Würzburg in Germany, at La Trobe University in Australia, and at the American Studies Research Centre in Hyderabad, India, I worked up additional materials. In essence, I was trying to make one brief volume that would answer the most pressing questions foreigners asked me about American culture. The results were published in 1990 by the Finnish Historical Society. Shortly thereafter I returned to Helsinki for another year, and so I had a fresh opportunity to profit from criticisms in making this revised and expanded edition for American readers. It incorporates numerous small editorial changes as well as new sections, most obviously on American culture since the middle of the twentieth century.

I have profited from dozens of colleagues and a great many students and friends in determining which subjects were important. In Helsinki, I must especially mention Jerker Eriksson, Markku Henriksson, Aura Korppi-Tommola, Marjatta Hietala, Keijo Virtanen, and Rauno Endén; in Würzburg, Gerhard Hoffmann, Alfred Hornung, Hartwig Isernhagen, and Rüdiger Kunow; at La Trobe, John Salmon, Alan Frost, Bill Breen, and Rhys Isaac; in Hyderabad, Prafulla Kar, Manoj Joshi, and Isaac Sequeira, not to mention all the participants in our seminars, most notably those who appear in the volume I edited, *Traffic of Ideas between India and America*, and those who contributed to the volumes of the *Indian Journal of American Studies*, which I edited. Foreign scholars of America get little recognition for their efforts, and only a small amount of their work gets into print even locally. This book is in many senses a product of their talk, which is where much of real history lies anyway.

In Austin, I have to thank Mike Cable, who found errors in one of the jazz analyses and corrected them with his personal experience, and Janice Bradley, who reduced several messy foreign typescripts to disc form. Rauno Endén oversaw the printing of the first edition, and without him the book would not be here. Peter Coveney offered one of the most thoughtful critiques I have ever received from an editor, and I also have to thank the three anonymous outside readers for their suggestions in Americanizing this second edition.

R.M.C.

Helsinki/Port Lorne/Austin, 1992

Prologue

England at the End of the Sixteenth Century

The most important single fact about American civilization is that it began in England as a revolutionary religious and political movement. This conjunction of British background, political means and religious ends proved capable of survival in a wilderness, and of dominance over a large geographical area. The essential characteristics of American economic behavior and artistic endeavor stem from these origins. Often challenged, they proved capable of overpowering alternative ways of expression to set a cultural tone accepted in most quarters as "American" until well into the twentieth century.

American civilization began in the England of Queen Elizabeth I. The final decades of the sixteenth century were a period of intense religious turmoil in England. Protestants in the London area backed the new queen, but pockets of Roman Catholic loyalty still remained throughout the less densely settled areas of the country. The queen and most of her citizens agreed that the religion of the monarch should be the religion of the country, but no one knew precisely how willing some citizens might be to oppose a monarch whose faith they detested. Elizabeth was not herself much interested in theology. She wished above all to remain on the throne and her statecraft was aimed at survival rather than doctrinal purity. She was willing to tolerate a certain amount of dissent so long as it seemed to dissipate revolutionary fervor. She seemed to know intuitively that the British people were traditionally not doctrinaire, and that if left alone they would not normally support a strong challenge to legitimate authority.

In terms of the future American settlement, the left-wing critics of the queen were the most significant. These were the people who were convinced that the Reformation had not gone far enough and who found Elizabeth's tolerance a dangerous trifling with God's plan for the world. They found everywhere remnants of Roman Catholicism and wished to purge the nation of the church's

dogma, ritual, and political influence. Because of this wish for further purifica-
tion of the church these radicals were called puritans. They were not a group
totally out of favor. Some of them remained close to the throne and others were
influential in the government and the upper social circles. As long as they
exercised a certain discretion, they could talk and act largely as they pleased. A
man might lose a university position or a comfortable pulpit for his dissent but
prison sentences or executions were rare and resorted to only with zealots
determined to martyr themselves.

The center of puritan feeling around 1750 was Cambridge University. Occasional lecturers there were preaching that God had been very specific in the
scriptures about what a church government should be like. God did not want an
episcopacy like that existing in England, with a monarch ruling through appointed bishops. Instead, God wanted a presbyterian structure, in which independent congregations each could elect their own ministers; then these
ministers would in turn elect leaders for the church as a whole. These leaders
then could determine doctrinal orthodoxy and give organizational unity to the
entire church. Such an arrangement would of course do away with bishops
appointed by the queen, and thus do away with the power of the queen over
church affairs. Indeed, given the possibly central role of these churches in the
daily life of the people, a presbyterian model of church government would also
provide a kind of local veto on acts of the central government.

Preachers who asked for these changes received just enough persecution to
give themselves feelings of martyrdom without the necessity of jail, exile, or
death. The result was a peculiar pattern of growth: Puritanism flourished
secretly and sometimes generated peculiar notions. No one was capable of
exercising doctrinal authority and no one assumed responsibility for an established institution. Schismatic ideas could grow; the Bible being an imprecise and
metaphorical book, untutored readers proved capable of reading it in a bewildering variety of ways. A charismatic leader only needed to disagree with an
orthodox doctrine, find a few followers in his local area, and a new heresy came
into being.

The major body of puritans and the one most important for American civilization did not wish to leave the orthodox church; they were "non-separatists."
Somewhat further to the left were a group of "separatists" who frankly did want
to leave the church and establish their own independent congregation. Also
known as "independents," the separatists usually wished to limit church memberships more strictly to those saints who had achieved a genuine religious
conversion. They also wanted their local churches to be as independent as
possible of presbyters or other outside restrictions, enabling the maximum
amount of local autonomy. Still further to the left were groups of radicals, each
with its own leader and doctrine. William Bradford's colony at Plymouth was one
of the best-known of these groups. Some of them, like the Baptists in Rhode

Island and Quakers in Pennsylvania, proved to be far more important in America than they could possibly have been in England.

These religious disputes also set important precedents for American creative achievement in the arts. The first and most important art form for the colonies was the sermon. The art of preaching had cut itself off from the tastes of the common Christian in England. A few Anglican preachers like Lancelot Andrewes and John Donne perfected an ornate style of preaching full of wit, simile, and metaphor. They might discourse about the authority of the church or the crown, or retell the story of Christianity. Any modern scholar remains impressed by the depth of learning they displayed. But to a plain, uneducated church member, such performances were all meaningless. Puritans demanded that preachers go back to an appeal comprehensible to a mass audience.

Often deprived of pulpit and professorship for their views, puritans frequently made a living as professional speakers to audiences who felt they had no place within the established church. In the process the dissenters came to emphasize a plain style that would not put literary excellence in the place of moral content. They might occasionally launch into a homely metaphor, but chiefly they developed a sermon form that set precedents for all the arts in early America. They wanted a sermon that stated a biblical text and a clear doctrine derived from that text, developed this theme through a few key examples, and then applied the idea to local circumstances. An Anglican might develop doctrine into an object of beauty and all but forget its application. A puritan stated the doctrine abruptly and then went on at length about the application. In effect, the "art" for a puritan was in the simple expression of a moral idea. Aesthetic beauty of expression thus became something identified with orthodoxy—possibly papist in tendency, but certainly a political as well as a moral threat. Roman Catholics appealed to the religious emotions of the Christian with their vestments, their incense, their statues, their hymns, and their words. The Church of England might have done away with the pope and portions of the ritual and "priestcraft," but essentially it still attracted the Christian to the Archbishop of Canterbury and the queen through the senses— a political as well as a religious attraction and thus doubly dangerous. The peculiarly puritan attitude toward the arts which dominated much of America for generations began in this way. The beauty of a work of art had nothing to do with style, tone, color, or sense impressions. The beauty was in the moral or the message of the work. A poem, a painting, a hymn, a statue: all could be judged in an essentially similar fashion. The puritan "plainstyle" became an American assumption about any aesthetic expression.

These religious arguments had a number of important corollaries for the American experience. The puritans were at least implicitly democratic in their orientation. They belittled educational and literary skills and emphasized the clarity of the message to everyman. If the mind of the average Christian was the target of the preaching, and if that Christian could vote for the preacher and have God bless the results of that vote, then that man was essentially the equal of the finest aristocrat. Modern liberalism was in no sense the goal of puritans, yet the seeds of liberalism were indeed implicit in their whole stance. Elizabeth and her successors were correct in seeing their challenge as a political threat.

Puritanism also deserves treatment sociologically and economically. Many of the ambitious, intelligent young people found that they had no obvious future in the England of 1600. The church was no longer the vehicle to wealth and status that it had been and no modern system of business and professional opportunities had yet developed. In effect, England was educating a discontented white-collar proletariat, able and yet placeless. Such men proved articulate and full of grievances and puritan pressures provided them with an outlet for nonreligious frustrations. They could become itinerant preachers, living by their wits and profiting from religious discontent even when not especially religious themselves. They often found that men of wealth and status who were opposed to the crown for reasons of their own might join them for specific protests. In effect, an opposition with a religious name and core could easily be a political alliance of many groups, each with its own grievance.

Soon after the accession of James I (1603–1625), the path to American settlement became clear. James proved both literal-minded and intolerant, suppressed the kind of dissent that Elizabeth had permitted and actually burned the last two heretics in English history. By this time, however, puritanism had had a good forty years in which to flower. Instead of suppressing it, James' persecution simply enraged a well-established group. For related reasons economic rivalry intensified as well, men felt increasingly alienated from the social system, and preachers took advantage of the discontent to become even more radical and outspoken. In his attempt to unify the church and the crown, James succeeded only in uniting them in the eyes of those most hostile to himself and his archbishop. In effect, he caused puritans to hate him because they hated his church. Puritanism thus came into a battle that united much of the gentry, business community, and independent artisans with the religious dissidents, in opposition to crown, bishops, and aristocracy.

The man who forced events beyond the point of tolerance was Archbishop William Laud, who became the most significant villain in puritan eyes. An able man, Laud took all too seriously the idea that church and state should work as one to save souls. He was willing to censor, jail, and execute in his pursuit of his goals. At the same time he revitalized the established church, reestablished higher standards of clerical behavior, and rebuilt decayed churches. Intellectually, he also helped to define the orthodox position as one of his means for fighting off the puritan challenge.

He and his later American Episcopal Church followers argued that the Christian church was unitary throughout the world, however much difference in practice might separate worshipers at a local level. If a person believed that God existed and had revealed his word in the scriptures; if a person believed in the atonement and resurrection of Christ and the indwelling of the Holy Ghost, then the rest of Christian doctrine did not matter that much. Over the years, the Church of England established itself as one of the most liberal and even apathetic of churches—"God's frozen people" as the old joke put it—but in this early phase it worked up quite a passion in defense of these ideas and the very real power of the bishops and king.

However unattractive he appears in puritan polemics, Laud was essentially correct. He may have been rigid and dogmatic as well, but he perceived the threat to his power posed by the puritan alliance. Not only was much of the puritan message inherently democratic, it had elements which modern students would call populistic and even fascistic. In the hands of Cambridge-educated intellectuals, such dangers were remote, although developing a speaking style appropriate for uneducated audiences and demanding them all to convert and then to vote for their ministers were dangerous enough. But given a volatile situation and a text open to many interpretations, it was only a matter of time before one of those who had converted decided that he should also be a leader. He might even decide that education unfitted a man for leadership and that only a mind unspoiled by the institutions of this corrupt world was fit to lead people to God. The seeds of anti-intellectualism were present in puritanism as well as those of democracy. Such tendencies remained in the American tradition, where they broke out over the years to vex the educated, the elite, and the wealthy.

The situation became impossible under Charles I (1625–1649). Less tactful and more dogmatic than James, he took a certain glee in tormenting puritans. He insisted that he ruled by divine right and that all who opposed him opposed the will of God. Since a puritan usually wanted to believe in his king almost as much as he believed in his God, Charles' course placed the puritans in an excruciating dilemma. Their God and their king seemed to be mortal enemies. If they obeyed their God, their king might torture, jail, and otherwise deprive them of their rights. If they obeyed their king, they clearly risked eternal damnation and for many of them a permanent hell seemed worse than an earthly jail. Neither alternative was especially attractive, and escape to America was one of the few plausible ways of dealing with the situation.

PART I

A LOCAL CULTURE
1630–1815

Chapter 1

Boston, 1630–1776

John Winthrop was the most important political figure to make the transition to America. Born into the gentry in 1588, educated in Cambridge, he succeeded easily into the position expected of him: marriage in his own class, legal studies leading to a justice of the peace position, an apprenticeship in the managing of family lands. Yet despite this outward conformity and comfort, Winthrop had achieved an intense religious conversion and deeply wished to remake the world to meet puritan demands. With Winthrop as with so many puritans, it is impossible to separate religious, economic, and social motivations. By 1629 England as a whole was sinking economically into a depressed period and Winthrop seriously doubted that he could retain for long the position he already possessed. He was forty years old; three wives had provided him with eight children and he doubted their economic as well as their religious future under Charles I and Laud. The group that wished to form what became the Massachusetts Bay Company recognized his ability, asked him to join, and quickly came to recognize him as their leader. The trip might well cause further financial loss, but it also seemed likely to save the immortal souls of his children. In 1630, he and 1,000 puritans sailed from England and arrived just to the north of modern Boston several months later.

The first important contribution to American political thinking was Winthrop's sermonlike address, "A Model of Christian Charity," which he gave to his fellow passengers on the way over. Their society had a collective covenant with God. Every one was bound together by love and each should expect to bear one another's burdens as well as to tolerate a conformity stricter than anything they had known in England. If his fellow Christians lived up to this covenant, then God would be among them and they would serve the world as an example of a Christian nation in action. Their settlement would be a "city on a hill," to use the modern sense and spelling of a phrase that became absolutely central for understanding the civilization of the American nation. "We must consider that we shall be as a city upon a hill, the eyes of all people are upon us; so that if we

3

shall deal falsely with our god in this work we have undertaken and so cause him to withdraw his present help from us, we shall be made a story and a by-word through the world." The document marked the beginning of American exceptionalism and gave the colony a foreign policy even before it had a town. America as a civilization was founded to fulfill God's intentions and thus peculiarly set apart to provide the rest of the world with guidance. The religious, economic, and political practices thus were to be an example to everyone, even those who were not Christian.

Strictly speaking, the government developed in the colony was not a theocracy, since the clergy were not themselves magistrates. But the ties of church and state could hardly have been closer. Those regarded by the community as saints, or converted Christians, gathered themselves into small groups and elected their ministers—many of whom had already been ordained in England but who were legitimized by this process. Winthrop, already named governor in London, organized a political structure by admitting over 100 planters to the franchise, but thereafter limited the vote to saints. Thus, in effect, the colony functioned democratically but was democratic only for those who earlier church members had accepted as converted. Winthrop proved dictatorial, keeping rigid social control over deviant behavior and punishing or expelling those given to disobedience, frivolity, or heresy.

Winthrop's period as governor, which lasted almost twenty years with occasional interruptions, set precedents for his successors. The key event that illuminates many of these precedents was the argument which Winthrop had with the people of Hingham in 1645. He had tried to make them accept a militia captain whom they did not want and he found their reluctance "mutinous and seditious." In the court action that followed, he won only the smallest of majorities for his views, yet used the occasion to lay down the law. The great questions that troubled the country, he told them, were about the authority of the magistrates and the liberty of the people. He insisted that people had elected him to his position and that "being called by you, we have our authority from God." His logic duplicated the logic used to justify the process of electing the preacher. Once a magistrate or a preacher were legitimately installed in office, God intervened to bless the election. The people had to obey the official and had no right to challenge his decisions. He was a flawed man like anyone else and would make mistakes. Only if he were guilty of bad faith could he be challenged. If the case were in any way doubtful, "yourselves must bear it."

Such a view was intensely conservative. However radical the puritans seemed in opposition to England, in power in America they felt most comfortable in an authoritarian democracy. The right of rebellion, so recently exercised by the puritans themselves, was forbidden. In effect, the divine right of kings was replaced by the divine right of minister and magistrate. "Liberty" turned out to have two discrete meanings: "natural liberty" to behave as an animal, uncivilized and non-Christian; and "civil liberty," or the right to obey freely chosen magistrates the way any converted Christian did normally. American puritans had "a liberty to that only which is good, just and honest." In an illuminating example, he compared the proper citizen to the proper wife: Just as the wife chose the husband freely but had then to obey him and put up with his vagaries, so must a citizen choose his minister and magistrate and then live with the results. Such was the will of God and such was the beginning of American ideas of liberty.

II

While John Winthrop was establishing the key political attitudes, John Cotton was formulating the key religious doctrines. The son of a struggling puritan lawyer, Cotton attended Cambridge and came to Boston to be the teacher of the new church there. As teacher, Cotton was the arbiter of puritan doctrine and from him the puritans heard in detail about the covenanted status of their church. Cotton frequently appeared inconsistent in his doctrines, seemingly radical one minute yet compromising the next. Essentially, he argued that man was hopelessly incapable of earning eternal life. The only thing that he had to offer God was his faith and good intentions. John Calvin might insist that man was irredeemably wicked and could not possibly deserve anything from God, but like most English puritans Cotton believed that the world was more rational than that and that God was not entirely a mystery to man. One could never be sure what God would do, but a resident of Boston who felt he had experienced conversion and lived a blameless life in all probability had received God's grace and would enjoy life everlasting. This covenant of grace became the core of puritan religious teaching and living up to its demands the most important duty of a citizen.

In England, Cotton had been a radical persecuted by Archbishop Laud; in America he became a conservative even among fellow puritans. In the spectrum that ran from a Calvinist emphasis on man's total depravity to an eighteenth-century unitarian emphasis on man's reason and ability to earn salvation by good works, Cotton was far closer to the first than to the second. He tended, most of the time, to stress man's utter depravity and inability to deserve much of anything from God. The problem in such a context is what a poor Christian is expected to do. If he is totally depraved and capable of nothing, if God's will is mysterious and unpredictable, then a man could ask with some justice why he should do anything. If going to church, being moral, and obeying the minister did not help him to deserve God's approval, he seemingly had full license to do as he pleased on earth. Cotton sincerely believed that a covenant of works that permitted men to work their way to heaven, opened the door to Roman Catholicism, universalism, and other horrors too terrible to contemplate. If a man could sin happily, confess, and be forgiven, then church discipline meant little; the community rapidly became immoral; and the devil reigned. Only in a prelapsarian society could such a covenant of works be plausible.

The dangers inherent in Cotton's doctrine appeared clearly in the mind of his devoted disciple, Anne Hutchinson. Born into the family of a dissenting minister, Hutchinson transcended the normally passive role of an Englishwoman to become one of the more learned of the colonists on biblical issues. She could also be rigid, naive, and censorious. John Winthrop unsurprisingly found her "fierce" and disliked her "ready wit." In England, she had married the rather pliant businessman William Hutchinson, and the union produced fifteen children in twenty-two years. Displaying remarkable physical vitality, Hutchinson not only pursued religious ideas zealously, she became an accomplished nurse and midwife—a profession which enabled her to visit many people. In comforting them she spread her own version of what John Cotton preached. For John Cotton became the great authority figure in her life and no matter what controversy she found herself in, she insisted that she was following the preaching of the most popular religious teacher in the colony.

Theologically, she was different from Cotton in two key respects. John Cotton believed that, being human, a saint could sin. Anne Hutchinson insisted that, being a saint, he could not sin by definition. Cotton insisted that men were patterned after Christ. Hutchinson insisted that a saint was of the same substance as Christ. From these basic differences she developed the Antinomian heresy. She insisted that being a saint, she was of the same substance as Christ and could not sin, and that the Holy Ghost spoke directly to her and guided her actions. To an orthodox puritan these were unacceptable ideas which verged on Godless anarchy. If the Holy Ghost spoke directly to saints, then magistrates and clergy had no power over them and the whole rationale of the covenanted colony collapsed.

Hutchinson was highly critical of many of her fellow citizens and regarded them as believers in a covenant of works. But perhaps more to the point was the economic substructure of much of the controversy that resulted. Most of those who followed Hutchinson were merchants like her husband or in loosely related areas. At the time, agricultural groups, sure that inflation was hurting their interests and that capitalists were usurious price-gougers, were attacking them. Preachers and magistrates tended to side with the farmers and one way for the merchants to rebel against this assault was to follow Hutchinson. For them, their wealth and success were signs of God's approval and not something that earthly institutions should control. God had granted them grace and wealth was its outward and visible sign. Winthrop was outraged and in the resulting trial he was both prosecutor and judge, banishing Hutchinson from the colony and establishing the persecution of dissenters as one of the many legacies he left to the nation. His own church was hostile to him on this issue, however, and he found it necessary to establish as well that the acts of a magistrate could not be censured by a church. In so doing, he set an important precedent for the separation of church and state in America. The demands of the law had to be followed regardless of the demands of a church, assuming always the good intentions of the magistrate.

For Hutchinson, the court's decision proved to be a delayed death sentence. She went briefly to Rhode Island, always a haven for dissenters, and then into the New York area in a place technically under Dutch control. In 1643, rampaging Indians tomahawked her and five of her children to death.

III

Anne Hutchinson deserves mention because she was the first woman of importance in America. In a masculine environment she became a charismatic figure even for many males in the business community. With the other great dissenter in Massachusetts Bay, the situation was more theoretical but the personal impact was even more striking.

Roger Williams was in many ways the most compelling puritan in American history. Despite his obsessive radicalism and unwillingness to compromise, his personality was so charming and his abilities so obvious that people sometimes seemed to follow him insensibly, as if they did not perceive the seditiousness of his thought. Educated for the ministry at Cambridge, he arrived in Boston in 1631 and began acting as he always would: he was so impressive a person that he was offered one of the most important positions in the Boston church, yet he refused to take it because he felt that that church was not pure enough and not separate enough from English churches. He also felt that its members had not expressed adequate repentence for their former ties to the Church of England. This was more than merely personal extremism. Roger Williams was in the process of becoming the most ardent and perceptive advocate of the separation of church and state before Thomas Jefferson. He could see no reason why the crown should ever have authority over something so important as the souls of men. For him, the state defiled the church and the church needed to retain distance and independence from all earthly, political influences. He was in fact the exact opposite of the way he sometimes sounds to modern ears. No liberal, he was a perfectionist puritan, unwilling to compromise church purity in any way. Not for over one hundred years would more liberal arguments insist that church and state should be separate so that the church would not corrupt the state.

Despite being a personal friend, John Winthrop could not tolerate the consequences of Williams' thought. Winthrop may well have wanted the churches separate enough from the state so that they were unable to discipline him as chief magistrate, but he was quite willing to have clerical influence supreme in the colony and to use the state to punish heresy, blasphemy, and other religious crimes. Williams moved from Boston to Salem to Plymouth to Rhode Island, seeking a haven for his views. He was soon insisting that the state should compel no one to attend church, because the presence of non-saints in a church defiled it. Because "Christenings make not Christians" a man had to experience his own genuine conversion and thus even baptized children of saints should not be present in a covenanted church. He came as well to doubt the genuineness of the conversion of anyone but himself and his wife and preferred to worship alone or with her. No one could possibly institutionalize such a man and in his own way he has come to typify the frequent anarchy that seems inherent in many Americans. Just as John Winthrop represents the authoritarian democrat defining liberty as the right to follow his laws, so Roger Williams represents the individualist democrat, unsure of anyone but himself and forced by the rigor of his conscience to go it alone.

The secular consequences were many. Williams opposed the swearing of oaths, convinced that these took the name of the Lord in vain and that non-saints all too easily swore them hypocritically. He came out against some of the acquisitive land policies of Winthrop and the elite and insisted that land be set aside for the poor and newly arrived. He denounced the wealth of certain individuals and insisted that economic divisions were inappropriate to a godly colony. Cotton, setting precedents that many Americans followed over the next three centuries, assumed that the gaining of wealth was just reward for pursuing a godly calling, and that while a puritan should not enjoy his wealth and live luxuriously, he could take it as an outward symbol of his presumptive sainthood. Williams preferred the spirit of Christ's life and thought a poor carpenter more likely to enter heaven than a wealthy landowner.

Williams' restless mind led him also into Indian studies and he became the first American anthropologist and linguist. When banished from Massachusetts Bay and Salem, he made his long trip to Rhode Island in the middle of winter on foot. Had he not had help from friendly Indians he might well have died. Williams could befriend almost anyone and he repaid his debt to these Indians for the rest of his life—the only white man they trusted in many cases. In addition to making peace, he compiled the first guide to Indian customs and language, a volume good enough to make a scholarly impact in England as well as a practical impact on colony–Indian relations.

Under his leadership Rhode Island developed into something resembling a genuine democracy. No one had to go to church; non-saints could hold office; Sabbath-breaking was not a crime; tax money did not pay ministers; women enjoyed many civil rights; church and state were separate in spirit as well as technical fact; land policy was reasonably egalitarian. Heads of households, regardless of saintly status, and new immigrants could vote once they had settled into colonial life. Terms of office were short and rotated frequently so that no one became a ruler like Winthrop. Towns had some local control to avoid laws they did not wish to adopt. Gentlemen explicitly had to face the same punishments for crimes as the poor—in contrast to Massachusetts Bay. Prisons were less brutal and fewer acts were crimes. Death was not as common a penalty. The mutilations, whipping, branding, and ear-chopping, so favored in Massachusetts Bay for penalizing people like the Rhode Islanders, almost completely ceased.

Williams and his colony thus demonstrated one ironical way in which a modern sensibility could come to life in America. Motivated by religious extremism, combining both charm and fanaticism, he came to toleration because he felt that no man and no government could safely judge the religious status of another, and a man's religious condition was the most important thing in his life. The colony he produced looked deceptively like a prelude to the Enlightenment, and perhaps it was in a paradoxical way. His stance was neither liberalism nor apathy. It was an example of religious intentions having secular and unintended results. That was a true lesson for America and remains an essential part of understanding the American experience. If God had intended to found a secular democracy in America, surely his first attribute was a sense of humor. Williams' intentions died out in the hands of his successors, but the seeds of American secularism remained inherent in the puritan experience.

IV

John Winthrop's death in 1649 marked a convenient end to the power of the first generation in Massachusetts Bay. Individual members lived on throughout the next two decades, but they were the first to declare that the colony was in a state of declension and apathy. The zeal that had fired the immigrants no longer fired their children, growing up as they did in a colony isolated from the English civil wars and reasonably secure for the congregational way. These children commonly received baptism, yet such was the peace and quiet of their lives that few later worked up the energy to have a conversion. Harvard College, founded during the first decade of the settlement, was little more than a dogmatic academy designed to indoctrinate the young in puritan ideas. Far from being a city on a hill to guide the world to a Christian commonwealth, Massachusetts Bay became merely a forgotten colonial outpost, so unimportant to Europe that even its enormous presumption was unworthy of notice. In any such society, elders sense the decay and stress the legal enforcement of manners and morals—when internal faith is weak, legal power must be strong. Formality replaces intensity; a sense of history replaces a sense of current importance. Where early puritans thought their greatest dangers came from Archbishop Laud, Quakers, or Roman Catholics, subsequent puritan generations worried about drunkenness, dancing, and adultery. Sin became synonymous with social disorder.

One example can stand for many. Lack of conversions presented the church with an agonizing dilemma. If it refused to accept prosperous and useful citizens as saints and voters, it automatically reduced its own power and prestige and implicitly recognized that sanctity and earthly reward were not connected. If the church accepted such citizens and retained its social prestige, then it watered down its own doctrine and went perilously close to theological hypocrisy in its efforts at compromise. The puritans may have been ideologically doctrinaire but they were not politically foolish and after much controversy they institutionalized a compromise. They lowered the requirements for sainthood and began accepting those who lived blameless lives and who claimed to be converted Christians. In effect, this compromise opened the door for people to join the church who merely assented to a certain style of living, who in effect performed good works and did not offend anyone. In the Half-Way Convenant, 1662, they further decided that the baptized children of saints could achieve partial membership in the church, and their children as well. But no one could vote or receive the sacrament unless he claimed conversion and was accepted as a saint by his predecessors. By the late seventeenth century church practice was no longer uniform, however, and deviations developed that marked the end of puritan unanimity even in theory.

Increasingly, the puritans took on the censorious image so popular in later history books. Originally a highly intelligent, well-educated, bibulous, and sexually uninhibited lot, fascinating for all their idiosyncracies, they became all too frequently the killjoys of colonial life. They enacted countless blue laws, forbidding anything that seemed likely to give pleasure or encourage dissidence. They outlawed public drunkenness and Sabbath-breaking, forbade singing and dancing in public places, and gave fathers astonishing power over their families. They forbade most of the more imaginative sexual activities. Social classes slowly hardened and a kind of puritan tribalism settled on the land. Just as the magistrate was the stern father of the community, so the biological father was the magistrate of the small unit. Young people and even unrelated itinerants were expected to associate with established families until they could form their own. Each of these families held daily prayers that included servants and guests. Religion excused a great inquisitiveness into the lives of other families—if anyone escaped this discipline, the community might disintegrate. Squabbles over land distribution became more common than squabbles over doctrine and by the end of the century Americans were well on their way to their reputation as being one of the most litigious peoples on earth.

The family of Increase and Cotton Mather provides posterity with examples of the concerns of the colonial leadership. Increase was one of the innovators of the jeremiad, the sermon form that developed in this period as a means of bewailing the loss of virtue in a covenanted commonwealth. While to any visitors from Europe life in Boston appeared decorous to the point of collective social neurosis, Mather found "great Sensuality" in his flock for its lamentable habit of going "to haunt Taverns" and to "squander away precious hours, many days in publick houses" which had better be spent "in Meditation, Secret Prayer and Self Examination." He was especially offended by "strange Apparel," where "the haughty Daughters of Zion" could be seen "with their Borders and False Locks and such like whorish fashion," and where men wore "monstrous and horried Perriwigs." Such sermons could also be tribal rituals: a preacher could condemn all those who were not in his audience, thus comforting those who were with a specious sense of virtue, superiority, and separateness from those so unfortunate as to have been born non-saints.

A more cosmopolitan figure than many in his generation, Increase lived for much of his early career in Ireland and England while the puritans were in power, but persecutions after the Restoration drove him back to America to become teacher of the Second Boston church. For two decades after 1676, he found himself in a running battle to protect the charter of his colony from attempts in England to change it radically. The British wanted more control over the colony, less connection between the Congregational church and the state, less severe laws regulating family and church practice, a more open ballot, and more of a place for the Church of England. In 1688 he returned to England to fight his battle, and at least in part because of the British Revolution he managed to negotiate a charter he thought he could live with. It eliminated the popular right to elect the governor and made him a royal appointee; it gave the king a veto over local laws. The governor became commander of the militia and appointed its officers. He also appointed judges for colonial courts and controlled naval affairs, the post office and the customs house. The colony gained local control over taxes and many functioning legal procedures which had never been formalized were made so. Land titles were guaranteed, the vote freed, and toleration proclaimed for all but extreme Protestants and Roman Catholics. Here, as elsewhere in American history, democracy and toleration developed not because of any feelings of liberalism and the beneficence of freedom, but because of competing zealotries. The clash of fanaticisms was slowly producing the tolerance of fanatics.

While Increase was in England his son Cotton faced the crisis of his life. In 1692 a group of children in Salem apparently were tormented by the devil. In a manner known to Christians in Europe for centuries they identified the forms of the people tormenting them. People made the usual assumption that each person thus used by the devil was a witch. Many puritans felt that America had been the devil's country before their arrival and that he was making a comeback. They did not doubt their right to try such people and put to death those convicted, in accordance with long-standing Christian practice. From England,

Increase counseled prudence and skepticism about the charges, but his thirty-year-old son went along with the crowd and twenty persons were executed. Himself a hysteric with personal problems for which he blamed the devil, Cotton surely offered his advice to the magistrates and may well have written the public statement of the ministers that urged prosecution of the witches. In the aftermath of the executions, when many people felt grave doubts over the propriety of the proceedings, this act of Mather and the clergy stood out. It marked the last time that the civil authorities formally asked them for their opinions on anything. Whatever the level of private piety, orthodox puritanism was in decline as a social and institutional force.

V

By all the expectations of history, puritanism should have died quietly in western Massachusetts, eccentric in manner and sterile in creativity. Until the 1730s it gave every sign of doing this, but in less than a decade it revived with an intense theological vigor. The Great Awakening was a radicalizing experience that marked many American attitudes which have perplexed foreign observers ever since.

Jonathan Edwards came directly out of the Connecticut countryside. Related to some of the most distinguished colonial families, he was a precociously intelligent child fascinated by nature and the way God's plans for the world seemed evident in material objects and natural processes. He seemed fascinated equally by the science and by the mystery of life, finding no conflict between church doctrines and the newest ideas of Isaac Newton and John Locke. His conversion came in a quiet, peaceful way when he was about seventeen. His record of the event, one of the illuminating creative achievements of the period, emphasized the word *sweet*, and Edwards clearly had a streak of intellectual sensuality that was all the more remarkable for appearing in the mind of a young man seemingly isolated from both emotional and intellectual stimulation.

Edwards' more mature formulations all but returned his listeners to Calvinism. Not for him the comforting covenant theology of a hundred years of puritan compromise. He insisted repeatedly on the doctrines of the majesty and inscrutability of God and the incapacity of man to do anything to deserve salvation. His mind, so logical in the presentation of his ideas, seemed to reach them through his emotions. In one extraordinary passage, he talked of his terror of thunder and lightning, but how he came to rejoice at the appearance of a storm because it revealed to him the majesty of God. Fear and grandeur appealed to Edwards and while observing the spectacle he "would speak with a singing voice." Nature was replete with the images and shadows of divine things: In his reading the nature of an inscrutable God through the elements, in his combination of mysticism and science, in his eagerness to make order out of chaos, he summed up much of the American experience.

In his revolutionary application of conservative doctrines he was even more significant. In 1727, the young graduate of Yale went to Northampton, in western Massachusetts, where his grandfather Solomon Stoddard was in need of assistance. The intellectual leader of the back country, Stoddard had terrorized the Mather orthodoxy by his use of the Sacrament as converting ordinance. Fearful at the declining number of conversions among his flock, Stoddard had gone far beyond the Half-Way Convenant and admitted into his church all who applied and who led blameless lives. He hoped that such acceptances would lead more people to experience conversion; he was right, but the Mathers were horrified. In time, Northampton also experienced small revivals of religious fervor. Jonathan Edwards apparently accepted these circumstances without a murmur and quietly replaced Stoddard after his death. Far from being emotional or stimulating in any literary way, his sermons proved to be meticulous examples of the standard puritan sermon form. God was never more unpredictable than when he granted this intensely intellectual young man the central role in a great emotional upheaval.

The first stirrings came in 1733, with an early climax in 1735. Stressing God's sovereignty and man's unworthiness, Edwards gave the town a thorough inventory of its many sins, mostly the usual catalog of disrespect, Sabbath-breaking, disobedience of parents, and sensuality. A few unlikely souls experienced conversions and soon the whole town seemed to experience a mass conversion. The town also had dissenters who disliked the proceedings. Many experienced a kind of emotional hangover when the outburst had passed, but Edwards preferred to pass over these problems when he wrote up his narrative of events. His book spread the word and five years later the Great Awakening began. Edwards was too fixed in his own pulpit and too intellectual to be a rabblerouser, but by 1740 new recruits were in the land, itinerant ministers who went from place to place stirring people who had felt themselves dead to divine experience. In different ways, George Whitefield, Gilbert Tennant, and James Davenport carried to their listeners the message that most established clergy were deaf to the true word of God, that their sermons encouraged sleep more than grace, and that Harvard and Yale taught more atheism than true religion. For many established clergy, this was a bit stiff. They had to deal with covenanted churches for life and could not go from place to place giving the same emotional performance to new audiences. They lived lives that by European standards were marvels of sobriety and had founded what still remains the most remarkable colonial system of higher education the world has ever known.

The Great Awakening was an event of extraordinary importance for the shaping of American civilization. It taught people to subsume their economic and class conflicts into what appeared to the world to be religious categories—

the urban, prosperous, and educated clearly preferred to be Old Lights, or conservative supporters of the established clergy. The more rural, poorer and less educated preferred to be New Lights, radicals in favor of social egalitarianism and the understanding of the heart over the head. The experience of the Awakening taught people to question authority for the first time in their lives. The rebellion against ministers was an act closely related to later acts of rebellion against British governors and customs officials. The Awakening taught also a mean-spirited anti-intellectualism to the rural poor, and a contempt for the rural poor to the urban elite. The deceptively bland exterior of a unified colonial civilization was gone forever. America was developing the same kinds of educational, social, and class differences that Europe had always known.

VI

Much about the American Revolution remains exceptional in world history. European nations had revolutions with more social impact due to the class divisions in their societies. European revolutionary leadership tended to be more ideological and less able to cope with the demands of institutionalizing success. Often enough, European nations exchanged one monarchical regime for another or substituted a dictatorship for an autocracy. Meanwhile, other colonial regimes like those in Canada and Australia evolved peacefully toward Dominion status, in which freedom and self-government seemed to be the gifts of their rulers, not rights acquired by force. Twentieth-century situations in Africa and Asia are too different in too many key aspects to warrant extended comparison.

    In the American experience, however, four aspects of the larger situation had lasting consequences for American culture. First, many of the events occurred because of the meddling of the British government in an area where things had been going smoothly. Many Americans had come to America to escape the religious and class antagonisms of Europe and the settlers were always suspicious of governments. Governments seemed to act in mysterious ways to deprive citizens of liberty. Such an attitude lies at the root of the long-standing American hostility to European social democracy in the twentieth century. Second, Americans disliked the corrupt, nepotistic relationship between the British government and capitalism, most obviously the East India Tea Company. Americans perceived British taxes on tea and molasses as attempts to raise profits for private companies as well as graft for customs officials, not legitimate tax revenue. The nation that resulted retained this hostility to government-assisted business ventures in ways that contrast strikingly with modern attitudes in Japan or Germany. Third, Americans could not look to their governments to assist them because the governments were controlled by the king. Therefore,

Americans managed the revolution through private, *ad hoc* organizations. Private committees sprang up to organize boycotts, spread propaganda, and influence elections in ways quite independent of conventional political machinery. This emphasis on private group action remained a deep strain in American psychology, unthinkable in either continental Europe or the British Commonwealth. There, presumably benign governments made worthwhile endeavors possible and modern social democratic regimes could take over the old functions of the aristocracy or the colonial administrators. Finally, America was that rarity among revolutionary societies, one with leaders of genuine substance and conservatism both before and after the violence. Occasional radicals provided exceptions to this generalization and conservatives often came to regret what they helped start, but the fact remained that the comfortable classes provided the most significant leadership. This stabilized the fighting and minimized social disruption. It also continued to influence modern American perceptions of colonial revolutions: Americans often do not see parallels between colonial leaders and societies and their own, in terms of education, experience, or stability. Americans are thus often unfriendly to contemporary revolutions. They genuinely believe that their revolution was unique and in many ways they are correct. Whether this uniqueness justifies their modern attitudes remains quite another matter.

Considered economically, the revolution was a record of British interventions in a functioning imperial system. Before 1763, the colonies enjoyed the "salutary neglect" of London—in effect they were too insignificant economically or strategically to warrant close supervision. Largely distracted by conflict with France, the British regarded the colonies as a place where friends and relatives could grow rich off bribes and related considerations of public office. The colonies could thus develop undisturbed by onerous taxes. A few bribes were not too high a price to pay for reasonably secure rights to worship and trade as they pleased, protected from Europe and Indians alike by the British military. In the North, a prosperous and educated commercial society developed, concentrated in Boston, New York, and Philadelphia. In the South, a plantation petty aristocracy evolved, dispersed along waterways. Problems of taxation and communication being what they were, British policy changes inevitably affected the cities in the North first, with their customs houses, import-export businesses, newspapers, and taxable wealth. But resistance found quick support in the South, for plantation owners were often deep in debt to British merchants. Popular support came quickly because the British were so inept as to tax the rum and tea that most citizens drank in excessive amounts.

Britain had long insisted upon close regulation of the colonial trade. On paper, strict laws restricted the cargoes as well as the nationality of the vessels carrying them. In practice, so many colonial businessmen found that they could make a great deal of money anyway and that the most bothersome laws were not too difficult to evade. The *Sugar Act* (1764) tightened up the laws relating to sugar, molasses, and rum and made evasion more difficult. Economic crisis developed in several areas and people of all classes joined in sending protests, organizing boycotts, and thinking in a preliminary way about the political principles that might protect a colony from this unwarranted intervention. The *Stamp Act* (1765) made the situation both broader and more severe: it taxed all pieces of commercial paper, from wills to newspapers, with stiff penalties for noncompliance. Lawyers, journalists, and businessmen—the most educated, wealthy, and articulate men in the Northern cities—were thus united at a stroke by dislike for this extra expense and red tape. The first organizations developed to encourage local manufactures not subject to tax and to systematize protest to London. Anyone foolish enough to accept a patronage job administering the Stamp Tax was in danger of physical violence and a burned home. The British, intensely irritated, nevertheless gave in and things quieted down.

VII

All this religious and economic activity led to the development of an American political science. Colonists had previously taken their rights as loyal British subjects for granted and had scarcely worried about trying to codify them. Once they found themselves fighting for those rights they found defining them unavoidable and within a decade Americans began the arduous process of telling the world what, in political terms, they stood for.

At first their position was not at all clear because Americans most frequently identified themselves with an almost lost school of British Whig political science. The most important figures in the school were John Locke, the great Enlightenment philosopher; John Milton, the puritan poet; James Harrington, author of the utopian fantasy, *Oceana*; and the team of John Trenchard and Thomas Gordon, whose book, *Cato's Letters*, turned out to be the single most important influence on early revolutionary thinking. The points of connection between these thinkers and the colonists are now beyond dispute. Both Jonathan Mayhew, the great Old Light preacher, and John Adams, the greatest American political scientist of the revolution, explicitly recalled these men by name when trying to recall formative influences on their thought. Benjamin Franklin, as an adolescent helping his brother James run a Boston newspaper, actually set the type when that newspaper published long excerpts from *Cato's Letters*. Perhaps the most convincing evidence of this pervasive influence is the presence of long quotes and close paraphrases throughout many of the pamphlets published in support of the revolution.

Being the descendants of puritans, both the British Whigs and the American revolutionaries were seriously concerned with power. Their own lives and religion had been in danger because their enemies had power and they always feared the return of unsympathetic authority. Yet they were authoritarian themselves and clearly understood the need for executive authority. In their writings, "power" became a kind of original sin, corrupting even the best men and governments unless properly controlled. Most colonists accepted a social compact theory of government in which people had freely gathered themselves together and given up some of their individual freedoms in return for the protections of society. If a legitimate government received the support of citizens, then they could emerge from a state of license into a state of Christian liberty. They had less liberty if they preferred a state of nature; they had more liberty if they were true Christians and understood the kind of life God intended men to live as Christians.

Not even Sigmund Freud believed more firmly in the Id than the puritans did. For them, uncontrollable drives motivated people and governments, and the goal of their political science was to channel these drives so that they did the least harm to society. The striving for power corrupted the best men and turned them into tyrants once they attained public office. Americans frequently used alcoholic and sexual imagery to speak of the lust for office and the intoxicating nature of the possession of power. They became obsessed with that most obvious of symbols of governmental power, a "standing army," and pointed repeatedly to nations who had lost the precious jewel of liberty because they had allowed a standing army in their midst. Like Rome, England could find itself awash in gangs of restless mercenaries who would gradually destroy English rights, laws, and liberties. America could be next.

In colonial eyes, Britain had escaped these dangers as long as she had because of her sturdy Saxon ancestors and the unwritten British constitution which they had evolved. Like Isaac Newton's famous clock, the British constitution worked because of its built-in checks and balances. Royalty, nobility, and democracy represented key vested interests in society and helped keep each other honest through power in the monarchy, lords, and commons. The danger was that one faction would get too much power and put the whole system out of kilter. Britain would then suffer a tyranny, an oligarchy or mob rule. Unfortunately, the American view was hopelessly complicated because America was governed by its own local and colonial governments, governors appointed by the crown and the British Parliament as well. Jurisdictions seemed to overlap in a serious way, and Americans desperately needed to codify the power relationships both as they were and as they thought they should be. Probably the only way to solve these problems amicably was the one suggested by Benjamin Franklin and later developed in the British Commonwealth of Nations: allow complete local autonomy but retain the crown as chief of state and allow the mother country at least for a lengthy period of time to control foreign policy. That was too radical a suggestion for the 1770s.

At home, the British were mired in problems of their own which had little direct reference to America. Her leaders were inept, ill-informed about American conditions, and seriously in need of funds. To them, the colonial position was selfish and unreasonable and they seem scarcely to have considered American protests. To the colonists, however, the inconsistencies and ineptitudes of the British government fitted all too well into the patterns they had learned from Whig political science. The colonists became convinced that British aristocrats had developed a conspiracy to crush American liberties. They wanted to place their relatives in lucrative American positions so they could grow rich. They wished to destroy American religious independence and install pliant English judges loyal to London and not the local community. The landing of troops in Boston in 1768 was very nearly the last straw. This was clearly a military conspiracy and hardly a literate colonist was unaware of the terrible symbolism of a "standing army." Even so conservative, sensible, and enlightened a figure as George Washington could decide in 1774 that the troubles between Britain and her colonies were the results of a "regular, systematic plan" of oppression and that the British government was "endeavoring by every piece of art and despotism to fix the shackles of slavery upon us." He was quite sure that these actions were deliberate. "I am as fully convinced as I am of my own existence that there has been a regular, systematic plan formed to enforce them." When an imperial government has lost its conservative military leadership in the colonies in this manner, it is indeed in bad shape.

Three ideas with lasting political results came out of this ferment. First, Americans modified the British idea of representation. British defenders stressed the notion of virtual representation and insisted that each elected member of the House of Commons represented all the interests of all the British people everywhere. Americans thought this nonsense and could not understand any way in which a fox-hunting drunkard from some forgotten rural borough could represent any plausible American interest. Americans ever since have insisted that each representative must actually live in the district he wishes to represent. Second, Americans lost their admiration for the unwritten British constitution. It had not protected them when they needed it. Instead, they insisted on a written constitution that specified in detail what a citizen's rights and obligations were and how the electoral system would work. Under it, a president, a senate, a house of representatives, and ultimately a judiciary divided among them the powers of monarch, lords, and commons in England. Third, the Americans insisted that the power of sovereignty did not lie with Parliament, the monarch, or the church. Instead, the source of sovereignty was in the people and there for democratic theoreticians it has remained. Unlike the British system, where the various branches of government represented separate social interests, the American system evolved in such a way as to have the president, the senate, and the judiciary, as well as the house, all represent the people. Each may check the power of the other, but each represents "the people," and not a special class or interest group in society. No European society had ever had such a radical theoretical basis.

VIII

This intellectual revolution in political science in turn gave meaning to the economic and religious events of the next decade. In economic matters, people had learned that England had its own interests and that these were not the same as those of the colonies. Britain seemed to regard the colonies chiefly as a source for tax revenue to support military or bureaucratic goals of no concern to the colonies. The respect Americans had once had for their local governments in Plymouth or Massachusetts Bay seemed irrelevant and even dangerous when transferred to London and it began to fade. One evident example of this was smuggling. Wine still retained a high duty and so smuggling wine became as much an act of patriotism as a pleasant way to satisfy the palate. When the East India Company raised tea prices and profits, smuggling undutied tea became popular. Such activities led easily to disrespect for all law and authority and a reliance on private, extralegal economic channels. Wine, tea, and molasses were all vital ingredients of American independence.

In the early 1770s things were relatively peaceful throughout the colonies and yet the image of the military began to change as well. The British army had originally been a useful force that kept the French and Indians from harassing British subjects along the frontier. The navy protected American boats from attacks of privateers. But the use of troops to protect governors and customs agents and the use of boats to enforce the tax laws and confiscate cargoes made the British military resemble the Roman. It was the instrument of an imperial tyranny. In this context, a peculiarly inept British ministry enacted a new tea law in 1773, not only to save profits for the East India Tea Company but also to eliminate much American business profit. The law made tea in the store cheaper, but it also threatened the life of many British and American businesses. Many dependent Americans interpreted the law as a means of wiping out independent American commerce in order both to enrich a British monopoly and to put more money into British tax funds. Paradoxically, cheaper tea symbolized British tyranny and British taxation without consultation with the colonies. Everything seemed to come together: tax policy, economic cartels, troops, loss of local autonomy.

A series of events then moved revolutionary sentiment out of the hands of the conservative businessmen and into the hands of more radical forces. Late in 1773 a boat full of tea appeared in Boston harbor that for legal reasons had to be unloaded quickly. Governor Thomas Hutchinson was also deeply involved with the cargo and refused to work for compromise. Samuel Adams, one of the leading radicals, gathered a group of citizens disguised as Indians and they dumped that tea and some from other vessels into the harbor. No one was hurt, the great majority of local people approved, and the news spread quickly to other colonies. The infuriated British government retaliated with a series of laws that closed the port of Boston and suspended many civil liberties. Intended to break American rebelliousness, these laws only encouraged it and radicalized people elsewhere. What had begun as an administrative, economic measure designed to rationalize British imperial policy had become a systematic British repression with impact far beyond simple economics. By 1775, the issue was whether or not Parliament could wage war on a colonial city inhabited by British subjects, suspend constitutional rights, and ignore the wishes of citizens. Economics had become political science and repression had brought war.

IX

Such a stress on economic matters, however, leaves out the religious concerns that remained central for many descendants of the puritans. For them the issue of political freedom was inseparable from the issue of religious freedom and the clergy became the most articulate of political leaders. Congregationalist and Presbyterian churches often became centers of revolutionary activity.

This religious revolution took place against a background of the whole peculiar American custom of established dissent. In colonies like Massachusetts Bay, the established religion of congregationalism was the dissenting version of puritanism in England. Through neglect, disorganization, and impotence the British had permitted colonies to support through taxation churches which were in open rebellion against the Church of England. Even in areas like Virginia where the Church of England was legally established, it was weak in structure and seemed congregationalist in practice. Local vestries kept far more power than comparable bodies in England, ministers tended to be on one-year contracts, and no American bishop enforced discipline. So pathetic was the Church of England that at the end of the seventeenth century it appointed Societies for the Propagation of the Gospel in Foreign Parts and for Promoting Christian Knowledge. The first body, known as the SPG, played a key role in several colonial developments.

With unimportant exceptions, relations between congregationalists and Anglicans in both England and America were smooth for much of the eighteenth century. Dissenters had an important place in Hanoverian English society and the Whigs under Robert Walpole seemed tolerant of dissenting interests. Toleration as an idea made progress and many influential British dissenters came to prefer toleration to frustrated attempts at dominance. Yet in both British and

American minds, bishops and kings had an identity of interest that no tolerant climate of opinion could change much. The British regarded the church as an arm of the state and the king appointed its bishops. Americans could hardly be blamed for believing them and assuming that the presence of a bishop assumed the hidden presence of the king and royal troops. Many of the favorite Whig pamphleteers preferred by the colonists, like Trenchard and Gordon, in *The Independent Whig* (1770–1771), could produce strong warnings about the inevitable connections between popery in religion and arbitrariness in government.

In England, strong influences developed on the tory side in Parliament and within the Church of England that boded evil for colonial religious independence. Thomas Secker, the eminent and forceful Bishop of Oxford, was the key figure; he firmly favored putting bishops in America as soon as possible. Occasional eminent Americans publicly converted to Anglicanism over the years. Clergy like Jonathan Mayhew were openly telling their Boston audiences by the early 1760s the political lessons of these events: that God did not intend that kings should act in an arbitrary manner, that reason had to govern in politics as well as religion, and that every people had the right of revolution if misgoverned by either bishops or kings.

Even Enlightenment rationalists were deeply affected by these currents. William Livingston, the leading intellectual in the New York City area, evolved from Old Light Presbyterianism to something resembling deism. In the process he became an ardent advocate of simple toleration, not so much out of eagerness to protect an alternative religion as out of eagerness to be left alone by all religions. Even before Thomas Jefferson became the most famous of American defendants of toleration and disestablishment, Livingston and his colleagues on *The Independent Reflector* (ca. 1752) established many key arguments not only for toleration but also for the development of secular institutions of higher learning. They pointed out sensibly enough that America had too many competing religions and that the only solution was to allow none of them to dominate the colleges.

Livingston, however, did not try to rewrite American history; many clergy and their followers did. In their reinterpretation of the American experience, they usually ignored puritan intolerance, dogmatism, the exiling and mutilating of dissenters, and the whole unpleasant story of puritan attempts at building a monolithic community. Instead, they pictured their ancestors as men deeply desiring freedom of worship and the separation of church and state. The city on the hill, originally a symbol of strictly religious conversion through American leadership, began its peculiar transformation into a democratic political symbol. In effect, Americans urged other societies to follow their political example: to establish freedom of religion and the separation of church and state and to institute a political version of the freedom of the vote that began in convenanted churches and town meetings. A religious procedure had evolved into a political procedure and both demanded an evangelical enthusiasm from citizens. That peculiar American invention so puzzling to foreigners, the secular religion of democracy, was being born. Now God blessed secular elections and freedom of choice and anyone interfering with these institutions defied the will of God. To oppose democracy became blasphemy.

Thus for various reasons Americans wore religious spectacles when they viewed British tax laws and military interventions. To them such interventions were first signs of the establishment of a colonial Church of England and the end of established Congregationalism. Taxes supported bishops and all issues of liberty and taxation implied religious tyranny. America did not yet stand for freedom and toleration in the world, but it had always stood for the freedom of Congregationalist-minded people to ignore both bishop and king on local issues. To take up arms in the 1770s was indeed an act in defense of religious and political liberty. When many Anglican clergy supported the quiet payment of the taxes, many of the worst colonial suspicions were confirmed.

That such a situation had little basis in fact was hardly relevant. The mistakes people make in their beliefs have far more relevance than simple truth. Archbishop Secker was not Archbishop Laud and Jonathan Mayhew did not face the same problems as John Winthrop. Apathy, secularism, and tolerance had made more progress in England than in America. English church authorities knew very little about American conditions and frequently sent oddly inept men to represent their views. Ignorance was great on both sides and thus here as in so many areas, the revolution occurred in an atmosphere of incomprehension and suspicion verging on paranoia.

X

Suspicious circumstances were hardly enough to energize a people to revolution by themselves. But the suspicions about the Church of England took place against a backdrop of the divisions of the Great Awakening. Religion, politics, and social tensions combined to create a mental environment increasingly hostile not only to England and its established church, but also to local authority figures, both secular and political.

Many of the Old Lights, having been in positions of authority in 1740, had used their power to harass the evangelicals, thus creating a local "enemy" for New Lights that included members of both church and state. By the 1750s, many New Lights had themselves come to positions of power in the state as well as the church and they were inordinately suspicious of the right of any state to tell any church what to do. The long-forgotten precedents of Roger Williams regained relevance: the church and the state had to be separate because the state defiled the church. Evangelicals in the 1750s thus began their continuing policy of strongly opposing any official contacts between church and state. So strong does this tradition remain in America that major state universities, such as the University of Texas, may not contain departments of religion, because each church fears that a competitor will gain control over the instruction and misinform the young. For true apathy in religious matters, one has to look at established Lutheranism in Scandinavia or Catholicism in Italy.

The crisis of authority extended even into local churches. Congregations which had submitted willingly to the demands of clergy denounced their ministers for being numb to grace and their social superiors for snobbery, exploitation, and sterility of thought. Combined with the insistence that any man of any educational level could find truth in Scripture by himself, the result was a loss of deference, passivity, and doctrinal purity. The church and its minister had long been the key force in America and suddenly the churches were splintering and the ministers feuding.

The political lines hardened accordingly. The Old Lights, with their permanent churches and covenanted ministers, their preference for status, deference and sermons in traditional forms, tended to become a colonial haute bourgeoisie. Living in cities and informed about European ideas, they became easily frightened about what had happened. Having found the Awakening democratic and radical, they found the revolution a difficult trial. Some of them joined the revolution, fearing the tyranny of Britain more than the tyranny of the masses. Others became Tories, sometimes leaving the country. After the revolution, such people tended to recombine behind the banners of the Federalist party, to stress the authority of the national state, the need for discipline within the country, and cultural ties with England.

The New Lights followed a different course. With the occasional exception of someone like Jonathan Edwards, they were less likely to be educated and preferred emotional to intellectual religion. Blooded by the Awakening, they proved to be the most furious opponents of the Stamp and Sugar Taxes. They often became vigilantes threatening violence against anyone foolish enough to become a stamp tax collector. Easily mobilized into support of the revolution, they came to form the backbone of Jefferson's political grouping in the 1790s. Indeed, Jefferson's running mate in 1800 was Aaron Burr. Usually remembered as the man who shot Alexander Hamilton, Burr was also the grandson of Jonathan Edwards and the son of Edwards' successor as president of the college now called Princeton University. The political ticket in 1800 symbolized the alliance within American democracy of the forces of Jefferson's Enlightenment and Edwards' evangelicalism.

Religion, economics, and politics by the end of the eighteenth century had become so closely connected in people's minds that no one could say where one left off and the next began.

XI

The American Revolution was not especially radical by comparison to such later revolutions as the French and the Russian. One major reason for this was the way the Old Lights interpreted the events. They may not have been as violent in their dissent as the New Lights and would probably not have come to actual fighting by themselves, but in fact much of Enlightenment thinking was inherent in conservative puritanism and this thinking led many sober men to take up arms.

Throughout the eighteenth century, conservative New Englanders slowly adopted positions identified with what church historians call the Arminian heresy. It got its name from Jacobus Arminius, a Dutch Reformed theologian, whose position was set forth in 1610. Against the Calvinists, who held that Christ died only for the elect, Arminians thought he died for all humanity. In the American context, the heresy developed out of the vexed issue of the gift of grace. For a true Calvinist, God was the sole author of grace and man could do nothing to encourage God to grant grace. Man could prepare his heart and life but he never bound God by his actions. This state of ignorance about his ultimate fate proved more than an orthodox puritan could tolerate and he gradually came to believe that he could perform good works, live in a Christian way, and thus all but obligate God to reward him with heaven. Some people converted to the Church of England on this issue, but many stayed within their Congregationalist churches and took them slowly along the path to Unitarianism and deism.

Seeds of Arminianism appeared as early as Cotton Mather, but real growth occurred only after the Great Awakening. The most articulate preachers were Jonathan Mayhew and Charles Chauncy; a convenient milestone was Chauncy's attack on New Light excesses, "Seasonable Thoughts on the State of Religion in New-England" (1743). Sober, scholarly, and usually sensible, Chauncy was upset at itineracy in ministers, ill-bred behavior among both clergy and congregations, spontaneous exhortations, and personal attacks made on established ministers. He preferred to think of conversion not as something violent, personal, and emotional, but as a gradual process of doing good in the world, having faith in God, and not fretting about the state of one's soul. Live a Christian life and a person would become a Christian. God did his share if a Christian did his.

Chauncy and his followers developed several positions that marked the death of puritanism in America as a coherent body of doctrine. They attacked original sin and insisted that men were capable of both good and evil. They decided that the Calvinist position on the freedom of the will was so confused and self-contradictory that people should stop worrying about it. In a predestinarian world, God seemed to be the author of sin and this seemed an unwise position. They attacked the notion of "disinterested benevolence." For Edwards, benevolence was always disinterested because God never took it into account before he saved or damned people. Arminians replied that of course God noticed and that when he saw that a Christian had faith and performed good works he was pleased and rewarded the person. Arminians also stressed man's capacity to reason; this faculty was where people most resembled God. Nature to them was explicable and even when people could not say what caused a given event, accumulating knowledge would someday explain it without resort to divine intervention. God could be read in nature. Even the personality of God changed: he proved to be kind and not the thundering Deity of old. It was only a short step to the ideas that any man could be saved, that the Trinity was a nonsensical notion, and that toleration of dissenters was the only civilized religious policy.

These doctrines had revolutionary implications in politics as well as religion. If a man could use his reason and depend on himself for salvation, then he was capable of solving political and social issues. If God were kind and nature benevolent, then people could strive for and achieve happiness. If God wanted people to do this, then any government that prevented them from exercising their reason, free will, and faculties in general was against God's will and contrary to nature. If people and God seemed to live by rational convenants, then people and governments could live by covenants as well. God worked through his ministers for the common religious good; the king should work through his ministers for the common political good. If God could be reasonable, it surely was not too much to ask for the king to be reasonable as well. The Old Light sermons for the period often contain as much discussion of the social contract, natural rights, and the right of revolution as they do of grace and justification.

As early as 1750, in his "Discourse Concerning Unlimited Submission," Jonathan Mayhew had already worked out the conservative rationale for revolution. Once magistrates acted contrary to the legitimate demands of their office they immediately ceased to be ministers of God. No one needed to honor them. In his most quotable sentence, "Rulers have no authority from God to do mischief." Tyrants and oppressors had no right to claim the protection of God. A citizen had the duty to obey his king only if he ruled for the public welfare. If he ruled oppressively, then he was interfering with God's plans for his people. People must be able to use their reason and live happy lives. If a king prevented this through taxation, injustice, or irrational behavior, then he was a tyrant and must be overthrown. Such a rebellion "is not criminal; but a reasonable way of vindicating their liberties and just rights." Indeed, not to rebel would be criminal. Mayhew did not exempt the church. His distrust of the Church of England verged on paranoia and he later insisted that historically bishops were but the instruments of kings. "The old cry, *No bishop, no king*, has indeed been of mighty efficacy in times past."

Thus Old Lights and New Lights could join hands in fighting Britain. Due to British incompetence the religious passions of a century and a half became channeled into political activity. Wronged businessmen and nonbelievers often had their private reasons as well, but the passions of those years would have been hard to sustain without the black brigades of Congregationalist clergy urging their flocks into something very close to a political Armageddon.

Chapter 2

Philadelphia, 1740–1800

The hegemony of Boston over American civilization lasted more than a century. Essentially based on religion, it included significant thought on literature, science, and politics; toward its climax in the revolutionary era it was discovering fine arts as well. Boston and its intellectual suburbs like Concord never lost their importance for American creativity and during the three decades before the Civil War enjoyed a renaissance of literary and political ideas. But even Boston never quite equaled the swiftness of growth and brilliance of achievement that occurred in Philadelphia during the last six decades of the eighteenth century. The creative environment of Boston came to dominate the North before the Civil War and the nation after it, but for many Americans Philadelphia in the Age of Franklin was the place and period in their history of which they were most proud.

In its larger contours, Philadelphia and the Pennsylvania colony as a whole provided something of a paradigm for the characteristic American experience. A persecuted group found no place for itself in Europe and imagined that in America they could realize their utopian dreams. Through good luck they managed to find the means to begin a functioning colony. The original emigrants were not plentiful enough to control the colony and keep outsiders under discipline; they also feuded too much among themselves. Success, prosperity, and the apathy of the new generations insensibly dried up the utopian energies and diverted people to secular pursuits; pragmatic adjustment became the pervading theme. The unintended consequences proved to be the most important of all.

The Quakers were essentially a radical religious splinter group with roots in the sixteenth century. Controversy still surrounds the early days of the sect, but in essence it appeared in the person of George Fox in the 1640s and developed behind the leadership of William Penn in the 1660s and after. Puritanism frequently had a strong emphasis on the individual experience of the human heart as it strove for grace and Quakers were the group that carried this tendency to an extreme. In revolt against everything popish—vestments, art, ceremonies, elaborate sermons, music—they came to emphasize two related doctrines. First, they made a radical distinction between a wholly passive man and a truly omnipotent God. In Calvinist fashion, they stressed the vast gulf between God and man and denied the utility of puritan covenant theology. Second, they emphasized the gap between the "carnal" and "spiritual" and denied that sense perceptions or the study of nature could tell a person anything about God. Only the inner spirit of Christ could do that. They thus deemphasized the Scriptures and the elaborate sermons which applied them. Christ was in the heart more than he was in history or a book. Their ideas had much in common with the antinomianism of Anne Hutchinson.

Appearing in London first as a Seeker and then as a recognizable Quaker, Fox stressed the "inner light" through which men could find God and urged men to ignore creeds, clergy, and churches. They should also abolish frivolity, social inequality, and injustice. In the 1650s his followers worked to rid the language of class distinctions, refused to swear oaths, and avoided using pagan names for the days or the months. Having no betters, they refused to lift their hats to them. Governments as well as churches were "fallen" and Quakers refused to take up arms either to attack or defend them. They resembled the puritans on aesthetic matters. Offended by the licentiousness of Restoration comedy and the vogue for love sonnets, they opposed all art that did not focus the mind on eternal subjects.

William Penn (1644–1718) was born into a sturdy Anglican naval family. Affected by puritan students at Oxford and the disturbing environment of the plague, Penn went through a severe religious crisis. His father tried to interest him in healthier topics like Europe, the law, and public affairs, and for a time Penn managed the family's Irish estates. A term in the Tower for blasphemy focused his mind and he emerged to become a Quaker leader with unprecedented social status. Because Quakers could not swear oaths, vote, hold public office, or sue in court, they needed men of influence to lobby their cases for them. Penn used his education and his father's contacts where he could and proved remarkably successful. His great opportunity came with his father's death. King Charles owed the elder Penn a large debt for naval services and decided that a tract of land in the New World would not only discharge that debt, it would provide a place to dispose of many troublesome citizens. William Penn began to plan his own city on a hill along the west coast of the Delaware River: a radically consensualist community with both religion and government under divine power. Unanimity would reign and God's presence be in every heart.

Penn intended to run the colony as a joint stock company financed by wealthy London Quakers, with much of the real power retained in his own hands. People were to agree and of course that meant that they would agree with him.

He expected to appoint the key officials and to make the colony financially profitable. Unlike the puritans, he hoped to have religious toleration for other sects and Pennsylvania never had the persecutions that so marred the history of Massachusetts Bay. But like so many pioneers in America, he combined radical ideas with a conservative temperament. His intentions were clear, but in practice not only did human nature prove recalcitrant, but Quaker principles proved inconsistent and difficult to formulate coherently or apply successfully. The successive constitutions of Pennsylvania, called *Frames*, tinkered frequently with the machinery of government without basically changing the fact that a conservative Quaker clique of early settlers wished to run things to suit themselves. Subsequent Quakers and all nonbelievers were expected to defer to their accumulations of wisdom, experience, and property. The vote was restricted to adult males with adequate property and the ruling clique expected them to return candidates of stature. Penn's temperament and the pressure of the investors kept liberalism out of political affairs.

Penn was soon bogged down in administrative and financial problems and the colony rapidly acquired a population largely non-Quaker. Penn often was away for long periods of time, he found debt collection difficult, and he turned out to be a poor judge of character when appointing subordinates. Land hunger and greed permeated much of the colony; religious enthusiasm quietly waned; and a prosperous, provincial life settled over the land much as it had in Massachusetts Bay. The French and the Indians harassed the port areas and the backwoods, but Quakers militantly refused to take up arms—and got away with it chiefly because they lived in areas that remained largely unthreatened. For perhaps a decade at the beginning of the eighteenth century, rebellious elements under the leadership of David Lloyd seemed to be on the verge of democratizing the government, but the prosperity that followed the end of Queen Anne's War in 1713 muted discontent.

Three explicitly Quaker achievements deserve note. Unlike the puritans, the Quakers got along well with the Indians. Penn himself dealt with them fairly and abundant evidence shows a general amicability between the races that was all too often missing from later American contacts along the frontier. Religiously, an atmosphere of polite incomprehension frustrated any attempts at conversion. Later settlers, like the Moravians, had more success along these lines..

The slave issue was more significant. The leading Quaker thinker after Penn was John Woolman (1720–1772). His dates mark off the significant period of Quaker concern for slaves and a growing commitment to emancipation. Quakers really inherited slavery as a problem. Slaves and slave trading were customs of the time and few people questioned their presence in Pennsylvania and nearby New Jersey. But as early as George Fox Quakers had expressed doubts about the propriety of holding men in bondage and the topic came up repeatedly in Quaker meetings. It proved relatively easy to go on record against slavetrading, but the possession of slaves was a more complicated issue. Many Quakers inherited slaves or married the owners of slaves; laws of entail made it difficult to emancipate them. Some large estates seemingly could not function without them. Like many Quakers, Woolman disliked compromise on moral issues—good Christians did not compromise with sin. Under his pressure Quaker meetings came slowly to the conclusion that slaves had to be freed and by 1758 Quakers who did not work toward this goal were in danger of expulsion from the sect. Thus, as happened so frequently in later American history, one or two men had a reform idea and ceaselessly worked to have a religious group adopt it. That group slowly adjusted itself to reform, its debates aroused the public conscience, and a political issue was born. Slavery lingered on among society at large in the area for a brief period, then disappeared by law. The spread of this area of freedom led in time to the Civil War.

Attitudes toward Indians and Negroes were part of a larger pattern of toleration, perhaps the greatest of all Quaker legacies. William Penn hardly intended a liberal democracy, but he was a more liberal figure than anyone in Massachusetts Bay. Even Roger Williams, in many ways a more compelling person, came to toleration by the back door, through excessive zeal and despair at separating saved from damned. The forces of a diverse population in Pennsylvania made severe repression all but unthinkable and the result was a sane, pleasant society in which people could be peculiar in a great variety of ways. A fiasco like the Salem witch trials was not possible. The one case of witchcraft that did turn up was handled as an example of regrettable insanity rather than criminality. The Quakers may not have directly contributed many individuals to the great flowering of Philadelphia after 1740, but the mental and emotional universe they evolved made such a flowering possible.

II

In 1723 a rebellious young newspaper apprentice named Benjamin Franklin stole away from his job in Boston and went to Philadelphia to make his way in the world. His success and his ability to convey that success in words made him a legend long before his death, the first American genuinely to symbolize to Europeans the possibilities of human development in America. Franklin's departure conveniently dates the decline of Boston as an intellectual center of first importance and his intellectual maturity around 1740 marks the start of the Age of Franklin in Philadelphia. His personal connection between Boston and Philadelphia also usefully connects those two cities as twin centers of the early American Enlightenment. A man could be enlightened in Boston, for the roots of enlightenment were certainly there. But one could be genuinely liberated in Philadelphia.

The Enlightenment in Europe and America shared many attitudes. Educated men revolted against the irrationality and violence of post-Reformation Europe and stressed the way human beings could become more and more perfect through the use of their reason to improve society. They insisted that God need not be as inscrutable and unknowable as many Christians believed and that the scientific study of nature would reveal the truth about religious questions. Kings and priests did not deserve the respect of mankind unless they could communicate clearly the rational bases for their actions; personal whim no longer seemed a rational way of conducting church or state. Freedom, knowledge, and humanitarianism all become touchstones: people should be free, they should use their freedom to acquire knowledge and they should use that knowledge to improve society.

In Europe, Enlightenment thinking tended to be a private affair of drawing room and personal correspondence: any outspoken attack upon a European monarch could result in censorship, exile, or prison. In America, the king was far away and so was his bishop. Local clergy, businessmen, academics, and professional men were often quite publicly enlightened; the Enlightenment and the establishment were often coextensive and puritan preachers the first to proclaim many new ideas to their literate congregations. The bulk of the citizenry might remain evangelical and only vaguely aware of these currents, but just as Thomas Jefferson and Aaron Burr could share the same presidential ticket, so evangelicals and secular leaders could share similar values and goals if with quite different emphases. Public figures wrote the Declaration of Independence and the Constitution, not prisoners or members of a discontented intelligentsia.

America was also more practical and less abstract in its Enlightenment. Europeans like Isaac Newton, Francis Bacon, and John Locke had done most of the technical thinking necessary for religious and political reform and so the extensive, abstract controversies of the European Enlightenment never made much of an impact in America. Americans perceived English taxation and military intervention as catalytic acts and did little original thinking until forced to justify their rebelliousness after 1763. Within a remarkably short time they produced the political science that helped change the way multitudes far away from America viewed their own government.

In its turn, America helped Europeans locate their myths. Utopian fantasies needed a plausible place to take root and America was the playground of the European imagination. It had no real aristocracy or monarch and by the middle eighteenth century no established church comparable to European establishments. Americans could grow up to lead rational, virtuous lives because their social environment did not oppress them. In this context Benjamin Franklin played his key role. To countless Europeans who had never met an American and who would never see the country, Franklin was the embodiment of their utopian fantasies. The rustic sage, the plain-spoken man of folk wisdom, the natural man of scientific inventiveness—he was an institution, not a real person of flesh and blood. He affected Quaker expressions and a coonskin cap and played his role with the skill of a Talleyrand. He was the European intellectuals' foil against the vapidities of aristocratic life, the proof that freedom from priestcraft brought virtue and progress. When he and Voltaire finally appeared together, the Old and New World Enlightenments came together in one of those fleeting moments of aesthetic perfection in history: two wily old men, loving their own legends, acting out the public fantasy. Rationality was the great myth of the age and America supplied its own saints; even more incredible, it put them into public office.

The American Enlightenment was also far more nationalistic than the European. In Europe, philosophy, literature, and science tended to be international; nations all too often were under the domination of irrational monarchs. But America was new and free from much of this and an American could plausibly intermingle ideas about democracy, rationality, nature, a benign Deity, and his own country. America was the place where these things could happen, in fact were already happening. In this manner intellectual positions like freedom to worship, the right to trial by peers, or the right to vote became identified with an "American way," and this way took on religious sanction. To Canadians or Australians, by contrast, such ideas were not relevant. Settled largely at later times, they avoided many eighteenth-century issues. Settled often with government police, military, and bureaucratic assistance, they associated freedom, prosperity, and even their own identity with Home—i.e., the Mother Country, England. Neither religion nor revolution came up in this context at all.

III

Philadelphia made its first contributions to the creative life of the world in the natural sciences. The old "natural philosophy" was in the final stages of its evolution into "the sciences" as the modern world knows them. The first specialists in fields like botany and geology were emerging, chiefly in continental Europe. British science was somewhat laggard, but the formation of the Royal Society of London (1660) marked the beginning of serious British contributions in a systematic and organized way. The Royal Society immediately formed a Committee for Foreign Correspondence and Americans were present in significant numbers—fifty-three names appeared on the list between 1663 and 1783, many of whom had genuine scientific interests. Over this period the American contribution was to collect new data, classify it, and give it proper nomenclature. For most contributors the emphasis was on flora and fauna, with only passing attention to other areas. For example, John Winthrop, Jr. (1606–1676), although frequently elected to public office because of his famous name and diplomatic disposition, was a chemist and physician who dabbled in alchemy. Over the years he sent the Royal Society reports on maize, cornbread, and beer; on one occasion he shipped over the first hummingbird nest ever seen in the Old World, along with a report about the characteristics of this strange new creature.

Boston provided the first genuine scientific community in the colonies. Increase Mather had had a fascination for comets. Cotton Mather accumulated a decent library on science and medicine and wrote at length about the more nauseating ways to cure oneself of various ailments: *The Angel of Bethesda* has a whole chapter on ways to use urine and dung as internal specifics to cure diseases. During the Presidency of John Leverett (1708–1724), Harvard University was a center for scientific investigation. Cotton Mather, Leverett, and William Brattle were all fellows of the Royal Society, and Mather won a secure if small place for himself in the history of medicine when he read about the practice of inoculation against smallpox in a medical journal, ignored the best medical opinion of the day, and inoculated his own children among others in the early 1720s. A later John Winthrop (1714–1779) was Hollis Professor at Harvard and the first genuinely productive scholar on its faculty, making significant contributions to the study of earthquakes and comets. None of these men felt the least conflict between their religious and their scientific ideas. For them the natural laws were as much a part of the laws of God as the covenant theology and Christians had a duty to discover those laws as an act of fealty to the Divinity. All assumed that scientific knowledge and biblical knowledge complemented each other.

Young Benjamin Franklin was certainly aware of the scientific work going on around him as a teenager in Boston, but nevertheless he found a far freer intellectual and social climate in Philadelphia. William Penn had been the second American Fellow of the Royal Society (1681), and the period of Franklin's early maturity was one in which public attendance at scientific lectures and general interest in the subject were remarkably high. Science enjoyed an enormous prestige after Isaac Newton and Francis Bacon: men were eager to discover the rationality of their natural environment, which not only encouraged someone like Franklin, it used his insights and made a hero out of him as well. When Peter Kalm, a student of Karl Linnaeus, visited America, Franklin was one of the figures he wanted to meet, and some American contributions appeared in the *Systema Naturae* (1735). More typical of American emphases, John and William Bartram developed their famous botanical garden, the kind of investigation that seemed the most productive of insights, given the state of botany at that time.

Franklin seemed an improbable figure to give the age its name. He was the son of an elderly candlemaker who intended him for the church. Instead, Franklin early felt an aversion to both religious controversy and ceremony. As an apprentice on the *New England Courant* of his brother James, he watched his brother experience the attacks of the Mather forces on the smallpox issue and even serve a term in jail for offending the magistrates. Once safely started upon his career in Philadelphia, Franklin began his famous Junto, a kind of social club that met on Friday nights at local taverns for thirty years to discuss public questions. In time the Junto organized a circulating library and Franklin became the official printer of Pennsylvania. A practical interest in science went along with a curiosity that came in the years 1745–1752, when he pursued his work in thunder gusts and electricity and made his famous experiments with kites. His invention of the lighting rod received recognition in Europe and when Europeans replicated his electrical experiments he became well-known and even translated into German and Italian. Immanuel Kant referred to him as the new Prometheus who had stolen fire from the heavens. Simultaneously with his conduct of many other interests, he pursued experiments with ants and memory, weather, cyclones, agriculture, the Franklin stove, and light.

In the 1750s he became deeply involved in public affairs, reorganizing the postal network and making a beginning toward a more rational and unified colonial organization. His work took him across the country and his experience made him the logical choice to be representative of the Pennsylvania Assembly in London. Franklin took the opportunity to explore Europe as well, continuing his scientific interests and experimenting in the new area of musical glasses. Oxford gave him an honorary degree. But as the political situation deteriorated in the 1760s, Franklin became the key colonial spokesman in England and his scientific interests faded under pressure of current events. An eager supporter of an English-language empire, he worked hard to reconcile the colonies and the mother country. Early in the 1770s he began work on his *Autobiography*, which despite its structural flaws and omissions became the first work of American literature to be of permanent importance—not only because the author was well-known, but also because his book so simply formulated American myths of industry, utility, and upward mobility. He returned to America to become the oldest delegate to the Second Continental Congress and then went on to France for his astonishing old age as the Sage of the New World and the embodiment of Enlightenment Man. By the time his aging eyes had led him to the invention of bifocal glasses, he was quite possibly the most famous man in the Western world.

IV

The focus of aesthetic creativity shifted from Boston to Philadelphia at much the same time. The puritans had long disapproved of sensual secular music and art but made a definite place for creative work that seemed likely to help a person to focus his mind on God and his achievements. Samuel Sewall, the greatest puritan diarist, loved chamber music, quartet singing, and psalms. Both John Cotton and Cotton Mather wrote brief books on musical subjects, and Cotton's son Seaborn copied into his commonplace book sentimental love ballads that were in the air in Boston. Puritans contributed most directly to church music. As with Anglican sermons, they found Anglican compositions too complicated for plain people to play or sing, and one of the earliest aesthetic acts in Massachusetts Bay was to print *The Bay Psalm Book* (1640), the first book actually printed in English North America. The puritan verses eliminated anything resembling aesthetic beauty and thus concentrated the mind on the meaning of the words. Singing instructions were included but actual music did not appear until the ninth edition (1698).

Many rural Americans gloried in their crude singing and felt no need for musical polish. But as colony became province and provincial mothers coveted social position for their daughters, even clergy found ways of justifying a more professional standard. Choir schools increased the effectiveness of the Sunday service and required the musical expertise more appropriate for a settled urban culture. Choir schools meant music teachers, the giving of performances, and soon societies devoted to the music of Handel and Haydn. Men and women had to meet and train together to put on a piece like *Messiah* for a devout public. In effect, some of the first performers in America came disguised as choirboys.

Painting in Boston was even more primitive, yet paradoxically produced a major figure. English Protestantism was peculiarly hostile to the visual arts, associating them with Roman Catholicism. Both Henry VIII and his daughter Elizabeth I caused the destruction of many works of art as well as religious buildings and the British developed a genuine mistrust of anything symbolic in art. The one art form to survive was medieval manuscript illumination. Out of this tradition came a vogue for portrait painting, a literal, representational art form that appealed to both the aristocracy and the newly wealthy commercial classes. The puritans in America found this vogue congenial because it fitted well both with their hostility to the sensual and their tendency to hero-worship ancestors. A portrait of John Winthrop was to the puritan the psychological equivalent of the chapter on Winthrop in Cotton Mather's *Magnalia*. Such works, like puritan hymnody, helped focus the mind on suitable, nonsensual topics. Artists in general, however, did not enjoy any more social status than other artisans and the standard of aesthetic judgment was usually that of truth to nature.

The only solution for those wishing genuine talent in their painting was to import it from Europe, and Europe was the only possible place to obtain adequate training for native talent. The two best mature painters of the colonial period were John Smibert, the favorite painter of the Boston aristocracy, and Peter Pelham, a man perhaps most noted at the time as the founder of a dancing school which charmed the women and scandalized the clergy. Both men were born in England. Pelham's quite untypical attitude toward the arts bore unexpected fruit when his stepson, John Singleton Copley (1738?–1815), became the greatest painter America produced in that century. Receiving only primitive training at home, Copley nevertheless proved remarkably competent as a portraitist and later broadened his subject matter to include history as well. Shy, depressed by the low social status of his chosen profession, Copley matured artistically only with great difficulty. He was also something of a pacifist whose father-in-law was a wealthy merchant who was a consignee of the tea dumped in Boston harbor at the start of the Revolution. Copley agonized about his allegiance at length but finally migrated to England as the war broke out. With appropriate patronage, he became the greatest English painter of his generation.

On the surface Philadelphia was no more fertile ground than Boston for the nurturing of an artist. The Quakers were if anything even more deaf to music and blind to painting than the puritans, even as they too became provincial bourgeois casting furtive glances at urban pleasures. Because they did not sing psalms at meetings they lacked even the most rudimentary church-music tradition and so sacred composition concentrated in the Anglican and Roman Catholic churches. John Adams, his curiosity besting his upbringing, visited a Catholic chapel in 1774 and wrote afterwards that "the scenery and music are so calculated to take in mankind that I wonder the Reformation ever succeeded." He found the chanting "exquisitely soft and sweet." But the real force of musical culture was secular, the concern of cosmopolitans and immigrants. Benjamin Franklin, being interested in everything, brought back an interest in the glass harmonica from Europe. Musical glasses were popular enough in Europe for even Mozart to write several charming pieces for the instrument, and Franklin developed his own version, the glassychord. He also did some random theorizing about music that gives him a tiny place in the history of musical criticism.

A typical representative of Philadelphia musical culture was Francis Hopkinson, a gentleman amateur who made his living at the law and thought of music as entertainment and avocation. A good patriot during the revolution, the friend of Adams, Jefferson, Franklin, and painter Charles Willson Peale, Hopkinson played the harpsichord and the organ and composed a respectable quantity of two-part songs, church music, and simple training exercises for students of the keyboard. A minor American musical version of Laurence Sterne, he liked especially to compose mournful, pathetic songs that could move the hearts of young girls—one of which, Jefferson reported to him in some amazement, had indeed caused his younger daughter to cry while the elder played it on the harpsichord; the future president at first thought she was ill.

Europeans, rather than dabbling amateurs, became the salvation of American musical culture. The first serious pieces of genuine merit written in America were the six string quintets of Johann Friedrich Peter, a migrant from Holland of

German background who worked chiefly in the Moravian settlements near Philadelphia. A composer chiefly of church music, he also introduced European standards of training to the performances of the organizations he directed. More significant to musical life in the city if a lesser composer, Alexander Reinagle had been born in England, the son of an Austrian immigrant, and he in turn settled in Philadelphia when about thirty. He lent a great dignity to the performances he led and had a kind of charismatic respectability that helped to quiet residual Protestant fears that the arts led quickly to immorality. No less a figure than George Washington attended Reinagle's concerts whenever he could and personally chose him as the man to give music lessons to his adopted daughter.

One example of artistic creativity in America stood out before all the others as an example of the problems of an artist in American civilization. Benjamin West (1738–1820) was born into a rural Pennsylvania Quaker family, the tenth child in a family hostile to art. Placed by chance in the least nurturing environment conceivable in the Western world, he began to paint when very young. Demonstrating what was really American about American art, he went after the family cat when he could not get paintbrushes, cutting off hunks of fur to make his own. The family noticed the strange disease the cat seemed to have, but Benjamin found an alternative only when a tolerant relative provided some drawing equipment and several engravings to copy—the first pictures the boy had ever seen. West went to Philadelphia to receive what little instruction might be available, while his people called a meeting to determine what church policy should be toward this peculiar child somehow born in their midst. They noted that God frequently did things for reasons of his own that seemed wildly improbable to mortals, and that Quakers should not question God's judgment. They offered him encouragement and commissions.

His opportunity came in 1759 when he received the chance to go to Italy for further training. He was appalled by the religious and moral atmosphere of Rome, but he discovered the rudiments of a new style of painting that he helped impose on the entire English-speaking world for two generations. Johann Joachim Winckelmann was then the curator of an influential religious art collection in Rome and busy writing his seminal books on the history of classical art. At the time the excavations of Pompeii and Herculaneum helped create a vogue for classical archeology and the art forms it discovered. Winckelmann insisted that these new discoveries should influence all future art. Uncorrupted by Roman Catholicism, classical art was pure and democratic.

Already far more democratic than most Europeans simply by his upbringing, West found himself drawn to these theories. Such art avoided the sensuous and the voluptuous and appealed to Protestant consciences. Winckelmann insisted that painters should not draw those human bodies which had been corrupted by modern aristocracy. Rather, they should study the newly discovered Greek statues, for Greeks had been ideal human beings

uncorrupted by evil governments. The color, light, and shadow that were important to aristocratic painters of his time were no longer important. Instead, a
painter should imitate this sculpture and paint what was universal in human
nature, what was untouched by corrupted modern times. "Noble contour" was
more important than literal accuracy. Lessons of antiquity that taught moral
virtues were the great subjects for painting.

In 1763 West brought these lessons to an England that seemed barren of
talent. English art had migrated to the Continent under the Tudors, and with
the exception of Hogarth no new talent had appeared. Through an accidental
occurrence, West impressed Colonel William Howe with his skill at ice skating
and when Howe's aristocratic friends found out that he was also a skillful painter
they showered him with commissions. George III, whose simple bourgeois
tastes in painting made him seem remarkably kin to Americans, made West a pet
painter of the crown for the forty remaining years of the king's sanity. West
joined with Joshua Reynolds, the grand old man of English art criticism, to
found in the Royal Academy one of the most influential of all art schools. The
two men taught classical theories of painting to the Empire and in 1791 West
replaced Reynolds as head of the Academy, to rule unchallenged until his death.

In his capacity as teacher, West was the natural figure for Americans to work
with. Painters as competent as Copley and Gilbert Stuart did significant periods
of study at the Royal Academy. But for the history of American civilization,
West's greatest success was with Charles Willson Peale (1741–1827). Son of a
somewhat disreputable father, apprenticed to a saddler at twelve, Peale was also
an ardent democrat who never seemed able to avoid the very political commitments that were most offensive to the few people actually willing to pay for
pictures. Living chiefly in the Maryland area in his early days, he was a characteristic man of the Enlightenment; a deist, a democrat, a rationalist, and a fighter
in the revolution who then became a radical member of the new Pennsylvania
legislature. Peale had great talent but too many interests for the history of art.
He carried his Enlightenment principles over into the study of nature and his
wish to read God's will there. He immersed himself in natural history and
anthropology. He began a museum that he wished to stock with specimens of as
many animals as he could find. He remained convinced that if men studied
nature long enough they would discover there the rational principles which they
needed to live lives of peace and benevolence, pleasing to God. Personally
friendly with radicals from Jefferson to Tom Paine, he also painted portraits of
more conservative heroes like George Washington and the Marquis de
LaFayette. One of his characteristic paintings has Liberty standing by the sea,
next to a classic column, trampling down tyranny, taking hold of death, thrusting
slavery aside, over the title, "Representation or No Taxation." The democratic
American version of the Enlightenment could hardly go further—and it even
remained true to Winckelmann's principles.

His museum institutionalized the Age of Reason for Philadelphia. The first attempt to convey science to the whole of American democracy, it absorbed Peale's art in the hundreds of landscapes he painted to be the backdrops for his animal displays. He advertised the museum as a pleasurable way for people to find God in nature. Peale had no taste for biblical revelation or the lessons of the local clergy. He thought natural laws taught men how to live, govern themselves, and come to peaceful terms with each other. Unfortunately, the bloody course of the French Revolution and the publication of books like Paine's *Age of Reason* scared even as liberated and tolerant a community as Philadelphia and Peale often found himself under attack for encouraging immoral tendencies. He denied it. The contemplation of the works in his museum, he said publicly, should "confirm your faith in his being and providence, exalt your conceptions of his nature, and lead you to look up to him without superstitious terror." He did not encourage "fanatical familiarity" nor "mystical enthusiasm," but rather he hoped that his patrons would adore God and "worship him with reverence as the first of *all beings*."

Chapter 3

Virginia, 1763–1815

Virginia was the first of the colonies to have a permanent settlement but slow to develop a civilized culture. In its early days it resembled colonial experiments elsewhere: economic greed, shameless exploitation of the land and original inhabitants, large turnover of population, few long-term inhabitants with education, and no sense that the task a person did contributed to anything of long-term importance in the history of the world. Compared to John Winthrop or William Penn, the first leaders in Virginia resembled a group of pirates.

In contrast to colonies that developed a town and city life originating in convenanted churches or the economic needs of farming or fishing, Virginia developed into a plantation economy based on tobacco. Large plantations decentralized the colony so effectively that Virginia never developed a genuine urban core of its own and had to make its contributions to institutional civilization first in Philadelphia and later in the swampy capital of its imagination, Washington, D.C. Each planter was a cultural unit, often acquiring his education abroad, buying a library for his extended family, hiring a tutor for his children and paying in whole or part for a clergyman. All too often he did too few of these things and the life of the mind had little chance to flourish. Only after the middle of the eighteenth century did this cultural desert begin to bloom, financed by a more settled plantation economy and goaded by British ineptitude. By then Virginia had also acquired a fatal flaw: the slavery that was giving way to public opinion farther to the north became too integral a part of the economy and the white mentality to abolish peacefully. Some of America's most acute philosophers of freedom lived daily with reminders of what lack of freedom looked like.

Racial prejudice was largely absent in early Virginia history. No consistent pattern of Indian relations emerged and on many occasions settlers displayed more prejudice against Spaniards and Roman Catholics than they did against Indians. Indians were possible allies, suppliers of food, possible converts to Christianity, and sexual companions. Few people gave the problems much of frustration at the untrustworthiness of agents, the machine that arrived but did not function, clothes that came and did not fit, bills that came and could not be paid.

Washington's commitment to revolution came gradually. From personal experience he disliked American economic dependence on Britain and came to the conclusion that the two entities should be separate and independent. He thought the British government inept and deep in a conspiracy to deprive the colonies of liberty. When the war started he was the only experienced general available. He got along well with most factions and was ever willing to eat, drink, and party with convivial people. Most of all he was a Virginian in a war dominated at least at first by men and events from Massachusetts and his presence meant a semblance of colonial unity to the American war effort. He hated to leave his plantation, knew the problems that were in store, and generally disliked Yankees, but he reluctantly accepted. He matured quickly if inarticulately into a nationalist and tried desperately to get the inherent local-ism of the colonies into some semblance of unity. Himself as near bankruptcy as the collective colonies, he worked out banking policies with Robert Morris and Gouvernor Morris that set important precedents for postwar economic policy.

By the time of the Constitutional Convention his military skill and personal charisma seemed to dominate the minds of the delegates as they evolved their ideas of what type of government the country should have. Some wanted to make him king or at least a military dictator. Most had a great fear of centralized power of any kind. The office of president evolved almost as if tailor-made for his brooding presence. The people might elect their representatives, but President Washington could veto their laws and command their armed forces. Washington himself did not much care for the Constitution at first. Made extremely skeptical in his views of human nature both by the war and by the squabbling localism of the delegates maneuvering before him, he came to accept it only under the influence of Alexander Hamilton and only after reading defenses like *The Federalist Papers*, written for New York newspapers by Hamilton, James Madison, and John Jay in support of ratification. Once the Constitution was accepted he became the inevitable choice for president, and only his force of personality kept the country together over the next eight years (1789–1797). He bequeathed three key legacies in this period to the new nation: he left offic[e] voluntarily, giving democracies everywhere a much-needed precedent; warned against European entanglements as likely to destroy American lib[erty] and unity; and he began gradually to free his slaves, convinced that slaver[y] and freedom could not long coexist. The first precedent lasted until 1940, the s[econd] till 1917; the third was not followed and in time all but tore the countr[y] because it was not.

thought. Indeed, the real problem at first was the abysmal quality of the English immigrants. Overpopulation in England and the resulting poverty and criminality caused the shipment of groups of settlers with none of the education, intelligence, or sense of purpose that permeated Massachusetts Bay from the beginning. The whites frequently spread disease among themselves as well as the Indians, proved remarkably lazy, and were unwilling to obey authority. They had no concern about making a permanent settlement, were willing to cheat and murder Indians and kept their eyes on the main financial chance—which due to severe myopia they never could seem to grasp. They had rarely worked at a serious job in England and did not want to learn in Virginia. If they took one lesson from their earlier existence to heart, it was that English gentlemen did not need to work. They intended to be gentlemen.

Such an economy and such an economic attitude demanded the importation of large numbers of manual laborers. The system that developed was to import indentured servants, people who agreed to work for a specified term of perhaps seven years in exchange for passage money, food, and shelter. Unfortunately, not only were the men running the plantations unused to executive authority over others, the men arriving were frequently the least promising human material obtainable from British streets. Legal relationships were unclear, the labor was hard and brutal habits easy to fall into. A certain amount of violence was inherent in the system and no traditional customs of humane discourse prevented it. In England, servants could sell their services for a year at annual fairs. Virginia did not have towns or fairs and servants soon found they had few rights. Masters could sell their contracts and force them to move, or insist that they stay whether they wanted to or not. Men got into the habit of thinking of other men as being like animals—useful if stubborn, something to be sold if necessary.

The first Negroes arrived in 1619, but for a long time most servants were white. Neither law nor custom made for different treatment based on race. But one key difference proved important: Blacks normally arrived as slaves, war booty bought from a slave trader in Africa. They could not ever expect to serve out their terms and the assumption seemed to grow that their children inherited this permanent status. Slaves had other advantages: They were more stable as a work force and did not seem to aspire to social equality with white men after a term of service. No one much thought about it and when white labor became scarce, boatloads of slaves filled the gap, reproduced, and helped whites achieve the wealth and social status they so yearned for. By 1682, Indians and slaves became lumped together in laws that tied the color of skin to the status of freedom. After that date, the assumption always was that a dark skin meant slave status or at least slave origin; a white skin meant a more acceptable origin and the freedom to rise in status.

By the early eighteenth century, Virginians developed mental lives not all that different from those in the North. They too tended toward low-church

Protestantism; what they lacked in zeal they imported, in the form of Scots Presbyterian tutors for their children. They too read the Whig commonwealthmen and absorbed their puritanical notions about high taxes, established churches, tyrannical kings, concentration of property, restricted voting, and a standing military. They did not even need to look to Rome for examples of what slavery meant, although they could and did; they needed only to go into the next room or look out the window. In effect, when the British neglected to respect the rights of white Virginians, they were trying to treat them like blacks in a society still socially insecure and very touchy about such things. With less influence of church and minister, there was less talk of the inhumanity of slavery. By the time public opinion mobilized on the issue according to humane, secular Enlightenment ideas, it seemed to be too late. A whole class had developed set apart by skin color and history that would be quite unassimilable if suddenly set free. Whites could not bear the thought of competition from such people. Having only recently emerged from primitivism themselves, they had no firm traditions or civilized resources to fall back on. The economy needed blacks and wholesale exile was the only way of freeing them. The dilemma seemed unsolvable.

The goal of the successful Virginian was to recreate English country gentry life. After 1700 a relatively fluid aristocracy developed a definite local culture that reflected well the Virginian's understanding of what a comparable Englishman did. He was in all probability unaware of how independent he was of higher governmental and religious authority or in how many ways his mind resembled those to the north. Imported books arrived with little delay, tutors educated in England or Scotland brought the latest religious and educational ideas. Children could go abroad to complete their education or go to the new College of William and Mary. Nothing especially creative or original came out of such an environment except the whole style of life; for the comfortable white class it would be hard to imagine a better place to live. Evangelicals, liberals, and deists coexisted peacefully under an apathetic Anglican establishment, local vestrymen obtained competence in practical politics, and the general tolerance was not complicated by Congregationalist or Quaker pressures. French Huguenot, Scots, and Scots-Irish blood leavened the earlier Anglo-Saxon mixture, reenforcing the already strong Protestant bias. In Virginia, too, the clergy were among the leaders when the Revolution broke out: Scots had little reason to love a British king in any case and the French had not come to America out of sheer love of ocean travel. Especially in Virginia, America attracted the very people who made the best revolutionaries.

So many Virginia revolutionaries were deists that the evangelical passions that motivated many less prominent Virginians sometimes are forgotten. The concentration on William and Mary as the key educational institution has meant a

stress on its atmosphere of toleration and its competent teaching of science, political science, and a generally democratic liberalism. But a number of leading Virginians went to Edinburgh for training, especially in medicine, and even more went to the College of New Jersey at Princeton, which remained securely Scots Presbyterian through the presidency of Woodrow Wilson in the early twentieth century. Evangelical pressures helped establish Hampden-Sydney and Washington colleges as cultural colonies of Princeton. Presbyterians increased in social respectability as Anglicans went into temporary decline; Baptists and Methodists expanded with remarkable rapidity once they established a toehold. The vast preponderance of the evidence seems to point toward religious independence and recalcitrance as providing much of the energy to political radicalism. Far from usually going together, political liberalism and religious liberalism went together only in a few highly visible leaders. The Washingtons, Jeffersons, and Marshalls of Virginia were *sui generis*. A comfortable Anglican did not easily give up his allegiance to king and bishop even when he regarded current policy as shortsighted.

II

Few people any longer remember the names of the evangelicals or the Anglicans. Vast numbers know something about George Washington, Thomas Jefferson, and Alexander Hamilton and have at least heard of John Marshall and James Madison. These five men in different and often conflicting ways are the greatest contributions Virginia made to American civilization. Without them, early American history would have been quite different.

Washington remains the hardest to come to terms with. In many ways the perfect embodiment of Enlightenment man, he possessed charisma without ever seeming to have uttered an original sentence or even one that was striking if derivative. He simply and sensibly went about the practical, utilitarian life that others preached about. He was frankly American, with none of the French connections of Jefferson or the British affectations of Alexander Hamilton. He never had much of an education, never went to Europe, and never studied medicine, law, or the classics on his own. He was basically a product of the comfortable backwoods who learned human nature while pursuing a military career during and after the French and Indian War. He was not a very talented officer, but the British undervalued him and he left the army to marry well, run a large farm, and speculate in western lands. Like many Virginians, he found that the system of selling his tobacco through traveling factors and buying on long terms of credit from British merchants was a recipe for financial disaster. Washington's letters often become long wails

III

Virginia, by itself, could never have produced a strong centralized government for the nation. Virginia was too proudly local, too suspicious of national power, too wealthy and too self-sufficient. But Virginia's leaders, often in spite of their professed principles, proved remarkably adaptable to changing circumstances. When their own ideas proved inappropriate for a given problem they assimilated others, however grudgingly. Washington became a nationalist through his military experience and the demands made on him as president. He bequeathed a potentially strong and growing nation to Thomas Jefferson and James Madison largely because he ignored their advice and followed the advice of Alexander Hamilton.

Hamilton (1755–1804) was essentially placeless and statusless. Born illegitimate in the West Indies, he had neither a native state to which to feel allegiance nor money or land to locate him within American social contexts. He apparently became a rebel upon landing in New York in 1772 to attend King's College. Brought up a zealous Scots Presbyterian, he found himself among that most fractious of all rebel churches and began publishing revolutionary pamphlets when still an undergraduate. Like many Enlightenment thinkers, he placed the British–American relationship within the larger plans of a rational God for his creation and insisted that the British tax policy violated natural law. Only by exercising local autonomy could Americans exercise their faculties the way God intended. He took these principles, a great military zeal, and an enormous ambition into the army and became personally close to General Washington. Since Washington could not have a son of his own, Hamilton in many ways played that role for him.

Hamilton's experience in the war made him a nationalist like Washington, but it also made him a currency expert. Appalled by the chaos of rebel finances, he read widely and mastered the best economic thinking of the day. He never cared much for Francis Bacon, John Locke, or Isaac Newton, however. Instead, he took his most useful insights from the extraordinary Scots skeptic, David Hume. For Hamilton, reason played a small part in the lives of men. He thought people lived by custom, prejudice, and convention and that the greatest motive force of human behavior was avarice. People could be governed only if statesmen ruled them by channeling their greed into constructive paths. If greed coincided with patriotism, then the state was safe.

In certain ways, Hamilton remained a mercantilist in his economics. He believed in a powerful nation-state with tight control over citizens at home and imperial demands abroad. He wanted protected industries and a strong military. Like Hume, he valued a powerful state far more than the transitory happiness of individual citizens. In essence, Hume showed Hamilton how the corruption of the human heart could make for the greatness of nations: tie men to the country through bond sales, financial interdependence, tariff protection, and military assistance, and they will in turn be model citizens if only to protect their investments. A strong centralized government and a stable national currency were two keys to this relationship and between 1777 and the middle 1790s Hamilton worked ceaselessly to have his policies made into law.

His connections with Washington were all the passport he needed into American society and Hamilton managed to marry into the well-established Schuyler family in New York and develop an influential legal practice. For a while, no one listened to him. The war had been fought to keep George III and Parliament from exercising central control over local colonies and most Americans of the 1770s and 1780s had no desire to trade one despotism for another. They preferred to err on the side of anarchy at least for a while and did so under the Articles of Confederation. Army and navy remained weak and taxation ineffectual. State legislators proved vulnerable to pressures from debtors and enacted laws that delayed the collection of debts, which permitted payment of debts by commodities instead of cash or which simply inflated the currency by printing money not backed by specie. Small backwoods rebellions of infuriated farmers scared people in more settled areas. Men who had fought for their just liberties against the British came to fear the loss of those liberties to tyrannous democratic majorities. The rights of property came to seem more relevant than the rights of man.

In 1787 Hamilton had his way and the Constitutional Convention enacted many of his suggestions at least in part. No one commanded that gathering, and possibly Madison, Franklin, and John Adams were more influential as individuals. Certainly Hamilton represented an extreme point of view: He wanted a president for life with an absolute veto on legislation and two electoral bodies to name the president, each one more removed from popular control. He was willing to settle for what he could get, however, and certainly the Constitution was far more centralizing in tendency and reflected a far greater skepticism about human nature than did the Articles of Confederation. Hamilton then joined with Madison and John Jay to write a series of election arguments for New York voters telling them why they should accept the new document. Published later as *The Federalist Papers*, they became the most influential statements of American political science. The system of checks and balances—dividing power among the president, congressmen, senators, and judges—promised to keep human greed from disrupting the power relationships of the state. No one faction would be able to control all the others—the nation was too big and the factions too many. If all else failed, then the courts would annul laws that conflicted with the Constitution. The Constitution itself never explicitly said this, but Hamilton felt his view sensible and a great Virginia lawyer named

John Marshall used *The Federalist* to justify this highly original American contribution to world legal practice.

As Washington's first secretary of the treasury, Hamilton had a unique opportunity to shape the institutionalization of his ideas into the American system. In key position papers he argued that the nation should fund and assume state debts, establish a strong central bank, stabilize the currency, and keep banking policy insulated from angry debtors. Essentially he was using Hume's psychology to shape economic policy: focus the attention of the men of wealth and property on the nation and they will have a vested interest in its success. Their debts, the validity of their money, and their own physical safety depended on the soundness of the nation: of course they would become patriots! He was perfectly right. The country desperately needed a strong guiding hand economically, and local governments were too small, weak, and subject to pressure to enable most of them to pursue sound monetary policies. Hamilton thus constructed the perfect Enlightenment machine for the American government: a rational mechanism that ran itself and was all but immune to irrational pressures.

Thomas Jefferson, the key representative of Virginia thinking, disapproved. He felt that Hamilton reflected the business and commercial interests and that his policies would hurt farmers. He feared that many speculators, including some embarrassingly close to Hamilton personally, would profit while legitimate debtors would receive little or nothing. He feared the centralizing economic power and thought it open to corruption. Above all, he feared any strong institution. The Jeffersonians codified their position largely on the basis of "strict construction" of the Constitution, meaning that the Constitution explicitly specified certain government tasks and that government could do nothing except these tasks. Hamilton argued for "loose construction," meaning that the government could do anything not expressly forbidden by the Constitution. Hamilton carried the day with President Washington and the country acquired a strong, flexible central government. Hamilton and his party were soon out of power, however, and Hamilton lived to see his mechanism in the hands of his Virginia enemies. Both Jefferson and his leading intellectual supporter, James Madison, lived to become president. Both found loose construction of the Constitution essential for the execution of their policies. In effect, Virginia could rule as well as it did in the early nineteenth century because it assimilated the principles of the man it hated perhaps most of all the founding fathers.

IV

The leading Virginia intellectual in politics was James Madison, Hamilton's collaborator in writing *The Federalist Papers* and a reasonably ardent nationalist in many of his views. But Madison was shy, retiring, and politically uncharismatic and preferred to work behind the scenes. Thomas Jefferson, despite his frequent protestations to the contrary, became the leader of the Virginia agrarian forces. Opponents of Hamilton's economic schemes muted their own differences to establish some kind of solidarity behind Jefferson's leadership.

Jefferson was in many ways sheltered in his political background. He rarely left plantation Virginia if he could help it and was in France when many important issues arose during the revolutionary years. His great charm of character, astonishingly broad-ranging mind, and ability to phrase effectively the thoughts of others made him the chief author of the Declaration of Independence and the preferred voice of the Democratic-Republicans as they formed themselves into something resembling a political party to combat Hamiltonianism. He could also be weak and vacillating in making up his mind and following a decision to its logical conclusion, was an inept administrator, and like many Americans of conservative temperament he basically hated politics. His eight years as president were thus to him a "splendid misery," splendid because of the achievement of democratic nationhood, but miserable because they tore him from his home and kept him from the intellectual and aesthetic pleasures he preferred.

Jefferson's leadership of Virginia and his assumption of the presidency in 1801 marked a major shift of cultural dominance. The Boston that had been so creative through the life of Jonathan Mayhew had reached its climax in the essentially derivative and often unreadable political science of John Adams. The city had little more to say and entered the deep sleep of High Federalism, not to reawaken creatively until the 1830s. New York, still bustling and mercantile, occasionally attracted an intellectual like Hamilton but seemed incapable of growing any of its own; except for an occasional minor writer, New York did not become important until the emergence of James Fenimore Cooper in the 1820s. Philadelphia seemed at its height in 1800 but within ten years was clearly exhausted, deprived of the national capital by politics and of many of its most creative figures by death or loss of creative power. Virginia was the only creative environment that remained vital, but due to its lack of an urban center it had to focus on Washington, a diseased swamp that might be a city of the future but was hardly one in the present.

Just as Hamilton represented a right-wing tory Enlightenment, stressing greedy human nature and the need for government mechanisms that harnessed avarice usefully, Jefferson represented a liberal Enlightenment. He was convinced of the basic rationality of many people and thought that a well-informed citizenry could be trusted to choose a competent leadership. In many ways fully as skeptical as Hamilton, he aimed his skepticism more at religions, kings, and governments and remained convinced that science and reason could progressively solve most social problems. He also had important cultural differences from opposing leaders like Hamilton and Adams. For Hamilton, life was mostly money, status, power, and glory; for Adams life was constant striving toward public and private virtue combined with a middle-class yankeeism that made heaven seem like having all his family around him on his Braintree farm. But Jefferson came out of Virginia and brought with him a kind of Epicureanism. He liked music and architecture, good conversation and beautiful women. He was serious without being earnest, and unafraid of enjoying himself. For Hamilton this attitude was hypocrisy, for Adams a trivial frivolity. Neither man, nor those for whom they spoke, could ever really understand Jefferson and Virginia.

Jefferson contributed to more areas of American civilization than anyone else except Benjamin Franklin. Outside politics, his greatest impact was on architecture. His passionate fondness for the classics, especially Roman history, gave him a preference for Roman architecture that has shaped political building in America to the present day. Learning much of what he knew from the *Four Books of Architecture* of the sixteenth-century Italian architect Andrea Palladio, Jefferson also loved the Roman forms because they illustrated so well his Enlightenment preconceptions. He had a Newtonian faith in a rational and harmonious universe, and the austere, rational designs of Palladio seemed the perfect means for carving scientific order out of the Virginia wilderness. He did not pretend to be genuinely original in architecture any more than he did in politics, but he felt that a painstaking assimilation of the best of Roman aesthetics was appropriate for a democracy trying to shuck off the decadent forms of medieval and Renaissance Europe. The visual results remain at his home, Monticello; the University of Virginia; and a few structures in Washington, D.C., and its imitators across the country. Jefferson's Roman ideas, combined with the strong bias toward Greek architecture of his good friend Benjamin Henry Latrobe, produced a composite classicism that came to symbolize American Enlightenment democracy in architecture.

Jefferson's liberalism had four main sections. He felt that all men were created equal, not in ability but in potential for rational thought and in moral sense; therefore each person should be free to develop his abilities as best he could. He modified John Locke slightly to insist on the natural rights to life, liberty, and the pursuit of happiness. He insisted that the sovereignty of the people replaced the sovereignty of the crown. He asserted the right of revolution against tyranny. Expressed in clear prose, these ideas form the core of the Declaration of Independence, and that document begins the history of liberalism in American thinking.

Jefferson also made three concrete contributions to American politics after writing the Declaration. He returned to Virginia to fight first against the laws of primogeniture and entail that gave the state at least a resemblance to the British class structure. He thought that the comfortable classes had governed well in the past but feared that in the future they might not. In the long run, the state would be better off if such undemocratic vestiges of the past disappeared. He then worked for the disestablishment of the Anglican Church, another vestige of the British past and one that could not help but be offensive to a deist like Jefferson. Successful in disposing of these largely symbolic issues, Jefferson was less successful in his third campaign, to set up a ruthlessly meritocratic system of public education. The state did little to enact his ideas in education at the time. When it did it went far beyond anything he had intended, joining the country in a more egalitarian, indiscriminate system of free education for all regardless of ability.

V

Jefferson genuinely believed in many of the principles long associated with his name; unlike most intellectuals he had the opportunity to try them out as president. He found no valid constitutional passage that permitted him to annex Louisiana, yet decided that he should do so. He found no way to do without Hamilton's Bank of the United States, but decided that under Jeffersonian control such an institution might have its uses. He successfully reduced public debt and the military forces, but in no material way altered the course Hamilton had set for the future of the country. He tried an embargo policy rather than war to get his way with Britain and France and found that high-sounding words and policies did not always do what they were supposed to do. This one at least caused severe sectional animosity that possibly threatened the unity of the new country. He left even more severe trials for his successor. In surviving those trials, Madison quietly adapted Jeffersonian principles to the realities of the young nation and in effect Virginia dominated American civilization for a generation.

Madison's career in many ways summed up the basic themes of the period. Growing up in a Virginia gentry family in the Piedmont, he experienced a system whereby the vestry of the local Anglican church provided Virginians with roughly the same experience in self-government as that experienced by Massachusetts Congregationalists. The vestry not only had power over the hiring and firing of the minister, it also regulated town morals, took care of the destitute, and supplied the community with local leaders like sheriffs and country lieutenants. Madison took this democratic culture with him to the College of New Jersey, where he found it reinforced and revolutionized in the New Light Scots Presbyterianism of President John Witherspoon. School revolutionaries included two men of letters, Philip Freneau and Hugh Henry Brackenridge, both friends of Madison. He absorbed the prejudices against a possible Anglican bishop and read widely in the Whig Commonwealthman tradition. Madison never was especially zealous in his religious practices, but like many of his generation put all such energies into the battle for independence. Prevented by poor health from a military role, he fought hard for liberty of religion and separation of church and state in Virginia, in the process becoming close to Jefferson.

During the 1780s he seemed to find compromise positions that permitted alliances with both Hamilton and Jefferson. He also began his lifelong efforts to curry the favor of France as a long-term ally for America to use in neutralizing excessive British influence. Such pro-French attitudes made a man seem a violent radical in the years after 1789, yet Madison combined them with a genuine nationalism. The support of France, in his view, was simply a necessity for a strong America. Many of Madison's ideas went into the famous Virginia Plan, probably the key submission to the convention that wrote the Constitution. He worked hard for a strong currency and two houses of Congress, one democratic and one more restricted; he also wanted some kind of a federal veto on state laws. He became the preeminent analyst in America of the dangers of factions controlling the nation and formulated the then highly original argument that republics as large as America could succeed because their many competing groups effectively prevented any one from gaining control.

Always prominent but behind the scenes, Madison became close to President Washington and was in fact the author of important works like Washington's first inaugural. He proved far more willing to compromise than many others from Virginia. He could support Hamilton for secretary of the treasury, for example, because he was the "best man," while still opposing Hamilton's pro-British foreign policy bias. He also supported Jefferson on key issues like the need for a Bill of Rights in the Constitution and hostility to a national bank. The events of the 1790s polarized everyone, however, and even Madison finally had to choose sides. He chose Jefferson's and in 1801 became secretary of state, with the extraordinarily difficult job of keeping America from being swept to disaster during the course of Britain's war with Napoleon. The task was difficult, for many Jeffersonian policies had been formulated in simpler colonial times, when the problem was British colonial policy, not American foreign policy. The agrarian ideal, public debtlessness, and a weak military were ideas of genuine relevance in the 1770s that did not necessarily retain that relevance in the 1800s. Madison not only had to compromise these positions, he had to do so while being attacked from the New England Federalist right and the irreconcilable Virginia left.

Madison persevered under great British provocation. Britain treated America insultingly, while Jeffersonian dogma prevented strong military retaliation and demanded an end to the nationalist bank when its charter ran out. Federalists threatened secession and a trade embargo to cut down much-needed tariff receipts. Madison recognized that he did not have the national unity, troops, or currency system vital to a war, yet he felt that the republic was in peril and that only a war might possibly unite the country. American democracy was too precious a heritage to allow the British to harass Americans in the West or impress American sailors on the seas. The nation was in danger of seeming a laughingstock to all Europe and the very idea of a workable democracy was in danger. The War of 1812 was a desperate gamble that America did not deserve to win by any rational military standard of judgment. But the British were too preoccupied in Europe to pay America much attention and the war ultimately ended with neither side obtaining much advantage. The country did emerge relatively unified and a new issue soon absorbed popular attention. The Virginians had fought a war, enacted tariffs, and decided that a national debt might have its uses. They even rechartered a second Bank of the United States in 1816. The Madisonian compromise had become accepted national policy.

VI

Simultaneously, to the horror of most of the Virginia "cousinage" who ran the public life of the state with an almost hereditary right to elective office, the most creative Virginian of them all succeeded in defeating every attempt to unseat him or lessen his influence. Long after James Monroe, the last Virginia president, retired from public office, Chief Justice John Marshall was serenely persuading Jeffersonian Democrats among his colleagues to follow his Federalist lead in the law.

Despite his birth in a log cabin, Marshall was related to Thomas Jefferson and a member of the famous family that came to include John Randolph and Robert E. Lee. The family was important for Marshall's quick rise to political prominence, but the backwoods did more for his mind: deprived of conventional schooling, he was largely self-taught. Having in a sense made his own mind, he never had that craven feeling of inferiority toward British legal precedent that seemed to predominate among the lawyers of his generation. He took pride in casual manners and sloppy dress and never pretended to be a scholar. Those who took the pose too seriously missed the fact that they were dealing with one of the most original minds in the history of law and a man whose only American peer was Oliver Wendell Holmes, Jr., a century later.

Piedmont Virginia had been hostile to Britain since the Stamp Act, when Marshall's father, Patrick Henry, and other future radicals first made their appearance. Marshall was in his early twenties when war broke out and he joined up to fight for four years alongside the family friend George Washington. During the course of the war the men became devoted both to a strong central government and to each other. The reluctance of the states to work together even to ensure their own survival haunted Marshall for the rest of his career and in many ways his legal biases all stem from this war experience. Here too began his contempt for cousin Thomas Jefferson: while Marshall was with the troops freezing at Valley Forge, Jefferson was safe in Virginia and then in Europe, a utopian statesman and diplomat developing ideas quite inappropriate to the brutalities of daily existence.

Two early controversies helped shape his later career. Before the Revolution many Virginians owed large debts to British merchants. The war had of course changed financial circumstances and many debtors clearly thought that victory in war meant forgiveness of debts. British creditors understandably took another view and they had the terms of the peace treaty to back them up. Contrary to the national treaty Virginia and other states passed laws voiding these debts and thus in effect posed a clear case of local law in conflict with national authority. Marshall was appalled at such behavior and insisted that people must honor valid contracts regardless of inconvenience or popularity. He never forgot the willingness of people to dishonor just debts nor the willingness of the Virginia legislature to bow to such pressures.

The other issue on which he had strong opinions was that of frontier Americans accused of crimes. America bounded British, French, and Spanish territory and usually some kind of extradition treaty governed legal relations in the areas. Western Americans committed crimes from robbery to murder in areas far from courts and often in places of doubtful jurisdiction. Americans handed over to foreign courts lost their democratic rights to jury trial by peers, one major reason for fighting the Revolution. But the national law said that accused persons had to be handed over. Not to hand them over meant that national authority was impotent and incapable of negotiating treaties or enforcing its own laws. Once again Marshall sided with national power. In both cases, James Madison agreed with him.

Almost at the end of his presidency, John Adams appointed Marshall chief justice of the Supreme Court, then a post of small prestige. The Federalists knew that they were going out of power and wished to have a strong man on the Court to keep Jefferson in line. The atmosphere was soon tense. The Federalists had exercised power first and had thus been able to place their own judges in all the key positions. Many Jeffersonians were furiously ideological and demanded the right to appoint their own men when they took power. A number of laws and legal cases exacerbated feelings and some Federalist judges proved to have blatantly unjudicial temperaments. Worst of all, Congress had not enacted laws to cover many cases and judges trained in British legal tradition normally enforced British common law in American cases. In effect, many Americans found that they had won the Revolution only to be condemned to jail under laws enacted by the defeated enemy in London.

Marshall was the main target in these battles and President Jefferson had already picked out Virginia lawyer Spencer Roane to be Marshall's successor. But Marshall outwitted the Jeffersonians and managed to keep his job and the judicial system largely intact. In the process, he decided case after case in favor of national supremacy over state laws and decisions. In one case, he established the right of his Court to declare acts of Congress unconstitutional, something Hamilton had stressed in the *Federalist Papers* but never succeeded in having included in the Constitution. In another case he insisted that valid contracts undertaken by state governments could not be repealed by state legislatures; in the process, he established the right of the Court to invalidate state laws. In a third case, he invalidated state taxing laws which were aimed at driving the Second Bank of the United States out of various states. He insisted that when state and national laws clashed, national laws prevailed.

In these and other cases Marshall prevailed, often winning the support of justices who might otherwise have voted against him, so great was his personal charm and logical power. The last of the great Virginians, he lived on into the Age of Jackson to bequeath that great American contribution, a Supreme Court equal in power to the Congress and the presidency and separate from each, to other times and other countries.

PART II

A SECTIONAL CULTURE
1815–1901

Chapter 4

Cultural Nationalism, 1815–1865

The new republic proved fascinating to foreigners. One after another they arrived to see the democratic state that presumed to function without a national church, an army, an aristocracy, or a rigid class structure. Like most travelers, they missed most of what was important and instead wrote down excited examples of odd behavior or personal prejudice. "Little more reflective than a bee or an ant," as Henry Adams later observed, they often used what they encountered to warn their own countrymen of the dangers of democracy. America for them could not work because it had not been tried before.

To the foreigner, "America" was a presumptive unity. The new nation had fought a revolutionary war, had established a constitution and government, and had then fought England yet again to establish the fact of its existence. Whatever the variations that might exist from town to town, or from section to section, to foreigners at least the country really was a country. It might not last very long—it probably should not last very long—but the first visitors did not really concern themselves with much beyond the matters that were most on their minds: whether or not American principles had any possible future in their own lands. To many visitors, America symbolized a possible future for Europe; they responded largely in terms of what would happen to themselves and their own interests should "America" happen to France or England.

Among these visitors was one of the most perceptive of all the students of American civilization. Alexis de Tocqueville had grown up in a French family that had never accepted the French Revolution. The product of upper-class comfort and Roman Catholic education, he seemed an unlikely prospect to become the foremost analyst of a secular democratic culture. But Tocqueville read deeply in Enlightenment thought, became a liberal idealist in politics, and was soon critical of his family's Bourbon political views. When the Revolution of 1830 put his family out of power and installed the bourgeois monarchy of the house of Orléans, he found himself in a difficult situation. To continue his career in law required a public oath of allegiance to a regime that his family hated;

although willing to take the step, he preferred to escape the conflicts by leaving the country for an extended visit someplace else. France had long been curious about America, and Tocqueville himself had developed an interest in the issue of prison reform. He decided that the way out of his problems was to go to America to see how prisons worked in a new and more liberal society. Also curious about America as a civilization, he recruited his friend Gustave de Beaumont to accompany him on a trip that would ostensibly examine American prison reform ideas but that was in reality an effort to determine whether or not America was providing possible precedents for the future of France.

He was genuinely puzzled at first. France had an obvious national character that one could examine by isolating the *moeurs* of family, church, and state. America seemed to have little of this sort of cultural cement, but the young Frenchman soon noticed that, although "there are no American *moeurs* as yet a restless temper seems to me one of the distinctive traits of this people." Americans seemed always on the move, self-reliant and largely free of tradition, and he concluded that "the American has no time to tie himself to anything, he grows accustomed only to change, and ends by regarding it as the natural state of man." Somewhat to his surprise, he also noted that the culture of the country seemed remarkably unified: it was the culture of New England that had moved slowly westward, obliterating the differences that Tocqueville had expected to encounter along the frontier. Residents of a Southern plantation or inhabitants of a city like New Orleans would hardly have agreed, but Tocqueville was nevertheless correct in his analysis of the most obvious of the aspects of the American culture that he saw. Even in the backwoods of Michigan he found the same kinds of people, books, and attitudes that he had found on the East Coast. "In America, even more than in France, there is only one society," he concluded. "It may be either rich or poor, humble or brilliant, trading or agricultural; but it is composed everywhere of the same elements." Somehow, the "plane of a uniform civilization" had passed over it. "The man you left in New York you find again in almost impenetrable solitudes: same clothes, same attitude, same language, same habits, same pleasures." New England had conquered the wilderness, and French romantic notions about primitivism seemed to have no foundation in fact.

Tocqueville made his greatest contributions in two areas of analysis. In discussing the middle-class nature of the people, he noticed repeatedly that European notions of class did not seem to apply to American statesmen, clergymen, or the wealthy. No one in America seemed to stand out and yet no one seemed ill-bred either. The country had assumed a *"merchant"* character, and everyone seemed to share a passion for getting rich. Self-confident and optimistic, Americans also assumed that theirs was obviously the best way to live, and that foreigners would naturally emulate them once they saw how things were. The new religion and morals that went along with this middle-class self-reliance especially struck him. He could not get over the great variety of American religions, all unprotected by the state, and the great freedom that seemed to exist between unmarried members of both sexes fascinated him. In France, religion meant an established Roman Catholicism and any sort of dissent seemed to threaten political stability. The sexes socialized separately until marriage, and only then could women expect any kind of social freedom. Americans seemed quite happy believing anything they pleased and associating with anyone they pleased, and he spun wild theories in attempting to explain why American morals were "the purest existing in any nation."

The national state also fascinated him. In Europe, it initiated, financed, and controlled most of the important aspects of life, and nowhere in America could he find anything that fulfilled this seemingly essential function. He missed a great deal, including the whole middle layer of state as opposed to federal government, but he was nevertheless perceptive in his remark that "the greatest merit of American government" was to be "*powerless* and *passive*." All America seemed to need in order to prosper was "liberty and still more liberty." "What a point of comparison between such a state of affairs and our own!" Instead of petitioning a government official when something needed doing, Americans formed a private group: in short order, they had their bridge, their road, or their hospital. The conceit that this self-reliance fostered was something he could have done without, but the sense of self-worth and the willingness to rely on individual initiative were valuable national traits.

To look back at *Democracy in America* is to realize that the early 1830s were a key period in the history of the country. Tocqueville saw the present and the immediate past, and he wrote before the issues of Southern slavery and Western expansion tore the country apart. For him the great threat was not slavery, but middle-class conformity. He noticed the lack of literary and artistic achievement and feared that the oppressiveness of middle-class conformity would strangle young talent before it could emerge. He could not know that, even as he published his book, Transcendentalism was achieving its first important formulations and that soon the first important generation of major American writers would be producing works of permanent value. But what he did note, in one of his most acute analyses, was that abstract thought seemed to have no place in such a culture. Americans did not seem to have a philosophy of their own and were unfamiliar with most European thought. Not until the rise of pragmatism after the Civil War did a school emerge that made this distaste for abstractions into something of a philosophical postulate, and not until Daniel Boorstin over a century later did a writer emerge who could extend Tocqueville's insights and make them into something resembling a philosophy of American history.

The nation that emerged from this analysis was a mixed one. It had a great openness and a willingness to experiment. It was self-reliant and questioning of authority. But it was also a country that often refused to look at the past or to learn from experience. Citizens seemed to take nothing on faith and to demand that all ideas be reduced to the level of the average citizen. The majority exercised a benevolent tyranny; they meant well but were hostile to genuine political debate, were educated only in the most primitive sense of the word, and were often unable to govern themselves properly. Clearly attracted to America, Tocqueville was also repelled. He was also sure that France had little to learn from the American precedent.

II

In many ways, the nation Tocqueville found really *was* a nation. The issues that had divided people in the years between 1789 and 1815 had certainly had their sectional qualities, but disputes about strict construction versus loose construction, or over whether or not to establish a national bank, were the kinds of issues that made for broad alliances that crossed local and sectional lines. George Washington and Thomas Jefferson had won significant political support in most sections of the country, and while political parties in the modern sense of the term did not exist, national issues did. The War of 1812, while the object of violent opposition in New England, was also a unifying force if seen in a national context. The nation had fought Great Britain twice and the second "victory," however marginal militarily, ratified the existence of an entity larger than any single state. Madison had been right; the war had revived the nation.

Creative people in any young nation have something of a vested interest in national unity. In politics they wish to have an important entity with which to deal and major issues that require definition. In literature they need large topics and audiences, and the international recognition that comes from having dealt with themes that transcend a merely parochial importance. In art they like to think of themselves as part of a larger tradition, contributing in some small way to the vast history of creativity and perhaps, in the case of America, producing something which the world would remember as both original and democratic. As far as the American of the 1830s was concerned, however, only politics had produced these genuinely important issues, but literature was rapidly increasing in sophistication, and in time would produce more that was memorable than any other creative area.

The most visible of the national issues that dominated political life was the role of banking. Thomas Jefferson and Alexander Hamilton had fought many of their major battles over the need for a national bank, and Jeffersonian ideology had triumphed to the point where, in 1811, the first national bank had quietly expired—on the eve of a war in which its services were greatly needed. In 1816, the somewhat repentant Jeffersonians quietly installed a successor, hoping that their control of such an institution would prevent it from becoming a threat to states' rights. Unfortunately, they made it so weak that it served little purpose and the country suffered through several years of economic chaos before the government changed its policies enough to restore order to economic life. The lessons should have been clear to everyone: A nation needed a national economic policy that would keep local greed under control; otherwise, business rapaciousness destroyed itself and the country would never achieve economic greatness. Having let an ideology strangle a national bank once, Americans should avoid ever letting ideological purity dominate economic reality again.

Unfortunately, things never appear so clear to the people involved as they do to later observers. American banking policy had evolved over many years and was as much a product of morality and memory as it was of any empirical observation of what the country needed. British legislation like the Tunnage Act (1694) and the Bubble Act (1720) had created the Bank of England to make the raising of money for war more efficient, and to prevent the repetition of speculative fiascos like the infamous South Seas Bubble, and these two laws had been the crucial precedents in the mind of Hamilton as he developed American banking policy. The Bank of England was the model for the two Banks of the United States, and prejudices against speculation would always be a part of American rhetoric.

In practice, of course, most citizens never gave these larger issues a thought, and for years Americans needed to pay little attention to banks. The agricultural economies of the colonies did not demand much circulating money, and people could remain smugly convinced of the evils of business and speculation without really suffering from their essentially simple-minded views. But the developing economy of the new nation made conventional ideas of morality and thrift obsolete, and by the 1830s debate on the issue had a peculiar air of unreality about it. Politicians most often used rhetorical tricks to mask economic greed and debates over banking policy all too often degenerated into a mudslinging contest over who should lead the country and who would profit the most from thus controlling the White House.

An issue like paper money provided a good example of the level of debate. Any new nation is short of specie; colonial status normally means an underdeveloped economy and whatever hard currency local people do earn tends to find its way back to the mother country in return for manufactured goods that would otherwise be unavailable locally. Paper money of some kind is all but inevitable for the functioning of both the nation and the economy, and both the Hamiltonians and the Jeffersonians had accepted paper money as vital to American development. But under many circumstances, paper money depreciated in value, and in so doing could provide irresponsible politicians with an obvious issue: paper money might seem obvious and necessary to an urban businessman, but to a farmer it might just as obviously seem a trick, something that city people invented to steal food, raw materials, and land from country folk. Necessary for any sort of commercial or tax system, paper money could easily come to symbolize exploitation in economics and oligarchy in politics.

In practice, as always, things were much more complicated than in folk theory. Banking regulation in America was never really an instrument of democracy, free trade, or ideology; it was instead, as it had been in Britain, the attempt by certain favored institutions to control economic policy. State and local banks wished to restrict competition and to retain their own monopolies under the guise of orderly commerce. Paper money, as a concept, got caught up in these feuds; it was easy to feel the effects of inflation and to assume that paper money rather than irresponsible investment practices was the culprit. Even American bankers did not seem to understand banks or the role of credit in a commercial economy, and so it is no wonder that ordinary citizens were mystified and irritated. Politicians with eyes on the main chance could thus exploit them.

By the 1820s, the political scene had also changed since the early days of the republic. Then, the issues between Hamilton and Jefferson—between commerce and loose construction on the one hand and agriculture and strict construction on the other—had been relatively clear. But the Federalists had gone out of power in 1801, never to return. As time went on, young business and banking people entered the Jeffersonian party and transformed it. The party that once represented agriculture became a party of young commerce as well, using the old rhetoric of rural morality to mask commercial greed. The old language was useful to these new men, because it enabled them to attack the second Bank of the United States for reasons quite different from their real ones. They hated the bank because it worked: it prevented their more outrageous attempts to grab speculative wealth and so they wanted it out of the way. Rural morality became a hypocritical means of justifying their acts politically and an excellent way of confusing voters. Only with this in mind do the banking wars of the 1830s make much sense.

Established in 1816, reorganized several years later, the second bank did its job reasonably well during the 1820s under Nicholas Biddle. It helped the government run the country and kept local banks from excessive speculation. But the bank never quite avoided an air of favoritism; its style of operation seemed too comfortably Eastern and even aristocratic both to young men on the way up and to farmers fearful that they were on the way out. When General Andrew Jackson became president in 1829, he found that the bank did not respond favorably to some of his requests, and it soon found itself embroiled in a political feud that killed it as an institution; its death put the country into the worst depression it had ever suffered. The supporters of the president insisted that it was all a battle against established wealth in the effort to achieve a more equitable democracy, but that was nonsense. It was instead a battle to put New York Democrats into control of money that had been in the hands of Philadelphia Whigs; to expand credit in general; and to allow local business interests a freer hand in making investments. As the chief historian of banking in the period has noted, most of the leading Jacksonians were either wealthy men at the time they held office or would soon become wealthy, and they "were interested in banking for the good, earthy reason that it was a fine way to make money." What the Jacksonians really did in the name of democracy and morality was to destroy an economic policy that had been working and a dollar that had been stable. Not until the establishment of the Federal Reserve System in the early years of the twentieth century would a system emerge that seemed in some ways superior to that which was destroyed in 1836.

III

The Jacksonians claimed to speak for the common man as he took control of the great democratic experiment and in a political sense they were correct. They won elections repeatedly under the leadership of Jackson and his successors, while their Whig opponents won the presidency only in those rare instances when they managed to steal Democratic issues for themselves and to unite behind generals of their own. But the Jacksonians did not really have anything like a coherent ideology; they captured the language of equality successfully, but as far as new ideas were concerned they merely repeated slogans about states' rights, hard currency and the wickedness of national banks and wrapped themselves in the mantle of agrarian virtue. In addition to representing the new forces of capitalist enterprise based in New York City, they also spoke for numerous laboring groups as they struggled for political maturity, and for Southern slaveholders in their attempts to make cotton into the most important American export.

Their chief opponents took the old British name of Whigs. Never as coherent as the Jacksonian Democrats as a group, the Whigs tended to represent the older money of Philadelphia and the East Coast, the business interests of New England, and the Western push for internal improvements. Where Southern agriculture wanted free trade and minimal government, Northern capitalists wanted a high tariff to protect their vulnerable new industries and to pay for the roads and canals that would open up the West both as a market and as a source of raw materials. Less successful than the Democrats at winning elections, the Whigs nevertheless produced several of the most important figures in nineteenth-century political life whose ideas shaped the development of the party system in America, won the Civil War, and remained dominant in the country until the 1930s.

The most important of the Whig thinkers emerged even before the existence of the Whig party. The son of former president John Adams, John Quincy Adams was a Federalist who had shifted into the National Republican party of the Jeffersonians because he supported the foreign policies of Jefferson and Madison. Probably the most important foreign policy intellectual in the country during the nineteenth century, Adams managed to serve both as secretary of state and as president despite a personality that was not politically attractive and a primitive political organization that had unity only in its opposition to Andrew Jackson. His fate was to be the author of ideas for which others received the credit. In foreign policy, he was the key formulator of the Monroe Doctrine, and in domestic policy of the American System. President James Monroe won fame for the first, and Senator Henry Clay for the second, but Adams was the man who deserved the credit and the larger place in the history books.

As a teenager, Adams had served in Russia as secretary to Francis Dana, an American then on a mission to Catherine the Great. He had then served his father for two years when John Adams, Franklin, and Jefferson were in Paris negotiating treaties with the French. The younger Adams' education included fluency in Latin, Greek, French, and Dutch and he could read simple Spanish; he was thus one of the few Americans of the period who could talk directly with influential statesmen in their own language about books which they all knew. In the process Adams learned firsthand about the dangers of the French Revolution and firmly resolved that his country should never involve itself closely with any European power. Like Poland and Holland, America was a small country in danger of losing its liberty if it involved itself in quarrels which were not directly concerned with its own self-interest. His views came to the attention of President Washington and apparently played some role in the composition of Washington's Farewell Address, that famous statement of America's noninvolvement in the European scene.

For the next two decades, John Quincy Adams served most noticeably in Russia and as a delegate to the conference that established the Peace of Ghent in 1815. By the time he became secretary of state in 1817, he was probably the most experienced person ever to hold that post, and this experience served him well in his efforts to strengthen American independence at home and to keep Europe from excessive intervention in the Western Hemisphere. Adams was especially eager to secure the Florida territories from Spain without a war and he rightly feared the problems that could result for America if European powers continued to colonize in Latin America. Like many Americans, he sympathized with Latin American attempts to follow the precedents of American independence, but he also knew that his own country was militarily weak and in no position to offer much more than moral support in the case of war. The British, at the time, were eager for some sort of cooperative alliance with America, and Adams greatly feared that, should America actually ally itself with England, England would inevitably dominate that alliance and America would appear insignificant and impotent before the world.

The policy document that emerged from these concerns late in 1822 was called the Monroe Doctrine because it was included in a presidential message. It had three main points: (1) Noncolonization, which meant that European powers should not establish new colonies in the New World, nor should they take over colonies then under the control of some other European power; (2) Isolation from Europe, which meant that America would not intervene in European quarrels unless vital interests were directly at stake; (3) European nonintervention in Latin America, which meant that the United States would regard its own interests as at risk if any European power meddled in the affairs of the countries to the south. Simply phrased and of no immediate applicability, the policy nevertheless went into American history as a basic statement of what would be best for America and continued to represent the essential American position until World War II.

The American System that Clay and Adams developed to set forth their domestic goals was also quite simple. They had a vision of an expanding democratic nation that would cover the North American continent and spread the blessings of democracy. A protective tariff would raise the necessary money, and then Congress could use that money to open up the West. Industry would develop, canals and roads would promote business interests, and a stronger and more unified nation would result. They also planned to organize and sell off the public lands of the West, which would not only supplement tariff revenue but would also encourage new settlement and thus the development of new markets. Although other goals were not properly integral to the American System, Adams himself went far beyond this in his ideas of what the responsibilities of democracy were. In contrast to the Democrats, who were always trying to minimize national governmental activity, Adams wanted to have an activist government on the Hamiltonian model. He wanted a national astronomical observatory, a naval academy, nationally sponsored scientific expeditions, and a new department of the interior that would bring together administratively all his concerns for the internal development of the country. His vision of federal activism became the core of Whig ideology in the 1830s and after, provided the intellectual basis for the emergence of the Republican party in the 1850s and served as the basis for Republican domination of the country through the presidency of Herbert Hoover (1929–1933).

The other prominent thinker to emerge from Whig political activity was William Henry Seward. Like Adams the product of a family that was rigidly moral in its approach to life, Seward quickly took his stand against the "dictatorship" of President Jackson in Washington and his New York supporters, the "Albany Regency" of Martin Van Buren. Seward's policies not only included those of the American System, they advocated an end to imprisonment for debt, repeal of state militia laws, and temperance reform. Unsuccessful at first, Seward forged an alliance with political manipulator Thurlow Weed and newspaperman Horace Greeley to become a potent force in mid-nineteenth-century politics. The men soon managed to elect Seward governor of New York, where he supervised the building of railroads and the Erie Canal. He was less successful in his other efforts at reform, which included improved schooling opportunities for immigrant and black children. Meanwhile, Greeley became the chief spokesman for more radical Whig positions, including his own peculiar version of utopian socialism.

The most important development over the next two decades within American politics was the slow shift of people like Seward from a generally friendly attitude toward many reforms to a firm concentration on the slavery issue. The Democrats were the party of Southern slaveholders in a moral sense as well as an economic sense, and so the development of antislavery in political life took place within the Whig party. In the 1830s, former president John Quincy Adams stood almost alone in the House of Representatives as the advocate of the abolition of slavery in the District of Columbia and as the chief conveyor of petitions which opposed slavery. Southern congressmen were furious at this attack on their "peculiar" institution and tried to prevent Adams from delivering the many petitions which he received. It proved a fatal error, because such attempts at censorship quickly changed the nature of the argument from the rights of black people to the rights of whites. If slavery drove Southerners to attempt to restrict the civil liberties of whites in a democracy, then perhaps slavery really was a menace to the whole country. Adams' heroic old age, spent in battling for his beliefs, earned him the nickname "Old Man Eloquent" and an honored place in the history of antislavery. By the time of his death in 1848 he was one of the most prominent of the Conscience Whigs who were slowly moving to a more outspoken and even radical position on the subject of slavery.

Antislavery developed slowly in national politics. It lay behind some of the battles of the 1840s, but did not begin to seem permanently important until Seward went to Washington in 1849 as United States senator. The expansion of the country westward had opened up the issue of whether or not new states like Texas and Oregon would be slave or free, and thus send advocates of those positions to Congress. While some Whigs, like Henry Clay of Kentucky, worked ceaselessly for compromise, Seward rejected it and insisted that the Southern position endangered freedom everywhere. For Seward and the other Conscience Whigs, freedom was the permanent contribution of America to the world and slavery was tolerable only if it were clearly dying out. If allowed to spread into the West, slavery would hurt natural rights, restrict the diffusion of knowledge, and shackle industrial development. Democracy would suffer. In words that gave reformers their most important rallying cry of the 1850s, Seward declared that "there is a higher law than the Constitution, which regulates our authority over the domain, and devotes it to the same noble purposes." Christian morals as well as common sense demanded freedom for everyone.

New leaders like Charles Sumner and Abraham Lincoln emerged during the 1850s, but Seward remained the chief Whig spokesman for the abolition of slavery. The Whig party disintegrated under the issues of the decade, but the new Republican party soon took shape, with a far more outspoken policy toward freedom in the West. Because Seward had been too outspoken in his views to be politically acceptable in many parts of the country, the new party nominated explorer John C. Frémont as its presidential candidate in 1856 and Abraham Lincoln in 1860. Even as it did so, Seward continued his gift for making phrases that rang through the country. Convinced that the country was developing two incompatible political and economic systems, he declared that there was "an irrepressible conflict" between freedom and slavery and that either one or the other had to prevail. Lincoln, then a less controversial figure, won the presidency and the larger place in conventional history books, but Seward was the man who made a Republican victory possible. He also became the most obvious example of the continuity between the Whiggery of the 1830s and the Republicanism of the years after 1865. As secretary of state under Lincoln and Andrew Johnson, he continued to dream the noble dream of John Quincy Adams, of America as an area of freedom that could conceivably include Mexico, Canada, Hawaii, and other distant areas. He was the individual most responsible for the acquisition of Alaska, and his general attitude pervaded the Republican foreign policies of later leaders like Theodore Roosevelt and Henry Cabot Lodge.

IV

In addition to these national political issues, American literature also showed some signs of a national rather than a sectional orientation during the early years of the republic. Conventional ways of organizing the country usually divided it into thirds: the East, including New England; the middle, including New York, Pennsylvania, Delaware, and Maryland; and the South, including everything south of Maryland, which meant culturally an emphasis on Virginia and South Carolina. Insofar as national literature meant anything during the early years of the republic, it meant chiefly work that came out of Philadelphia and New York, those commercial centers most able to bridge the gap between the free societies of the East and the slave societies of the South.

In 1800, Philadelphia was clearly the literary center of the nation. During the height of its political and scientific eminence of the 1790s, it had attracted a cosmopolitan group of local and emigré figures who took for granted the European world of deism, skepticism, and science. Philadelphia had the best theaters, the best museum, and a botanical garden that had won considerable respect in Europe. Figures as well-known as Samuel Taylor Coleridge and

Robert Southey lived part of their imaginative lives in the area and even pondered schemes for emigration to the banks of the Susquehanna River.

Literary life existed, but on a less spectacular scale. Americans very much wanted to have a national language and a national literature, but the gap was great between wish and achievement. Existing European literary forms—the epistolary seduction novels of Samuel Richardson, the journals of Daniel Defoe and Laurence Sterne, the picaresques of Cervantes and Fielding, the novels of sensibility like Sterne's *Tristram Shandy*, or the Gothic romances of Horace Walpole or Ann Radcliffe—seemed oddly inappropriate to American eyes. They could perhaps take some inspiration from a work like *Robinson Crusoe*, with its world of lonely exploration, but America lacked the materials that European history and society provided. As James Fenimore Cooper noted in 1828, America had "no annals for the historian; no follies (beyond the most vulgar and commonplace) for the satirist; no manners for the dramatist; no obscure fictions for the writer of romance; no gross and hardy offenses against decorum for the moralist; nor any of the rich artificial auxiliaries of poetry."

The earliest American efforts were obvious imitations of these European forms. Susana Rowson was clearly indebted to Richardson in *Charlotte Temple*, and Hugh Henry Brackenridge owed an equally obvious debt to Cervantes in *Modern Chivalry*. Not until the earliest successes of James Fenimore Cooper in the 1820s did Americans begin to transcend their European inspirations and exploit successfully the history and the landscape of the new country. Indeed, such was the power of European fiction on an American writer like Charles Brockden Brown that Brown seems to have lived his life as if he actually were a character in one of Richardson's novels trying to write a Gothic romance at the same time. He not only cultivated the persona of the lonely and misunderstood writer, he courted the woman of his choice in a long series of letters that seems to have replaced any drive for sexual or domestic satisfaction.

Brown was the most important Philadelphia contribution to literature. Despite a nominally Quaker background, he read widely in the literature of the French Enlightenment and absorbed its ideas from the many emgirés living in Philadelphia during the French Revolution. Religious skepticism and utopian political science were in the air, and Brown's work came out of the same intellectual upheavals that produced William Godwin's *Caleb Williams* and Mary Shelley's *Frankenstein*. But Brown found little interest in his work in Philadelphia, and in a move relevant to the larger flow of cultural history, he spent most of the 1790s, when he was at his most creative, in New York City, where a small group of figures provided congenial support. From people like William Dunlap, the chief impresario and historian of the early American theater, and Charles Adams, the second son of President John Adams and a cultivated lawyer, Brown took what nourishment he could find and wrote the books which make him the first novelist of any importance in American literary

history. *Wieland* and *Ormond* and the rest are moralistic and rhetorically excessive, and Brown goes to great pains to generate an air of mystery; what strikes
modern readers most clearly is less their pseudo-Gothic trappings than their
commitment to political reform and their concern for the sensibilities of
women. But he never reached the stature of *Caleb Williams*, and quickly burned
himself out as a novelist. By the time of his early death in 1810, he had
degenerated into something of a journalistic scold, and few Americans seemed
to notice either his novels or his passing. Europeans were far kinder and quickly
translated his work into French and German, where both his themes and his
prose style doubtless seemed more appropriate.

V

Insofar as the nation, as opposed to any given section, had any cultural life at all,
William Dunlap was the individual most responsible. The son of an Irish soldier,
Dunlap had studied painting in London with Benjamin West while at the same
time beginning his long association with the theater. Once settled in New York,
he became a theater manager, portrait painter, playwright, novelist, diarist,
historian, and plain gossip. Never of the first rank in any one activity, he
managed to be second-rate at a great many, and such people are always vital to
any functioning cultural life. Dunlap not only helped sustain the creative impulses of Brockden Brown, he also introduced the country to the works of
Shakespeare, Schiller, and Kotzebue. Where young people in other parts of the
country remained unfamiliar with the larger cultural world, young New Yorkers
discovered a genuinely functioning theater that paid little attention to the
disapproving Protestantism that blighted efforts in other cities.

One of those young people was Washington Irving (1783–1859). The product
of a Federalist-Calvinist family that disapproved of all pleasures including the
dramatic, Irving habitually stole away to Dunlap's theater, where he could live
imaginatively in far-off lands. Never in good health, he managed to combine his
interests and disabilities in a recuperative trip to Europe, where he became
friendly with American exiles like the painters Washington Allston and John
Vanderlyn. He decided that his true gift was in literature, but a literature that
was sketchy and anecdotal like much of the painting which he saw. The word
"sketch" indeed described what many artists were attempting at the time; that is
what a gentleman would create as he traveled, in order to convey his impression
of distant lands to those less fortunate. As an art form, a work like Irving's *The
Sketch Book* also owed something to the traditions of the British eighteenth-
century essay of the type associated with Joseph Addison and the *Spectator*. But
Irving had come on the scene as that art form was in decline, and he did not
share its usual tone of rationality and confidence in the progress of human

nature. Irving instead adapted this decaying form to the New World, and examined instead the old Dutch legends he had heard as a child, casting a languid eye over the tensions he saw daily between the raw commercial society that dominated New York and the wild frontier that was not so far away. He adopted names like Jonathan Oldstyle and Geoffrey Crayon, but used them to muse and wander parodically over topics that might have been quite serious two generations earlier. Irving thus became something of a sport of cultural history, recording the end of the Enlightenment and the birth of romanticism without feeling much identification with either. Much of his work in this vein appeared in the journal *Salmagundi*—the name meant "hash" and the journal not only made hash out of previously sacred Enlightenment ideas, it did so in bits and pieces of art forms: making hash to convey hash, the medium and the message agreeing disgestively.

Like many American conservatives, Irving had contempt for politics of any kind; he not only satirized the follies of his own day in works like the *History of New York*, he also invented a past for the area which seemed to indicate that time meant nothing to an American either. After the manner of Laurence Sterne, he wrote as if burlesque and profundity coexisted side by side and made a mockery of any notion either of a factual past or of any possibility of serious scholarship. Not having much history to write about, he nevertheless disapproved of what he found, from Dutch bourgeois greed to the persecution of witches. What triumphs America supplied to her children were clearly accidents, with no intrinsic meaning for the new nation. In this despair, the genial Irving soon had important company among men of letters. Cooper's *The Crater*, Herman Melville's *Mardi*, and Mark Twain's *A Connecticut Yankee in King Arthur's Court* all belong to this tradition, as do a whole series of other books, ranging from much of Nathanial Hawthorne's work to John Barth's *The Sot-Weed Factor* (1960) and T. Coraghessan Boyle's *World's End* (1987).

Irving soon returned to Europe, and his seventeen years there put America on the literary map of the world. His art became genuinely cosmopolitan: writing ostensibly about New York in stories like "Rip Van Winkle" and "The Legend of Sleepy Hollow," he nevertheless borrowed many themes and details from German sources, as if he could give life to a new culture by borrowing from an older one. He devoted much time as well to the novels of Sir Walter Scott, and the past of England quite possibly meant as much to him as the past of his own country. Yet, like many visitors, he never felt more American than when he was abroad. His obsessions have many modern qualities about them: fascinated with decay and death, he also seemed happy in a world of bourgeois marriage and rosy children. He worked out his tensions in dreams; the line between the real and the imaginary is never clear and modern students of psychology find his fantasies beguiling and contemporary. Like many modern sensibilities, he seems to have feared a loss of identity, and neither he nor his creations seem to have a firm grip on themselves. More than a century before the term became a cliché, Irving intuited something of the meaning of the identity crisis for modern man.

Irving was also both seminal and modern in some of his formal innovations. Most earlier narrators made at least a pretense of reliability, and readers did not normally feel called upon to analyze the source of their information as well as the information itself. But Geoffrey Crayon was not reliable; he was whimsical, insecure, and not to be trusted. He became the father of a whole line of unreliable narrators in American literature, from Miles Coverdale in *The Blithedale Romance* to Gilbert Long in *The Sacred Fount*. He was also the progenitor of the voyager toward self-discovery, that peculiarly American literary figure which Henry Thoreau made famous in *Walden*. It is perhaps no wonder that Irving found more success in Europe than in America. America as a culture knew little of these concerns and cared less. But when Irving fled from his unimaginative native land, he was peculiarly qualified to build up legends in the lands he visited. Conscious of what his country lacked, he all but invented what he wanted in Spain and England. The most famous success of all was his description of the British Christmas. The yule log, wassailing songs, and visits from Santa Claus were not all that common in the English homes he visited, but such was the force of his pen that he all but made them come true. Life could imitate art long before Oscar Wilde made epigrams about it.

VI

Because he was away for such a long period, Irving contributed to cultural New York chiefly in spirit, but other figures attached to the Bread and Cheese Club confirmed the city in its new cultural hegemony. As the name of the club implied, it did not take itself too seriously, but it nevertheless came to include not only Irving in absentia but also the first important American poet, William Cullen Bryant; Chancellor Kent, the Federalist legal scholar; Samuel F. B. Morse, talented at painting but known now as the inventor of the telegraph; and Gulian Verplanck, an editor of Shakespeare. Others now obscure added a vital bulk to the group, and for the first time in close to a century, an American city could rival Philadelphia in the Age of Franklin as a creative environment.

The member of the group who became best known abroad was James Fenimore Cooper (1789–1851). Cooper's father was a wealthy judge, Anglican in religion and Federalist in politics, and like many such young people Cooper was too high-spirited to seem quite respectable. Never especially reverent, he was also given to practical joking, and Yale College only tolerated his attendance for a brief period. Unrepentant, he went off to sea to pick up the lore that later went into many of his novels. Inheriting more land and money than was necessary for a comfortable life, Cooper also married into yet another wealthy family and settled down to life as an indolent country gentleman. One evening, however, he read a novel so bad that he was sure he could do better himself. He turned out a novel of manners that was nothing special, and published it anonymously with some success in 1820.

Once he had the taste for literature he seemed unable to stop. He abandoned the style of Jane Austen and turned to the style of Scott; the publication of *The Spy* in 1821 marked the beginning of a number of important themes in the history of American writing. It introduced the American Revolution as a topic worthy of treatment as a historical source; it treated the American landscape as a serious inspiration to the imagination; it introduced the whole genre of flight-and-pursuit to American art, with its ancillary motifs of the solitary horseman on his mission, the families divided by war, and the women who seem to be either overly sensitive or mentally defective but never merely competent. Cooper always wrote much too quickly—a wealthy gentleman could please himself and ignore criticism—and his language was verbose and clogged with detail. His plots were inconsistent and his love scenes awkward enough to convince a reader of the virtues of celibacy. An immediate success in French and German as well as English, the book not only made the American novel possible, it proved that the American Revolution could play a role that was the functional equivalent of the Middle Ages for Scott.

The members of the Bread and Cheese Club were encouraging and *The Pioneers* (1823) attempted still a third type of novel, the American pastoral. In it Cooper looked at the life of his own father in Cooperstown, New York; in the process he made the first imaginative presentation of the quintessential American theme of the tension between "civilization" and the frontier. One memorable scene, the massive pigeon-shoot, has become something of a *locus classicus* for the condition of being an American, as the forces of settlement wantonly slaughtered the bounties of nature. But the real achievement of the book was the creation of Natty Bumppo, the aging hunter with the yellow tooth and the vulgar manner who was apparently based in part on Daniel Boone. Not all that impressive in this volume, Natty found himself in legal trouble for hunting deer out of season and served a brief term in jail. Not until later volumes in the Leatherstocking series did Cooper return to Natty's youth and make him into something of a holy innocent of nature, the symbolic bridge figure between nature and civilization who never quite seemed comfortable in either place and who was doomed by the unstoppable forces of history. As *Lederstrumpf* he entered the folklore of Germany especially, and was soon the inspiration of young imaginations in lands remote from the American frontier.

Having succeeded in books about history and the frontier, Cooper turned next to the sea to establish yet another province for the novel that also seemed peculiarly American. Using both the career of John Paul Jones and his own experiences as a teenager at sea, Cooper wrote *The Pilot* (1823). As subsequent writers like Richard Henry Dana and Herman Melville soon proved, the sea was as much a frontier for the American mind as the woods, and a young citizen of a new country could venture out into the unknown to test himself against the elements, or to find God, heroism or his own identity in the middle of nowhere. Cooper also locked the American novel into a single form. Where English writers had Jane Austen and Anthony Trollope to provide examples of social realism in all its mundane detail, Americans did not have anything similar until the works of William Dean Howells later in the century. What was "real" to the American writer was the mystery and adventure of life in a new world, a new world of the imagination where a man might have to face himself as well as hostile Indians and frightening storms at sea. Thus the romance became the first American fictional form of permanent importance and romanticism—however that vague and all-encompassing term may be defined—the first genuinely productive climate of creativity in America.

VII

Romanticism had many strangely divergent achievements in America, from the sketches of Irving to the poems of Walt Whitman, but surely none so strange as those of Edgar Allan Poe (1809–1849). To most Americans in the century and a half since Poe's major work, he was a man famous for being a drunk in private life and a creator of art for adolescents when he was functional. Few read his criticism or valued his work for its literary qualities: they knew of "The Raven" because generations of schoolchildren had to memorize its thumping rhythms and perform it as a final-examination ceremony; and they knew a few of the tales of horror and of detection, but did not regard them as truly adult. Poe did not seem to teach Americans anything important about their country or about morality, and most literary scholars ignored him until the 1930s. Poe has recovered, in large part because for a century the French insisted on treating him as a major artist, and American critics began to ask why. The line now seems clear from Poe and Baudelaire down to the modernist writers of the early twentieth century, and when even so august a literary presence as T. S. Eliot stressed the connection, Americans had to take notice. But Poe will always remain a problem for native scholars because he not only did not seem to be a sectional literary personality, he did not seem to be American at all. Cooper and Irving could explore the world and still write about America in ways that Americans and foreigners could recognize. Poe's world was internal and had no geographical location at all.

Poe was a Southerner by rights but a cosmopolite by upbringing and choice of residence. The son of an English actress and an American actor, he grew up largely in Richmond but had five key years in England. An orphan from an early age, his adoptive parents were a narrow-minded and obstinate Scots merchant and his neurasthenic wife. The mixture of nation and social class left scars that never really healed. Poe seemed hardly to know which country he belonged in, whether he was to be a Southern gentleman, an artist, or a Scots businessman; he never had, at any time, much sympathy for his desire to be a man of letters. He read Byron, yet also entered West Point; his family had money, yet he had little or none. He wanted to write poems, yet no one wanted to read them. He wanted to edit literary journals, but no one wanted to buy them. A Southerner, he spent most of his adulthood in Philadelphia and New York. Poe was a deracinated person who never could find his place, and instead made his place through his art. In doing so, he became not only the closest America could come to producing a romantic poet, he became a vital influence on later literary history. His status in the 1840s seemed to speak with great relevance to the modernists of two generations later, and Poe joined with Whitman—of course a very different artist—in presenting modernism with an American version of the artist ignored by his society and forced to create a habitable universe through his art alone.

Poe's earliest work was poetry that had no apparent roots in America. Most of it was not especially good, but through it he began the habit of developing masks that enabled him both to present himself to the world and to hide himself from the world. He developed the notion that the poet could will into existence any world that he wished; since reality had so few attractions, reality could not be all that important; the imagination was the true means of grace for such as he, and through it the wronged, innocent, scapegoat poet could find the only kinship he would ever know. He wrestled regularly with philosophical ideas that were too big for him to master, and he insisted on expressing himself all too often through literary forms that were inappropriate vehicles for what he wanted to say. In a manner similar to that of Emerson, he worried about the relationship of fact and idea, of nature and God, and emerged with a sense for the symbolism of all things, the correspondence between discrete data and the structure of the universe. Neither writer was ever especially clear about these issues, and Poe only made matters worse by his constant resort to an apocalyptic tone, an overwrought rhetorical style that seemed to resemble all too clearly his frequently temperamental behavior, his "drunkenness," and his extraordinarily insulting book reviews. Like many romantics and modernists, he seemed to have no clear idea of when to stop.

He also was something of a case of arrested adolescence. His home was enough to make anyone of sensibility neurotic, and his early separation, both emotional and financial, from his adoptive parents certainly never helped him achieve stability. He never matured sexually, and instead luxuriated in some of the worst literary habits of the age: the Gothic romance was bad enough as an art form, but to live life and create short story plots that revolved around pubescent maidens whose sole future seemed to be to become nubile and doomed simultaneously was not the way to literary greatness. Poe also had a fascination for embedding his neuroses in easily remembered physical structures: because he felt he lived in a prison, he could write with great effect about people in prisons; because he was hopeless with sexually mature women, he could write with extraordinary verve about the hot tensions between brother and sister, or between women socially unobtainable and the males who admired them. For an age when actually consummated sexual relationships were not subjects thought appropriate to fiction, this writing had some attraction, and it still does to adolescents who have not quite figured out what adult life is all about. For a developing artist, however, the problem was insuperable. Since Poe himself never really grew up, his art never did either, and he remains a favorite chiefly for those for whom immaturity is a compelling topic.

Instead of analyzing the American landscape or the Revolution, Poe ransacked world history for his themes. A Southern education concentrated on the classics and, like Jefferson, Poe was fascinated by Roman legends. The excitement which Europe felt over the discoveries of Pompeii and Herculaneum was still in the air, and the thought of whole civilizations frozen in time like those cities was far more compelling to Poe than a revolutionary love affair or the progress of American enterprise. Timelessness was a positive value, and great distance enabled the poet to do what he wished. A close reader of Coleridge's literary criticism, he insisted that a poem or a story was a symbolic way of unifying the world; everything except words was an illusion. Nothing in his own life seemed to cohere, and so it was doubly important to create art that did cohere. Otherwise, a man could split in two, like the house of Usher.

Poe will always be a fascinating problem if not a great artist. Obsessed by the dark side of the human personality, by the irrationality of normal-seeming life, he put into a few tales the heart of his neuroses. In some of his most influential work, the mystery tales, he effectively initiated a popular literary form simply by positing the existence of a chaotic and meaningless world, and then by demonstrating that a man who could intuit the workings of the universe, proved that things made sense after all. A detective like M. Dupin was thus a poet in disguise. In effect, the rational, philosophical side of Poe's mind warred with his vision of chaos and the irrational, making art of personal anxiety. In his one long work, *The Narrative of A. Gordon Pym* (1837–1838), he came close to making an effective and sustained statement of these themes. All people, like poor Pym, were literally "at sea," traveling in small prisons, threatened by mutinies, buffeted about by the unknown, and doomed to deception and possibly death when encountering supposedly friendly natives. The novel petered out in a vision of blinding whiteness; neither Pym nor Poe knew the answers to the questions that obsessed them. Most Americans never asked the questions and so of course paid no attention.

Chapter 5

The Religious Pressures on Literature and Politics, 1815–1876

Until perhaps 1830, the country did have a unity that made Tocqueville's analysis plausible and talk of "American politics" or "American literature" seem sensible. But the existence of slavery proved to be a problem that the new democracy could not solve peacefully. From Russia to Brazil, other societies managed to rid themselves of equally pernicious social arrangements, but in America things were different. Both North and South took their major cultural ideas from the spokesmen of a conservative Protestantism. The humane values of the revolutionary generation all but died out in both sections of the country, and a religious absolutism replaced them. The same essential religious orientation in both North and South made compromise impossible, for both came to identify the existence of slavery with divine sanction. Men could have compromised an issue that was merely political or social, but the issue of slavery became a religious one. Only the West remained relatively free from this theological cast of mind, and the West was still underpopulated. It provided the two chief political figures of the years around the start of the Civil War, but in the end never found an acceptable compromise.

The beginnings of this holy war went back to roughly 1800, when the first signs of a resurgent puritanism appeared. The first Great Awakening of the years around 1740 had been astonishing enough; while Western Europe was settling comfortably into an age of skepticism and science, much of America was returning to an orthodoxy that seemed an intellectual disaster. Occasional divines appeared who seemed quite as intelligent and educated as any in the opposing camp, and a figure like Jonathan Edwards remains impressive two and a half centuries after he wrote his major works, but the impact of revivalism was pernicious. Religious beliefs became both more simple and more rigid, and arguments that deserved dispassionate scientific investigation instead existed in theological contexts. Although many clergymen were amateur scientists, theology limited the possible areas for future investigation; although many clergy were not without literary and aesthetic interests, theology likewise limited any perception of aesthetic achievement. Outside a few cities the American public followed their lead and blighted the forces of intellectual and aesthetic liberation. Not until the 1920s could New York emerge as a cosmopolitan center of creativity that challenged Philadelphia in the Age of Franklin in its potential.

The second Great Awakening was no single event, but rather a series of outbursts of conservative religion that marked the spread of New England values westward. Beginning about 1800 and continuing until the later 1850s, these revivals Christianized a West that had seemed in danger of becoming pagan. First acquainting people with the fundamental doctrines of Presbyterianism and Methodism, itinerant clergy soon expanded their interests. Americans experimented with a bewildering variety of new ideas for reforming prisons, restricting the consumption of alcohol, educating the deaf and blind, and rehabilitating the insane. People might take up wild schemes for chewing their food scientifically one day and then spend the next looking for bumps on their head in an effort to analyze personality. The treatment of women and children came in for serious examination, and utopian socialist colonies put into practice ideas that a few years earlier would have seemed unthinkable. In time, the condition of slaves preempted this attention and absorbed this energy. Northerners increasingly identified slavery with wickedness and the devil, and demanded that such a blot on democracy be put on the path to extinction. Southerners responded in self-defensive anger: slavery had always been a part of the world, sanctioned both by the Bible and by two centuries of American custom. To white Southerners, slavery was what made American democracy and a cotton economy possible. Slavery, they argued, was a positive good and worth defending with arms.

The small white churches of Congregationalism were as old as permanent American settlements. Bare of ornamentation and ritual, they were churches of the people. Originally having state support, by the early nineteenth century they were all independent financially. Church members raised money among themselves, chose their ministers, and formulated what doctrines they needed as they went along. No Rome or Canterbury told them what to do or what to think. Being dogmatic and litigious, Americans and their churches showed a regular tendency to form new sects and to involve themselves in feuds that lacked Christian charity. Presbyterian groups emerged, dominated by Scots and Scots-Irish theological and governmental ideas; Baptists insisted on their own varieties of independence, evident most obviously in their demands that true baptism meant total immersion of the body in water. Even groups like the Episcopalians and the Roman Catholics developed in oddly American ways, and local church practice often varied wildly from the ideal set forth in official church regulation. As far as the Second Awakening was concerned, the key event was the arrival of

Methodism in America. The Methodists did not do everything by themselves, but they provided most of the energy and set the examples that energized a number of other churches and thus dominated the culture that emerged before the Civil War.

The Methodists were chiefly British in origin, followers of John Wesley wishing to revitalize and reform a Church of England that had become intellectually lazy and largely irrelevant to the emotional needs of the lower classes. When Wesleyan preachers began arriving in America, they found fertile ground; the Church of England had never been especially central outside Virginia, puritan ideas of predestination and election had been dying of their own absurdities, and people were ripe for a new faith that took them as they came and that injected a new emotionalism, a new sense of meaning and importance into their lives. Arminian in their theology, they believed that sinners could work for their own faith and salvation and that saints could forfeit their places in heaven if they acted immorally. Such ideas, heretical to a thinker like Edwards in 1740, seemed obvious by 1800. The key institution became once again the revival, but this time a revival pregnant with possibility. Now a citizen could decide intellectually that he lacked faith and commitment but that he wished to belong to the Christian community. He could attend a revival, pray openly for assistance, and allow the nervous energy of the proceedings to overwhelm him. Where for someone in 1740 a revival could merely confirm a saint in status which he had always possessed, after 1800 the status of sainthood was something that a person could choose; all he had to do was acquiesce and let a revival follow its natural course. With Methodism, theology had become truly egalitarian.

Appropriately enough, the Second Awakening began in Yale College under the influence of a grandson of Jonathan Edwards. Timothy Dwight (1752–1817) was appalled at the influence which French revolutionary deism had at Yale, and devoted his life to rechristianizing that institution, and through it the world of New England and points west. A man of great personal magnetism and some literary talent, Dwight was a compelling figure, and he made a name for himself in politics as well. He detested a great many things, from Thomas Jefferson to alcohol, and he worked desperately to keep state money committed to church activity. He lost many battles: Jefferson won his election campaigns and the state of Connecticut ceased its support of the church, but Dwight won the war even as he lost the battles. Yale remained under the shadow of his influence into the twentieth century, and only the arrival of great numbers of Roman Catholic immigrants enabled the state to become the multiethnic democracy that it became a century later. The ideas Dwight championed spread as far west as Iowa, as the sons of Yale went over the land to remind people of the religion of their ancestors.

Dwight's influence worked most obviously through his best-known student, Lyman Beecher (1775–1863). Insofar as any man stopped the spread of Unitarianism and secularism in America, Beecher was that man. He worked frantically, from Boston to Cincinnati, to make his own conservative but theologically uncomplicated Protestantism the faith of the American people. At the core of his work was the revival and the new notion of grace that went with it. Beecher convinced many Americans that heaven was open to them unless they were opposed to God, to holiness in general, or to the idea of eternal life. The way for a citizen to demonstrate that he was not opposed to these things was for him to go to a revival in the hope that God might choose that very day as the occasion for granting grace. Once grace descended, a Christian could rest more easily in the assumption that any reasonable effort at a Christian life would lead to life everlasting.

The revivals that resulted are essential to any understanding of the meaning of America. Activity came to a halt for days when a preacher came to town. Neighbors worked upon neighbors, and family members on each other, and only the hardiest of souls could resist the pressures to convert. The carefully prepared sermons, the learned quotations from the Bible, and the sober air of notetaking in the congregation all disappeared from much of the normal routine. Instead of an established minister who cared for his flock throughout his lifetime, an itinerant would come to town, set up a tent, and begin a passionate, emotional, and frequently mindless exhortation. As the darkness came on and the torches provided a type of lighting all too evocative of hell, erstwhile Christians might moan and groan in their convictions of wickedness; one would fall on his knees to pray aloud while another would shout to no one in particular. A third might lie as if dead on the ground, while a fourth ran madly into the woods close by. Some went into trances, while others convinced themselves that they were dogs and diverted themselves by barking at the feet of trees in order to scare the devil up into the distant branches. Whether a person sang, laughed, or cried, all such expressions were evidence of God's grace as it worked in ways inexplicable to human intelligence.

Outside of church history, the second Great Awakening had much the same effect as the first: it radicalized several generations of citizens as they settled the central portions of the continent. Just as the first united common people in rebellion against British religious and tax interventions, so the second united them against any vestige of a British, or Eastern, or élitist sense of the nature of the American experience. Whatever the democratic implications of the original American puritanism, it had also been rigidly hierarchical. It had separated the saved from the damned, the Christian from the citizen, and demanded that everyone respect the authority of minister and magistrate. Learning was essential in ministerial training, and respect for learning a presumption of sainthood. But with the Second Awakening this changed. The complexities of theology vanished and almost everyone who could find someone to listen to him could declare himself a minister and go on the road. Sermons ignored ideas and stressed emotional response. A man was supposed to feel, not to think, and the emotions of an untutored backwoodsman might be more authentic than those of a B.A. from Harvard. These attitudes affected not only religion but institutions from education to politics as well. Schooling deteriorated as it spread west, as every little church and every little town seemed to want its own college—even if that college was little more than a ramshackle building with a president, two tutors, and a large debt. Politics deteriorated accordingly. The nation that had elected presidents like George Washington, Thomas Jefferson, James Madison, and the two Adamses began instead to vote for temperamental generals, machine politicians, and genial nonentities. Intelligence and sobriety went out of style, and few survived in public life capable of educating the democracy in its own best interests.

II

The new religious impulses saturated the culture and shaped many of the attempts to institutionalize the citizens of the democracy. Nowhere were the fruits of religion more obvious than in the attempt to educate the country in free public schools that would instruct the young in how to live in accordance to God's will.

Horace Mann remains the figure who stands out among the many reformers of the 1830s and 1840s both for his typical background and his long-term impact on America. The product of a family staunch for religion and rigid in morals, he rebelled against the dour puritan God and came to believe in the benevolence of the Deity and the ability of Christians to work their way to heaven. Full of guilt about this change of religious faith, he labored ceaselessly in secular areas to prove himself worthy of an eternity in heaven. His goal was the perfection both of himself and his society, a kind of heaven on earth that would come to America if men followed his example and began the noble effort in that direction.

Having little formal education of any kind as a child, Mann was largely self-educated when he entered Brown University in Providence. There he encountered the typical American college in all its depressing inadequacy. More of a sectarian academy than a college and in no sense a true university, Brown was as rigid in its teaching methods as it could be. Everyone entered in a class and stayed with that class until graduation; the curriculum had no flexibility. A student lived, ate, and studied with his classmates under strict supervision; he faced a class routine that was almost entirely memorization, with no lectures, seminars, and discussion sections. A student had an assigned text for each course, and each day a passage he was expected to memorize and be able to recite on demand. He was even expected to memorize the typographical errors, no matter how ludicrous, since correcting authority was a sign of serious rebellion bordering on actual creativity, and not to be tolerated in a Christian institution. If you memorized enough and avoided expulsion for behavioral quirks, you could expect to graduate, and Mann did so in 1819.

For several years he vacillated between career choices. He studied law and considered teaching; he listened to Lyman Beecher and had a more than passing interest in his daughter Catherine, but the ministry did not appeal. He became instead, with seemingly no specific decision, a "reformer": not a profession at all, but rather a general attitude toward an imperfect society and its imperfect citizens. Although willing enough to consume alcohol himself, he settled on drinks as the worst of the social problems America faced; if you could stop men drinking, the jails and almshouses would empty and a perfect society come that much closer. You could not educate a man's conscience if it had dissolved in alcohol, and so alcohol had to go. One reform led to another. He became deeply involved in reform of insane asylums—which really were a disgrace to the nation; he helped his old friend Samuel Gridley Howe, in Howe's important pioneering efforts at reforming the education of the blind; he tried to improve the condition of blacks; he cooperated in efforts to end imprisonment for debt; he wanted strong restrictions against any activities that would mar the peace of the Sabbath.

Only in the middle-1830s did Mann begin to concentrate on the reforms that made him famous. Anyone who believed that better institutions would help the deaf, blind, insane, and the black become better citizens obviously believed that public schooling was a key to the achievement of a perfect democracy; Mann was soon the most visible educational reformer in the nation. In 1837, the state of Massachusetts established a statewide board of education and authorized it to investigate the conditions of schooling. It was prestigious but powerless, but as its secretary Mann discovered that he had an important platform from which he could preach the sort of reforms that were so important to him. Young people, after all, were the future citizens of democracy; if you could shape their minds you could usher in a Christian democracy in installments. Although Massachusetts had what many regarded as the best educational system in the country, Mann found it miserably inadequate. Teachers received no special training. Many schools operated out of single rooms little bigger than a modern dormitory bedroom, and had little equipment beyond a few benches, tables, a stove, and a water dipper. Many of them lacked even an outhouse, and so students had to answer the call of nature even in the winter behind a frozen bush. Farmers in Massachusetts cared for their livestock with more care than for their children in school.

His findings did not excite much support. Poverty and lack of hard currency in the state made many voters opposed even to minimal taxes for public schools: their ancestors had fought a war to avoid British taxes and they thought the precedent excellent. Many wealthy citizens disliked the democratic aspects of the matter, fearing that education might sow social unrest and encourage the growth of egalitarianism. Even many poor people refused to support public schools; they needed their children on the farms to help with the harvesting and refused to spare more than from four to six weeks of their children's time for any school at all. Many religious leaders feared that secular schools would lead to a secular society and a decline in their own authority.

Mann persevered. Through marriage to a sister-in-law of Nathanial Hawthorne, he moved in influential social circles. He worked with wealthy businessmen to establish teacher-training schools. He toured Europe and studied with special care the schools of Prussia, becoming one of many Americans to bring back German models for institutional reforms. Through it all, he retained an attitude characteristic of himself and his class. As he wrote a friend in 1843, "If I had a few thousand dollars I know I could . . . hasten the millennium. God having time enough on his own hands lets these things drag along strangely; but I confess I am so constituted that I feel in a hurry." God had chosen the schools to be the chief tool for the reformation of the world. All the reformers were in a hurry to help things along.

Mann had help, but he was the man most responsible for the public school and teacher-training systems that Massachusetts and soon the whole country adopted. He himself went into politics, as a Conscience Whig holding the seat left vacant at the death of John Quincy Adams. He became something of a figure of fun to less earnest observers of the American scene, and readers of Hawthorne's *The Blithedale Romance* will find him caricatured in the figure of Hollingsworth, the compulsive and egocentric reformer. But Mann persevered—yankee reformers usually persevered—and worked for equality for the blacks and better education for all. He ended his career at the new Antioch College in Ohio, an experimental college that combined a rigid morality with an extraordinarily open mind about the education of the poor and the female. His last bequest to the nation was a functioning institution that no longer made memory the test of education; the lectures and discussions of the Antioch method soon became an ideal standard for colleges around the country.

III

Admirable though it was, educational reform did not have the immediate impact of abolitionism, and in this area the force of religious revivalism was obvious and effective. The greatest of the revival preachers to emerge from the Burned-Over District of New York—the place most directly affected by the new religious impulses—was Charles Grandison Finney. Largely self-educated, Finney was a lawyer who at twenty-nine experienced a violent conversion of the sort that made a man go out onto the streets to buttonhole people and ask them about the state of their souls. Barely literate in theology, he developed a highly effective preaching style capable of transfixing crowds with his strong voice, his waving arms, his wild pacing about the stage, and his vivid descriptions of the life in hell that awaited those who did not pay him close attention. He practiced the total revival: he expected business to stop when he came to town and he wanted everyone there to hear the Lord's latest word. He was also quite capable of attacking local clergy whose views did not match his.

More than any other leader, Finney confirmed the shift from the educated clergy to the amateur revivalist in America. With him, the center of Protestant activity moved into the West and lost its respect for Harvard, Yale, and higher education. Instead, Americans learned to rely on the Bible. Finney had converted himself by reading the Bible, and he was convinced that any American could do the same. No man able to read really needed the guidance of ministers or schools of divinity; they needed only to read the Bible. Fundamentalism had entered American culture, with results that still shape the social and educational views of millions of Americans. Its emergence marked the death of the old theology. No longer could men feel that they were passively dependent on God's electing them to the sainthood; the precedents Lyman Beecher set at Yale had spread into the West, and men everywhere became convinced that getting to heaven was the responsibility of each individual Christian, and what he could do to encourage reform in this world. Finney's converts imitated Finney, telling all who would listen about their faith and the need for still more conversion and reform in this world. The results soon tore the country apart.

Real abolitionism, as opposed to the many attempts to improve the life of blacks or to send freed blacks back to Africa, began when Theodore Dwight Weld heard Finney preach and was converted. A strange, absent-minded man with a psychosomatic eye problem, Weld had toured the country lecturing on memory aids; in the process he had seen slavery and come to hate it. The son of a Harvard-educated Congregationalist minister, Weld was a college student in the Burned-Over District when Finney came to town. Weld had long been a staunch supporter of established ministers like his own father, and no friend either to an itinerant clergy or to abolitionism. But Finney converted him to an evangelical attitude, and Weld was soon involved with a utopian colony, with temperance reform, and with efforts to stop the delivery of mail on Sunday. He was already slightly interested in antislavery work when he met Arthur and Lewis Tappan, and the key alliance of abolitionism formed. The Tappans were extreme examples of the odd workings of the Protestant Ethic. Grasping, arrogant, provincial, and opportunistic, they were the kind of capitalists who paid pitifully small wages to their employees so that they could themselves become rich and devote their time to social reform. The product of a fanatically moralistic home out of the world of Jonathan Edwards, they resembled in many ways the workings of puritan theology. They strove for success in their calling, they became wealthy, and then did not enjoy their wealth at all but instead tried to encourage the development of a radically consensualist community where every citizen had a place and all agreed about the proper path to heaven. Merchants with significant connections to the Southern trade, they nevertheless worked for the rights of blacks as well as for better treatment for the hand-icapped and insane. Unable to enjoy life by any standard known to most people, they seemed fascinated by the vices of the poor: idleness, alcohol, and sexuality seemed equally abhorrent to them, yet equally fascinating; Arthur in particular had a fondness for accompanying police on their raiding expeditions to houses of prostitution. They also conducted their business accordingly: clerks had to live in boardinghouses run on the strictest Christian principles—they had to be home by ten at night, attend church at least once a week, and avoid the environment of the theater or the companionship of actresses. Despite normal business practice at the time, the Tappans also did not believe in usury or even credit, and so the business ran awkwardly if profitably on a cash basis.

Above all, the Tappans were social conservatives in their reform interests. Unemotional and traditional in their religious views, they had none of the evangelical enthusiasm that contributed so much to the triumph of their reform efforts. In conducting their business, they abhorred labor unions and made no effort to give labor any voice in the governing of workers' lives or the functioning of the business. They were Christians, and they used their money as they wished, and that meant authoritarianism at work and Christian regulation in society. They put their money into reforms like the banning of mail delivery on Sunday or the many missionary attempts then being organized to Christianize the West. The most ludicrous of their reforms was the campaign against the production of gas on Sundays—even as the gas in question supplied heat and light to the church in which they were conducting their campaigns!

Antislavery was one such Christian reform. The Tappans supplied money to Charles Finney, despite obvious differences between the men on both religion and tactics, and they also helped finance William Lloyd Garrison, the famous yankee pamphleteer, in his efforts to publicize the cause. The basic area of agreement between these men was on the Christian context of the slavery issue: slavery was an unforgivable sin, a conscious disobedience of God's will that implicated the whole community. If the members of a Christian community did not protest against slavery and work to destroy it, then they were in complicity with evil and their souls were in danger. Here lay the crux of the abolitionist campaign and its greatest political weakness. For the abolitionist leaders, sin and evil were the real issues, and Christian conversion the goal. The political and social problems involved with the introduction of abolition received little atten-tion, for they were not religious problems. No one seemed to give much thought to how the Southern economy would function after freedom, how blacks would receive their education and become citizens, or whether or not, given the racism endemic in American culture, blacks could ever become citizens at all. The abolitionist speech was a revival speech, conversion was the goal, and mundane problems were irrelevant. The disastrous treatment of blacks in America during the century after abolition was inherent in the revivalist context of antislavery agitation.

Despite severe business disruption, riots, boycotts, and the vandalization of Lewis Tappan's home, the brothers persevered, their money supplying significant antislavery funding throughout the 1830s. Events followed each other quickly for a few years: in December 1833 the American Antislavery Society formed, and shortly thereafter the Lane Seminary in Cincinnati opened; these organizations focused the antislavery efforts for about five years.

People and themes came together most obviously at Lane, situated as it was on the border between slave and free territory. Cincinnati was a key Northern entry point for Southern business; it provided holiday opportunities for Southerners as well as educational instruction to the young. Being in the North, it also was an obvious place for escaped slaves to hide and for free blacks to settle. Friendly to Christian principles in the abstract, it had many business and social reasons for disliking abolitionist agitation. Lane and the city were due for a clash from the start.

The president of Lane was Lyman Beecher; his salary was guaranteed by Arthur Tappan. The atmosphere was that of evangelical New England, and when Theodore Weld heard about it he came to enroll as an aging theological student. He no sooner arrived than he had the school in an uproar as he worked to bring the students to a commitment to abolition. According to Beecher, who had severe doubts about the effort, the students thought Weld was "a god." Even heirs to slave plantations found themselves committed to antislavery, and soon Lane became more an association for the improvement of black life than a theological seminary. As Weld summed up his work to Lewis Tappan: "We believe that faith without *works* is dead." The students financed a library for local blacks, began night-school classes for them, and then set up three large Sunday schools to help them on the difficult path to equality in America. Local businessmen were upset, the school was soon deep in controversy, and Lyman Beecher fled to the East to avoid a situation he could not control. In time, the students most involved left to find a more congenial location farther north.

They settled on an almost bankrupt little Presbyterian college near Cleveland, took it over, and with Tappan money made it into Oberlin College; almost overnight, it became a center for both abolitionism and for radical educational ideas. Friendly to integrated and co-educational schooling, it remained for a century one of the key experiments in American higher education until the country caught up with it. Charles Grandison Finney became the chief professor, and as he took up his post, Theodore Weld went out on the road and used

Finney's techniques to bring abolitionist ideas to the rest of the country. Enduring great personal discomfort, his audiences harassed, Weld nevertheless persisted, and soon the ideas of Lane and Oberlin were everywhere. A nation with its head full of puritan ideas about sin, guilt, complicity and redemption had avoided thinking about slavery long enough. Weld was speaking a language that everyone understood, and soon he had followers that took his message to places he did not have time to visit. People found that they had to take a position for or against slavery; neutrality became less and less respectable or defensible. It was terribly hard for the descendants of the Calvinists to compromise between right and wrong on earth, or between heaven and hell after death.

IV

The path from evangelicalism to reforms of all kinds to abolitionism supplied much of the energy to American cultural activity between 1830 and 1860, but evangelicalism was not alone. Even in the Boston area, the home of a socially conservative Unitarianism, a parallel pattern persisted. Boston intellectuals displayed more decorum but their perception of the logic of events paralleled the perceptions of Christians farther west. In the process, they helped supply America with its first coherent, creative group and a number of the classic works of American literature. Indeed, Transcendentalists were active in an astonishingly broad range of important cultural activities.

Romanticism came late to America. Some elements of the new climate of creativity were visible in occasional writings of Thomas Jefferson and Philip Freneau, and the painter and poet Washington Allston sampled European romanticism through his close friendship with Samuel Taylor Coleridge in England and on the Continent, but truly romantic ideas do not have much meaning before the early poetry of William Cullen Bryant and the early novels of Cooper in the years around 1820. As a conscious literary position, romanticism did not become really seminal until 1836 and the publication of Emerson's *Nature;* serious work then continued into the 1850s in the publications of Henry Thoreau, Nathaniel Hawthorne, and Herman Melville.

The ideas of John Locke and the Enlightenment had seemed ideal for fighting off the British church and state. British behavior had seemed capricious and the Enlightenment philosophy of reason and science had its own plausibility; the revolutionary generation shaped the country on corollaries to its central doctrines. But within a generation, young people were growing up who had never heard a shot fired in anger. The excitement had gone from American life and even the War of 1812 had not affected most citizens, especially in the Boston area, which had detested the whole affair. To the young people of the 1820s, the older generation seemed dull and bourgeois, all too safely British, classicist, and complacent in its views, and much too respectable to bear close examination. The corpse-cold Unitarianism of State Street could not move the imagination and other ideas seemed more promising and even vital for the functioning of the imagination.

The romanticism that developed was in many ways the opposite of the classicism that bored the young. It stressed the emotions and the imagination and tended to ignore the rational faculties and science. It stressed the importance of the individual instead of society. It stressed the dignity of the common man and his infinite capacity for growth if nurtured in a supportive environment. It always looked to nature for inspiration, and that inspiration was emotional and intuitive. It looked to the past, to the primitive, to the unusual and the far-off, and tended to downplay the immediate social context of real life. In the Boston area and its intellectual outposts in the West, it found its most important expression in the Transcendentalist movement, but romanticism went far beyond that rather precious group of figures to include painters, musicians, architects, and other writers who did not, most of the time, contribute work of permanent merit but who constituted an important part of the American culture that was slowly struggling toward visibility.

The Unitarians who dominated the life of the mind in Boston had turned their backs on their Calvinist ancestors. They no longer believed in the mysterious Trinity, but assumed that God was one and that Jesus, while in many ways an ideal man, was not the stuff of God. They believed that men had God-given faculties of reason and morality and were infinitely capable of good. The idea that a church ought to be run by saints seemed outmoded, since any man could be a saint if he made a sincere effort. No one needed to experience a violent conversion, and anything resembling the antics of a Western revival meeting was in bad taste. In short, the patterns of behavior appropriate for a settled business environment had become the norm in respectable Boston; people wanted nothing more out of life or religion than that they might grow to resemble their much-loved leader, William Ellery Channing, in thought and deed.

The Unitarian church was the key intellectual institution in Boston and Transcendentalism was in large part a revolt within the church against the attitudes and ideas of the Enlightenment. Henry Thoreau found it hard to join any group and Margaret Fuller as a woman faced severe vocational discrimination, but otherwise most of the Transcendentalists were Unitarian clergy and the first meaningful decision they had to make was whether to leave the ministry like Emerson, or stay within it and fight from a pulpit, like Theodore Parker. Their most talented opponent, Andrews Norton, accused them of heresy, and of course the arguments had more than their share of theology beneath the more obvious references to literary, philosophical, and esthetic matters.

Because so much of the reading of the older generation had been British and Scots in origin, the younger generation preferred to turn instead to the

Continent for inspiration, occasionally to France but chiefly to Germany. Unfortunately, except for Frederick Henry Hedge they did not read German with any fluency, and so they had to rely on translations, trots, and discourses brought in by boat from England. English writers, especially Thomas Carlyle and Samuel Taylor Coleridge, were making detailed studies of the German romantic thinkers and writers, although subsequent scholarship has made painfully clear the fact that their work was often either plagiarized or inaccurate; ideas once clear in Königsberg became muddled by the time they arrived in Boston. Because Carlyle and Coleridge were primarily men of letters, American romanticism took on a decidedly literary look, and so what was essentially a battle over philosophical terminology within a local church looked in the end much different from what it really was.

The necessary intellectual hero for the Transcendentalists was Immanuel Kant, an obvious foil for John Locke. But they did not have anything resembling the modern English translations now available, and so they simplified and distorted Kant's complex categories. To the Americans, the key terms were *Vernunft*, or Reason, and *Verstand*, or Understanding, and much intellectual discourse in the period was incomprehensible without keeping simple definitions of these terms in mind. Reason was that faculty of the human mind that dealt with topics not related to experience. Concepts like God, space, the sublime, and form were not something that you saw every day, and so Transcendentalists insisted that John Locke's philosophy was unable to cope with them. His philosophy dealt only with the sense data, with what you could see or hear or smell, and they referred to that realm of experience as Understanding. Romantics, above all, wanted to know God and feel the sublime and they used the word *Reason* to bring together whatever it was inside them that functioned in this way. Understanding was everything else, the fruits of the everyday Unitarian world of Andrews Norton that bored them senseless. "There belong to human nature, passions, emotions, sentiments, affections, of which, the understanding properly so called, can take no account," Orestes Brownson argued. "The feeling which we have, when contemplating a vast and tranquil sea, distant mountains with harmonious outlines, or, when marking an act of heroism," comes to us "without any dependence on the understanding." In contrast, "the understanding cannot feel; it cannot love, hate, be pleased, be angry, nor be exalted or depressed. It is void of emotion. It is calm, cold, calculating. . . ."

The most important early statements of the Transcendentalist position came between 1836 and 1838, when Ralph Waldo Emerson published *Nature* and delivered his talks on the American scholar and the role of the church. In the first, he adapted Emanuel Swedenborg's theory of correspondences for American audiences, explaining that people could look at nature and through nature perceive the presence of God. "Every natural fact is a symbol of some spiritual fact," he proclaimed; everything in nature and in life meant something, for God spoke to men in everything they perceived; nature, in short, was symbolic of Reason and not confined to Understanding at all. For the literary imagination, such ideas could not help but be fruitful, and the evidence of the creativity is plentiful not only in key Transcendentalist works like Henry Thoreau's *Walden*, but in the historical fictions of Nathaniel Hawthorne and the sea novels of Herman Melville.

In the subsequent talks, Emerson spoke movingly about the need for Americans to break their intellectual and literary dependence on Europe and to develop a warm, nurturing religion. He declared that God and America had a special relationship and that the American landscape in particular was a source of inspiration which could enable Americans to cut themselves off from Europe, its wars and its industrialism, and develop their own national vision of what life could be. The context was literary more than political, but the document could easily be read as justifying much of what came to be called Manifest Destiny, the right of Americans to bring their civilization as far into the West as they could travel. Praised by many scholars with parochial interests, the talk remains a stunning example of American self-centeredness, since it ignores the European sources from which Emerson himself had borrowed so many of his ideas. The talk on religion was more relevant; American religion in the Boston area had lost much of its creative life and was sorely in need of new ideas and a new sense of both individual and social relevance. Whether all men could become the gods that Emerson wanted them to become was quite another matter.

Emerson and his friend Henry Thoreau represented one side of the Transcendentalist intelligence, but they were far from being the whole story. Books like Emerson's essays and *Walden* have since become the best-known texts of the movement, but at the time one of the most visible fruits of the urge to perfection was the creation of utopian colonies. The writing of Emerson's cousin, George Ripley, supported the creation of experiments like Brook Farm in its aim "to substitute a system of brotherly cooperation for one of selfish competition" and "to diminish the desire of excessive accumulation by making the acquisition of individual property subservient to upright disinterested uses"; such statements read at times like Marxist propaganda, yet they appeared in America well before Marx or his influence made any impact. In its efforts to treat all people as members of one corporate body, each with obligations to the larger group, Brook Farm managed to pursue romantic and Transcendentalist goals that seemed as far from the individualism of Walden Pond as it was possible to go. To the surprise of many skeptics, it was also a success. It was not only intellectually exciting, it pioneered new ways of educating the young that antedated the better-known work of John Dewey and Maria Montessori by many years. In time, an excessive devotion to the ideas of Charles Fourier caused a needless regimentation at Brook Farm, and a fire ultimately destroyed it, but not before it had given Americans a rare alternative to the implicit urge of any bourgeois society to accumulate possessions as the great goal in life.

In other areas as well, Transcendentalism left a legacy to American culture. The unpredictable Orestes Brownson not only made significant contributions to American thought about labor and class issues, his eventual conversion to Roman Catholicism and his influence on fellow convert Isaac Hecker also enabled that "foreign" religious group to gain its first generation of native American intellectuals. Margaret Fuller was instrumental in bringing German literature to the attention of readers hitherto unaware of much beyond the British and her writings on the role of women effectively began women's studies as one approach to the study of civilization. John Sullivan Dwight went on to become America's first music critic of any importance. The list of minor figures and lesser achievements was quite long and in no way merely a series of footnotes to the role of Unitarianism or of nature in the American mind.

For many subsequent scholars, in fact, the most impressive of the Transcendentalists was Theodore Parker, the greatest intellectual in the group and a reform clergyman of great charisma. Probably the most learned man in the Boston area, his library stuffed with the wisdom of several other cultures, he was capable of viewing local events as if from a great distance. Contemptuous of both Calvinism and conventional Unitarianism, he was the man who made the most forceful case for bringing theology up to date and then making it into an instrument for social reform fully as potent as anything that developed among the evangelicals.

At the core of Parker's thought was a deep sense of calm about the religious differences among men. Sure that Reason was eternal, Parker could be extraordinarily cavalier about the products of Understanding. He liked to compare the religions of the world to theories of astronomy. Just as the theories of Ptolemy, Copernicus, and Descartes changed over the years, while the true nature of the universe remained permanent, "so the Christianity of Jesus is permanent, though what passes for Christianity with popes and catechisms, with sects and churches, in the first century or in the nineteenth century prove transient also." He told friends that it did not matter if someone proved that the Gospels were full of myth; the Resurrection might be a myth; the miracles might all be myths—it hardly mattered. He declared that Christianity itself "will stand forever," but admitted that he thought at times that "it would stand better without the New Testament than with it." Indeed, so far did his relativism go that he was willing to declare that, "if it could be proved . . . that the Gospels were the fabrication of designing and artful men" and that Jesus of Nazareth had never lived, he remained convinced that "Christianity would stand firm, and fear no evil." Few Americans were willing to go that far, even behind the leadership of a man they deeply respected.

For Parker, true religion was pure morality. It declared that man should believe in God and imitate him: "Its watchword is, Be ye perfect as your father in heaven." The implication could be, on the one hand, to attempt the private perfection of Thoreau at Walden Pond, or on the other hand to leave society for the communal perfection of George Ripley at Brook Farm. But Parker was not temperamentally attracted to these extremes of American perfectionism and he asked instead for a social perfection. He accused the Boston churches of ignoring their social mission to go out into the world as Christ did, to serve the poor and the suffering and to help usher in a whole society worthy of comparison to heaven. "A Christian Church should be the means of reforming the world" and it should judge the habits and ideas of the day "by the universal standard." "The noblest monument to Christ . . . is a noble people, where all are well fed and clad, industrious, free, educated, manly, pious, wise and good." He was soon advocating reform in the treatment of criminals, greater sensitivity to the rights of women, the need for temperance reform, and more legal guarantees for labor.

With Parker as with most Northern Christians, slavery soon became the paramount issue. He came to insist that the law of God was paramount in human relationships and that slavery was in clear violation of it. If the government were foolish enough to protect slavery, then the government should be ignored. Christians should obey God before Congress, and if faced with a Fugitive Slave Law that required them to disobey their consciences and help return slaves to the South, they should follow his example and "trample it underneath my feet." To those who wished always to obey the law, he brought up the precedents of Pharoah and his laws about murdering newborn Hebrew boys, and the decree of King Ahab that the Jews should worship Baal. Turning in a fugitive slave resembled the turning in of Jesus, and conservative Massachusetts citizens heard themselves compared to Judas.

In this fashion, Parker's theology came to support the Whig reform positions of William Seward and the evangelical abolitionism of Theodore Weld. "To say that there is no law higher than what the State can make," he insisted, "is practical atheism." A Christian who accepts God must accept God's laws, and God's laws have never been subordinate to the laws of the state—in a country descended from English Protestants, Pilgrims, and revolutionaries, the whole concept was preposterous anyway. In effect, Parker brought the American version of Kant's Reason into social thought: If man had these innate qualities, if these qualities were what man shared with God, then man had no choice but to use these divine insights to achieve social perfection. The outside world had to resemble the inside world, and both man and society had to imitate God and ceaselessly work for perfection. No one with his wits about him could believe that slavery was compatible with perfection, and so slavery had to go. Parker was soon deep into abolitionism and an active assistant of fugitive slaves as they fled north to freedom. His ideas spread into the West, and there is at least some evidence that Abraham Lincoln, as he emerged into the leadership of the Republican party, knew of them and admired them. Seward, Weld, and Parker all agreed that there was a higher law than the Constitution, and by 1861 they had a president who agreed with them.

V

At odd moments in history, a single work can focus the attention of almost everyone on a social issue, whether it be reform, war or revolution. Such a work was *Uncle Tom's Cabin* (1852). Leaders in both North and South had been taking stronger positions on the slavery issue and the attitudes toward it proper to convinced Protestants; Congress had held divisive debates. But the public at large had never been deeply concerned and had had few unforgettable ways by which to understand the issues involved. After the book swept the nation, this was no longer true. The war broke out in 1861, and no less a figure than President Lincoln shook the tiny hand of Harriet Beecher Stowe two years later and made his famous remark: "So this is the little lady who made this big war?" Often dismissed as propaganda, the book was actually great art of a certain kind. The evidence for this should be obvious: no one who read it could ever forget it, and for the rest of the century it was the source for Tom shows, songs, and then films, each of which seemed to get farther from the original. Such a fate did less than justice both to the work and its author.

The family of Lyman Beecher remains one of the most remarkable in American history. Unlike the Adams or Roosevelt families, they had no patrician lineage and held no political office. Instead, they embodied the central religious concerns of most Americans, as Protestantism flirted with Unitarianism and skepticism, but then reverted to a diluted version of traditional puritanism. The Beechers spoke for the hinterlands: Lyman pushed its theology to its limits, and the children seemed to transcend it. In doing so, Harriet was hardly alone. Catharine became a pioneer of feminism and the reform of home and school; Henry Ward became one of the most eminent clergy of the era after the Civil War, and their brothers Charles, Edward, and Thomas were only slightly less visible for a time. Most of the family struggled with skepticism and all had doubts about their father's orthodoxy. The country evolved with them, worrying about antislavery, saving the Union, and adjusting to the economic as well as the ethical problems of American Darwinism.

Family life essentially began in Litchfield, Connecticut, during the reign of Judge Tapping Reeve and his law school. Reeve's first wife had been a granddaughter of Jonathan Edwards, and the persistence of orthodoxy in the relatively isolated area allowed members of the two families and their associates to form what was known as the Standing Order, the name of the elite, conservative hegemony that fought off anything that smelled of Thomas Jefferson, France, skepticism, or modernity. Yet even here, children could grow up with larger concerns than such a statement might imply. Harriet wrote later that her first horrible feelings about slavery came to her as a very young girl when she listened to one of her aunts tell stories about her life in Jamaica. She had married an English settler in good faith and complete innocence, only to discover upon arrival at his plantation that he was already the father of mulatto children, thought nothing of it, and was mystified by her revulsion. She left him after a year, to fill the Litchfield air with tales of the fruits of slavery: this has to be the phraseology here, because she died when Harriet was two, and the child could not possibly have remembered such tales from direct exposure. But such stories never die, families repeat them endlessly, and they point directly to the impact of *Uncle Tom's Cabin*: the horrors not only of the violations of the laws of sexual morality but of the lives of women and the sanctity of their homes.

In literature, family taste defied the expectations of posterity: at a time when the reading of novels was forbidden in most conventional homes, Lyman exempted the work of Sir Walter Scott, and one summer Harriet recalled reading *Ivanhoe* seven times. Even more important and less likely was the family obsession with Lord Byron, the poet as well as his work. Harriet discovered "The Corsair" (1814) in her Aunt Esther's room one day: "I shall never forget how it astonished and electrified me," and she went about for days with the verses reechoing in her head. Even Lyman was under the spell, and when Byron died, he lamented: "Oh, I'm sorry that Byron is dead. I did hope he would live to do something for Christ. What a harp he might have swept!" Elements of the Byronic hero remain in *Uncle Tom's Cabin* and in Stowe's later works, recalling these early enthusiasms and reminding readers that great literature works in the imagination in ways not only mysterious but also theological, political, and sexual.

Life in Litchfield appears to have been idyllic; life in Boston was combative, as Lyman almost singlehandedly tried to stem the advances of Unitarianism and cosmopolitanism. He largely succeeded, and Unitarianism remained a small, urban, and East Coast affair when at first it had seemed likely to sweep the country. But the crucial spot where Harriet lived was in fact Cincinnati, where she remained from 1832 to 1850. She never wrote about it, but she absorbed what it had to offer: while her father struggled with Lane Seminary, Theodore Weld, and the pressure for abolitionism, Harriet absorbed literary influences from Dr. Daniel Drake, the urbane physician who was the cultural as well as the medical leader of the city; from Salmon P. Chase, not yet the political and legal figure of Civil War fame; and from other members of the Semi-Colon Club, which flourished in the 1830s and kept European books alive in the new West.

But Harriet had a tropism for slavery. She couldn't stay away from it. She took one trip into Kentucky, which gave her her only firsthand experience of plantation life, descriptive material that she used to advantage in *Uncle Tom's Cabin*. But most of all, she absorbed antislavery through stories both written and oral. She all but memorized Weld's *American Slavery as It is: Testimony of a Thousand Witnesses* (1839), later telling Angelina Grimké that she "kept this book in her work basket by day and slept with it under her pillow by night, till its facts crystallized into Uncle Tom's Cabin." The Reverend Mr. John Rankin told her tales. The pastor of a Presbyterian church in nearby Ripley, he always kept a light burning so that slaves escaping Kentucky could find their first sanctuary on the Underground Railway to freedom farther north. Rankin was the man who told Stowe the story of Eliza Harris, a young slave mother whose owner treated her cruelly. Deciding to escape, she took her child and headed for the river. A Scots riverman along the road told her about the light, and assured her that if she could reach it, she would be safe. The winter had been severe and the river remained frozen, but a thaw had settled in for several days, and water was running over the ice. She kept slipping and falling, but emerged on the other side with her baby miraculously dry. She found Rankin's house and received food, dry clothing, and a quick trip to the next stop on the Railway. As he helped her, the preacher heard thundering in the background and realized that the river was breaking up. By the next day, it was all ice floes. Slavecatchers at first assumed the woman had drowned, then found items of clothing on the northern side that suggested that she had somehow crossed on a floe; but she got away despite them. A few weeks later her husband escaped as well, and the couple fled to new lives in Canada. This story became the basis of the most memorable event in *Uncle Tom's Cabin*, and thousands who probably never looked at the novel could repeat the miraculous tale of Eliza crossing the ice with her infant in her arms.

The Beechers disliked Cincinnati; not only was it full of slaves, slavecatchers, and abolitionists, it was a wild, thug-ridden city where it was scarcely safe to walk the streets. Lane was always in turmoil, and teachers worried as well about the frequent fires and the descent of cholera. Harriet and her husband, Calvin Stowe, were more than glad to move to Brunswick, Maine, when Calvin received a professorship from Bowdoin College. There, according to Harriet, God dictated her great book, merely using her as intermediary. One of his other instruments was the Reverend Mr. Josiah Henson, a black clergyman whom she met at the home of her brother Edward. Henson had been a slave in Maryland when a brutal master had so beaten him that both his shoulders had been broken; his arms remained crippled for life. Josiah had forgiven him. Another master promised him freedom upon payment of six hundred dollars, then reneged on the agreement and was in the process of selling Henson down the river when the slave escaped. Harriet absorbed these details and those from other sources, and the result was Uncle Tom, the saintly slave of her book's title.

By conventional critical standards, the book lacked art: its form was imperfect, its characters seemed stereotyped, borrowed from Dickens if not from Scott or Byron, and it was clearly a tract. Professional critics profess not to like tracts. It was also a travel book, a common genre of the day, and a sentimental novel that exploited domesticity and the family shamelessly. It was melodramatic, with sex and violence always in the wings if not center stage. Such criticism seems odd, coming as it does from readers who usually profess elsewhere to admire the work of Melville or Faulkner, not to mention Shakespeare. In fact Stowe was an important writer who proved her skill in subsequent works as well, most obviously in *The Minister's Wooing* (1859). Here, the plot wryly ties theology to domesticity, producing one of the few religious novels in American history worth examination. Aaron Burr, Ezra Stiles, and other figures pass in and out as the tale revolves around the legendary efforts of the Reverend Dr. Samuel Hopkins to find a suitable wife. Fiction and history fuse in an effective way, and Stowe displays her greatest penchant: to write convincingly about New England life. She was no George Eliot, but she was firmly in the second rank of competent writers. She deserved her fame and deserves better of posterity. No one else tied the personal to the political in such a memorable way. She had only a pop theology of love to offer as a solution to the world's problems, and as such it was hopelessly inadequate, but the male leaders of society were not doing noticeably better, as the next twenty years demonstrated.

VI

A focus on Transcendentalism and such examples of post-Calvinist sentimentalism as *Uncle Tom's Cabin* can leave the impression that Americans were producing nothing but religious tracts disguised as art; this was not true. Since the days of Washington Irving and James Fenimore Cooper, New York City had been going its own secular way. In prose, the results were respected in Europe by the 1850s, but poetry lagged behind. Only William Cullen Bryant (1794–1878) remained an exception to this. Chiefly a journalist by profession, Bryant had begun as a precocious poet who had first admired the work of Alexander Pope and his generation, and then, under the influence of Wordsworth's *Lyrical Ballads*, turned his attention to nature in America. Between "Thanatopsis" (first version, 1811) and "Autumn Woods" (1824–1825), Bryant wrote several romantic poems that were first-rate, dwarfing anything churned out by Poe, Emerson, Longfellow, and the rest over the next decades. But the muse did not linger, and Bryant focused most of his mature energies on the policies of the Jacksonian Democrats and then on antislavery, where he was a supporter of President Lincoln from the radical left.

The poet who picked up Bryant's journalistic and political positions picked up his poetic ones as well, and when he did so, Walt Whitman took them to a truly international reputation. Whitman (1819–1892) had grown up in a family chiefly of English, Dutch, and Welsh puritan stock; his father was a carpenter in Brooklyn, devoted to the radical politics of Tom Paine and the visionary painting of Elias Hicks. As a boy, Whitman assumed the validity of their ideals, and lived the democratic life of a hunter and fisherman that was still then possible in the New York area. Hedonistic, sensuous, and narcissistic, he would scarcely have been conceivable in New England, but in the bustling commercial city he could take life as it came and leave Angst to yankees. He left school at age eleven to work as an office boy for lawyers and printers, and even as an adolescent was trying his hand at occasional bits of Democratic propaganda. Reform movements were all around him, and of course someone of his background was sympathetic, but he preferred loafing about the city to wasting his time improving the morals of his neighbors. The 1840s were a time of great expansion in the newspaper industry, and Whitman had no trouble finding all the work he needed to live comfortably and the space he required to publish his own attempts. Like any radical Democrat he was patriotic without having to think about it, simply assuming the greatness of America as a country and the excellence of the opportunities available to anyone who wished to take advantage of them. He was soon editing newspapers, writing stories, and advocating reforms; on one occasion he turned out, for money, a temperance novel. He favored women's rights, civic improvements, and an end to capital punishment; he wanted a better educational system; he supported Manifest Destiny in foreign policy. He was not interested in Europe and seemed hostile to its influence.

The boom times of the 1850s were his period of great poetic growth. He worked out rough principles that equated aesthetic and moral beauty, and like any British Victorian became certain that art expressed the life of the nation and that its production and consumption made the nation freer and better. He was fascinated by both political oratory and the theater: the first kept him in touch with people, and although a man of many solitary habits he always retained a rather abstract love of the masses; the second exposed him to influences ranging from Shakespeare to Italian opera and opened his mind up to ideas, languages, and verse forms that were more inspiring than those at home. Like many Americans of that period, he developed notions about the divinity of man and of infinite possibilities for his own aesthetic growth; unlike them he expressed his sense of his own genius in verse of considerable quality, and in 1855 the first edition of *Leaves of Grass* arrived in the hands of those he admired. Emerson in particular welcomed it, for Whitman's celebration of democratic man in relatively ordinary language made a significant step away from literary dependence on Europe.

Whitman's egotism and immodesty offended Emerson and any number of other people, and his emphasis on sexuality and sensuality offended them even more. But then the nation went to war, and as Whitman was a devout believer in the Union, these disturbing aspects of his life and work seemed less significant than his ability to sum up what the soldiers were fighting for. President Lincoln became one of many public men to express admiration, and Whitman returned the compliment. He did not enlist, but rather preferred to visit hospitals, comfort wounded men, and to write poetry that expressed his convictions. The events of the war permeated his work, and when Lincoln died he expressed his grief in one of the major works of American poetry, "When Lilacs Last in the Dooryard Bloom'd" (1865). His enumerations of material data, his assumption of the importance of common men as well as common objects, his refusal to bend his work to fit conventional ideas of meter all appealed to the larger public, and after the war a growing number of English writers helped introduce Europeans to this untypical American; the reception in France was especially enthusiastic. Homosexuals were of course receptive to some of the sexual implications of Whitman's work, but his matter and manner were both among the few significant counterweights to the conventional assumptions current in English writing at the time.

In his odd way, Whitman managed to combine the role of prophet with secular subject matter. Americans used to receiving Truth from their ministers could be receptive to prophecy from poets as well. Whitman after the war increasingly slipped into legend; he became, as the title of a book defensive of him had it, *The Good Gray Poet*, the bard of democracy as it emerged battered but optimistic from the carnage of the Civil War. Increasingly, too, Whitman published prose, and *Democratic Vistas* (1871) became a convenient shorthand phrase for recalling his democratic idealism as it struggled against the pressure of the new ideas of the 1870s.

The Civil War thus became a dividing point in American culture in ways that transcended the social and even the political impact. Before the war, Protestantism had provided much of the energy as well as the principled context for discussions of capitalism and democracy. Citizens finally opted against slavery because it was sinful. After the war, ideas of public sin seemed to be in bad taste. Economic exploitation became an end in itself, and for a long time few people paid attention to its moral effects. Politically, the Union had been saved, and democratic man could presumably prosper with few restrictions. Christianity in its traditional Protestant sense still retained an honored place in American lives, but increasingly it was like a picture on the wall, of an ancestor revered but largely forgotten in the daily round of secular events. Religion would return with the progressive years after 1900, but by then the shift had become permanent: American life was one where capitalism and democracy had religious sanction, but where religion itself seemed diffuse, lacking in coherent theology, and largely ceremonial.

Chapter 6

The Defeat of the South and the Appeal of the West, 1815–1901

Opposing the North and the spread of New England values into the West, the South changed radically during the early years of the nineteenth century. At first, the existence of slaves had not been a sectional issue, since Northern states had permitted slavery and few political leaders were willing to use slavery as an issue. But the abolition of the slave trade was written into the Constitution, and points of friction were inevitable. Northerners disliked the formula that permitted Southern states to have political representation for three fifths of its slave population; since slaves obviously could not vote, Southern whites thus effectively had more political influence per voter than did Northern whites. The District of Columbia was another problem: slaves at work and slaves for sale were on view daily to Northern eyes in their own national capital, which after all was a Southern city. You could not visit the president of the nation without a vivid reminder of the blot that remained on the face of the democracy.

Culturally, the South at first consisted of two distinct areas. The Virginia of the Enlightenment was at first preeminent, with its cavalier leisure, its deism, its political supremacy, and its ease with European things. No cities worthy of the name could challenge Virginia until the 1820s, but soon Charleston and its rather different values took over the lead. Scarcely more than a village, Charleston still had a population of only about twenty-five thousand in 1840 and grew to only forty thousand by the outbreak of the war in 1861; roughly half of these were slaves. The only conceivable place capable of challenging Charleston was New Orleans, but that city was largely cut off from the rest of America by distance and its French language. In the long course of cultural history it contributed far more than most cities through its music, but jazz and its antecedents did not come into public awareness until the twentieth century.

II

An occasional gifted individual could make a creative mark outside the genteel provincialism of the cities and the obsession with slavery and its defense. One figure in fact did so, although few today think of him as especially Southern. John James Audubon (1785–1851) was actually born in Santo Domingo, the son of a wealthy French planter and his Creole mistress. Jean Audubon had led an adventuresome life. From the Nantes area, he was born to the sea. His father had taken him, age thirteen, as cabin boy on a boat that was running war supplies to the beleaguered outpost of Louisburg, in present-day Nova Scotia. Such activities, in such a war-ravaged time, all but inevitably led to capture by the British, and within a year Jean Audubon was in a prison. Released, he made up for lost time, but during the Revolution in America he was captured once again, and spent over a year (1779–1780) in detention. He understandably loathed the British for life, and celebrated his release by joining the French navy, commanding a corvette during the Battle of Yorktown. Tough and shrewd if essentially uneducated, he made his fortune in the Caribbean. While his wife waited dutifully in France, he led the life of a "big white" in Santo Domingo. In time, revolutionary forces in both France and the Caribbean cost him his wealth, but he had invested meanwhile in a farm outside Philadelphia, and that farm served as a beachhead for his son a generation later.

John James Audubon was willful and undisciplined. His father took him and his half-sister back to France, where Mme. Audubon raised them as if they were her own. While her husband made up a series of engaging myths about the origins of the children, thus confusing biographers for years, Mme. Audubon spoiled them. Jean tried to maintain discipline, even at times using naval personnel to keep the boy at his books, to no avail. As family fortunes deteriorated and Jean retired on a meager naval pension, the farm near Philadelphia loomed larger in significance. In 1803, Jean sent John James to America to take charge of its possible development, learn English, and begin taking care of himself.

In his feckless way, the teenager was charming, and no matter how badly he behaved, people kept taking care of him. He arrived ill with what he thought was yellow fever, and the ship's captain arranged to have two Quaker ladies nurse him to health. They did so, then passed the boy on to Miers Fisher, the agent who had been taking care of the farm for Jean Audubon. Fisher was also a Quaker, and despite the boy's thoughtlessness, he proved a kind and useful friend. As soon as he was able, Audubon began to explore his patrimony, quickly developing his fascination for birds and wilderness life in general. Most of all, he liked being free of authority to do what he wished, when he wished. "Hunting, fishing, drawing, and music," he said later, "occupied my every moment" during this period.

The scene appears entirely romantic from a distance, but from close up it does not match modern assumptions about romanticism. For one thing, Audubon had a capitalist streak that would ruin much of his adult life with ill-conceived schemes for becoming rich. On the farm, the project was a lead mine, which absorbed his energies for several fruitless years. Later on, life as a merchant appealed to him, and he opened stores and passed out business cards like any upstart booster, with no sense either for commerce or the impact of national policies: from Jefferson's embargo on trade (1807–1809) through a series of banking crises to the severe depression of the Van Buren administration (1837–1841), fate made it all but impossible for most businessmen to prosper for long, and Audubon lacked business sense and discipline. After the lead mine and the stores, a steam mill and then a steamboat absorbed energy and money. Much of the money was not his own, and the failure of the steamboat scheme in 1819 cost English poet John Keats the money he hoped to use to marry Fanny Brawne—Audubon had charmed brother George Keats out of investment funds, and the relationship proved a total loss all around.

Audubon was, as well, a hunter with none of the squeamishness about death that modern lovers of nature seem to have. The animal and bird population of America seemed inexhaustible, and he found he could not draw effectively while birds moved. Besides, he clearly loved the whole ritual. He laid in a stock of wire, took the limp carcasses and reshaped them into the lifelike positions that he later immortalized. "This is what I shall call my first drawing actually from nature," he wrote, pleased by an early effort. As for preserving his specimens, he developed a trusty American substitute for formaldehyde: "Yankee Rum is the only proper thing to Keep them well," he informed a friend.

Audubon was a foreigner without a cultural base within continental America, but he was fascinated by the Southwestern frontier enclosed by the Ohio and Mississippi River valleys. He opened his first store in Louisville in 1807, and the center of his life was either there or down the Ohio at Henderson until the early 1820s, when a scheme to move to New Orleans failed and he settled, more or less, in Natchez. There his wife ran a school on the estate of the well-established Percy family, while he wandered as far as Paris and Edinburgh in search of new species and gifted engravers capable of doing them justice. Insofar as he belonged anywhere he was, like many a Southern entrepreneur, a citizen of the waterways, exploring the rivers, the Gulf of Mexico, and the Caribbean Sea in search of birds and friends who shared his interest. Most of his letters of any importance, for example, went to the Reverend Mr. John Bachman, who lived in Charleston. Clearly, Audubon proved that it was possible to live in the South, to live in fact all over the South, and still be creative.

Artistic skill had been evident even in his spoiled adolescence. Despairing of his ever doing anything useful, his father had allowed Audubon to study drawing; the boy claimed that he spent a few months under the famous Jacques-

Louis David; if he did, that was the extent of his formal training. But *art* is probably the wrong rubric for categorizing Audubon's contributions. In those days, barriers between disciplines scarcely existed, and Audubon was really more of an ornithologist, a scientist chiefly interested in establishing new species and in describing them with accuracy for the information of the scientific community. He rarely had anything to say about art per se, and when he did his language was caustic in its stress on realism. Confronted by a famous work portraying the death of a stag by Sir Edwin Landseer, he dismissed its effective brushwork and declared that "nature was not there, although a stag, three dogs, and a Highlander were introduced on the canvas." The stag, the experienced hunter noted with disgust, "had his tongue out and his mouth shut! The principal dog, a greyhound, held the deer by one ear just as if a loving friend; the young hunter had laced the deer by one horn very prettily, and in the attitude of a ballet dancer was about to cast the noose over the head of the animal." To anyone from Kentucky, "such a picture is quite a farce; not so here, however."

As a scientist, Audubon met two of the most important of his colleagues in the business of naming new species. Alexander Wilson (1766–1813) was the great pioneer in ornithology, his *American Ornithology* (1808–1813) important not only as a contribution in its own right but also as a work Audubon had to admire and wanted to make obsolete. They met one day when Wilson wandered into Audubon's Louisville store, introduced himself, and put two volumes of his work before Audubon's admiring eyes. Wilson wanted subscribers and had heard that Audubon was his most likely prospective customer in the area. An eccentric Scots weaver and poet, Wilson already knew Charles Willson Peale, William Bartram, and others in the Philadelphia area, and his drawings were more than skillful; they were superb, a tough precedent even for Audubon to follow. Constantine Rafinesque (1783–1840) seemed both more eccentric and more scientific. Born in Turkey of French and German parentage and a sometime resident of Italy, he was in and out of America from 1802 to 1815, living chiefly in Philadelphia while he dabbled in ichthyology and tried to make a living selling medicines. In 1818, he too visited Audubon in Louisville, arriving penniless. The two exotics got on, the fishman and the birdman each knowing that the other was a species unto himself. Rafinesque won an appointment at Transylvania University but lost whatever chances he might have had for greatness as a scientist by an excessive enthusiasm and gullibility. A naif, the perfect victim, he provoked his new friend into practical jokes that had unfortunate consequences. Audubon began to draw imaginary fish and to talk all too convincingly about them to his friend. Ever eager to find new species, Rafinesque swallowed each one whole, taking notes for three weeks for his future publications. He then disappeared without a word, to put ten of Audubon's imaginary fish into his *Ichthyologia Ohienses*; each one was carefully credited to its creator.

Few in America paid much attention to Audubon or the other men of early science; fewer still subscribed to their works. Audubon spent most of his time during the coming decades traveling about trying desperately to line up subscribers to *The Birds of America, Ornithological Biography*, and *The Viviparous Quadrupeds of North America*, as they struggled onto the market in the 1830s and 1840s. But while Audubon had little luck in business of any kind, he managed quite well in finding engravers. The Scot W. H. Lizars was the first, a man not only skilled in his craft but also in the managing of odd colonials in the fickle European marketplace. Lizars not only developed the installment purchase strategy that kept the books appearing, he also transformed Audubon into the second Benjamin Franklin of the European imagination: the eccentric man of science, come to bring new knowledge to Old Europe. Audubon kept his hair long at Lizars' instruction, wore a wolfskin coat, and maintained the most picturesque look he could manage, cutting quite a swath through the philistine aristocracy that might be willing to pay for a myth more willingly than for pictures of odd birds. In time, Audubon and Lizars clashed, and the artist moved on to Robert Havell, and Havell's name went onto many of the best-known Audubon creations.

Much like Alexander Wilson, Audubon became famous in inverse proportion to sales of his art. While money only trickled in, even the greatest of authors proved eager to meet the man who was master of at least part of the nature of the New World. Audubon had studied ornithology, Sir Walter Scott wrote after a pleasant visit in 1827, "by many a long wandering in the American forests. He is an American by naturalization, a Frenchman by birth, but less of a Frenchman than I have ever seen, — no dash, no glimmer or shine about him, but great simplicity of manners and behaviour; slight in person and plainly dressed; wears long hair, which time has not yet tinged; his countenance acute, handsome, and interesting, but still simplicity is the predominant characteristic." After a second meeting, where Audubon displayed a portfolio of his work, Scott wrote as if he had just met Natty Bumppo: "This sojourner of the desert had been in the woods for months together. He preferred associating with the Indians to the company of the settlers; very justly, I dare say, for a civilized man of the lower order—when thrust back on the savage state—becomes worse than a savage." Like most Europeans, Scott had his preconceptions about Americans and saw what he wanted to see; the Americans just went along with the game: democratic man, after all, was supposed to be an entrepreneurial capitalist, and if he had to sell himself in order to sell his new species and his drawings, then so be it.

Indeed, Audubon was so American, and so much a product of the Southwestern frontier, that he could not resist occasionally adding the odd tall tale to his supposedly realistic and scientific reports. In the same spirit in which he invented new fish for Rafinesque, he contributed a whole mythology to rattlesnake lore. Europeans had enough trouble imagining a snake that rattled warnings to enemies, but Audubon could not resist going further. "The mode of copulation used by these reptiles is so disgusting," he told Europeans who normally could not even dream of discussing such things, that "I would refrain from any mention of it were it not my chief purpose to record any facts regarding them that may be uncommon or little known." It could have been a standard introduction to a gamy Gothic romance; all the snakes needed was a castle to crawl around in. "Early in spring, as soon as the snakes have changed the skin that contained their last year's growth, they issue brightly coloured, glistening with cleanliness and with eyes full of life and fire." Then enter the Marquis de Sade, as it were. "The males and the females range about, in open portions of the forest, to enjoy the heat of the sun, and, as they meet, they roll and entwine their bodies together, until twenty, thirty, or more, may be seen twisted into one mass, their heads being all turned out, and in every direction, with their mouths open, hissing and rattling furiously, while, in the meantime, the secret function is performed." This sort of thing went on for days, Audubon warned, and if you came upon this writhing heap by mistake, they quit what they were doing and gave chase. Such were the ecstacies of science along the Southwestern frontier.

III

But even so detached and itinerant a figure as Audubon had trouble staying in the South. He did not have the capacity to succeed at anything but scientific exploration and art, and the South scarcely had the resources to sustain business activity, let alone the colleges, museums, or publishers that creative figures needed. For conventional native sons—daughters had no chance at all—the picture was not only bleak, it was forever tainted by an obsession with religious orthodoxy and its application to slavery. At Transylvania University, Horace Holley was the leading intellectual and more important in context than his eccentric colleague, Rafinesque; he lost his job in a spasm of Presbyterian indignation in 1827. Kentucky also produced Cassius Clay, one of the rare Southerners to take a strong stand against slavery later in the period. An occasional figure like Jesse Burton Harrison emerged from Virginia to achieve a European education and return to his native state to lead the unsuccessful battle for gradual emancipation. An occasional Southerner emerged, like scientist Joseph Le Conte or painter Washington Allston, who made significant careers in the North; and an occasional talented Northerner attempted to make a career in the South, like Frederick A. P. Barnard, only to fail and return. What remained missing everywhere was any sense of the community of cultural endeavor, any intellectual or institutional framework capable of nurturing the young so that they took for granted the importance of painting, biology, or education and could feel secure that lives devoted to research or to art were both intrinsically worth living and worthy of social approval. Few creative people were eager to give up friends, family, plantations, and social life to pursue creative lives, but that was the prospect before them in the Old South.

Things closed down mentally about 1830. Until that time, distinctions between North and South, while valid and worth making, were not all that serious. The legacy of the Jeffersonians remained strong into the 1820s, and an easy intellectual commerce remained between Charleston and the North. Northern books sold in the South, Southern boys often went north to college, and travelers went back and forth bridging the gap between the two regions. But the debate over gradual emancipation in Virginia in the early 1830s failed to accomplish anything constructive; the rebellion of Nat Turner in 1831 scared many liberal Southern whites with visions of being murdered in their beds, and a new generation seemed abruptly to be in political and educational control. Contacts with the North declined, social discourse became more difficult, political differences sharpened, and leaders seemed to lose their senses of humor. By the time war began in 1861, each side seemed to be screaming at the other, and neither was listening. Culture had become sectional and Southern culture unproductive and obsessed with the slavery issue.

Insofar as the career of one man could comprehend the decline of the area, that of Thomas Cooper could. An Englishman from Manchester, he was opposed to slavery from an early age and friendly to the principles of the French Revolution long after most intellectuals stepped back from its violence. A farmer, doctor, and lawyer, he was opinionated and incapable of reticence. Despite the fact that he served six months in jail under the Sedition Act for an outburst against President John Adams, he went on to become a Pennsylvania judge and then a professor of chemistry at Dickinson College and the University of Pennsylvania. By 1820 he was so obviously an outstanding educator that Jefferson maneuvered his appointment to the chair of chemistry at the new University of Virginia, only to find that clerical opposition to such a skeptic was a serious obstacle. Cooper wrote Jefferson that he feared that the preachers would defeat all his plans and that the leading Protestant groups would only be satisfied if they could divide the professorships among themselves. He feared that "the reign of ignorance, bigotry and intolerance" was fast approaching and that he would not outlive it. He then noted that "in this country there is much of theoretical toleration, but far more of practical persecution" and that any public figure found himself condemned to silence: "simulation and dissimulation become points of prudence, if not of duty." Cooper went to South Carolina and the presidency of its university, only to be forced out in 1833 when pressure from the clergy became too great. Despite his anticlericalism, deism, and defense of a liberal education, though, Cooper was also hostile to Northern industrialism, universal suffrage, and natural rights theory. In casting him out, the South was being self-defeating: he was outspoken in his defense of states' rights, preferred local liberties to the preservation of the union, and could easily have been a leader in the ideological battles of the 1830s. When a region refuses even to tolerate its most articulate defenders, it is in the hands of leaders too stupid to be worthy of extended examination.

IV

Intellectual life in Charleston was in the hands of a small group of close friends. William Gilmore Simms was a novelist, James Henry Hammond a politician, Edmund Ruffin an agricultural reformer, and Nathaniel Beverley Tucker and George Frederick Holmes both professors. Having grown up in a society in which basic literacy was a privilege of caste and public education nonexistent, these men quite naturally felt beleaguered intellectually. They had no decent newspapers to keep them informed and no publishers to keep them supplied with recent works or to print their own. The religion of most citizens was as narrowly puritanical as anything in New England, nightlife was nonexistent outside private homes, and as the saying went, no one took anything seriously except "cotton, oratory, horses and elections."

Simms became the best-known of the group and his literary and journalistic productions about all that remain of Southern culture before the war. Charleston had taken its literary and intellectual tone from eighteenth-century England, but the poetry of Sir Walter Scott began to make its way in the South late in 1810, and *Waverley* appeared in a local edition in 1814. Southerners could easily see local parallels to Scott's rivalries between Highlander and Lowlander in their recent past: Were not these divisions similar to the split between Tidewater and back country? Faithful slaves seemed plausible substitutes for Scott's retainers, Indians and frontiersman could stand in for his outlaws, and a reader in Charleston could feel himself kin to all the British Empire in its fascination with this most popular of novelists. In *The Heart of Midlothian* (1818), Scott even had a Highlander outlaw go off to America to become an Indian chief, and the local offspring of such fantasies included George Tucker's *The Valley of Shenandoah* (1824), William Alexander Caruthers' *The Cavaliers of Virginia* (1835), John Pendleton Kennedy's *Horse-Shoe Robinson* (1835), and Simms' *The Partisan* (1835). Lord Byron and Tom Moore were also popular in the South, but Coleridge, Keats, and Shelley had to wait a considerable period before they achieved much of a local audience. By the time they did, the intellectual gates were closing and the obsession with slavery making it hard to tolerate ideas from anyone to the left of Thomas Carlyle.

Where a typical Northern literary man emerged from a clerical family and often studied for the ministry himself, a typical Southerner emerged from agriculture, the law, or politics, and quite frequently was involved in all three.

Simms' father was a business failure, but the family retained houses in Charleston and a plantation in Mississippi, and Simms' vocational goals were always those expected of a prosperous white man of the area. But he was never especially interested in making money, and instead he traveled widely, observing Indians and frontiersmen to the west and becoming friendly with a broad circle of literary men in the North. Politically, he identified himself with the circle of Jacksonian Democrats who called themselves Young America, and his novels often contained Jacksonian propaganda about the West and the mission of America to settle the area for American democratic principles. These novels began to appear in 1833, in two rough groups: colonial romances like *The Yemassee* (1835) and revolutionary romances, of which *Woodcraft* (1852) is probably the best.

Life was never especially kind to Simms. His works sold reasonably well in the North, but not in the South. He worked hard to establish local journals that would put Charleston on the literary map of the world and defend its institutions, but no one paid much attention and the financial rewards were meager. His letters contained frequent laments about the state of Southern culture, which seemed all but synonymous with his own circumstances. "A literary man, residing in the South, may be likened to the blooded horse locked up in the stable, and miles away from the Course, at the moment when his rivals are at the starting post," he moaned in 1853. He seriously considered a permanent move to the North, but decided against it because of family ties to South Carolina. He defended states' rights; he defended slavery. No one seemed grateful. By 1858 he was sure that his life's work "has been poured to waste in Charleston, which has never smiled on any of my labors, which has steadily ignored my claims, which has disparaged me to the last." Indeed, "with the exception of some dozen of her citizens, who have been kind to me, and some scores of her young men, who have honored me with a loving sympathy and something like reverence," Charleston has seemed to regard him "rather as a public enemy, to be sneered at, than as a dutiful son doing her honor." The war ended his career, and with him all that was left of Southern culture for two generations. General Sherman's army burned his private library of over ten thousand books, and a few years after the war Simms died, never having recovered his literary power. He had never created a character as memorable as Natty Bumppo; he had written too much, too fast; he had spread himself too thin; but he did not deserve the fate that was his, and at least a few of his works belong on the shelves next to Cooper's.

V

By the 1850s, the South and the North seemed so different from each other and so hostile to each other that it was hard to remember the nation that everyone once shared. The issue of slavery had shaped men's minds fully as much as it had shaped economic and political policy, and no point of compromise remained. From a great distance, however, things looked rather different; from such a perspective North and South shared many qualities to the point where each treated the other in the same shabby way, from similar premises. The nation in many ways remained a nation even as it tore itself apart. In both religion and political theory, the two regions were reenacting the feuds of the late eighteenth century, feuds that had shaped America at the time and that continue to shape America in ways unnoticed by the living.

The key example for these generalizations was the intellectual leader of the South for most of the period, John C. Calhoun. Calhoun came from religious and ethnic stock that was indistinguishable from many Northern backgrounds; he received the same education in the same place as many of them; and he formed his ideas about sectionalism and states' rights while studying with Northerners. All he did was to take ideas once conventionally American in origin and New England in development and apply them in a new and more specialized way to the situation of slavery in the South.

Born in 1782 in South Carolina, John Calhoun was the son of an old Indian fighter in the back country. The family heritage was rigidly Calvinist Scots-Irish Protestantism, indistinguishable from the puritanism that pervaded rural areas in most of the country. Calhoun's father was as separatist in his political science as he was in his religion, and was willing to tolerate no outside interference in any area of his life. The family was not only strong for the Revolution, it was strongly opposed to the ratification of the Constitution, because it felt that such a document would only enable Americans from outside to tax South Carolinians. Calhoun thus grew up in an environment that, in its practical effect on a young personality, was as "American" as it could be.

He also received his education largely from himself. His brother-in-law ran a school and he did receive some formal education there, but most of the stories of his growing up retell the same tale, of how he picked up what books he could, strapped them to the back of his plow, and read them while tilling his fields. Several local people noticed this unusual devotion to learning and helped send him north to a higher education; Calhoun chose Yale and arrived in the midst of Timothy Dwight's regime of revivalist exhortation. Calhoun admired Dwight but refused to treat him as anything but an intellectual equal, and the two apparently became as friendly as a Federalist Congregationalist and a Democratic Presbyterian ever could. Calhoun then went on to Tapping Reeve's famous law school in Litchfield, where he absorbed some of the key lessons for Southern separatism. New England at the time was deep in its hatred for Jefferson, Madison, and the policy of naval opposition to England, and Reeve's law school was the center of intellectual dissent from the majority in Washington. Calhoun was an ardent nationalist and remained one for over a decade, but every argument in favor of states' rights that he would ever need after 1830 was in the air of Connecticut at the time he was studying law.

Back in South Carolina, Calhoun rose quickly from the law to the state legislature to the House of Representatives, where he established himself as one of the War Hawks eager to assert American nationalism against Britain. He joined with Henry Clay to demand, in addition, a larger military establishment, the building of more roads throughout the country, internal improvements, the enactment of tariffs, and a strong national bank. In ways totally at variance with his later policies of Southern sectionalism, he wanted Washington to assert its authority over the nation and do everything possible to unify the country and fuse it into an instrument fit to fight against England. Had his career ended thirty years before it did, he would have held a firm place in the history books as an American statesman of national vision, a Democrat fit for a place near John Quincy Adams, Henry Clay, and William Seward.

But even in the years after the Peace of Ghent (1815), Calhoun was making distinctions between liberty and union that pointed the way to his intransigent positions after 1830. The two abstractions were the greatest goals the country could pursue. *Liberty* meant self-determination, and the term could apply to a person, state, region, "interest," or country. Slavery was not then central to political discourse, but Calhoun seemed to be arguing that if a region like the South or an economic interest like cotton needed a "peculiar institution" like slavery to function properly, then it deserved to have the liberty to retain or impose such an institution. The union came second and disunion was preferable to loss of liberty. The heritage of religious separatism, Anti-Federalism, and New England secessionism was creating yet another version of the eternal American desire to find salvation in one's own way, without outside interference.

Like many talented American politicians, Calhoun wanted to become president, and while in pursuit of this goal during the 1820s he displayed many flexible qualities and was willing to compromise on many issues. But as the decade wore on, he became increasingly concerned about the impact the protective tariff was having on his state. He served as vice-president under both Adams and Jackson, but this service marked the end of his career as a national leader. His low-tariff views made him unacceptable to many economic leaders in other sections, and he became involved in a feud with President Jackson that came close to tearing the nation apart. The enactment of the "Tariff of Abominations" and the attempt by South Carolina to nullify it by state action in 1832 marked the beginning of the end for Southern allegiance to national economic policies. As far as the South was concerned, it had to sell its agricultural produce in the open market, at low prices; it then had to buy manufactured goods in a protected market, at high prices. This situation was intolerable, and an imposition Northern merchants placed on Southern farmers. The price was too high; the Union was not worth it. From that point on, Calhoun and other Southern leaders worked out their defense of Southern separatism; they chose liberty instead of union.

The South clearly had a legitimate grievance, but it refused to recognize two things. In terms of its voting population, it had a far greater influence in Washington than it had any right to expect, and in practice could prevent the enactment into law of most measures it disliked. The White House had occupants sympathetic to slavery most of the time, and never held a president who openly advocated abolition or even the restriction of slavery while in office until the 1860s. Congress had any number of Southern leaders able to frustrate the few weak Northern attempts to inject the slavery issue, and the tariff came up for revision and was never permanent. The Supreme Court had been under two Southerners, John Marshall and Roger Taney, throughout most of its existence and was friendly to Southern interests in the 1850s.

But to balance this influence, the South had the incubus of slavery. Slaves had been there as long as anyone could remember; restricting the expansion of slavery might cause economic hardship; abolishing slavery would certainly cause disruption; but the civilized world was disgusted with slavery, and its abolition was an issue upon which most civilized men outside the United States agreed. Slavery was a relic of outmoded ethical and economic ideas, and Southerners should have spent their time trying to make a transition to freedom as painless as possible. They did not. They chose instead to glorify the existence of a genteel aristocracy and to assert the virtues of a white yeomanry that relied on slaves to do its least attractive jobs.

Calhoun and Jackson personalized the feud between them, and North and South learned to think of each other as tyrannical destroyers of freedom. While Jackson asserted the supremacy of the Union and threatened military action against secession, Calhoun turned his mind to the philosophical issues. He compromised grudgingly in the early 1830s, but on other issues he hardened. He wanted to shut off the flood of petitions against slavery that came to Congress, thus abridging the rights of whites to petition against grievances. He insisted on wedding the Southern identity to the slavery issue, and denied that slavery was an issue that Congress could concern itself with at all. Any attack on slavery was an attack on the South; any positive interest in the South was a part of its slave system. He got so entangled in the dilemmas imposed by this needlessly rigid position that he found himself asserting that the South could advocate the spread of slavery wherever it wished but that the North could not advocate the spread of freedom. His position was logically and morally ridiculous, and it led directly to the conclusion that a Northern democratic majority could not free slaves even in states they controlled. Since Northern states had been free for years and since such a position was unenforceable on its face, the argument clearly backfired; Northerners like Seward and Lincoln began to fear that slavery was expanding and the rights of Northern white voters shrinking and that the country could not endure much longer half slave and half free.

Calhoun spent his spare time in the 1840s developing a political science that would support his views. Never published while he was alive, the *Disquisition on Government* and the *Discourse on the Constitution of the United States* have received occasional attention over the years as serious contributions of political science. They do not deserve it. Calhoun essentially wanted to protect the interests of his section, or other minorities with substantial interests at stake in America. He developed a theory of a "concurrent majority" for his special interests, which required each interest to agree to legislation that was crucial to its self-preservation. He ignored the fact that, in practice, the South already had such a veto. He ignored the practical impossibility of identifying significant factions or of constructing a mechanism that would allow them to function without paralyzing the country. His argument looked philosophical, but it was merely special pleading.

Calhoun did not believe in natural rights or majority rule, and he convinced himself that slavery was a positive good. Natural rights theory had its problems; majority rule often did violate individual liberties; slavery certainly had its benign side; but these things said, America as a nation existed on principles that demanded a rough equality before the law for everyone, and a majority vote in some form as the basis for collective action. Calhoun seemed to be willing to tear the country apart in order to deny the very principles that made it worth fighting for. American practice might not always measure up to American theory, but the theory was important. Too many immigrants had come too far, and too many revolutionaries had died fighting, for the nation to accept such views. Slavery was too shabby an issue for a man of such intelligence to defend to the death.

VI

In contrast to concepts like *the North* and *the South*, which in time became definable because of the existence or nonexistence of slavery and the economic and social customs that went with it, *the West* was harder to pin down. In its simplest form, it was the wilderness that began on the edge of the first settlements and then slowly receded before the expansion of "civilization." But the whole idea of a West had more to do with European concepts of Atlantis or Utopia than it had to do with lands occupied by Indians or by no one. Europeans came to America with their minds filled with expectations of wildly varying kinds, and the West was really the vacant area where their imaginations played. It was the future, the unknown, the timeless, the salvation or damnation of the race. It was somehow both intangible and what the United States was all about, and the creative imaginations of both American and foreign artists found it inexhaustible. By the nineteenth century the West had become an imaginative staple of the world through dime novels that sold in the hundreds of thousands, and by the twentieth the revolution wrought by film enabled young people to grow up watching cowboys make their heroic ways through the unknown.

After 1815, immigration increased. Peace in both Europe and America provided enough stability for people to reassess their circumstances and make the decision to try something new. Older settlers had been predominantly British, French, Spanish, and African, and the English language was predominant at least along the Atlantic seaboard, but Germans had always provided settlers to the Pennsylvania area, and soon Scandinavians, Irish, and various Central European groups joined them. Toward the end of the nineteenth century the mixture was clearly changing, as Mediterraneans and languages far from English predominated in small areas from the Yiddish of Brooklyn to the Chinese of San Francisco. Second-generation Americans could grow up speaking Finnish in Duluth or German in New Braunfels, and only the passage of time and the spread of the English-language media enabled English to remain the first language of most of their descendents.

In the nineteenth century, the Atlantic seaboard seemed to be relatively settled. Newcomers arrived there, but they normally continued on into the old West before settling. New cities like Cincinnati, St. Louis, and Chicago challenged New York for the domination of their world, although at first rural life exerted great appeal. These people wanted independence, land, and freedom to work and worship, and so they went to whatever area was opening up. They brought with them new customs, especially new religions, and often did not bring with them much that older English-language settlers took for granted. The legacy of puritanism, which virtually defined the culture of New England and parts of the land farther west, was often unfamiliar to these new settlers. America was the country of their dreams, and those dreams often included neither the slavery of the South nor the abolitionism of much of the North. It did not include the fruits of revivalism, with its yearning to improve the morals of neighbors or the treatment of the handicapped. Many of these new Americans were fleeing obligations to the church, the tax man, and the military, and they had no desire to take on new obligations to authorities closer to home. The West seemed a prize for both North and South, but it also had interests of its own.

Before the Civil War, the West had too few people and too brief a history to be a genuine equal to the older sections. The states from Ohio to Iowa slowly organized and sought admission to the union, even while in the Far West California and its neighbors began to march eastward from the Pacific. The Southwest seemed to be excellent slave territory to Southerners, capable of sending an infinite number of new senators and representatives to Washington to defend the interests of the peculiar institution; the Northwest appealed similarly to the Northern economic interests. Northerners had the better case on both moral and practical grounds. Newcomers were unfamiliar with slavery and ignorant of cavalier virtues. They wanted land and independence, and slaves hurt the economy. A European was confident that he could survive free competition and prosper, but slave competition was another matter. Few immigrants went to the South; they preferred the Northwest that resembled the Europe they had just left. Particularly after the European revolutionaries of 1848, the Northwest attracted settlers whose bias was naturally Northern if not especially evangelical. They were Free-soilers at heart before they knew the meaning of the term. They had come a long way to escape conditions of penury and even serfdom, and they provided significant numbers of soldiers to fight a Civil War to save the Union from the expansion of slavery.

The West had long supplied occasional leaders to the new nation. As mature politicians, Andrew Jackson and Henry Clay, the key political leaders of the years after 1815, were from Tennessee and Kentucky; but they had national visions for their country and neither was an ideologist for any sectional interest. Abraham Lincoln grew up chiefly in Kentucky and Illinois, and only the events of the 1850s drove him to the position that he came to represent—morally firm on the issue of the expansion of slavery yet never dogmatic enough for evangelical abolitionists. But insofar as the West produced one leader who summed up its instincts, who above all wanted to forget the problems of the older settlements and get on with economic development, that man was Lincoln's great opponent, Stephen A. Douglas. Occasionally inept and frequently insensitive, Senator Douglas was the quintessential Western politician and as such he came very near to a compromise position that could have prevented the war. Another decade or two, more settlers providing more votes, and the West might have avoided the worst catastrophe in American history.

Douglas had been born in rural Vermont, and spent much of his early life in the midst of the evangelical enthusiasms of New England and New York, but they never touched him. He seemed to have been born secular, and no religion ever had much impact on his thinking. His two chief enthusiasms were Andrew Jackson and the making of money. Finding nothing that appealed to him as a way of life in the East, he went west like countless other Americans, picking Jacksonville, Illinois, as a likely place in which to prosper. He studied law in the haphazard way common at the time and came to know the area as a circuit-riding prosecutor, going from town to town as legal circumstances required. The wild speculation that marked the second Jackson administration was at its height in the middle 1830s, and Douglas emerged as a Jacksonian leader, favoring hard money, opposing any national bank with much power, and tolerating internal improvements only if locally administered. In the early 1840s he went to the House of Representatives in Washington with a general position that was "Western": when it came to legislation on any issue, he always preferred the smallest unit possible. If a city or town could tax and administer a road, a canal, or a railway, then it should; if the problem were larger than a local area could handle, then the state should do it; only failing both should the nation intervene. If the nation did become involved, it should be on the principles of Jefferson and Jackson: it should be strict constructionist, and only operate in those areas where the Constitution expressly said it should. Money should be hard and tariffs low; most other issues would solve themselves in the private sector of the economy.

During the 1840s, this general position picked up the name *popular sovereignty*. The term summed up the common sense of what was already happening in Western America. If the people should rule, then they could manage the job best if they kept it close to home. They should listen to the politicians, debate among themselves, and make democratic decisions. Popular sovereignty was the systematization of Jacksonian rhetoric, giving value to the choice of the citizen and keeping issues of manageable size and solvable proportions. Only if local people violated the Constitution should a higher authority intervene.

This procedural position combined in practice with economic expansion and a foreign policy stance. Like Douglas, most people in Illinois had come there from somewhere else; they were acutely conscious of what the freedom to travel and to settle in a new area had meant to them, and thought that that was what American democracy really meant. If they could open up a new land, then self-respect and political power would follow without any ideological justification being necessary. They were, then, eager to keep the lands yet farther west open, if not for them, then for their children. The obvious power in the way was Great Britain, which had historical and economic claims in the area, and which had been the hereditary enemy of Americans all along. Manifest Destiny brought the issues together: for a Jacksonian like Douglas, the destiny of America was to keep expanding the area of freedom in politics and in economic opportunities; any opposition to this stance was a threat to the meaning of America.

By the time of Douglas' political maturity, the railroads were becoming the central problem of economic expansion. They had not yet become the dominating force that they became in the 1870s and after, but their importance was obvious and the clash between local, state, and national jurisdictions a serious legal problem. Internal improvements like roads and canals had always been political issues; followers of Jackson and Clay had fought over them for two generations, and the sheer size of railroads and their obvious importance made the issue acute for the 1850s. Each new city wanted to get a Western railroad for itself; each state wanted the commerce of the West to flow through its area, thus enriching its economy and its base. Milwaukee, Chicago, and St. Louis were obvious places for the domination of the West, but other cities were growing fast, and fearful that if the central railroads bypassed them, then economic disaster would follow. Railroads were an important symbol, two bands of metal tying together a huge nation and a diverse, multilingual people. Few failed to notice that Milwaukee and Chicago were in free territory and St. Louis in slave territory. Construction of major railroads could materially alter the social and economic system that developed in the West, and thus dictate the votes of the politicians that the area would be sending to Washington.

Since Douglas was himself personally involved with the financing of the railroads, his career brought together clearly these conflicting strands of greed, mission, politics, and sectional diversity. While Congress debated the admission of Texas and Oregon to the Union, one presumably slave, the other free, railroad interests launched their campaign for federal help. Other cities both north and south of Chicago wanted to be the terminal point for the roads, but Douglas naturally favored the major city of his own state. Not only would both he and the city gain from railroad development, but he could then help dictate the political pattern of settlement. Douglas wanted to keep the issue of Western settlement out of the dangerous slavery controversy. The best way to settle the West was to organize the territory west of Illinois, put it on the path to statehood and allow it to become a state as soon as possible, sell land grants along the way to future settlers, use the money to pay for railroad construction, and then solve all remaining issues by local vote. This would combine politics, economics, and personal profit in an appealing way and avoid the hostilities that were poisoning national issues remote from slavery.

By the late 1840s Douglas' legal position was clear. No one questioned the right of Congress to legislate for a territory, but he felt strongly that Congress could not have any valid say in the future of any territory once it became a state. Local voting, or popular sovereignty, should be the means of solving all issues. Such a position was consistent with his whole career as a Jacksonian Democrat, and also avoided the increasingly hysterical forum of national politics. His wife's family owned slaves; slavery was a well-established part of the American system; he experienced no religious twinges on the subject; people could vote it up or down as far as he was concerned, since their democratic rights were the most important consideration. He thought the whole matter overblown, anyway: slaves were inappropriate on the plains and in the Far West. Even if slavery were tolerated, it probably would not get much beyond some point in central Kansas– Oklahoma–Texas. If people left the issue alone, the normal course of economic development would effectively solve the problem. Most of the West would end up in free territory; the point was to get it organized and out of Washington as an issue.

The focus during the 1850s was always on the slavery issue and Douglas' attempts to make it a matter of local control. In the short run, Abraham Lincoln became his great opponent in the running debate; Douglas won the Senate seat in 1858, but then lost the presidency in 1860 to a man who sincerely believed that the country had to face the slavery issue even at the risk of war. War came, and with it Douglas' full support of the Union and the North. But the legacies of his position went far beyond the fighting of 1861–1865. Douglas did believe in democratic settlement, railroad organization, and government subsidies. He did not contemplate for long any problems that might arise from federal government financial assistance followed by local control. Theory was never important to him, and he could not foresee the circumstances of the postwar years, when railroads led the nation in making raids on the federal treasury. In terms of economic policy, Douglas had come close to the position of Seward and John Quincy Adams: government should initiate and finance improvements which the nation needed, but should not expect subsequent administrative control. He too wanted governmental encouragement of science and technology, because they would clearly be useful in aiding Western settlement. He too wanted the government to help the telegraph industry, to assist in the development of steam power, finance geological surveys, underwrite agricultural surveys, and subsidize the Smithsonian Institution. The precedents were in place for the vast economic expansion of the years after 1865 and the perversion of ideas that accompanied it.

VII

But the Douglas West of railroads and politics, of popular sovereignty and homestead grants, was the real West, and with the West in America, the real was the last thing many people cared about. The romance was the first important American art form, and the West was romance before it had a single white settler. It might contain anything from the Lost Tribes of Israel to the last area of freedom for democratic man, but it seemed to excite almost everyone who thought about it. People who actually lived in the West rarely wrote about it, but those who lived on its edge found in it the possible meanings for their own lives; those who lived far away peopled it with every conceivable utopian possibility.

These fantasies had many practical elements. The British colonial administrators had recognized quite early that the West was almost impossible to control, and that if Americans migrated too far from the royal navy, they might migrate out of both the British Empire and authoritarian control of any kind. Jefferson was less given to fantasy than most men, and for him the exploration of the vast area between himself and the Pacific was the key to the passage to India, that fabled highway to the Oriental trade that had excited Christopher Columbus in the first place. Jefferson and those like him wanted above all to know, to find out scientifically what was there, and he was the man chiefly responsible for the explorations of Meriwether Lewis and William Clark to the mouth of the Columbia River. As other explorers followed, Thomas Hart Benton supported them with political visions while Walt Whitman supplied literary ones, giving a nation that was devoted to material progress a vision that stirred both the imagination and the pocketbook. The Mississippi River, the Rocky Mountains, and the Pacific shore all provided possible places for the end of America's manifest destiny in the West, but the imagination knew no bounds and somehow American democratic man wanted it all. He wanted ivory, apes, and peacocks, and he wanted bourgeois comfort too. Without inconsistencies of a monumental kind, nations seem hardly able to exist, and a large nation could tolerate large inconsistencies.

Jefferson felt ambivalence about the actual settlement of the West. For him as for most Americans, the real West was for trappers and explorers, wild men who could not tolerate settlements, neighbors, and the realities of farm life and politics. Life on the settled frontier was the reverse of romantic, and James Fenimore Cooper's ambivalence about the whole problem was what gave many of his tales the mythic believability they still retain. Great art frequently comes from unresolved tensions within the mind of the artist, and Cooper could never decide whether or not Natty Bumppo was more savage than free, more Indian than white, or more admirable than the character who represented Cooper's own father. Manners, grammar, and legal principles all seemed to deteriorate along the frontier, and yet the qualities of freedom somehow made it all worthwhile. The Atlantic coast all too often meant Europe, schooling, and history, while the West meant timeless possibility.

As the nineteenth century waned and the Civil War determined that Northern values would become national values, other heroes replaced Leatherstocking as Western archetypes. American folklore could never decide whether or not Daniel Boone was a hopeless misanthrope who could not stand the sight of his neighbors or the great pathbreaker for permanent settlement, but by the time of Kit Carson and the vogue of the dime novels, the formula had frozen into the Western. As the Western developed under the sponsorship of Erastus Beadle, the sons of Leatherstocking became benevolent hunters who never seemed to settle in one place, and who seemed to carry on the legacies of *The Prairie*: they were old, celibate, and sophisticated; they could follow trails or shoot with amazing accuracy. Living in the mountains and desert beyond the prairie, they were the last holdouts of the pioneer virtues, killing off the Indians yet themselves in danger from advancing settlers. As Deadwood Dick or Buffalo Bill, they circled the world with their exploits. Somehow they came to symbolize for Americans the virtues that men wished to preserve as civilization entered space and lost its few remaining roots in the land.

By the end of the nineteenth century, other ideas were competing with these standard ones. The West became for many people the garden of the world, so fertile that it could provide not only for its settlers but also for those less fortunate. The sacred farmer with his plow became a symbol less heroic but perhaps more appropriate, a mythical yeoman who could contain the qualities of democratic, independent man. Jefferson had worried about the natural rights of men to the land, and homestead acts had enshrined these worries into something like an American natural law. Americans seemed to feel that they had a right to life, liberty, and the ownership of the land. Labor gave them a valid title to a reasonable acreage and ownership gave them dignity; a life close to soil of their own was what made meaning in a world fraught with uncertainty. This legacy had its darker side even before drought and big business made a mockery out of the whole concept. Western writers finally began to contribute to the literature of their region, and the reports they brought back, from Ed Howe's *The Story of a Country Town* to Frederick Jackson Turner's historical addresses, were that the frontier was closing, that what had made Americans what they were was no longer there, and that the West had become gloomy, philistine, and unproductive. By the end of the nineteenth century, the West had gone the way of the South. *High Noon* and *Gone With The Wind* would keep regional messages forever pure, perhaps, but they were messages from the twentieth century about sections that no longer existed.

VIII

But while the West lasted, it made the first great American literature possible. The West began with the Eastern settlements, and so many works that seem to be about the East or the past are actually about the West. Many others, which ostensibly deal with the sea, really deal with the ocean as a West, a wet frontier where explorers sought passages to India while fighting savages of their own making. Those two great literary friends, Nathaniel Hawthorne (1804–1864) and Herman Melville (1819–1891), were both novelists of the West, and with both the true West was in everyman, the dark side of the human personality. Only with Mark Twain—finally, a man from the "real West"—did some kind of synthesis occur. With Twain, the West as place met the West as imagination, and the results seemed so unattractive that Twain married an Eastern woman, lived chiefly in the East as an adult, and spent much of his life in Europe.

Despite the emphasis on solitude in Hawthorne's writings and his own statements about his life, he was a man close to the affairs of his culture. Long a Jacksonian Democrat, he was a college friend of Franklin Pierce; for much of his life he was deeply involved in politics, received the consulship in Liverpool as a reward for the author of a campaign biography of his friend. Despite a puritan heritage that should have made him an abolitionist, Hawthorne on this issue as on so many others retained a certain detachment, and was willing to see merit in Pierce's tolerance of slavery in the South. Many of his short stories, furthermore, appeared in the *Democratic Review* of John L. O'Sullivan, one of the leading advocates of Manifest Destiny. Through his wife, Sophia Peabody, Hawthorne was the brother-in-law of one of the leading reformers of the period, Elizabeth Peabody, and Horace Mann was only a slightly more distant relative. Hawthorne was by temperament shy and retiring, but this was not a sentence passed on him by society and he was not the rejected artist of his own self-pitying analysis. The truth was that reform was in the air all around him and he had no taste for reform. He resisted Transcendentalism, utopian socialism, and Brook Farm, and when he did become involved in such movements, it was usually because of pressure from wife or relatives. Hawthorne was a born skeptic in an age of believers; he was skeptical about puritanism, progress, and Transcendentalism and thus had little use for Emerson, Margaret Fuller, or German literature. His lifelong creed was that a man had no claim on his fellow creatures for much beyond food and a decent burial, and that self-reliance was preferable to reforming one's neighbors.

Hawthorne was deeply involved in the American art form of the romance. His political involvement gave him an income from minor jobs, one of which was the position of Surveyor for the District of Salem and Beverly and Inspector of the Revenue for the Port of Salem—a prosaic spot for a brooding intelligence. But instead of wasting his time trying to write a novel of manners or of the vicarage, he took refuge in his family history along the frontier to write in *The Scarlet Letter* a study of original sin that gives that theological term a historical and national application far beyond its original emphasis. Hawthorne played with notions of the wilderness and the edge of civilization almost as much as Cooper did, and his too was a moral wilderness, full of doubts about the self, sexuality, and religion; his forest was a deceptive playground for neurotic memory, national as well as personal. Somehow the West was the meaning of America for him in ways he evoked rather than defined. The East was Europe and the Atlantic, the West was America and forest, and Hester Prynne's famous A conveyed far more than casual readers of a novel of adultery might notice. Beneath the placid surface history of a country that seemed to have no history, Hawthorne found an extraordinary undertone of random violence: maypoles destroyed, relatives bathed in tar and feathers, witches persecuted, lives destroyed because of a single trivial flaw. The Salem customs house thus became a useful symbol for an American symbolist: there was far more to America than routine governmental tasks. The wilderness and the soul were universal, and a bland democratic optimism concealed all the depths of irrationality that modern psychology thought it discovered only a century later.

Like Poe, Hawthorne had an uncertain grip on extended art forms. He was most effective in his early stories and in brilliant fragments of his work of the early 1850s, *The Scarlet Letter* and *The House of Seven Gables*. His four years in Europe provided excellent opportunities to expand his horizons and develop new themes, but Hawthorne was not up to the challenge. His letters and notebooks often had effective passages, but his subsequent attempts to create art went badly and he seemed unable to cope with Europe culturally, aesthetically, or morally. He could mock puritanism at home but turned out to be its prisoner abroad. He could not stand the condescension he received from Europeans, he found the class divisions beyond his analysis, and overt sexuality gave him the moral twitches. He could cope with women's rights neither in the abstract nor in the person of Margaret Fuller, and his remarks about Titian's Magdalen being "very coarse and sensual, with only an impudent assumption of penitance and religious sentiment, scarcely so deep as the eyelids," and of Titian himself as "a very good-for-nothing old man" have gone down in history as classic examples of American inability to appreciate anything sensual or erotic in art. He also had great trouble seeing a virtue in the Roman Catholic church, although one of his own daughters in time converted to that church to become Mother Alphonsa, a sister of mercy.

American criticism at the time was heavily derivative from European sources, especially the theories of Coleridge and the practice of Scott. Poe and Simms in particular had speculated in print about the way art should be constructed, but Hawthorne was the most important practitioner to make clear to Americans the problems involved with creating art in a young democracy. Cooper had touched on some of these themes, and Irving had written as if he knew them in his bones, but Hawthorne put them into permanent form in the introductions to *The House of Seven Gables* and *The Marble Faun*. When a writer calls his work a romance, he told his readers in the early 1850s, he obviously is claiming a certain latitude about what he would or would not do. A novel aimed "at a very minute fidelity, not merely to the possible, but to the probable and ordinary course of man's experience." The author of a romance, in contrast, could "present that truth under circumstances" of his "own choosing." Almost a decade later he refined the distinction. Life in Italy had stimulated his imagination if not improved his art, and he praised it as a place "where actualities would not be so terribly insisted upon as they are, and must needs be, in America." He moaned about the "difficulty of writing a romance about a country where there is no shadow, no antiquity, no mystery, no picturesque and gloomy wrong, nor anything but a commonplace prosperity," as was the case with America. "Romance and poetry, ivy, lichens, and wallflowers, need ruin to make them grow." Cooper had already proved him wrong with his work on the Revolution, the frontier, and the sea; indeed, Hawthorne had proven himself wrong with his earlier work, but his statement certainly had validity in terms of what an American writer felt. America did not feel full of what England or Europe seemed to have, although the Civil War that broke out almost as Hawthorne was writing soon supplied more topics for art than any romancer or novelist could wish.

IX

With Herman Melville, a great many themes relevant to the West, the North, and America as a nation came together. James Fenimore Cooper, especially in *The Sea Rover*, had been the first writer of importance to find the core of American experience along the frontier and to write as effectively of the sea as he did of the woods as a possible American space for practicing pioneer virtues. Richard Henry Dana, in *Two Years Before the Mast*, had carried the idea much further, seeing an unspoiled landscape, Indians, traders, hunters, trappers, and settlers as a part of his voyage to explore the route to California—the first area to be "west of the West." Melville read both books with enthusiasm and his early novels extended the notion of an oceanic West to the South Pacific. The Marquesas and Tahiti became frontier societies with "Indian" populations and white sailors encountered them with all the misunderstandings and mythifications inherent in any clash of cultures. By the time he wrote *Moby Dick*, Melville was so far into the spirit of the thing that he could call Captain Ahab a grizzly bear, a prairie wolf, and an Arkansas duelist; he could speak of a harpooneer who snatched up his weapon "as readily from its rest as a backwoodsman swings his rifle from the wall"; and compare a whaleman hunting for his oil to "the traveler on the prairie" as he hunted up "his own supper of game." He put Tashtego, an American Indian from Martha's Vineyard, on board, along with Daggoo to represent the African influence and Queequeg to represent an unmapped island somewhere out to the south and west of wherever America ended. Queequeg even refers to the god who created sharks as "one dam Ingin," and indeed such is the complexity and ambiguity of Melville's writing that it is not always certain who are the best Americans either on the boat or in the oceanic wilderness.

By birthright, Melville should have been a Barnburner Democrat, moralistically supporting reform at home and Manifest Destiny along the frontier, but nothing in the family worked out predictably. He was born in 1819 and as a boy knew the gentility of the upwardly mobile bourgeoisie in New York City. But his father overcommitted himself in business and the pressures of failure drove him to madness and early death. Financial woes remained forever after a theme in Melville's life; he had to withdraw from school at thirteen, clerk in a bank, and watch his mother and her eight children forced into less expensive quarters. A number of relatives had been involved with the sea, and it seemed an obvious way to lighten the burden on his mother and on himself when Melville signed onto a ship heading for Liverpool. He saw great poverty in that seaport but never suffered unduly himself, and returned to America to try schoolteaching and to explore the West. Nothing appealed to him vocationally, and he followed the path of many poor Eastern men when he signed onto the *Acushnet* for a whaling voyage to the South Pacific.

During the next four years, he served on four different boats, jumping ship, living among natives, joining the American navy, and storing up enough memories for the major books of his career. Many of the memories were unpleasant, and certainly two stood out in view of their effect on his novels. While in the South Pacific islands, he had ample opportunity to see Christian missionaries at work, and he quickly came to dislike both them and their effect on the natives. They seemed to him bigoted and authoritarian, corrupting native mores and not improving native civilization at all. While on ships, and especially on his navy ship, he also witnessed 163 floggings for all sorts of infractions, not to mention countless other petty brutalities. The sight never left him and became, in time, a literary symbol for the irrational power some men unjustifiably came to have over others. Increasingly, too, he came to put the authority system of the ship and the authority system of the church together, and neither clergymen nor captains would ever come out looking very admirable in his work. Both presumed political and moral control over men and both used a self-serving moral system to justify their vicious acts. Melville came to understand that he was something of a humanist at heart, and by the time of his greatest work had identified himself with the anticlerical libertarianism of writers like Rabelais and Pierre Bayle.

Upon his return, Melville had a fund of memories that enthralled his family, but no obvious career. They urged him to write up his adventures, and he did so; untutored in fiction, he made any number of false starts, but persevered and with remarkable luck and considerable native skill brought out *Typee* and *Omoo*, based on some of his more spectacular adventures. Exotic romances, they found an immediate audience in both England and America, and paid enough to encourage him to continue. The sexuality of some passages and the remarks critical of missionaries both irritated some readers, while others doubted the factual validity of the books, but on the whole Melville was well pleased. But he also had a certain contempt for what he was writing and wanted to do something more literary. Newly married to the daughter of Lemuel Shaw, one of the most important figures in American law, he enjoyed too much their mutual reading in German romances and English romantic poets, and the next volume, *Mardi*, displeased almost everyone in its shapeless vagaries and random commentaries on thinly veiled American issues. In 1848 the country seemed to be coming apart over the slavery issue, and Melville developed an enormous contempt for politicians on both sides of the argument; but writing a fantasy about the South Sea isles was an odd way to criticize America, and only well-trained literary critics have cared to make the journey.

The years around 1850 were the most crucial in his life. He ground out two further volumes of romance because he needed the money, took a lengthy trip to Europe, and then settled down for a while in the Berkshire hills of western Massachusetts. Lonely for literary companionship, he met Oliver Wendell

Holmes, Sr., James T. Fields, and—most important—Nathaniel Hawthorne. In one of those rare instances when two authors meet and find themselves compatible, Melville seemed all but overwhelmed that an American could look into the darkness, say "No! in thunder," and retain both his integrity and his talent in a country that seemed devoted to cant and hypocrisy in both religion and politics. He reviewed *Mosses from an Old Manse* to publicize his discovery—it has become one of the most quoted reviews in the history of American literature— but he probably misunderstood his new friend. While a dissenter from much held dear by majority American culture, Hawthorne was not nearly the gloomy heretic that Melville was, nor as adventurous in his reading or his formal experimentations. At the time, however, the relationship so flourished that Melville dedicated *Moby Dick* to his new friend.

Moby Dick is one of those books that will not bear brief analysis, and no two critics seem to agree for long about its meaning. It was clearly a romance of the South Pacific frontier. It showed the influence of Hawthorne, Dana, and Cooper. Its rhetoric seemed bathed in references to Shakespeare and the Bible. Its major figure, Captain Ahab, seemed Byronic. The literary contexts were all but inexhaustible, especially if a reader looked into the literature of whaling which supplied large amounts of factual data. But *Moby Dick* was above all about Melville's "quarrel with God," as one critic has aptly called it. Melville had been feuding with the Calvinistic God of his family for many years, and clung with stubbornness to the conclusion that God had put the world together badly. The Original Sinner, the person who put evil into the world, God was like Captain Ahab, in control over a boat that was a microcosm of the world, madly in quest of something better left alone. Men all wanted to think well of God and their captain, but if they were so simple as to trust in such authority figures, the results were fatal. A heroic man resisted this despotism, asserted reason and common sense against irrationality and will, and expected death for a reward.

Americans from then till now did not want to hear such a message, and such was the deviousness of Melville's style that they could read *Moby Dick* and many of his other works in quite different, more positive terms. *The Confidence-Man*, a few years later, permitted no such deception. A book that actually took place in the West, on a Mississippi riverboat, it combined the genres of the realistic Western narrative, allegory, and satire to offer a scathing picture of gullibility and deception. Once more, the ship was a world, this time on an April Fools' Day. Anyone in the book who believed found himself deceived. Always the note was of optimism and faith, and always the result was betrayal. If the two books were by the same man, then any optimistic or Christian reading of *Moby Dick* could have no basis. Totally heretical books like these were inconceivable to a Christian nation and Melville spent the rest of his life neglected. If people read him at all, they did so because they wanted a romantic narrative and preferred to assume that references to the Bible were always positive in their implication unless the author insisted otherwise.

X

With Mark Twain (1835–1910) the literary sections of the country came together in a literal sense. From Missouri on the borderland between South and West, he knew both slavery and the frontier at first hand; choosing a respectable Eastern wife and an adulthood in Hartford, Elmira, and in England, he became a pillar of respectable Eastern authorship. The nation he symbolized still had its divisions and inconsistencies and so did he. In the mind of the public, not to mention puzzled users of libraries ever since, he had two identities—the respectable novelist Samuel L. Clemens and the garrulous tale-teller Mark Twain—and in fact scholars have agreed that he was a man divided against himself. He could not decide who he was or what he was, and the long silence of his last decades was a tacit admission of failure to unify himself any more effectively than the country had unified itself.

In his youth he was Sam Clemens of Hannibal, growing up along the Mississippi, that mysterious river which changed its course with every major flood and that seemed both to bind the North and the South together and to divide slave territory from free. The contradictions of American culture were both social and linguistic: a democracy of white yeomen were firmly in control, yet that control included a subclass of slaves and a universal racial bigotry; the males talked a racy argot full of slang and tall tales, with frequent implications of the profane and obscene, while their wives and daughters censored them at the dinner table and kept the bookshelves full of romances in which the race seemed to reproduce parthenogenetically, stimulated by blushes and tears and hidden by long dresses and longer curtains. America appeared to have no class structure, and yet its mode of communication was as bifurcated as that of the speaker of Mandarin or Hochdeutsch. George Santayana soon made his celebrated distinction between the genteel tradition and the less refined layers of American culture, but Twain had it in his bones and he never got over it.

The first response of any young writer to such an environment was to flee, and Twain fled to the West, to Nevada and California, where he apparently led as rowdy and bibulous a young manhood as health permitted. He acquired journalistic experience and a fund of memories, but at thirty-one decided to head east and become a literary man in a more supportive environment. He was, in a relatively pure sense of the term, a Southwestern humorist, telling anecdotes in dialect that were full of outrageous inventions, surprising twists of plot, and mythical characters larger than life. Yet he was also desperate for acceptance in the older sections of the country, and there the traditions of the romance were in firm control of the magazines in which he wished to place books. He knew that he had to write a more elegant prose and to master longer forms, but throughout his life he never quite managed. At his best, he found that he had to work dialect and tale-telling into his plots; rather than shape a large work carefully, he preferred to string together scenes anecdotally that did not always add up to a coherent whole.

The form he knew best was that of the letter to a newspaper. It was short, impressionistic, anecdotal, and had to make its points quickly to a large, semi-literate readership who would throw the material away after a single reading. Such writing paid the bills but defeated any mastery of literary form. He could travel abroad and take notes, as he did to write *The Innocents Abroad*, but constantly lapsed into the sort of ignorant jeering that displayed his own sense of insecurity in another culture as well as the need to make quick humorous points with a readership that knew even less history and geography than he did. He could rework his Western adventures and early writings as he did in *Roughing It*, but here the problem was the reverse: he had to write about the raw and vulgar West in such a way as to be both amusing and genteel to an audience of Eastern bookbuyers. He was at his best when he ignored the strictly contemporary and allowed time and his memory to cover over the problems and unify the experience, as in some of the early sections of *Roughing It* or in the memories of his boyhood first published as "Old Times on the Mississippi." But he had decided permanently in favor of Eastern gentility. He married a respectable, neurasthenic wife with a wealthy father who would keep his language and his behavior pure, and he sought out literary friends like William Dean Howells, who could foster his career while tidying up his manuscripts. Mark Twain chose to become Mr. Samuel Clemens, literary gentleman, and to live in a style all too close to that of the very businessmen and speculators he castigated in a book like *The Gilded Age*.

Indeed, it is cruel but accurate to see money as the tie that bound North and West, as well as Clemens and Twain, together. Twain had an obsession with money that worked itself into his art as well as his life. He was no Melville or Hawthorne, detached from the scurrying about for wealth that seemed to be a national pastime. He adopted the life-style of his father-in-law with scarcely time to gasp at his good fortune, and spent many of his most productive hours deciding how to market his books so that they generated enough money to keep the family in servants and lengthy holiday trips. He went into the publishing business, not only to market his own work but also to make money on the work of others. A device known as the Paige Typesetter was his undoing; combined with his other business problems and his opulent way of living it drove him into bankruptcy—a word that had literary and moral applications as well as financial ones. He became as obsessed with God and the malevolent universe as Herman Melville had been and, like Melville, soon found literary production all but impossible. He spent more and more time in England and Germany. His old work continued to sell, and as a lecturer and literary presence he never lost an audience, but as far as new work was concerned, he was finished.

For most readers, the Twain worth remembering will usually be the Twain of the "boys' stories," of *The Adventures of Tom Sawyer* (1876) and *The Adventures of Huckleberry Finn* (1885). The man who was the son of slaveholders but who married into an abolitionist family, the crass Westerner determined to make it in the East, he divided himself between the conventional Tom and the unconventional Huck. The first book was a children's classic but nothing extraordinary, but once Twain let Huck loose with his slave companion Jim, they created an American classic out of Twain's divided personality and the opposing heritages. The book is a picaresque tale of escape and adventure of a style going back to Defoe and Cervantes; it is an initiation rite, with Huck becoming the archetypal American trying to cope with the institutions of slavery and civilization; it is a satire on Western violence and Southern sentimentalism, written from a securely Eastern perspective. But above all, the book is a celebration of the independent personality as it fled the demands of a culture that seemed divided against itself. Speaking a language of his own, forming a friendship of his own, traveling on his own, Huck became an embodiment of America trying to deal with moral and sectional divisions. Neither he nor Twain could solve the terrible problems of race the book posed: Huck lit out for the West, while Twain embarked for Europe. America wallowed in materialistic expansion for a generation and left its problems for later.

A sense of sectionalism lived on in America long after it had much validity in fact. By the end of the nineteenth century, the West was won. While Twain lost his artistic skills, the Mormons in Utah agreed to stop the practice of polygamy, the most obvious behavioral example of truly Western nonconformity to Protestant norms. The "forty-eight states" of the continent became complete in 1912, when Arizona joined Utah and the rest of the country.

The South died harder. The white South never admitted the injustices of slavery or the illegitimacy of the cause for which the Confederacy had fought, and remained distinct into the 1960s through the practice of legal segregation of the races. It also developed a self-consciously regional defense of its agrarian way of life, most famously in the volume by twelve southerners, *I'll Take My Stand* (1930). Professors in university history and literature courses persisted in using regional perspectives into the 1960s, but by then the whole affair was an example of cultural fossilization. Western films began to satirize themselves, while the last "professional Southerners" wandered off the stage of Tennessee Williams' dramas.

PART III

THE NORTHERN NATION
From Religious to
Capitalist Democracy,
1865–1917

Chapter 7

From Darwinism to Progressivism, 1865–1917

Between the Civil War and American entry into World War I the country went through a profound change. The religious ideas that had been so central to the nation's identity could not survive in their original form. They had to face the traumas of the war, then the brutalities of the rapid industrialization after the war, and they had to do so in the face of the skepticism generated by science, most obviously what became known as Darwinism. While America would always experience religious revivals and public approval of the role of the church would continue, the theological core was gone and religiosity had replaced the complex ideas and strenuous practices of earlier generations. Religious energies were channeled into economic activity and then into political faith. The "American Way" was the result: the belief that Americans were a people of diverse origins who believed in capitalism and democracy as if they were the decrees of Divine Providence. To question either became something close to blasphemy, especially in time of depression or war.

These were thus the linchpin years for the development of American culture, the years that divided the past from the present, so to speak. All dates for such analysis remain arbitrary, so the problem is to select one for good and sufficient reason, but always to remember that few things happen precisely in cultural history. The best year is 1901, in the middle of this major shift. America had survived a major depression in the early 1890s, and then gone through a brief, exhilarating spasm of imperialism, and in that year its public face changed with alarming abruptness with the shooting, on 6 September, of President William McKinley. An amiable man of mediocre ability, McKinley had fought in the Civil War and made his reputation supporting such nineteenth-century issues as high tariffs for the protection of industry and the sanctity of the gold standard. Eight days later he was dead and an entirely new sort of president took over. Theodore Roosevelt had been three years old in 1861, when the Civil War began. His mother was from the South, his father from the North, and much of his early maturity had been spent exploring and writing about the West. A faithful supporter of sound business values, he was nevertheless skeptical about much of what he saw happening in the world around him, and patiently worked out several ways of reforming society as he found it. He was patriotic in the most energetic and visceral sense and adept at using religious rhetoric for political purposes. As McKinley seemed to symbolize the nineteenth century, Roosevelt seemed emblematic of the twentieth.

Speaking culturally, two great shifts were in process during these years that led directly to modern American culture. The first was that from Darwinism to progressivism, from the survival of the fittest as applied to capitalist activity to a sense that Americans could intervene in both nature and society to shape a more moral, a more Protestant society. In this sense, progressivism became a third Great Awakening, with Roosevelt himself exhorting delegates to two national conventions in 1912 to stand at Armageddon and battle for the Lord, a rhetorically effective way of demanding progressive reforms. The second began with a rebellion against much of what was known as social Darwinism. Some Americans accepted Darwin, then rebelled against many of the economic and social corollaries of his ideas; others never accepted Darwin's ideas in a philosophical context at all. In trying to work out their own view of a morally satisfying democratic life, these thinkers developed the philosophy of pragmatism, the first original American contribution to philosophy. By the turn of the twentieth century, John Dewey and George Herbert Mead were working out important applications for these ideas in both city governments and schools, and in 1907 William James published the most important theoretical discussion in *Pragmatism*. By 1917, progressivism and pragmatism had come to complement each other, so much so that John Dewey came to symbolize for many people what it meant to be a democratic American. As the country went through these changes, other issues arose which laid the groundwork for a great outburst of original activity in the arts. Some Americans traveled to Europe to find stimulation away from the restrictions of Protestantism, economic exploitation, and democratic conformity. Others gloried in what was happening at home and saw indigenous materials equally worthy of attention. In the process, a national culture took shape in which issues of sectionalism no longer seemed relevant.

II

For Emerson's generation, life as they knew it made sense. The material world and the immaterial world coexisted happily; religion, philosophy, and literature agreed in assuring people that every little evil that they might experience in private life was a part of a universal good. Wars, diseases, and misfortunes might cause a temporary pessimism, but Americans believed that it all worked out and that on some distant day of reckoning they would have their reward. Most of them thought progress in some sense inevitable; a large number seemed to feel that the millennium might not be far off. God was rarely far from the thoughts of most individuals who left written records.

During the 1850s and 1860s, two men in England were at work fashioning ideas that ended this sense of personal security. Charles Darwin carried the ideas of a number of predecessors and coworkers to the conclusion that "natural selection" was the way that change occurred in living creatures. God did not plan much of anything or intervene to change things; organisms evolved in a way that was blind, unplanned, and chaotic. Species did not suddenly appear at the touch of a divine hand; species evolved into other species over an incomprehensibly vast period of time, and accidents of mutation determined the fate of vital characteristics, including characteristics peculiar to mankind. Nothing seemed to separate men from animals, and the warmth of a personal God who actually cared was suddenly absent from the lives of millions. Jungle warfare seemed to be the way the world evolved, everything seemed to be in flux, and man had nothing to depend on in a crisis.

Many scientists, not to say many theologians, greeted the new scientific ideas coldly. Led by the eminent Harvard geologist Louis Agassiz, they rejected Darwin's notions as unproven and unlikely. Religion denied such a universe, human nature could not cope with it, and the geological record did not support it. Other scientists and churchmen felt differently. Agassiz's equally eminent Harvard colleague, Asa Gray, was a botanist whose work by and large supported Darwin. He challenged Agassiz, defended Darwin, and convinced many people that Darwin's ideas need not be fatal to Christian doctrine. Gray developed the notion that evolution was in fact God's plan for the world. He admitted that Darwinism was compatible with a nontheistic universe, but he insisted that it was compatible with a theistic one as well, and that he saw no reason why God had not set evolution in motion as a perfectly sensible way of allowing change in his creation. God might seem depersonalized, but he was still there; people would just have to be more patient in their yearnings for final answers.

In most countries of the world, Darwin's ideas remained scientific and few dreamed of applying them to social thought. But to a certain extent in England and to a far greater extent in America, Darwinism seemed to have an immediate applicability to social and political life. Puritanism had left a deep legacy of ideas with which Darwinism seemed compatible. The puritans had instructed men to labor in their callings and assured them that if they were dutiful then God would reward them with wealth in this world and salvation in the next. Secularized over the years by figures as important as Benjamin Franklin, these ideas no longer appeared especially religious, but rather the common sense of democracy. If a decent man had a sober set of habits, if he worked hard and fulfilled his responsibilities, then the way to wealth was open to him. All men were equal in America, and most of them had a reasonable chance at success. Puritan ideas of election thus took on secular meaning, and wealth became emblematic of divine approval. If there was a God, then he clearly preferred those who worked hard to those who did not. The Protestant Ethic had found the one country in the world where it was most at home.

The result was a paralysis in social thought. If society evolved by blind chance, with random mutations doing their jobs over thousands of years, then efforts to change the world were not only fruitless, they got in the way. If wealth went to the most deserving, then it was immoral to take money away from those whom God had blessed. If poverty were the lot of the sinful and slothful, then it bordered on sacrilege to comfort them in their miseries. Whatever was, in business, was therefore right, and reform a notion almost blasphemous. To a nation of Northern businessmen, eager to exploit the new West and to build up economic empires in the North, social Darwinism was compulsively believable. It told them they were God's chosen few and that remedial legislation was needless. It allowed them to think of subsidies as helping them to perform the tasks to which God had assigned them, while allowing them to assume as well that taxation was an unjust penalty which the unfit imposed on the fit so that they would not have to work. Entranced by the air of science that surrounded the new ideas, many intellectuals adopted social Darwinism simply as a part of being up-to-date. It was regrettable that so much suffering existed, of course, but the war had hardened them to suffering and they adjusted.

The other Englishman to have seminal importance for American social thought after the Civil War was Herbert Spencer. In 1850, before Darwin's first significant publication, Spencer had published the *Social Statics*, and the book began a vogue for Spencerian thought that seems amazing in view of Spencer's opaque writing style and lack of a sense of humor. As the title of his book indicated, Spencer believed that the laws of society were static and that anyone who tried to meddle with them violated the requirements of nature. He insisted that progress was inevitable but that it came slowly, and that while it was occurring nature of necessity weeded out the unfit so that the fit could multiply themselves into a better society. Any state intervention to help the unfit was unwise, and he specifically opposed the regulation of industry, the imposition of tariffs, the bestowal of subsidies, the establishment of a church, the printing of money, the minting of coins, the carrying of the mails, the establishment of colonies, or the maintenance of schools. He did not even want public health measures unless there was wholesale contamination of the air.

Spencer insisted that the distresses of the poor were "the decrees of a large, far-seeing benevolence." Many things in life seemed hard, but when one took the long view, "these harsh fatalities" proved to be "full of the highest beneficence—the same beneficence which brings to early graves the children of diseased parents and singles out the low-spirited, the intemperate, and the debilitated as the victims of an epidemic." People should realize that "under the natural order of things society is constantly excreting its unhealthy, imbecile, slow, vacillating, faithless members" to leave room for the more deserving. Charity was a great error in most cases. It distracted the fittest from their proper roles; it kept the unfit alive longer and enabled them to reproduce more prolifically; and it encouraged people not to work when they would work if starvation were the alternative. The only charity Spencer could recommend was "helping men to help themselves."

Spencer had any number of American disciples, like John Fiske, Jack London, and William Graham Sumner, willing to translate his specific suggestions into American terms. But for the larger culture, the ideas of social Darwinism merged imperceptibly with those of the so-called Gospel of Wealth to form an American social philosophy that mentioned Spencer only rarely and that seemed to be merely the secularization of puritanism. The most vocal of these spokesmen was the Baptist leader Russell H. Conwell, who went about giving the speech known as "Acres of Diamonds" an estimated five thousand times, making the two-hour outburst a good candidate for the status of being the longest cliché in history. He told people that never in the history of the world "did a poor man without capital have such an opportunity to get rich quickly and honestly as he has now." He assured his audience that "you ought to get rich, and it is your duty to get rich," and anyone who complained when a Christian minister said such a thing should realize that "to make money honestly is to preach the gospel." Poverty was an irrelevant issue. "To sympathize with a man whom God has punished for his sins, thus to help him when God would still continue a just punishment, is to do wrong." He insisted that no one was poor in America "who has not been made poor by his own shortcomings, or by the shortcomings of someone else."

A world that has accepted the welfare state in its various forms finds it hard to accept Conwell, but every culture has popular figures who mystify succeeding generations. He and his intellectual superiors like Sumner served important roles in the post-Civil War world. When the traditional Christian attitudes were breaking down, people demanded figures who played the role of the minister: they assured everyone that things were working out, that everything was for the best, and that no matter how confusing the new world seemed to be, some principles were eternal. Contract had replaced covenant, wealth had replaced salvation, the fittest had replaced the saints, but the intellectual processes had not changed all that much. The economy had changed enormously, and laissez faire turned out to be a doctrine as erratic in its application as any of its predecessors in puritanism, but people had to have something to hold on to, and many of them held on to some variety of the Protestant Ethic, social Darwinism, or the Gospel of Wealth.

In many ways Spencer had been the founder of sociology in the English-speaking world, and Sumner was his foremost American disciple. Social Darwinism thus became the battleground for the formulation of much social science theory in the later years of the nineteenth century. As Sumner preached the middle-class values of the "forgotten man" who did his job, brought up his family, and never hurt anybody, he soon had his critics. Although many intellectuals were willing to consider some of Darwin's ideas as being applicable to social life, others insisted that Spencer and Sumner had gone too far, and that they should not apply such scientific ideas to sociology. The most important of these sociologists was Lester Frank Ward, a government employee who did not hate his employer and who regarded social Darwinism as intellectually indefensible. He did not, for many years, have much of an audience outside a small circle, but he worked out a compelling case against laissez faire. He and other "reform Darwinists" insisted that while Darwinism was true for the animal and vegetable kingdoms, the ideas did not apply to human beings. Men and women had minds, or "psychic factors," and they could use them to ward off the effects of natural events. Ward insisted that society was dynamic and not static, and that both the schools and the state were necessary ways which people used to foster growth and control evolution. The whole practice of medicine was in direct violation of social Darwinian principles, and only a fool would let someone bleed to death after an accident, or do nothing to prevent the spread of an epidemic. He also pointed out bluntly that the loudest supporters of laissez faire were big businessmen and their pet intellectuals, and that it was intellectually insulting to see them ask for government subsidies in one breath, and then howl with rage in the next at any attempt at exercising control.

Sociology went far beyond the university and the government in its early years. During the 1890s, as it took shape as a discipline, it also included many figures with no advanced training, but who were instead practitioners of applied social thinking. By the early years of the twentieth century, Jane Addams had emerged as the most visible leader in this area. No intellectual, she had only the undergraduate education permitted for young women of her class and generation. Frustrated at the lack of career opportunities, nagged by a Christian conscience, she went through her twenties fending off attempts to marry her off, to make her a missionary, or to make her merely a thinker of beautiful thoughts. Late in the 1880s she visited London and was deeply impressed by Toynbee Hall, the social settlement that was making an attempt to bring Christians and the poor together to mitigate the poverty and the class divisions that were so striking in British life. She returned to America determined to emulate the experiment, and with her friend Ellen Gates Starr she opened Hull-House in Chicago in the fall of 1889. Her example and her writings influenced countless men and women to change the direction of their lives and thoughts. With them, social and reform Darwinism evolved into a form of progressivism, and the first two decades of the new century became the "progressive years," devoted to finding some conservative Christian way of shaping evolution to the common benefit.

Unlike more academic theorizers, Addams tended to write in anecdotes rather than abstractions. She recalled in her autobiography, for example, several cases of people for whom the conventional American wisdom seemed inadequate. A shipping clerk, out of work and uncertain in health, came to her for advice about what he should do. She suggested heavy labor on the drainage canals and did not see merit in his insistence that his health would not be up to it. He accepted the job in despair, and was soon dead of pneumonia. He left two little children behind to remind her of the fact that a stern application of Social Darwinism to individual cases helped no one, killed perfectly capable human beings, and left the state with more of a burden in fatherless children than would have been the case had unemployment assistance been more available. In another instance, in contrast to Sumner's "forgotten man," she had her "forgotten woman": she remembered the case of the middle-class lady who remained in her house while her district changed from Anglo-Saxon to Italian in ethnic composition. Determined to remain aloof from her new neighbors, she saw no need to participate in local efforts at improved sanitation. Instead, she poured her money into her two daughters, who attended a proper Eastern college. One summer when both were visiting, a typhoid epidemic struck, and one daughter died from the disease. The lesson in progressivism was obvious: you could no longer remain aloof from society because the perils of modern life were social perils; if people did not cooperate, they could expect to die separately, each one independent to the end. Sumner and the Spencerians had a vision of human atoms, each independent of the larger society; Addams and the progressives assumed that society was an organism and that every part had to help every other part or life would not continue.

III

Progressivism was at its heart an effort to remoralize society, a secular third Great Awakening. Many of its leaders consciously thought of themselves as doing for workers in 1900 what their grandfathers had been trying to do for blacks in 1840: free slaves. At all political levels, politicians advocated laws to facilitate moral economic and political systems. They advocated city improvements, like pure water and sanitary sewage. They wanted honesty in public officials. They wanted the right for the people to initiate important legislation. They wanted the right to have referenda on laws that politicians enacted. They wanted the right to recall public officials who did not do what they had been elected to do. They wanted "gas-and-water socialism," meaning public ownership of natural monopolies such as natural gas, water supplies, electricity, and the telephone. They wanted regulation of the safety of food and drugs. They wanted railways to treat shippers equitably. They wanted free trade, a better financial system, and protection against monopolies. The list of reforms the progressives supported was very long, and most concentrated on only a few. Often they disagreed among themselves, leaving students confused as to which specific reforms were legitimately progressive.

The larger picture remains clearer. In their efforts to remoralize a society in danger of sinking into industrial slavery, the progressives were facing the problems of modernization with an inadequate institutional structure. They had to deal with modern industry, in other words, without professionals capable of fixing the machinery of government. Young people born between the middle 1850s and the middle 1870s had to choose their careers between the middle 1870s and the middle 1890s, and like Jane Addams and Ellen Starr, they faced few attractive choices. The professions as the modern world knows them hardly existed: the doctor, the scientist, the architect, the professor, the lawyer, and so on existed as words but not as actualities. Advanced education was not widely available, laws did not separate the capable from the charlatan, and people were as yet unable to think of "the professions" as respectable and worth rewarding with high salaries and social prestige. The progressives were the individuals who solved these problems. They made politics into a profession, electing presidents, senators, and mayors of far greater ability than earlier generations. They pioneered in opening better law and medical schools and then requiring degrees and examination results before permitting citizens to call themselves doctors and lawyers. They changed journalism from a seedy affair of yellow-press sensationalism into a responsible gathering of news that citizens needed to vote intelligently.

They also made social work a profession, one with special importance for women. This was the generation that pioneered the right of women to exist independent of the home. Women's rights had existed as policies since the 1840s, but reality had never matched advocacy. The issue of the 1840s was freedom for slaves, not rights for women; but more and more women thought the issues connected. Men, after all, did not want them even to speak in public, let alone vote or hold respectable jobs. Perhaps when the slaves were freed, men would pay some attention to women: if the poorest male workers in the land could legally vote and hold property in their own names, perhaps the most educated women could be allowed to do the same. It did have a certain logic, and by 1900 the time seemed ripe.

Suffrage seemed of central importance at the time, and in a symbolic sense it was: politicians only pay attention to voters, so women had to vote to accomplish much politically. But the proper place to focus upon was the professions: once women could receive advanced education and qualify for jobs, they had to win

assistant professorship. She insisted on teaching only half time so she could
sue her other interests, so the issue of a permanent appointment never came
she remained there until 1935. She investigated aniline dyes, carbon monox-
and mercury poisoning among other such problems, and in 1925 published
ustrial Poisons in the United States, which quickly took over the market. By
bining progressivism and pragmatism, she had become a leading example of
Americans could remoralize society to make it a safer place for everyone.

IV

issez faire had the power of myth, however, and progressive ideas took a long
e to grow. The reasons were many and complex, but at least a few of them
re obvious: some Americans actually were able to begin as uneducated
upers and live their old age as millionaire philanthropists. Probably no other
untry in the industrialized world was as open as American society from the
40s to the 1870s to a person of great drive and business ability. By the time
ese men had reached the top, however, the structure of business made it
ceptionally difficult for someone two generations younger to entertain similar
pes. As the "robber barons" were informing American voters that God had
ven them their money and that it would be immoral to tax it or regulate its
owth, the country went through a severe depression and emerged in the
iddle 1890s with a growing skepticism about the validity of such arguments.
mericans desperately wanted to believe in the virtues of unlimited competi-
on, but an increasing number were deciding that the social cost was too high.
No one illustrated the strange effects of wealth in America better than
ndrew Carnegie. Here was a man born to lower-class poverty in Scotland, to a
mily deeply involved with the Chartist movement, forced to emigrate because
f economic conditions in their home area. They were anticlerical in their
ligious views and antiaristocratic in their social views. Carnegie came to
merica as a child, began work as a bobbin boy in a textile mill, rose to the status
f messenger boy for the local telegraph company, and by hard work and native
kill became a railroad telegrapher, inventor, and ultimately an independent
usinessman. He worked hard but he was also lucky. Men went broke all around
im, but his key investments were in railway sleeping cars and his expertise in
ailways and telegraphs. All expanded rapidly under the pressure of war and the
reat boom of the 1870s. Oil and steel became the key industries in western
Pennsylvania and because of his experience with transportation, Carnegie was
oon deeply involved. His business methods were so conservative and his efforts
o great that his Carnegie Steel Company was almost embarrassing in the
amount of money it returned per dollar of investment. In time, it became a key
part of the first billion-dollar trust, the United States Steel Company.

those jobs, prove themselves up to the challenges, and render the issue of sexual equality dead. In this sense, the best way to understand what progressivism was all about is to focus on one woman in one profession, to show how women not only won their democratic freedoms but did so as part of the larger effort to remoralize society and mitigate some of the obvious effects of modernization.

Alice Hamilton (1869–1970) is one of many possible examples to use as a case study of how progressivism worked. A veteran of Hull-House, champion of several reforms, she had a distinguished career as a specialist in industrial poisons, a profession that did not exist when she was a girl. Considered sche- matically, her life illustrates the class-based nature of progressive reform, the educational problems women faced, the role of displaced Protestantism, the persistence of older Victorian ideals of womanhood, and the ways in which progressivism and pragmatism worked together to become a unified climate of creativity. She then established her expertise as a scientist and institutionalized her success by becoming a professor at a major university—one which did not at that time admit women as students.

Progressives most often came from the comfortable middle classes. They were not intensely ideological and their ideas were rarely extreme. In the Hamilton family, money was not a problem. Her grandfather had been a pioneer settler in Indiana, making a fortune in dry goods sales, land speculation, rail- roading, and banking; his wealth left his descendants comfortable. Her father was a wholesale grocer, ineffectual but not so much so that he squandered all the money. The family was active in the Democratic party, a bit unusually so since most progressives came from Republican ranks. All the children in this family could afford to go to college and pursue careers if they wished. Alice had three sisters and a brother, and all went into education. The most famous was Edith, who became headmistress of a preparatory school and a world authority on Greek myths, with the sales of her books reaching into the hundreds of thou- sands.

Women at that time were supposed to marry and have children, or if they remained single to help relatives who needed them. While men had few profes- sional options, women had none. As the graduate schools opened for men, their sisters naturally wanted places as well, but few institutions wanted them. Ham- ilton's problems were thus not unusual: she went to Miss Porter's School in Connecticut to be "finished," meaning that she prepared for gentility rather than a profession. She then enrolled in a third-rate place called the Fort Wayne College of Medicine, where she studied anatomy, helped doctors, and read a bit of chemistry and biology on the side. Only after almost four years there did she get into the University of Michigan to do serious work, taking her degree only a year later; requirements were relaxed in those days. Only later still, at the Johns Hopkins Medical School, did she get attention from the best teachers in the country, which she supplemented with research in neurology at the University of Chicago. This patchy record indicated all too obviously that neither family members nor society really wanted its women doing professional work, although they permitted it if the women kept at it.

Religiosity was as strong an element in the Hamilton family as it was for Jane Addams or John Dewey. For generations, the family had been chiefly Presbyterian, with a strain of Episcopalianism occasionally blended in. Alice was herself intensely religious as a girl, intending to become a medical missionary. She wanted a life of her own, on her own, and the chances in Persia seemed more interesting than in America. The medicine and the religion went together: such women were "doing good" in the traditions of Christ, Toynbee Hall, and the various societies for promoting Christian missions. They would worship Christ the Physician, curing bodies along with souls.

Hamilton was very much a young lady, anything but the humorless feminist of hostile male folklore. All graduates of Miss Porter's were ladies—the title went with the otherwise worthless diploma—but she had no problems with femininity. She appears in her own letters and those of her friends as fragile, ladylike, demure, cultured—a whole list of Victorian virtues. Men never found her strident or pushy, and perhaps she got her way as often as she did because she played so well to their expectations, which she shared without hypocrisy. What remains odd, however, is that she regarded many of the requirements of medical training as degrading and sordid, and seemed not to approve of them for most other women even as she slogged through them herself. She even complained about the freedom which her classmates enjoyed; she disliked seeing them in male company without chaperones.

In short, Hamilton believed that the sexes really were different, and that equality was not a proper goal as many understood the word. Each sex had its special skills, and she thought it silly to confuse them. Further, she thought that women, in those days of messy and unsafe contraception, really did have to choose between having careers and having families. Her own father had been a prima donna who drank too much and never accomplished much, and she regarded most men as problems, if not obstacles. She expressed no desire for a life of sexual freedom, and presumably went serenely celibate to the grave.

Such matters are not just gossip. One of the great goals of women progressives, after the winning of suffrage, was the enactment of special protections for women workers. They should not do certain types of heavy work, because they were not strong enough; they should not work more than a set number of hours because it would injure their health. All such legislation assumed that women were weaker and needed special protection, and many women reformers were as one with men on such issues. Others did not agree. Led by Alice Paul, they soon began efforts for an Equal Rights Amendment (ERA) to the Constitution, which would require equal treatment for all workers; being female or pregnant was a private matter of no concern to an employer. Hamilton opposed the ERA

and fought it into the 1950s, when she finally decided that v for everyone had improved to the point where it made sense

Having decided against having a family, Hamilton move where she stayed for twenty-two years. Through the close pe which Jane Addams had with John Dewey and George H became involved as well with the University of Chicago, its p phy department, and its Laboratory School. She practiced running the well-baby clinic which Hull-House maintained fo that crowded the neighborhood.

Hamilton's skill did not even have a name until she became one: she became an "industrial pathologist," an expert on the di with modern industry. She noticed that the combined effects mains and corrupt politics brought typhoid fever to the ci involved in the cause of tuberculosis, because the problem aff sought help at Hull-House. As a woman she had a woman's spe family issues like vaccination and proper diet. Because she fou inextricably bound up with industrial issues and urban political i become interested in them as well. This was what a progressive d pragmatist did. They were all remoralizing a democratic society to cure its economic problems.

In 1910 Hamilton became the medical investigator of a gr state legislature established to conduct a two-year investigation diseases. She took the use of lead as her special interest. Lead everywhere in industry; small doses caused no immediate probl lead accumulated in the system, victims came down with colic, co temporary blindness. They developed wrist drop, the limp wris poisoned nervous system and incipient senility. Less severe case pallor, loss of weight and appetite, constipation, indigestion, ar pains associated with rheumatism and gout.

Hamilton had trouble from the start, since she had little idea wh were even using lead. She proved a relentless interviewer and gos up data from workmen, inspectors, doctors, chemists, and anyone find. After visiting 304 establishments, she found more than seve industrial processes that used lead and exposed workers to possib She found it in car-seal manufacturing, in polishing cut glass, in wr in what was called tinfoil, in laying electric cables, and so on. H discovery came when she found out that the enamel paint used on lead in it, which no one outside the industry had ever suspected. He led to a 1911 Illinois law that regulated occupational diseases.

By World War I she was the greatest expert in the world on indust In 1919, Harvard University Medical School failed to find a man as she was, try as they would; but they wanted the best, and she accep

Yet Carnegie seemed an unlikely candidate for the status of robber baron. He was far more literate than one would expect, given his meager educational opportunities, and he seemed at times to yearn for the life of a leisured intellectual. He read Herbert Spencer, quoted him often, and helped subsidize the spread of his ideas in America. In England, he was a soft touch for liberal politicians, and figures like John Morley and William Gladstone profited from his contributions. But Carnegie seemed to feel that because America had no aristocracy and no state church, that reform behavior was unneeded there. America was an example of triumphant democracy, and when you lived in the best country in the world there was no point in belittling it. Carnegie remained willfully blind to American business and labor problems, and his own mills experienced some of the worst labor violence of the 1890s. He preferred to retire to his castle in Scotland, issue general statements, and let his employees order the strikebreakers to do their messy jobs. Like a good puritan, Carnegie preferred to keep his wealth available to his whim, and his charities included retirement plans for teachers, church organs, and a number of free public libraries scattered about the country.

For all his wealth, Carnegie was nowhere near the most important influence among the American wealthy upon American society. He not only did not have a vast enough fortune, he did not have an imagination adequate to the task. A figure like J. P. Morgan, for example, could take what in this context was a small amount of money and use his opportunities to control much of the activity of the Metropolitan Museum of Art and to acquire a personal art collection so large and so intelligently accumulated that its sale began the market for fine art in American culture. Other figures, from Henry Huntington to Andrew Mellon, made charitable contributions that will enrich American culture in perpetuity. The fortune of automaker Henry Ford has financed an astonishing array of social activities designed to ask questions and provide both answers and the means to implement them. The history of the charitable foundations in America remains an essential way in which American life has differed from life in countries where the state has preempted first place in educational and charitable activities.

The best example of how money worked in American culture came from the four generations of the Rockefeller family. John D. Rockefeller I accumulated vast wealth during and after the Civil War by working, chiefly in the oil industry, with great ruthlessness and a complete lack of charity for anyone else. Oil and railroad interests cooperated secretly to get preferential prices for Rockefeller oil and to penalize competitors through devious kickback and surcharging arrangements. By the 1880s, the Standard Oil Company had grown so large and had developed so many arcane legal ways of covering up its activities that few people could figure out how such a trust could be controlled. The conflicting jurisdictions of the local, state, and federal governments were too complex for politicians to master, and only well into the twentieth century did national legislation divide the company into units that seemed likely to compete with each other, and thus offer a measure of protection to the much-exploited American consumer.

But Rockefeller was far more important than his status as plutocrat implied. A devout Baptist, he was determined to give much of his money away: like many Americans, he thought giving a more legitimate activity than paying higher wages to his workers or allowing his competitors to operate in peace. In the late 1880s, Baptist church officials convinced Rockefeller to give six hundred thousand dollars toward the development of a major religious university whose influence would upgrade the standards of all its institutions of higher education. The outcome of the gift was the University of Chicago, which by 1910 had received forty-five million dollars from Rockefeller interests and had quickly achieved stature as a major university. Other funds went into the Rockefeller Institute for Medical Research, which was soon at the forefront of research into the treatment of meningitis, yellow fever, infantile paralysis, and pneumonia and into the General Education Board, which specialized in the assessment of Negro education in the South and the development of the means to improve it.

With these institutions a new phase in American wealth was clearly underway. As John D. Rockefeller II became increasingly central to the spending of the fortune, the formation of the Rockefeller Foundation in 1910 formalized the means by which American fortunes took their places in American culture. With original assets of a hundred million dollars, the foundation could change the whole course of educational or medical history in a large part of the country. In addition to the ventures his father began, the second Rockefeller was active in spending money on three projects still visible in America. Fascinated by the American past, he tried as closely as he could to recreate a part of it at Colonial Williamsburg in Virginia, which has long been one of the most important educational tourist attractions in the country. Less well known was his dislike of much modern art and his deep love for the medieval; the institutional result was The Cloisters, a beautiful small museum in New York City with some of the finest medieval art works in the country on display. His greatest achievement was probably the construction of Rockefeller Center in New York, a mammoth urban renewal project designed to reinvigorate a declining area in the country's major city entirely through private enterprise, and to make it self-sustaining through rental fees to corporations leasing office space. In no other country in the world would such a project be conceivable.

Between 1900 and 1915 a new generation of Rockefellers was born, and during the 1930s they began to take their places in the financial and cultural worlds. The five men and one woman, often lumped together as "the brothers," included David Rockefeller, the financial magnate who through the Chase Manhattan Bank was for many years one of the most powerful financial figures in the country, and not without influence even in places like Moscow and Beijing. Nelson became an expert on modern art and Latin America; after a period of service in the department of state he became both a formulator of policy statements and a political figure of increasing importance. His policy activities helped produce figures as influential as Secretary of State Henry Kissinger; his political activities as governor remade the face of New York State, from bridges to educational institutions. Winthrop Rockefeller had a significant influence on the business development of the state of Arkansas and served as its governor for two terms. Other siblings were active in museum work, conservation, and population control. In effect, money freed them to do what they wished, and their influence became considerable.

The fourth generation was another story. "The cousins" were a large and mixed lot, and with them the money seemed more a burden than a device of freedom. Some adjusted fairly well, John D. IV becoming governor of West Virginia. But others did not. Broken marriages and nervous breakdowns were not uncommon, and several cousins seemed to be guilt-ridden at inheriting the burden of so much controversial wealth. A number dropped out of society, while others entered professions like teaching where money could have little visible relevance. A few went so far as to send their wealth to radical causes, and one of the oddest things about the youth rebellion of the 1960s and later was that Rockefeller money supported a number of the student groups and their publications. The foundation lived on, seemingly impervious to change, but the people changed drastically and their influence on the larger culture dissipated.

Big business meanwhile had served its purpose as a cultural phenomenon. However inappropriate its ideas, however baneful its economic impact, big business had established the nation as a functioning entity. Within little more than a generation, the sectionalism of the years before the war was a memory, still present in political rhetoric but irrelevant to the plans of anyone under forty years old. The nation was a nation, for better or for worse. The North dominated the West and the South, and the former slaves were largely ignored.

Chapter 8

From Anti-Social Darwinism to Pragmatism, 1865–1917

Colonialism was far more a mental condition than a political one; those who lived far away from the mother country often remained under the control of customs and ideas that were ludicrously inappropriate under local conditions and that often became out of date in the mother country years before anyone in the colony discovered it. From clothes to religion, colonies seemed to exist in a time warp that only the establishment of mass airline transportation and modern communication equipment did something to break down. Even the establishment of political independence did little to end the cultural dependence of a new nation on its point of origin in Europe.

America was the first colony to establish its independence and to go on to major status on its own. It passed through a series of changes that in many ways anticipated the establishment of cultural independence for many younger nations. It asserted its political originality, it tried to work out a distinctive foreign policy, it feuded with its mother country, and it loudly proclaimed that it had its own artists, its own thinkers, and its own writers fully as much as it had its own political leaders. In most senses of these terms, the stance was ridiculous. America had its own political and cultural leaders, but no matter how great they might have seemed upon the local stage, in the larger view of history they were largely the creatures of European culture, and their originality lay largely in their efforts to adapt old ideas to the new environment. America itself was something of a European invention, and although its development was its own achievement, the materials that made up the new mixture were often merely the inventions of previous generations of Europeans. American puritanism, the American Enlightenment, and the American romance all had aspects of originality, but the very concepts involved were from somewhere else.

The same Civil War that eliminated sectionalism also eliminated much of this cultural dependence. Here again, it took a generation for the new ideas to develop, and only after 1900 did they begin to receive publicity beyond a small circle of intellectuals. But with the development of pragmatism, America finally achieved the sort of indigenous thought for which Emerson had called in the 1830s. Pragmatism had an occasional adherent in Europe, but what it had that was more important was influence: ideas genuinely original in America influenced Europeans and soon Asians as well. First William James and then John Dewey seemed to the world to be seminal figures. Over the years, the philosophy of Charles Peirce, the legal thought of Oliver Wendell Holmes, Jr., and the social psychology of George Herbert Mead also won significant foreign audiences.

Within the American context, the two most formative figures in the early history of pragmatism were hostile to the social Darwinism that sometimes seemed ubiquitous elsewhere in the culture. Charles Peirce always disliked it; William James was at first friendly, and then under Peirce's influence changed to the position of caustic critic. Only with the next generation of Dewey and Mead did the controversy quiet down. In the national culture of the years after 1900, both were pragmatists, both were progressives. The terms were not synonymous, but for most outsiders, what worked best was a moderate, reforming attitude to a generally moral, democratic, and capitalist culture.

II

The evidence is scanty, but pragmatism apparently began with occasional meetings of The Metaphysical Club in the Boston area around the Harvard campus. The most original member of the group was Charles Sanders Peirce (1839–1914), the son of a Harvard professor of mathematics and astronomy. Other key members included William James, the son of a Swedenborgian intellectual who was a friend of Emerson, and Oliver Wendell Holmes, Jr., the son of a prominent writer and doctor. As Peirce recalled many years later, they met in the early 1870s and agreed that their central task was the application of Bain's definition of belief as "that upon which a man was prepared to act." From this proposition of a British philosopher, pragmatism was "scarce more than a corollary." The air was full of science and agnosticism, metaphysics was in retreat, and the name of the club was intentionally ironic: Antimetaphysical Club would have been more literally accurate. As Peirce then pointed out, its first ideas were still derivative: most members were British in their orientation, although he himself "had come upon the threshing-floor of philosophy through the doorway of Kant."

Early pragmatism was grounded in the national agony of the war and the economic expansion that followed it. Holmes himself had been seriously wounded in the war, and members of the James family had fought; no one lived through the 1860s without having serious questions about the nature of American democracy and the value of the Union. The war settled political and social questions, but it did not settle intellectual ones, and many highly intelligent figures were disturbed by the impact of big business and social Darwinian ethics in their country. The shameless greed of figures like Andrew Carnegie and John D. Rockefeller and the blatant corruption of the Grant administration in Washington led to a serious reexamination of the nature of democracy, of community, and of the place of America in God's plans for the universe. A country which had been largely middle-class and honest seemed to be developing serious class divisions and a public acceptance of dishonesty. Pragmatism was one attempt to develop a means of coping with these issues. It argued against abstractions that had no results; it argued against an ethics that did not affect ordinary lives; it assumed that solving daily problems was more important than achieving abstract truths; it tried to tell people that what everyone thought and did was important, and that Americans did not need extensive technical philosophical training to lead meaningful lives. Europeans were entangled in class and metaphysical systems that were inappropriate for American democracy, and the pragmatists were trying to achieve a means of procedure which eliminated them.

In religion, the sense of unanimity was less apparent. Holmes, in particular, was a cynic who never wasted a minute of his long life worrying about the role of Christian love in the world, but Peirce and James were deeply concerned with religious problems. The science of Darwin and the social ethics of Spencer had given Americans what seemed to be a gloomy and depressing world in which to live. Progress might be inevitable, and perhaps God had planned evolution, but the roles that remained for human action seemed small. From the point of view of a philosopher of science, Peirce spent much of his life working out ideas of Christian community; from the point of view of a psychologist, James worked hard to establish the validity of religious faith and action. Neither was orthodox in terms of any one faith, but both insisted that faith was an important part of human life, that people had to act, and that neither science nor psychology provided any disproof for the existence of God. There was more to life than chance.

Peirce was the first to formulate pragmatic ideas in any public form, in a series of articles in the *Popular Science Monthly* in the late 1870s. "The Fixation of Belief" and "How to Make Our Ideas Clear" were the seminal texts for the development of pragmatism. Peirce began in the world of science and psychology, using words like *habit* and *action* to fight off any prior notions a person might bring to examination of the word *belief*. He talked about how scientific ideas changed and how no single belief was likely to last for long, and defended the assumption that if even scientific ideas changed over time, all other kinds of beliefs probably changed as well. He insisted that people should understand what they really meant when they talked about believing and doubting. If a person believed something to be true, he said, then he was basically comfortable with an idea. It became a habit for him and he acted automatically and did not question his assumptions. But if he doubted something, he was restless and upset. People did not like to be in a state of doubt and in fact would do almost anything to get rid of doubt and go back to the habits that went with belief.

Doubt, in other words, irritated people into an attempt to achieve belief so that the irritation would stop. This struggle to attain belief was what he called inquiry. People looked around and tried to find solutions, and when they found a solution they relaxed, they stopped the process of inquiry, and rested in the achievement of a new belief. Peirce isolated four ways of achieving belief: tenacity, or the stubborn dismissal of any information which might change existing ideas; authority, or the appeal to an institution like a church; a priori, or the appeal to an abstract idealism or ideology which eliminated the need for independent thought; and finally Peirce's preferred method, that of science or reality. Such a method "must be such that the ultimate conclusion of every man will be the same, or would be the same if inquiry were sufficiently persisted in." To restate this attitude into more common language: "There are real things, whose characters are entirely independent of our opinions about them; those realities affect our senses according to regular laws," and even though our perceptions may vary, by taking advantage of the laws of perception we can reason "how things really are, and any man, if he have sufficient experience and reason enough about it, will be led to the one true conclusion."

Pragmatism thus began as a denial of certain kinds of inquiry. It said that a person could not simply stop listening, assume established immortal truths, or take anything from institutional authority. A person inquiring into a subject could take a scientific approach, deal with the facts with an open mind, and have his work duplicated by someone else. That person had achieved belief when he accepted a new habit, a new way of behaving. Thus, if you asked such a person what an idea *means*, your answer must be a description of "what habits it produces, for what a thing means is simply what habits it involves."

From this, Peirce went on to the example of the idea of transubstantiation, the notion of Roman Catholicism that the consecrated wine and wafer of the Holy Communion service are really the body and blood of Christ; or whether, as most Protestants would insist, they only symbolized Christ's body and blood and reminded communicants of his sacrifice. Since the argument made no difference in behavior, since it did not change the habits of Christians one way or the other, then the argument was meaningless. Peirce then concluded with the words to which pragmatists have referred ever since. He said that it was impossible that "we should have an idea in our minds which relates to anything but conceived sensible effects of things. Our idea of anything *is* our idea of its sensible effects," and any other notion is self-deception. Thought only had meaning in relation to its function, and Catholics and Protestants wasted each other's time in arguing about an issue when in practice they agreed about the impact of the service. "It appears, then, that the rule for attaining . . . clearness of apprehension is as follows: consider what effects which might conceivably have practical bearings we conceive the object of our conception to have. Then, our conception of these effects is the whole of our conception of the object."

Pragmatism thus emphasized results, doing rather than thinking. Conceived by intellectuals deeply committed to a scientific view of the world, it adapted notions of science and experiment to common democratic behavior. It told people that most of the intellectual baggage of the European past was detritus of no value in a bustling young country. A state church had no right to impose views on a citizen any more than an aristocratic government had the right to impose taxes. A man had to work things out for himself and get others to agree with him. Just as America was a country in the process of formation, so too were ideas and truths in the process of formation, and anyone could participate and fashion his own. Americans were inventive and adaptive, and their inventions and adaptations were achieving the status of philosophical positions. God had not disappeared from the universe, he merely had an experimental attitude toward human life and wanted his creatures to work out their values in a universe of chance.

III

Peirce may well have been the most brilliant philosophical mind that America ever produced, but his personality was so difficult that he could never hold a regular academic job for long. But his friendship with Harvard philosopher William James (1842–1910) endured long after the Metaphysical Club was a vague memory. James may well have misunderstood some of Peirce's points, as Peirce later insisted, but he nevertheless had the personality and the professional stature to popularize the new ideas, and from a series of lectures late in his life produced the volume that gave a public shape to these seminal suggestions. With *Pragmatism* (1907) and his other philosophical volumes, James formulated the one truly American philosophy and applied it to religion and education as well.

The whole James family may well have been the most important such group in the history of American culture, surpassing even the Adams and Roosevelt clans in originality. Of Scots-Irish ancestry, early members of the family devoted themselves to business chiefly in the area around Albany, New York. With Henry James, Sr., William's father, the desire to make money died out completely, and literary, religious, and philosophical speculation replaced it. Instead of the dour Calvinism of his childhood, Henry, Sr., insisted on a religion of love and possibility; often inconsistent and even more often unclear, he was nevertheless optimistic, pantheistic, and idealistic in his customary approach to anything. A friend and correspondent of Emerson, he too stressed the harmonies of nature and the sacredness of individual growth; he too yearned for a society in which men could love one another without strife. Like many Transcendentalists, he was fascinated by Emanuel Swedenborg and the idea of correspondences and by Charles Fourier and the idea of a utopian socialism that might grow on American soil. Unlike Emerson, Henry, Sr., was also given at times to religious depressions and was firmly committed to belief in the presence of evil in the world.

Money and intellectual interests combined to make a home that was idiosyncratic in the extreme. Henry, Sr., never wanted to pursue a career and concentrated instead on being something, and upon writing about it. He traveled restlessly around the Eastern United States and Western Europe, sampling ideas and cultures in the hope that he and his family could grow into something organically fulfilled. The strain on the five children was enormous, and all of them seemed to suffer nervous debility and a kind of aimlessness. But the important historical point was that by giving his children such an unusual childhood and such limitless possibilities for "becoming," Henry, Sr., was breaking much of the hold of conventional religious and social ideas and opening up the minds of his children to new ways of exploring the universe. William took his freedom in the direction of psychology and philosophy; Henry, Jr., took his into literature. Both used their careers to explore the nature of freedom and chance that had been such central ideas to their own childhood development.

William James' childhood provided an excellent example of the strains involved in growing up creative in America. While other children had fathers with careers and never doubted the importance of material accumulation, William had a father who dabbled in whatever he liked and had plenty of money for reasonable needs. William tried painting and philosophy, psychology and medicine, and until Charles Eliot appointed him to the Harvard faculty he had no idea of what he might become. As for advanced preparation, he once remarked: "I never had any philosophic instruction, the first lecture on psychology I ever heard being the first I ever gave." The tone was both amused and rueful, and hinted at the pain involved in not having a secure place in the culture and work to give meaning to life. Like his father, James was also prone to religious depressions, with visions and nightmares that provided him painful examples when he wrote about the varieties of religious experience.

Like other members of the Metaphysical Club, James was deeply interested in science. He not only studied physiological psychology in Germany, he spent considerable time working his way through the works of Herbert Spencer, then regarded as the preeminent social philosopher with a scientific cast of mind. At first, James was impressed by Spencer, and at the request of his students he used

Spencer's work as a text for some years. But Charles Peirce ridiculed Spencer to him, and in time James agreed. Spencer never seemed to know the religious pain that so many Americans suffered; the results of his ideas seemed pernicious. But James retained for life a feeling of kinship for British empiricism of the sort represented by John Locke and John Stuart Mill. He called himself a "radical empiricist" rather than a Social Darwinist, and never forgot the hard facts of science or of existence when working out his philosophical ideas. He used the word *empiricism* because he was content to regard any conclusions to which he came "concerning matters of fact as hypotheses liable to modification in the course of future experience"; and he used the word *radical* because he treated "the doctrine of monism itself as an hypothesis," and unlike most agnostics or positivists, refused to affirm his version of the truth as something "with which all experience has got to square." Ever the good scientist, he thought everything in life was experimental, including even the faith in science to solve all problems.

James made his mark with the publication of his *Principles of Psychology* (1890). No American had ever made such a remarkable contribution to a field: the enormous volume synthesized all that was known up to that time, redirected the attention of specialists in the field, and attracted a large and enduring popular following with its engaging and occasionally even autobiographical tone. The book made a strong point about its physiological grounding in laboratory research that other scientists could duplicate. James ignored the soul and other such metaphysical and religious ideas openly, and insisted they had no place in such a book. Instead, he worked out two of his larger contributions to cultural history. He formulated his version of the James—Lange Theory, the important notion that the emotions are physiological and do not need religious or metaphysical explanations: "My theory . . . is that the bodily changes follow directly the perception of the exciting fact, and that our feeling of the same changes as they occur *is* the emotion"; and he developed the idea of the "steam-of-consciousness," which subsequently became so vital to the history of the arts. Philosophers since Locke had been cutting consciousness into bits and pieces of discrete perceptions, and this was incorrect. No one had ever had a single sensation all by itself, and an imagery of "chain" or "train" was imprecise. "Consciousness . . . is nothing jointed; it flows. A 'river' or a 'stream' are the metaphors by which it is most naturally described. In talking of it hereafter, let us call it the stream of thought, of consciousness, or of subjective life."

Between 1890 and 1910 James established himself as the most important thinker in America. In addition to the psychology, he made significant contributions to the history of philosophy and religion. In *Pragmatism* he attempted to mediate between the two currents of thought that were dividing America: the optimistic believers in free will and religion, and the pessimistic doubters who took their determinism from science. James himself was torn between the two camps: on the one hand a defender of religion and free will, but on the other a scientist devoted to facts and skepticism. Pragmatism, he told his audience, was a way out of this controversy. He suggested that whenever people confronted a religious or a philosophical question they apply the pragmatic method: they should "try to interpret each notion by tracing its respective practical consequences. What difference would it practically make to any one if this notion rather than that notion were true? If no practical difference whatever can be traced, then the alternatives mean practically the same thing, and all dispute is idle." In such a framework, truth itself was no longer something permanent, true for all time. Truth became an operational concept, limited to a specific time and circumstance, that dealt with events that were always in flux. Thus what was true changed constantly and depended on the problem involved. True ideas "are those that we can assimilate, validate, corroborate and verify. False ideas are those we can not. That is the practical difference it makes to us to have true ideas; that, therefore, is the meaning of truth, for it is all that that truth is known as." Truth was thus something which "happens to an idea. It becomes true, is made true by events."

Many religious people, already disturbed by the advance of science and skepticism, were not pleased by this cavalier disregard for permanent values. But James was sympathetic to religion; he had grown up in a house full of religious emotion, in a culture that was religious to the core, and could never be comfortable in a complete skepticism. In famous lectures published as *The Varieties of Religious Experience* (1902) he analyzed what one friend referred to as "wild religions I have known"—including some of his own periods of depression. In the book, James was tolerant of most kinds of religious expression, and refused to be judgmental about genuine human torment. He himself felt more sympathy for Buddhist doctrines of the karma than for any ideas in Western religions, but his readers could take solace from knowing that a man of science did not despise their ideas about the universe. James did dismiss most theological squabbling because it did not affect behavior at all, and no single denomination could find support for its program. Instead, he insisted that what was important was the way religion worked. If belief in God or a specific doctrine had results, then such was justified by those results. He assured people that "God is real since he produces real effects." Since a person could see the results of belief in daily living, that belief was valid, at least for the one person involved. Psychology, philosophy, and religion had come together in a distinctly American formulation: because every democratic citizen had a psychology, he could believe whatever he found productive in his own life. Americans had invented any number of mechanisms, from the Franklin stove to the cotton gin, to solve social problems; now they had a method of coping with problems of the mind.

IV

William James' influence on American life was enormous but difficult to measure. Common citizens flocked to his lectures and welcomed his books. The next
generation of intellectuals, many of whom went to Harvard, echoed his themes
and emphases. A century after he came to his conclusions, any number of
editions of his work remained available in cheap paperback editions, including
the unabridged *Principles of Psychology*, the *Pragmatism*, and *The Varieties of
Religious Experience*. A specialist could perceive his influence in areas ranging
from law to sociology to education. Scholarly assessments multiplied.

One excellent example of how this influence worked was the extraordinary
career of John Dewey (1859–1952). Dewey grew up in a small Vermont town,
the son of a grocer and his religiously fanatical wife. As a young man, most of his
intellectual friends were ministers, or educators who might as well have been
ministers, and Dewey entered philosophy as a Hegelian idealist. He tried briefly
to be a schoolteacher and then enrolled in the graduate program at the new
Johns Hopkins University. Of the faculty, Charles Peirce repelled him; Dewey
never realized the importance of his ideas until he encountered them in print a
generation later. But George Sylvester Morris, an idealist on leave from the
University of Michigan, inspired him and then brought him to the Midwest for
the next twenty years. Dewey arrived for his decade on the Michigan faculty a
devout Congregationalist in religion and Hegelian in philosophy, and his *Psychology* (1887) represented his commitment to the foggy language of idealism
that prevailed in social science before James. But Dewey read James' *Principles*
when it came out, and recorded his vast debt to James later in an autobiographical memoir. Dewey's writing changed its direction noticeably, and he was soon
deep in his study of the "reflex arc" and the way the workings of physiology were
continuous processes that could not be broken down into discrete components.
He stopped using metaphysical language and by the time he shifted to the
University of Chicago in 1894, Dewey was clearly something of a scientific
skeptic in religion, a pragmatist in everything but name. His interest in psychology waned, and he concentrated on pedagogy, technical philosophy, and liberal
reform.

The old schools had been primitive institutions relying on discipline and rote
memory to convey what they could to their reluctant inmates. The public was
ready for a more appropriate school system, and education as a field developed
as Dewey matured. He remembered his own educational experiences with
distaste and came to Chicago chiefly to experiment in a new school, attached to
the university, which he could use as a pedagogical laboratory. He rebelled
against the tyranny of print and words, and instituted the study of the city, of
science, of the practical arts from weaving to woodworking. Strong in his dislike

of the growing class divisions in America, he saw the traditional educational system as having a class bias which separated the highly literate into a privileged class that should have no place in a true democracy. He insisted that his school mix people of every talent together, in informal groups in open spaces, to emphasize the solving of group problems rather than the separating out of the highly intelligent for training that would in turn separate them from fellow citizens. The Chicago Laboratory School thus became a pilot institution for the realization of Peirce's community of Christian love, based on the pragmatic concepts first elaborated by James. A democratic culture should have a democratic school system, and children should grow up learning how to interact with fellow citizens and solve relevant social problems.

Dewey was also deep in political reform. He was friendly with Jane Addams and one of the most eminent supporters of Hull-House. He read widely in liberal and radical thinkers, and was especially impressed by the single-tax theories of Henry George. He absorbed a great deal from the English Fabian socialists. As he matured, he developed philosophical concepts appropriate to his reform activities. He insisted that ideas and values were generated by the affairs of daily life, and that no one should impose them from above. Most philosophy seemed as implicitly class-oriented as most educational ideas, and Dewey disliked any notion of permanence for abstractions. Real people faced problems; they solved those problems with whatever concepts seemed to have use that day; those concepts were then true for those problems, if not for others. If a philosopher faced large social problems, he solved them in the same manner. Everything became operational and relative, and nothing seemed permanent. Implicit in it all were the concepts so common to the 1890s: science was the proper method of procedure, reason was trustworthy, progress inevitable, democracy the appropriate goal. America was a society with fixable problems, and if educators and philosophers worked together, a better society would be theirs. Cherish every human organism, foster its growth, and a nation of sturdy democrats would emerge.

Dewey was a mature scholar of forty-five when he feuded so seriously with the president of the University of Chicago that he resigned and went to Columbia. There for thirty years he reigned as the preeminent reform intellectual in America. He worked out his nature philosophy most successfully in his *Reconstruction in Philosophy* (1920), and through the Columbia Teachers College he and his disciples sent forth into the country secondary school teachers of the new ideas. Some overemphasized the organic growth of each individual student, and for a while the fad for "child-centered" schooling threatened to make Americans into a nation of self-indulgent illiterates; others overemphasized the need for social reform and group cooperation, with unpleasant overtones of authoritarianism. Both stresses were implicit in Dewey's writings, and yet each tended to cancel the other out if only a sensible educator tried to foster both individual growth and social cooperation. But Dewey's ideas not only spawned these rather extreme distortions of his seminal concepts, they were also open to criticism because of their response to events like World War I. Dewey supported American entry into the war, on the grounds that the problem existed and that America should play a role in solving it. His own journal *The New Republic* accepted his logic, but many former disciples, led by Randolph Bourne, rejected it. They realized that Dewey's work had too many unexamined premises: that he assumed that situations were inherently manageable, that science and reason could solve any problem, and that in America at least, conditions were basically good. As time went on, pragmatism seemed to be a philosophy only suitable for small problems. Faced with savage war or the totalitarianisms of the 1930s, it tended to wring its hands and temporize. People demanded goals of permanent worth for which to strive. They needed to face up to the absolute evil of Nazism and Stalinism. Pragmatism retained many uses in American life, but its vogue was over.

V

James' influence also had repercussions closer to home. While John Dewey demonstrated how pragmatic ideas could reshape an institution like the public school, several less well-known figures in the Boston area prepared the way for the reception of Freud and psychoanalytic ideas. James was the person who taught or befriended several of these individuals, and his vast prestige and personal welcome to Sigmund Freud himself reassured America about the strange new ideas.

New England was an ideal laboratory for the testing of many new ideas. If Transcendentalism had done nothing else, it had established the notion that people had the right to think for themselves, and in particular to think out ideas in religion that went contrary to all orthodoxies. Emerson and Parker had questioned basic Christian tenets, and James carried this questioning much further with his public open-mindedness toward religious expression, no matter how odd. New England had an exceptionally literate population and many adults were drawn to experiments with psychic phenomena, mind-cure, Christian Science, the Emmanuel Movement, New Thought and other such groups. The "mental" was a traditional category of thought, and psychoanalysis at first was merely one more experiment with the mind and its power over nature. New ideas were in the air, many of the ideas were religious, and a pragmatic experimentalism made it possible for respectable people to commit themselves to a faith like psychoanalysis in ways socially unacceptable elsewhere. Insofar as anyone led in these experiments and gave them this social prestige, James was that man.

Historians have coined two terms to deal with the basic assumptions concerning mental illness before psychoanalysis. The "civilized morality" was the complex of moral values that Protestant America accepted without public questioning. Roman Catholics and Jews were quite as capable of such a morality, but in America, Protestants set the dominant tone until well into the twentieth century, and Protestants had developed a number of assumptions appropriate for the demands of a bourgeois culture. Men were to find themselves in business and to control their sexual appetites until they had the financial ability to support a wife and child in comfortable circumstances. Sexual activity outside marriage was immoral for men and unthinkable for women, and to uphold such abstinence society refused to tolerate public discussion of exceptional circumstances, or relevant topics like abortion or contraception. Men might learn the facts of life in a manner that would not bear close examination, but women should marry young and learn what they had to learn from their husbands. To protect them, novels and poems had to be purged of references to nonconforming behavior, and doctors learned to behave with great circumspection in anything relevant to the intimate details of a patient's life.

Having made sexuality as invisible as possible, society insisted on a morality that denied it any place in pathology. If someone were ill, the "somatic style" insisted that the cause was something physical. If a patient had a paralyzed limb, suffered hallucinations, or seemed unduly attached to horses, then the cause might be a hereditary defect or a lesion on the brain; it could not be a childhood trauma or the result of sexual frustration. Every seemingly mental illness had a physical cause; the method of science demanded it.

Physicians soon began to question the civilized morality and the somatic style much as social thinkers questioned the hegemony of Social Darwinism. Too many things seemed to be happening for which the reigning theories could not account. Physicians began to ask themselves why, in insanity cases, they could find no physical evidence to support the assumption of organic disease. They asked themselves why they could diagnose some patients as hopelessly insane or permanently disabled, only to find that in some cases they recovered almost overnight and led seemingly normal lives thereafter. If disease were really the cause, if the somatic style really explained everything, then this sudden cure should not have been possible. But if the true cause were mental, if in fact physical problems could have mental causes, then a whole new vista of medical science was opening up. The civilized morality prevented the discussion of such possibilities as long as it could, but doctors and patients in New England were literate and open to new ideas and no one who knew of William James could ignore even so outrageous a technique as psychoanalysis. If a method had real effects, if it worked, then a pragmatic scientist could ask no more.

James did not work alone. One of his most brilliant graduate students, G. Stanley Hall, had made a name and pioneered a new career for himself in the area of child psychology; although his advancement in academia had been frustratingly slow, Hall found acceptance at the new Johns Hopkins University and then went on to become the president of Clark University in Worcester, Massachusetts. Before Freud, Hall had developed notions about the children he studied that did great violation to common assumptions. He was convinced that children had some sort of sexual instinct as early as their third year; he recognized the mechanism of sublimation, where sexual drives become displaced onto activity in art or in business; he had studied perversions and considered the possibility that they were related to arrested development; and he was fully aware of the effect which unconscious drives seemed to have on the overt behavior of adults, and of how fragile the veneer of civilization could be. As a child, Hall had gone through a number of experiences dealing with the subject of masturbation and nocturnal emissions; the response of his family to anything of this kind had been repression and punishment, and Hall was too honest about himself and too skeptical about conventional morality not to believe that mind and body had far more intimate relationships than were dreamed of in puritan theology. Other scholars in the Boston—Worcester area had similar interests: Adolf Meyer at Clark, Josiah Royce and Hugo Münsterberg at Harvard, and Dr. James Jackson Putnam all were a part of the larger circle of Jamesian experimentation in this forbidden area.

Because of his great social and scientific prestige, James had a latitude of discourse that lesser men exercised at their peril. He was surely one of the few instructors in any American college who could ask his class a question, with obvious autobiographical reference, like "Why is it that a perfectly respectable man may dream he had intercourse with his grandmother?" But James' ranging mind went far beyond casual classroom questions. In both *The Principles of Psychology* and *The Varieties of Religious Experience*, he proved that he had investigated the relevant technical literature in detail, particularly the writings of the German-speaking world. Long before Freud became a household name, James referred to his work, and the names of Binet, Janet, and Breuer appeared in James' writing along with their American counterparts. He could write of how this pioneering work had explored "the subliminal consciousness of patients with hysteria" and inform Americans that their work revealed "whole systems of underground life, in the shape of memories of a painful sort which lead a parasitic existence buried outside of the primary fields of consciousness," causing "hallucinations, pains, convulsions, paralyses of feeling and of motion, and the whole procession of hysteric diseases of body and of mind." He pointed out that if you altered these unconscious memories by suggestion, "the patient immediately gets well." James' investigations in this area were not systematic; he was an abnormally acute intelligence who refused to accept old orthodoxies and who insisted on watching how theories and treatments really worked. The

pragmatist was working in the direction of psychoanalysis long before he knew what it was.

America, however, was not Boston. Most doctors were not William James. Men of science on the whole were as much prisoners of their culture as anyone else, and the culture permitted no theorizing about sexuality. No one had made much of a study about the relationships between family members, sexual or otherwise; no one knew how to analyze dreams, or even whether dreams were important enough to analyze at all. No one had a coherent theory about the relationship of sexuality, and the body in general, to the whole personality. Such topics did not come up in nice society, and medical school was the last place a person would look for any understanding of emotional or cultural problems.

Clark University planned to celebrate its twentieth birthday in 1909, and President Hall was determined to make the occasion memorable. At the time, Sigmund Freud was fifty-three, neglected in his native Vienna, and eager for foreign recognition of his unconventional approach to mental illness. He never liked America in theory or in practice, but he accepted Hall's invitation and made a good impression on his American colleagues with lectures that were conversational in tone, reasonable in their suggestions, and not at all like the writings of the more gloomy Freud of the years after World War I. Both the public and the scientific community responded well, and William James was among those who welcomed Freud not only as a fellow researcher of eminence but as a man who might well be a giant of the future. He and Freud were on the same side in their efforts to examine how the mind and the body worked together and their refusal to exclude any hypothesis, no matter how contrary to common sense it might seem.

In his lectures and the books that followed them, Freud clearly rejected both the civilized morality and the somatic style. His own training had been in medicine, especially neurology, and he knew from his clinical experience that no physical cause existed for many of the illnesses he saw. He noted one case after another where frightening events caused paralysis, blindness, deafness, or some similar physical disability, and that identifying the mental cause of these symptoms often led to a partial or even a full cure. Often the problems were sexual, and honoring the civilized morality by refusing to talk about them only made them worse. Freud wanted his patients to talk about sex, dreams, and forbidden thoughts about friends and family and was convinced that mental conflicts were at the core of much seemingly physical illness. Freud, in Jewish Vienna, had faced many of the same problems as young Americans growing up, and he put this insight before Americans willing to experiment.

Freud asserted that children were bundles of drives seeking gratification, and that the process of maturation involved restricting and channeling these drives in ways compatible with the requirements of the society. Conflict between child

and society was inevitable, and neurosis was the result of improper socialization. Children repressed their frustrations, only to have them reappear years later to disturb sleep, ruin sexual life, or cause mental illness. In particular, children experienced sexuality in its broadest senses, and went through phases where the mouth, the anus, or the genitals seemed to dominate outward behavior. He identified mature behavior as well as illness with each area: a compulsive smoker was an oral personality, a hoarder of money an anal one. He used the term *Oedipus complex* to describe the complex of emotions between children and the parent of the opposite sex, and insisted on the sexuality of such relationships. Male children tried to obtain exclusive possession of their mothers, and only after failing in this did they develop an identification with their father and begin to develop into adult males in need of appropriate sexual partners. Girls went through the same process, desiring possession of their fathers before imitating their mothers.

If such an emphasis on sexuality disturbed people the most in Freudian theory, two other areas were more immediately influential. The unconscious was a topic ripe for analysis at any time in New England, and Freud's insistence on the force of the unconscious, of how no one ever forgot anything and how these memories could emerge years later with important consequences, proved compelling. Likewise, much of Freud's early work was on dreams and their symbolism. No one previously had elaborated an acceptable theory for the interpretation of dreams, and Freud offered ideas on the subject that proved especially fruitful to writers and artists during the next generation. Indeed, once intellectuals got over their reticence, no one seemed able to stop cocktail party chat about how treetrunks and umbrellas seemed suspiciously like male sexual organs, while rooms or ships or other enclosed spaces seemed female. Given the number of objects in the world which were either long and thin or round and spacious, the possibilities seemed endless, and in time Freud had good reason for his suspicions about the American mind and the frivolous nature of intellectual life in a democracy.

Chapter 9

The Preconditions for Modern Art, 1865–1904

The struggles over how to interpret Darwin, and the resulting development of progressivism in politics and pragmatism in philosophy, dominated intellectual life. These issues did less for painting, literature, and the growing visibility of the most important minority group, the freed slaves. The fine arts always reflect their times to a certain extent, but artists can be fragile people and often prefer to create outside the normal institutions of society. To them, science was often a myth, business something someone else could do better, and complex ideas just what a person needed to ruin a work of art.

During these years, some Americans were closely involved with European artistic currents. They went into exile, they experimented with the forms of art, and their lives and works often implicitly criticized the business ethic of their country and the philistine democracy that was all too often its political expression. As black culture matured, it offered a new perspective: black religion proved to be a Christianity highly productive in the area of music and folk expression; blacks knew all about economic exploitation long before Herbert Spencer or Andrew Carnegie arrived to tell them how formative suffering was; and blacks knew what it was like not to be citizens in their own country.

II

Americans had been traveling back and forth to Europe since the earliest settlements, but the nature of that visiting changed in important ways over the years. At first, colonists from Roger Williams to Increase Mather assumed that they were still a part of Europe. During the eighteenth century, American society grew more provincial; Americans assumed that they were not all that much a part of Europe, and that it was a good thing: Europe meant taxes and

159

wars, and they had a continent to subdue. Few Americans visited Europe, but when they did, they were usually diplomats equal in status, education, and ability to the best that Europe had to offer. Franklin, Jefferson, and the two Adamses may not always have felt comfortable in their European posts, but they knew who they were; and when painters like Benjamin West or John Copley emigrated in search of larger opportunities, they too competed as equals if not as superiors to the best European talent. For a new nation with a small population, America had done well culturally in the late eighteenth century.

Things deteriorated over the next three generations. The new nation did not prove as productive as the mature colony. The most talented people focused their energies on the issues of settlement and expansion; artists faced poor training, loneliness, and misunderstanding. A steady stream of writers, painters, and sculptors went abroad, especially to Italy; scholars discovered the German universities; and almost everyone with an education wanted to travel in England and if possible to meet the likes of Coleridge and Carlyle. But with few exceptions, their work was not up to European standards and nowhere near the quality established by West and Copley. When important Americans did emerge, they flashed brilliantly but briefly and proved unable to sustain their early promise. Europe seemed to intimidate them. They could paint scenes that echoed the precedents of Greece and Rome; they could write novels about Americans searching for new values in the Holy Land or in Rome; they could sculpt Americans dressed in togas; but they could not in any sustained way produce work that Europeans respected and accepted as part of the larger heritage of the West.

Talented people still emerged, however, and if the circumstances were unconventional enough they proved able to join the ranks of European artists as equals. James McNeill Whistler provided the best example. The painter was born to a family that was British and military in its background. His father, George Whistler, was an army surveyor and engineer who specialized in internal improvements and had a special expertise in the building of railroads. In time he became a freelance engineer, and in 1842, when his son was eight, George was invited by Czar Nicholas I of Russia to supervise the layout of the Moscow–St. Petersburg railway. Because of the extraordinary recognition of American skill in technology, a family devoted to the values of Scots Presbyterianism suddenly found itself in the middle of the most opulent environment of all Europe. The czar took excellent care of his chief engineer, and James grew up accustomed to the pomp of court, the French language of the diplomats, and the moral assumptions of people for whom puritanism was a quaint American anachronism. Whistler's mother tried valiantly to keep her heritage alive, but American food, holidays, and religious habits were no match for the splendor of the city.

George Whistler died young and the family returned to the United States in 1849. His widow preferred the life of the ministry to the life of art for her son; he momentarily followed his father's example and went to West Point to begin a career in the military. His talent and his upbringing joined to defeat the attempt: He refused to accept military discipline and was thrown out. He worked briefly for the government but his mind remained in Europe. He stumbled across a copy of Henri Murger's *Scènes de la vie de bohème* (1848) and was enchanted. This was the life he wanted: happy poverty in the Latin Quarter of Paris, affairs with beautiful models—above all a life devoted to art, lived among fellow artists—that was his appointed destiny. He departed for a life that was as much like that in Murger's novel as he could manage.

In Paris, Whistler shed the remnants of Protestantism quickly. Members of the diplomatic corps remembered his father from their days together in St. Petersburg, and some even remembered Whistler himself as a boy. His charm helped make him friends and contacts. He soon learned that ideas about art that were unknown in America were common in Paris. In the work of Gautier and Baudelaire, for example, he discovered that an artist in France did not need to convey moral values to his audience; an artist could concern himself solely with beauty and the perfection of form. Art often began with the inspiration of the natural, but did not need to record or idealize it; art was itself more important than nature and had autonomous rules of its own. He found being taught in art school a useful methodology: students were asked to train their visual memories by looking out the window at nature, memorizing what they saw, then turning to their easels and trying to recreate their memories without further glances at the subject. The totality of the impression, not the precision of detail, was the goal. In many ways, Paris was worlds away from Transcendentalist Boston.

Whistler was soon spending much of his time in London as well, and art there was in some ways as backward as in America. Protestant moralism insisted that a painting could have no independent artistic existence: a painting told a story that conveyed some message. Paintings could not exist autonomously: they warned the weak that drink destroyed morals and that sexual license destroyed health. They asserted that hard work made the man, that a soft answer turned away wrath, and that the road to hell was paved with good intentions. They reassured viewers that their dogs were faithful, their horses fast, and their children adorable. Armed with his new French notions, Whistler refused to accept the notion that art was a three-volume novel in paint appropriate for the perusal of sixteen-year-old girls. For him, this was an obsession with the subject; a true artist began with a subject but then devoted himself to the formal qualities of paint and canvas. Form and color were important; children and morals were not.

Whistler first began to attract attention in France when he was part of a group that was refused a place in the annual salon exhibition. Emperor Louis Napoleon was currying favor with artists at the time, so he went over the heads of the customary authorities and sponsored a salon of his own, the famous Salon des Refusés, to give publicity to the new work. Whistler had recently completed a portrait of his current mistress, and "The White Girl" proved to be one of his more striking early works. No one attending the salon could take away much of a moral from the work, at least no moral compatible with conventional Christianity. It was an experiment in form and color, it attracted considerable attention, and one French critic called it a "Symphony in White." This so impressed Whistler with its formal, musical implications that he renamed the picture: "Symphony in White No. 1: The White Girl," and it became a milestone in his career. The musical term seemed to insist on the autonomy of the work of art and to play down the subject. Anecdote no longer trivialized formal experiments.

Whistler led as unconventional a life as his funds and the presence of his mother in London permitted. Already a part of the Paris art scene, he also had a significant place in London creative life, in the Pre-Raphaelite circle that at times included Dante Rossetti, Algernon Swinburne, George Meredith, William Thackeray, and John Millais. In this eccentric atmosphere he experimented especially with fading light. His eyesight was poor, the London air unpredictable; he studied Japanese art and experimented with new colors. The pictures that emerged continued to have musical titles: "Nocturne in Grey and Gold: Chelsea Snow," "Harmony in Grey: Chelsea Ice," or "Nocturne in Blue and Gold: Old Battersea Bridge." No painting told a story or conveyed a moral. Often the subject was scarcely perceptible off in the distance. The training in visual memory from his student days, the assumptions about the autonomy of art, and the experiments with color were combining into work that seemed hostile to everything traditional in British painting. Even when Whistler painted his famous portrait of his mother, he insisted on calling it "Arrangement in Grey and Black No. 1: Portrait of the Artist's Mother." The British might wish to think of this picture as yet another Victorian portrait, but to Whistler this bordered on impertinence. It was interesting to him as a picture of his mother, of course, but he insisted that as art it should be judged on its merits as an arrangement. London officials were so wary of Whistler by this time that at first they refused to display it; only pressure from an influential old man who had known George Whistler in St. Petersburg won the public the right to see the picture at all.

In 1875, Whistler displayed "Nocturne in Black and Gold: The Falling Rocket." It proved to be the last straw for John Ruskin, the critic who retained more influence with the British public than any other man. Ruskin had made major contributions to the criticism of art and architecture, and still retains an honored place in the history of social reform, but by this time both his mind and his temper were beyond rationality on many subjects. He looked at the latest affront and snarled that he had seen and heard "much of Cockney impudence before now," but that he "never expected to hear a coxcomb ask two hundred guineas for flinging a pot of paint in the public's face." Convinced that Ruskin was a charlatan, eager to publicize his ideas, Whistler sued. He seemed unaware of how unappetizing a figure he appeared to be to average British citizens, or of how revered a figure Ruskin was in the art world. Unable to cope with the larger issues, the debate in court sank to the level of how much work Whistler had to do to create a picture. In effect, a public event that was designed to inform the British about the autonomy of art informed them that an eccentric American with too many French ideas asked Englishmen to pay two hundred guineas for the efforts of a day or two. Whistler won his case at law but received only a farthing in damages; in time he had to file for bankruptcy—no one wanted to purchase the work of a man whose ideas ran so contrary to those of the art establishment.

Yet Whistler never lost a small group of supporters. He became something of a public figure in a circle that included Oscar Wilde, and in 1885 he made a rare gesture toward educating the larger public by scheduling a talk about his principles. He called it "The Ten O'Clock," after the hour at which he gave it, implying that gentlemen should have plenty of time for a good dinner and a glass of port before having to listen to a lecture. When they arrived, they heard the greatest artist living in London tell them that they had been preached to and harassed by art, that their homes had been filled with it, and that they had every right to resent the invasion of their privacy. Art, Whistler insisted, had no desire to teach; art was occupied only with her own perfection, "seeking and finding the beautiful in all conditions and all times." Too many people did not look at a picture, they looked through it at a moral. Whistler was bored with the language of Protestant art criticism: "the painting that elevates," "the duty of the painter," "the picture that is full of thought," and "the panel that merely decorates." Nature, he asserted, was almost never right; if anything, nature imitated art, for people saw what they were trained to see and only painters could train people how to see.

The British were not listening. Decades passed before Roger Fry and a new generation of critics could even begin the process of introducing modernism to a country so resistant. But in Paris, Whistler found his audience. His origins in America largely forgotten, the quality of his work unquestioned, he was an equal to the best in that first city of the art world. He came to know Edgar Degas, Henri de Toulouse-Lautrec, and Claude Monet. Marcel Proust based a character in *Remembrance of Things Past* on him and put the Whistler–Ruskin trial into *Jean Santeuil*. The most influential modernist in French music, Claude Debussy, became a good friend, and took to calling his own works by names like "Nocturne" and to attempting effects with new chord structures that matched those for which Whistler was striving with his tonal palette. An American, at long last, had once more entered the artistic life of Europe as an equal.

III

For sheer sustained achievement, however, the key figure in the American creative reunion with Europe was Henry James, Jr. The younger brother of William James, Henry provided the most significant link between the early-nineteenth-century world of his father and the modern world that was taking shape when he died in 1916. His physical presence in Europe for most of his adult life made America unavoidable at any discussions about who or what was important in literature. His innovations in fiction fused the novel and the romance, introduced the novel as theater and then the novel of consciousness. He pioneered in symbolism and in critical theory. The history of American civilization can scarcely point to an achievement equal to his in either bulk or quality.

His upbringing was as untypical of average America as Whistler's. William responded to it with indecision and depression, and only found himself intellectually when he became a Harvard professor. Henry adapted more easily, although as an adult he made clear how unsettling it had been to be a hotel child moving about the Western world, with no place in society and not even a religious orthodoxy in which to take comfort. William studied in Germany and dutifully sampled the delights of tourism in other countries, but yearned continually for the stability of a career and family in Cambridge. Henry kept his home in his head and remained free for life to arrive in a new city, check into a new place to live, and begin to write as soon as he had organized his desk. The delights of wife and children never much tempted him, and the most intellectual city in America, his brother's Cambridge, bored him. Henry never lost contact with American friends and editors, but preferred the physical presence of those Europeans who lived most of their lives in the London area. A cosmopolitan childhood produced a cosmopolitan adult; not since John Quincy Adams had an American been able to take Western civilization so for granted.

Because James voted with his feet and left what his fellow citizens regarded as the best country in the world, he seemed effete, deracinated, and genteel to many of his countrymen, and they were quick to assume that remarks in his novels critical of America were the opinions of the author. James was far more complicated and ambivalent than any of his characters, and his attitude toward America was appropriately complex. In private letters, he was perfectly capable of snorting about the vulgarity his countrymen frequently displayed. They assumed the superiority of their native institutions and the inferiority of things foreign—a trait neither original with Americans nor confined to them. But even as he made these criticisms, he insisted that Americans were "a people of *character*," and he praised American "energy, capacity and intellectual stuff in ample measure." He thought it "a great blessing" to be born an American, and found it "an excellent preparation for culture." Americans had the right to pick and choose among the cultures of the world, even if James himself were one of the few who consciously exercised the right. In time, he became acutely aware of how narrow the culture of even the most talented French writers could be, and painfully bored with the superficialities of the literary life even in his beloved London. A great intelligence was comfortable everywhere but at home nowhere, and in one of his most quoted remarks he said: "It's a complex fate, being an American, and one of the responsibilities it entails is fighting against a superstitious valuation of Europe."

More than any other American writer, James wrote from within this cosmopolitan framework. As a young man he traveled back and forth across the Atlantic, writing early fiction about both sides of the ocean, but one evening in a Boston hotel he made up his mind that his work had to lie in Europe. He decided that he could not write effectively about both cultures; he had to choose. "No European writer is called upon to assume that terrible burden," and it seemed hard that he should be. "The burden is necessarily greater for an American—for he *must* deal, more or less, even if only by implication, with Europe; whereas no European is obliged to deal in the least with America." Yet in many moods, what he called "the whole 'international' state of mind" wearied him, and he wrote William in 1888 that he did not have "the least hesitation in saying that I aspire to write in such a way that it would be impossible for an outsider to say whether I am at a given moment an American writing about England or an Englishman writing about America." Far from being ashamed about the cultural ambiguities involved, he would "be exceedingly proud of it, for it would be highly civilized." In that goal of civilization, in that tolerance and even delight in ambiguity, lay the seeds of modernism. James used his own personal circumstances to develop art forms that came to dominate the consciousness of the twentieth century.

James' first extended stay abroad as a writing adult was in Italy, and Rome and Florence retained a special place in his heart. In 1869 he wrote to William from Rome that he had been "roaming the streets," and that "at last—for the first time—I live! It beats everything." He went "reeling and moaning thro' the streets, in a fever of enjoyment." He was looking at every famous site he could think of, and assured his brother: "I shall go to bed a wiser man than I last arose." No doubt he did; and no doubt some of his tone was assumed for his skeptical brother's benefit, for William's pleasures were rather different. But Henry did love Italy, even if it was the Italy of his imagination, of tourists and expatriates. Of the real Italy, or even the Italy of native artists, he knew little. The work that came out of his stay began one of the great themes that will be forever associated with his name: the international theme of the American who comes to Europe to sample the art and the wisdom of the ages and who in some way fails to assimilate the experience. Occasionally, as in *The Europeans*, the work would be a light comedy of manners and misunderstandings, or deal with Europeans in America; more frequently, as in *Roderick Hudson*, there would be overtones of tragedy. Too many Americans were capable of seeing the flaws in their native country and feeling the attractions of Europe, while too few had the strength of character or the artistic talent to profit from the experience. James was one of those few. He also experimented with the form as well as the content of his work; as early as "The Madonna of the Future" (1873), he was writing about art and self-deception through the device of a tale told by a narrator, as told to him by yet another narrator. The distancing of artist from tale, and of audience from fact, was already underway long before Joseph Conrad made this procedure a standard device of modernist ambiguity.

By the middle 1870s James had decided that his love of Italy was not strong enough to claim his permanent allegiance, and he settled in Paris. The choice had a considerable impact on his taste, his fiction, and his criticism. He met the leading French writers—Flaubert, Zola, Goncourt, Daudet—and for a while was entranced. With certain members of the foreign literary community, most obviously Ivan Turgenev, he made friendships that affected his life and work. But even Paris soon palled. James realized that even the most catholic of French writers were uninterested in the literature of other languages, and that despite his relative youth and country of origin James was more truly cosmopolitan than most of the famous figures he was meeting. Like Whistler, he took up the new French ideas about the formal autonomy of art, and about the multiple perspectives that a brilliant artist could use to examine an object in the commonplace world; much of his work belonged as much to European culture as to American. But a writer could go beyond a painter in certain ways: Whistler could purvey atmosphere and point of view, but he could not really recreate consciousness, and James was soon doing experiments that paralleled his brother's work in psychology. Following the precedents of Flaubert, he worked at developing a style that could convey what a character was thinking at the same time that it conveyed false impressions to an outside observer and a vision of complexity to yet a third consciousness, that of the reader. Although James was not yet able to write fiction that was stream-of-consciousness in its style, he was on the path in that direction.

Before James became stylistically sophisticated, however, he had to work his way through the legacies of his predecessor Hawthorne and his friend Howells about the relationship of the romance and the novel. In the major work of his French period, *The American*, James seemed to be working in both traditions. The ostensible theme of the novel was the attempt by a rather innocent American businessman to marry into French aristocratic society, only to find that society more cruel and narrow-minded than anything he had left in America. But James also had a more important theme: the relationships between the romance, realism, and what people can "know." "The real represents to my perception the things we cannot possibly *not* know," he wrote in his later preface to the novel. The romantic, however, were those "things that . . . we never *can* directly know; the things that can reach us only through the beautiful circuit and subterfuge of our thought and our desire." The novel clearly had many problems, but in it and in certain of the works that immediately followed it, most obviously *Washington Square*, James moved beyond the terms of the debate. It no longer seemed important whether or not a fact were true, normal, or democratic on the one hand or improbable, fantastic, and aristocratic on the other. What became important was a state of consciousness: the consciousness of the characters, the author, and the reader. One of James' great contributions to the culture of the world was his attempt, over many years, to merge the three. The language that had mediated between author and characters, and between author and reader, seemed to become both a barrier and a means of transcending the barrier—it conveyed consciousness of self and of culture, but did so in increasingly complex ways that cost James much of his popular audience even as it helped initiate the modern in literature.

James soon left Paris for London; although he traveled frequently, he retained that first city of the English language as his "home" until his death. He loved London to the point of writing entire works where the city itself seemed to be the center of consciousness, and the characters important only as they evoked its ambience. Some, like "A London Life," were relatively unimportant as literature; others, like *The Princess Casamassima*, proved his willingness to experiment with literary naturalism and to spend considerable effort working on lower-class material far from his usual subject matter. It is hard to imagine Henry James, intense analyst of drawing-room perception, visiting a prison and taking notes for his next work, but so great was the fascination of this great city that he did exactly that, producing one of his best works, a volume that has not yet received the attention it deserves. Yet even here, in an experiment dealing with the effects of heredity on personality, and the shattering impact of a hostile environment that included such unpleasant topics as bastardy and bombings, James persisted in his concentration on the sensibility and on human consciousness. Hyacinth Robinson might have had a debauched aristocrat for a father and a French prostitute for a mother, but he was above all a sensitive soul aspiring beyond the sensuous possibilities of his birth toward something finer. The princess who befriended him did so in large part because she genuinely wanted to break out of the restricted possibilities for experience that went with a life of beauty, wealth, and title. London became the battleground for combats of consciousness; to an American, the extremes of perception were accessible in ways that seemed impossible in Boston or New York.

The great achievement of James' settlement in London was *The Portrait of a Lady*, with its cast of American and British characters moving across Europe seeking stimulation beyond their normal experience. The British seemed to be convinced that America was a land of infinite potential, and that above all beautiful young American women had opportunities for growth closed to those from older cultures. The Americans found Europe fascinating yet infinitely deceptive: from the superficial clichés of the journalist Henrietta Stackpole to the lethargic connoisseurship of Gilbert Osmond, Americans sought in Europe something indefinable which they seemed unable to feel at home. Yet behind this mature analysis of the international theme lay an even more important philosophical issue, an issue all but patented in the name of the James family. In this work Henry James, quite unconscious of the specific intellectual formulations of his philosophical brother, experimented with free will, determinism, and the pragmatic method. He posed the problem of an American girl made free with the inheritance of vast wealth to go with her beauty and intelligence; surely such a being were free if anyone were. Certainly Isabel Archer had the illusion of freedom, and like most Americans she was sure of her competence to handle its responsibilities. She turned down a solid, sensible American and a wealthy British aristocrat, because marriage to them seemed likely to restrict her perceptions and inhibit the organic growth of her consciousness. Yet such was her innocence that the first man who seemed sensitive and aesthetic in his interests won her, despite a lack of other noticeable virtues. Gilbert Osmond proved to be one of many unattractive Jamesian characters, taking the virtues of perception past the point of egotistical corruption. Instead of freeing Isabel, he imprisoned her in his museum; she found herself one more pretty object sitting there, inert among the porcelain of ages past. Her world had seemed free, but in fact had not been.

The implications of the book were enormous. By the middle 1880s, James had clearly come to terms with his American birth and his European environment and found both deficient. Americans were innocent and thought they were free; Europeans were imprisoned in their culture and no longer capable of exercising free will or creating new art. Each hemisphere fed on its illusions about the other, and only Henry James and his most perceptive readers found a stimulation in the spectacle that rewarded a searching imagination. For William, the problem had been one of consciousness in the religious and philosophical sense, and his suggestions those of a scientist anxious to justify the role of belief in a world desperate for guidance in its habits and actions. For Henry, the problem had been one of consciousness in the literary and cultural sense, and his suggestions those of a cosmopolitan anxious to transcend the illusions of time and place. Each sought to go beyond the limits of discourse that had fettered earlier thinkers, to use his American birth and sense of possibility to structure a present that seemed in chaos. Late in life, after William published *Pragmatism*, Henry wrote to him in pleased astonishment at how parallel their paths had been: the book cast a spell "of interest and enthrallment" upon him. He found it hard to write William about it because he "simply sank down, under it, into such depths of submission and assimilation that *any* reaction, very nearly, even that of acknowledgement, would have had almost the taint of dissent or escape." He became "lost in the wonder of the extent to which all my life I have . . . unconsciously pragmatised. You are immensely and universally *right*. . . ."

In terms of its form, *The Portrait of a Lady* seemed traditional, a long exploration of manners and morals tied together effectively by central characters and persisting themes. But in Chapter 42, James had his heroine sink into a long internal monologue that proved an important precedent. Isabel Archer sat before the fire, musing and dreaming about the illusions of freedom and the mess she had made out of a marriage and a life which she had consciously chosen. Nothing had worked out as she had planned, the surfaces of life and art had deceived her, and the people she trusted had proven manipulative and self-interested. The scene pointed toward the future of both James' art and the novel in general in two ways: it was theatrical, in that it made use of the soliloquy, that device so common in Shakespeare through which a character like Hamlet summed up his dilemmas before attempting to solve them for the rest of the play; and it was a successful early version of the stream-of-consciousness, written before William James had given it its first formal statement in the *Principles of Psychology*.

The theatrical experimentation soon led James in a new direction. Convinced he was losing his popular audience, he determined to recapture it by writing plays which would give him a new place in the public eye. He failed, but the time was not wasted. His true skill lay in the dramatizing of conscious states, not in the dramatizing of external relationships, and in a series of short novels during the last years of the century he pushed the art of fiction beyond anything which other writers had attempted. Fascinated by the work of Henrik Ibsen, he experimented with memories, delusions, and obsessions and became increasingly open in his use of unconscious drives as motive forces. Sexuality lurked everywhere, corrupting families and distorting relationships; most of all, these drives enabled the novelist to develop surfaces rich in ambiguity and deception. Nothing was as it seemed, and symbols proliferated in the work of an author who had previously made little use of them. Some works, like *The Spoils of Poynton* (1897), were relatively straightforward in their drama; others, like *The Sacred Fount* (1901), were so ambiguous that the reader could emerge unsure of the meaning of the action, the mental capacity of the narrator, or the intention of the author. The most successful work of the period, *The Turn of the Screw* (1898), managed to combine several levels of narrative complexity. Some read it as a ghost story, others as a tale of sexual frustration. It seemed as traditional as *Wuthering Heights* and as modern as *Ghosts*. It was the last work in which James succeeded in hitting both the public taste for straightforward narrative and the critical taste for works that stretched the mind beyond the normal range of aesthetic perception.

Having assimilated the modern theater, James returned to the long novel with three works that many critics regard as the triumphs of his career. In some ways, *The Wings of the Dove* (1902) *The Ambassadors* (1903), and *The Golden Bowl* (1904) were traditional Jamesian works: long international novels that once more examined the mutual perceptions of Europeans and Americans and the failure of Americans to assimilate the most rewarding aspects of European life. But the intervening years had made their mark. Isabel Archer's soliloquy had taken over much of the narrative, as readers found themselves deeply involved in the perceptions of a few characters as they tried to figure out the deceptive surfaces of the world around them. Laid out like plays in scenes, on stages, the works substituted perceptions for actions, in the process demonstrating why James did not succeed as a playwright; what worked in a complex novel seemed impossible as an actual play. The symbolism of dove and bowl were only the most obvious examples of James' new fascination with objects that could represent states of emotion and perception. The style, the content, and the point of view seemed to merge, and readers found themselves deep in the confusions of the characters, with none of the traditional guideposts of Victorian fiction. Fully as much as James Joyce and Marcel Proust, James had pioneered the modern novel of consciousness, gaining a place for himself and for America in the history of modernism in Western civilization.

IV

Running parallel to the artistic developments which found their inspiration in Europe were competing developments that found their inspiration in America. Ethnic groups which had long been excluded from American cultural life established themselves economically, advanced toward social equality, and began to produce work that demanded the attention of a broad public. In time, these groups combined to create a multicultural nation in which no single group and no single section could dominate the others.

The ethnic group which emerged first was the black community. Resident in the country almost as long as the whites, the blacks spent almost two centuries and a half as slaves, or as freemen whose skin color indicated a history of servitude. In Canada and in the Northern United States, small communities of free blacks existed long before emancipation legally freed everyone. But educational opportunities were few, and no black children anywhere could look forward to careers as rewarding as those open to whites. This condition began to change only with the articulation of abolitionist goals and the beginning of some understanding in the white community that the concepts of freedom and democracy upon which American civilization was based demanded schools, careers, and the privileges of citizenship for everyone. Even with freedom, however, blacks faced an uncertain future. Whites in both North and South refused to deal with them equally, and by the 1890s segregation—sometimes formal, sometimes merely customary—was common everywhere in the country. Blacks had trouble attending good schools, eating in good restaurants, riding on buses and trains, finding places to sleep at night. Everywhere a black child looked, America seemed to be a place full of promises that were never kept.

The first creative productions of black culture to receive wide exposure were autobiographical accounts of the slave experience. Frederick Douglass, to take the first black to achieve a place for his life story in American literature, told the story of a Maryland slave who had rebelled against exploitation, escaped from slavery, earned enough money to purchase his freedom legally, and became one of the most visible of the abolitionist speakers. He was an organizer of black support for the new Republican party, and in time became one of the highest-ranking black officials in the national government, serving in minor diplomatic posts. The *Autobiography* told his story in several versions over the years and made Douglass into a role model for young blacks. He was apparently even more impressive in person than in print, and in 1845 the white poet James Russell Lowell summed up the essence of Douglass' position in American culture with the remark: "The very look and bearing of Douglass are an irresistible logic against the oppression of his race." Over the years he spent periods of time in Britain and deeply impressed a number of British reformers; just as a century earlier Benjamin Franklin had demonstrated to Europeans that the American wilderness could produce men of genius in science and statecraft, so Douglass proved that free blacks were worthy of a place at the functions of any white group.

Douglass played an important role in moderating black demands before the Civil War and avoiding some of the extremes which hurt the abolitionist cause. He refused to follow the lead of William Lloyd Garrison and to denounce the Constitution as a fraudulent document unworthy of veneration. For Douglass, the words that initiated American history were so broad in their implications that even blacks could look forward to an equal place in American society. The founding fathers had been limited by their time and place, and had accepted slavery as unavoidable, but Douglass believed that with slavery gone his people could use that language to achieve equality in any aspect of American life that truly mattered to them. In the very long run, he not only proved correct in this assumption, he created the logic that other ethnic groups—not to mention women—could also use to point out those places where American reality did not measure up to American ideals.

A great gap still separated those ideals from the reality of the years after the Civil War, however. Where Douglass had been the great hero for blacks during the years before the war, Booker T. Washington took over that role during the Gilded Age; merely by his existence, he demonstrated clearly how far blacks had to go to win equality, and how high the barriers were along the way. Born a slave, probably in the spring of 1856, he grew up in the hands of white people originally from New England or from German-speaking Europe. Only whites of such backgrounds were willing to concern themselves with the educational and social welfare of the freemen, and thus figures like Washington received strong doses of puritan mores along with their new liberties. But the level of such training was perhaps unavoidably low. Washington was a houseboy and elementary student. He learned basic reading and writing, but he learned as well how to play up to whites: how to be respectful, how to appear pious, to stay clean, to seem helpful. His was a training in how to adjust to a permanent position in the lower classes of society.

Washington adjusted to this upbringing and never rebelled overtly for the rest of his life. He taught school, he worked at the Hampton Normal and Agricultural Institute, and in time became the leader of a new institute in Tuskegee, Alabama. From that position, Washington rose to be the chief black political and financial power in the country. Republican presidents consulted him on post office and customs appointments that were reserved for blacks. Foundation officials consulted him before they granted money to blacks or to institutions that served blacks. Washington served them well. He was always respectful toward whites, even as he was authoritarian toward blacks; he adjusted to custom and moderated his demands to those which seemed possible without public disturbance. Blacks looked to him for advice, and he in turn looked to Northern whites.

The advice he gave often cut both ways. He was quite willing to agree with whites that most blacks of the day were illiterate, politically naive, and not yet able to exercise the full rights of American citizenship. Yet he would also argue that after an adequate period of training at schools like Tuskegee, blacks of the future would indeed be worthy of full integration into society. In his judgment, blacks would earn the privileges of white society, and when they had done so, whites would permit them to exercise those privileges. Whites could see him as an advocate of segregation and industrial education, because for the short run that was what he was; blacks could see him as a leader who told them that equality was not all that far away, and that if they worked at it, they would get it. It was a clever game and Washington played it well. But the cost to the black community was high. Even as he worked behind the scenes to achieve political and social acceptance, Washington refused to criticize even the most outrageous actions of racists. Whites who listened to him understood that blacks were contented and making progress, and could thus happily turn to other subjects. The first requirement of change was sharp, persistent identification of legitimate grievances, and thanks to Washington, such criticism was not there until the end of the century.

Just as Douglass' autobiographies represented the intransigent spirit of the

1840s, so Washington's *Up From Slavery* represented the spirit of the postwar years. The book functioned in the black community in the same manner as the *Autobiography* of Benjamin Franklin had long functioned in the white: it was a handbook of the upwardly mobile survivor who knew how to cope with a society that did not at first seem especially open to new talent. The volume stressed the ethic of manual labor that Tuskegee had long taught. It said that blacks did not demand social equality. It sympathized with white former slaveholders, and assured them that not only did blacks harbor no grudges but that they had learned a lot as slaves and had much to be grateful for. It presented a model of self-help, in its explanations of how young Washington had taught himself how to spell, with only his mother's sympathy for assistance. It stressed the simple New England virtues of bathing and neatness, and hinted strongly that among the weapons that blacks really needed to fight for equality, the paintbrush and the toothbrush were at the top of the list. Finally the book was hostile to organized labor. Washington wanted self-reliance but not group action, and strikes in the book seemed distinctly unamerican. Outside observers might have had trouble seeing what American blacks had to conserve, but Booker Washington was a conservative and both the white and the black community respected him greatly. He never became rich, but he deserved a place in American history close to that of Andrew Carnegie.

Just as Carnegie eventually faced progressive criticism, so Washington had to face growing criticism from younger blacks who found him authoritarian to blacks and submissive to whites. Younger blacks had an excellent case; by 1900, Washington had been supporting segregation and industrial education for a generation, and yet the result around the country had been a worsening of conditions. White people did not think blacks equal and nowhere could blacks be sure of their rights to do much of anything. They faced suspicion at every turn, and lynching in times of crisis. Washington's lessons proved counterproductive, and blacks learned that if they acted like doormats a great many people would walk on them.

Criticism of Washington became endemic during the early years of the twentieth century, and the leader of it was a man who in some ways shared much with Washington and had once admired him. W. E. B. DuBois had been born in 1868 into a Massachusetts family that had French and Dutch blood on his father's side and black on his mother's. The baby never knew his father, and instead grew up in a small town as a light-skinned child in a community almost entirely white. He never knew the pain of segregation and received the same education as any white child. Indeed, if any ethnic group were on the bottom in that town, the Irish were, and DuBois for a long time had little conception of the role race would play in his life. Thus, for reasons totally unlike those affecting Washington, DuBois also internalized the norms of the New England middle class. He wanted a good education, a rewarding job, and political equality because he assumed he had a right to them, and when he ran into trouble, his rage was all the greater. He knew that not only was he equal, he was more than equal—more intelligent and better educated than all but a tiny group of whites. The frustrations drove him to the far left of American life and his autobiographies taught quite different lessons from those contained in *Up From Slavery*.

To cope with this complex background, DuBois first had to go south to find out what the problem was. He chose to attend Fisk University in Tennessee, and thus for the first time encountered blacks in large numbers in a segregated Southern city. He discovered black women, black laughter, and black frustration. He read widely in the classics and philosophy, and heard genuinely African-American music. He also perceived the undertone of violence everywhere, and remembered how customary it was for many of the students to carry guns.

He then returned to New England, for like white boys of his intelligence he wanted the best. A sense of his dual heritage dogged him throughout his years at Harvard, where he took his A.B. (1890) and Ph.D. (1895): on the one hand he remained an aloof black, knowing he was different, fearing prejudice and unwilling to face every day the knowledge that he could count on no one to treat him simply as a student. In *The Souls of Black Folk* he described the feeling as that of "a sort of a seventh son born with a veil, and gifted with second sight in this American world." He would always find the experience of seeing one's self through the eyes of whites odd: "One ever feels his two-ness—an American, a Negro; two souls, two thoughts, two unreconciled strivings; two warring ideals in one dark body, whose dogged strength alone keeps it from being torn asunder."

Yet DuBois did well at Harvard. He felt little prejudice among the faculty, and recalled with special praise the instruction of William James in philosophy and of Albert Bushnell Hart in history. "James with his pragmatism and Albert Bushnell Hart with his research method" were the forces which "turned me back from the lovely but sterile land of philosophic speculation, to the social sciences as the field for gathering and interpreting that body of fact which would apply to my program for the Negro." In time, he completed a doctoral dissertation on the suppression of the African slave trade, using his current training to discover his racial past. But even that achievement was not the only triumph of his graduate training: he managed as well to spend two years in Germany, doing precisely what the top white students wished to do, studying the social sciences with the best men in the world. He found that he was no odder in German eyes than any other foreigner, and the temptation was great to marry into society and enjoy a life that seemed likely to be free of the tensions of race in America. DuBois loved the wine, women, and song of Europe, and if the loneliness of many foreigners there affected him, he neglected to mention it years later. Instead, what stayed with him was the social science of his own situation. Under the scholars like Rudolph von Gneist, Adolph Wagner, and Gustav Schmoller, he became aware of the world context of the racial issue. He studied the black peoples of Africa and Asia, noting the economic and political relationships which tied them to the rest of the world. He also studied the writings of Karl Marx and attended meetings of the Social Democratic party. Yet he did not necessarily imbibe a revolutionary attitude at this time, regardless of how it might seem years later. Indeed, so great was his admiration for things German that he trimmed his beard so that it would resemble the beard of the young German Kaiser! The tensions of this dual allegiance again bothered him, this time more in terms of class than in terms of race: "I began to feel that dichotomy which all my life has characterized my thought: how far can love for my oppressed race accord with love for the oppressing country? And when these loyalties diverge, where shall my soul find refuge?"

He picked America and found no refuge. In the clerical atmosphere of Wilberforce College, he seemed exotic indeed—a new faculty member in a small Midwestern town, walking about in his beard, wearing gloves and carrying a walking stick, loving German art and music on a campus where men and women were not even allowed to share sidewalks together and where religious revivals were the chief form of spiritual exercise. He found no refuge at the University of Pennsylvania when he received a grant to study the local black community. The result, *The Philadelphia Negro*, was the first example of scientific sociology ever written by an American, and yet no university in the white world, including the one that sponsored it, was willing even to consider DuBois seriously for a professorship. He retreated to Atlanta and the black university there, sure that knowledge and time were all that were needed to improve race relations. He found no refuge there either. The *Atlanta University Studies* that emerged between 1897 and 1910 presented great quantities of systematic knowledge even as the condition of blacks deteriorated before his eyes. No student of William James could fail to notice the lack of results. As far as race was concerned, progressivism in America was a fraud; it yielded no worthwhile results. The American dream did not seem to be true.

DuBois had long doubted the doctrines of Booker T. Washington, but in 1903 he made his doubts public in *The Souls of Black Folk*. He acknowledged Washington's ascendancy and the logic of his emphasis on industrial goals, conciliation of the South, and submission to legal discrimination. The scars of slavery and civil war were painful and perhaps required a generation to heal. But things were getting worse for blacks and conciliation was hardly the way to deal with a lynch mob. DuBois had experienced the best education the white world could offer and he insisted that the top tenth of the black population was quite capable of doing the same. For these talented members of the elite, equality was essential; a generation so trained could deal with the rest of the black people, and thus the race could raise itself to the level of whites. Blacks, he insisted, did "not expect that the free right to vote, to enjoy civic rights, and to be educated, will come in a moment," nor did they "expect to see the bias and prejudices of years disappear at the blast of a trumpet." But he did not doubt for a minute that "the way for a people to gain their reasonable rights is not by voluntarily throwing them away and insisting that they do not want them." Blacks knew that they "must insist continually, in season and out of season, that voting is necessary to modern manhood, that color discrimination is barbarism, and that black boys need education as well as white boys."

DuBois became the most articulate race leader of his generation. He was the executive secretary of the Niagara Movement of 1905, an abortive attempt to organize black professional people into a pressure group. When it failed he became the most visible black in the interracial group of progressives who founded the National Association for the Advancement of Colored People (NAACP). In time, as frustrations and disappointments mounted, he turned out piece after piece on aspects of the racial problem. Always ambivalent about his sense of two-ness, his desire for integration with whites balancing his desire for black solidarity, he could never quite come to terms with America. His studies of Marx and his reading in the history of the third world in time seemed more promising, and when as an old man his own country harassed him in ways he found intolerable, he joined the Communist party and spent his last years in Africa. For at least one American, the American dream had not worked, and he refused to issue optimistic statements that said anything different.

V

Leaders, by definition, are exceptional; few could have been more exceptional than DuBois. The bulk of the black population, by definition, could not fit into the "talented tenth," and even members of that elite could entertain few hopes of an education or career that included so much. Most blacks had enough trouble making a decent living. The irony of their situation was that the cultural achievements of the black majority produced one of the great contributions of America to Western civilization. Jazz music did far more to gain American blacks international recognition than all of DuBois' anguished polemics.

In its public form, black culture began with the minstrel shows. The American theater developed in several directions in the early nineteenth century, and one of them was toward the portrayal of blacks, usually by white actors, in a variety of comic routines. People in those days did not have much by way of entertainment, and theaters were an important means of filling the night with something to do that provided topics of conversation the next day. Lower-class figures were popular on the stage, and audiences liked to see versions of themselves which were larger than life. Heroic figures like Davy Crockett,

Daniel Boone, Mike Fink, and Brother Jonathan reassured whites about the capacities of democratic man. The portrayal of comical blacks reassured them in a different way. If white audiences could fantasize themselves into the roles of heroic battlers, they could also comfort themselves with the knowledge that no matter how down and out they might be, they still ranked above blacks. Blacks were, by definition, slaves or the offspring of slaves, and a stage that made them appear simple-minded and animal-like served the sociological purpose of making whites feel superior.

The first appearances of white actors in blackface were before the Revolution, but in terms of minstrelsy as an art form the British actor Charles Matthews was the man who began it all. He had noted that American audiences, never noted for their quiet behavior, often hooted a performance of Shakespeare off the stage and demanded a sequence of black songs instead, and during 1822 he went about the country gathering data on black life and habits. By the late 1820s, it became common to interrupt long dramas with intermissions in which the actors came out as minstrels to keep these audiences pacified. Often enough, the songs were not black in origin at all, but merely English or Irish lyrics with local variations and accents added. One of the most popular of these actor/singers was Thomas D. Rice, and in 1828 he happened to see an old, deformed black doing an odd, jerky dance as he sang: "Weel about and turn about and do just so;/Ebery time I weel about, I jump Jim Crow." Rice quickly realized that such an odd, "genuine" dance had stage possibilities. He adapted the material to dress it up a bit, and soon enjoyed great public success. The actual melody combined an Irish folk tune and an English stage song, and of course Rice was white, but that was the way popular culture worked. Most whites had never seen a black off the stage and seemed willing to believe almost anything so long as it seemed amusing.

As politics heated up in the 1840s and 1850s, the minstrel shows became bastions of reaction. No one wanted to go to the theater to hear about reform; they wanted entertainment and reassurance, and in the theater they were told with increasing frequency that slaves were pleasant animals who were happy where they were and had neither the desire for freedom nor the mental competence to cope with it. The great writer of songs during the period was the sentimental Stephen Foster, who had begun acting in blackface at the age of nine, and who had tried unsuccessfully to write songs for "Jim Crow" Rice as a teenager. But by the 1840s Foster was a success; songs like "Old Uncle Ned" and "De Camptown Races" were catching on, and Foster found a place for himself writing for E. P. Christy, leader of one of the most popular of the minstrel groups. The world of these songs was generally a plantation where everything was warm and happy. No breath of rebellion invaded either the Big House or the slave quarters, and when Foster's old slaves left the plantation they seemed to spend their waking hours yearning for its security. The political implications were fairly obvious: life was better for blacks in the slave South than in the industrial North.

The Civil War made much of this irrelevant without destroying the audiences for vaudeville routines. It also freed blacks who desperately needed ways to make a living. The stage was an obvious place where blacks had long been present, at least as whites in blackface, and soon blacks were claiming the minstrel show for themselves. In doing so, however, they found themselves trapped. Whites had established the roles, and most of them had strong prejudices against blacks. They degraded blacks, but by the 1870s the wire hair, thick lips, clumsy gestures, and idiotic accents were what audiences wanted to see and hear, and so black actors and singers found themselves participating in their own degradation, authenticating stereotypes that made political progress almost impossible to contemplate. A black star like Billy "Big Mouth" Kersands specialized in primitive humor that included routines in which he somehow managed to get a cup and saucer or several billiard balls into his mouth. Whites seemed to love his act in part because it confirmed their stereotypes of blacks; blacks loved it because through it they could see a black entertainer making his way in part through the money and approval of whites. Like the Jewish schlemiel or the Southern redneck, he could appeal both to outsiders and to insiders, in effect putting on two rather different shows at once.

The minstrel shows also provided educational and vocational opportunities for young blacks with no alternatives. W. C. Handy, for example, was a black child from a fanatically religious family who faced great opposition when he made his first attempts at playing an instrument or getting musical training. But he had seen minstrel shows; he had seen Billy Kersands, the man who could "make a mule laugh"; he had watched the routines of Sam Lucas and Tom McIntosh, in their silk hats and long-tailed coats; he desperately wanted to join them. Despite family opposition, he went off with Mahara's Minstrels in 1896, because he quite correctly saw the group as one of the few ways he could leave the impoverished South. In *Father of the Blues* Handy readily admitted that to many blacks the minstrel shows seemed disreputable, but he insisted that "all the best talent of that generation came down the same drain. The composers, the singers, the musicians, the speakers, the stage performers—the minstrel shows got them all." He did not hesitate: "I took it for the break it was." He never regretted it. The minstrels made him a professional and took him all over North America, Mexico, and the Caribbean. They "taught me a way of life that I still consider the only one for me." He was not alone, for out of that tradition came a number of the greatest black talents of the succeeding generations: singers like Bessie Smith and Ma Rainey; a songwriter like Gussie Davis; a star like Bert Williams; a comedian like Pigmeat Markham. And out of it as well came some of the strongest of the influences which contributed to the development of jazz.

VI

The sort of music that will be forever associated with Handy's name, as the title of his book indicates, is the blues. Like many terms in cultural history, it meant many things to those who used it, and in a strictly musical sense was often so vague as to be undefinable. But the term was actually quite precise in its meaning at first. Most European music was written down in the seven notes of the diatonic scale, *C D E F G A B*. Each note had a half-note in between, the sharp or the flat, but other fractional notes were impossible on some instruments, like the piano. On others, such fractional notes sounded like mistakes of intonation. If the human voice sang or the cornet played off pitch, to Western ears that was an error, but to the ears of the early blues musicians, it was not. In much of the music of Africa, European folk music, and some Oriental and American Indian musics, a pentatonic scale was more common, with five notes, usually *C D E G A*, rather than seven. Fractional notes in such a system will come out sounding different, and other variations in pitch will sound systemless to conventionally trained Western ears. The "blues" as a term referred to these notes that sounded "wrong" to Western ears. A "bluenote" was a note that was off-key; usually it was a note a human voice hit intentionally, although instruments soon learned to imitate the human voice. Such "wrong notes" could not be written down effectively in Western notational systems, and properly trained musicians often dismissed them as naive expressions of folklore, refusing to accept them as legitimate musical expression.

Equally strange to Western ears were the "dirty tones" that Africans took for granted. A singer did not normally growl in Western music, or sing falsetto outside exceptional operatic circumstances. Drummers did not hang teeth or tusks from their drums and horn players did not use mutes to distort the sound. But Africans took these distortions for granted, and so did most black musicians. Jazz absorbed these dirty tones and even gloried in them; the most talented musicians seemed to go out of their way to invent weird noises that had a musical purpose. To Western ears, the musical purpose was chiefly to irritate audiences, but to blacks the use of various mutes, the addition of wordless song substitutes—growls, laughs, "scat" singing, and the rest—were all ties to a genuine heritage that belonged to them rather than to whites.

Indeed, African music was communal in a way that European music could never be. The music of Bach and Mozart was a music that separated the performers and the audience. In the concert hall, the pianist, the quartet, or the symphony played by itself, on stage. The audience dressed differently, it paid money, and it "was entertained," passively. It did not participate except in rare circumstances like the singing of a patriotic opener. Even in a church, trained choirs usually handled the burdens of hymn-singing, and the organ played most of its pieces alone. The African attitude was quite different. Africans all participated. They all swayed, or danced, or made audible contributions in some way. Theirs was a communal music that expressed the feelings of the whole community, and they had no such split between players and audience. In many ways, in fact, music supplied vital linguistic connections between people with acute problems of language. In Africa, dialects often made the inhabitants of one village all but incomprehensible to inhabitants of another, and music was the effective means of communication. Jazz musicians took over this communal spirit. The atmosphere was spontaneous, people might join in or drop out, and anyone in the audience was free to shout, moan, or otherwise make some contribution to the quantity of sound. These were not interruptions, as they would have been in an eighteenth-century ballroom; they were expressions of communality that were part of the heritage and were so understood by the players.

Africans could also take for granted rhythmic customs that European music did not absorb until the early twentieth century. Some African music had no discernable rhythm at all, and some religious and funeral music was free in form and seemingly impossible to notate in a Western manner. But more common were the various rhythms that Africans used simultaneously. A drum, clapping hands or some other percussive instrument set a beat, often a simple one, and then other instruments set up another or perhaps even a third beat that might be quite different. Beats that sounded uncomplicated alone became quite complex when played together; listeners became accustomed to various off-beats as the two sounded, each against the other. The term in Western music was *polyrhythm* but not until works like Igor Stravinsky's "The Rite of Spring" outraged Paris just before World War I did musicians have much idea of what might be involved.

Finally, Africans were far more accustomed to a call-and-response pattern than Europeans. Eighteenth-century composers experimented occasionally with multiple choirs that tossed themes back and forth, and churches did the same, but in African music such antiphonal devices were a common means of organizing communities that were untrained and did not know the proper words or even the language in use in the area. In African usage, a leader gave out the first line of a song, then the chorus came in with a reply; the leader continued, but all the chorus had to do was repeat its one reply. In this fashion only one singer had to know the words, yet all could participate.

The peculiar circumstances of slavery added elements to these African customs. Slave music tended to be functional: the cotton had to be picked or the corn shucked, and the tunes the slaves sang were essentially means to get reluctant bodies through an arduous task as pleasantly as possible. Other tasks, like pulling a boat through a canal, were essentially group tasks; songs helped to establish a rhythm through which men could strain on the ropes at the same time to concentrate their strength. Slave entertainments also added elements: the famous "ring shout," for example, was part of a common dance ritual that took place after religious meetings, as the participants shuffled about in a ring in jerking, hitching motions which worked them into all kinds of audible self-expressions. By such means, church music, work music, and entertainment music might come together, with no one at the time caring to differentiate between them. Conventional terminology might distinguish between spirituals, the blues, and various shouts and dance customs, but in practice the lines blurred and black music included all the expressions of an oppressed group in sound.

These African and slave developments constantly encountered the white community and white taste. Slaves were slaves, and they not only heard white hymns and popular tunes everywhere, they had to play for whites and please them. Black and white musical habits thus had to fuse in various ways. One obvious example was the cakewalk: slaves who had once been in the habit of putting on a show for themselves in the clothing of their white master became free performers who worked out exaggerated two-step routines, preening and clowning but displaying considerable musical and dramatic skill as well. The winning couple "took the cake" offered as a prize, but the music meanwhile went down in history as something fresh and genuine, a black art form that pleased white audiences. By the early twentieth century, no less a composer than Claude Debussy had put his "Golliwog's Cakewalk" into a suite of piano pieces for children, most of whom had never seen a black. The rhythms had not only been modified for the Western notational system, they had emerged as a means through which a leading modernist could modify the artistic expression of time.

The first recognizable art form to emerge from these musical cross-fertilizations was ragtime. Ragtime was essentially a piano music that domesticated some of the African effects which made cross-rhythms and polyrhythms sound so original to American ears. When the effects were too complex to notate precisely, what emerged was the idea of "ragging" the melody or producing the effect of syncopation, where a piece began between the usual Western beats and then continued with the principal notes falling between the beats. The resulting compromise between African sound and Western notational system was not technically all that original—Bach had similar effects in "The Art of the Fugue"—but it sounded new enough so that it could become a kind of public symbol of the impact of black civilization upon white civilization in America. By the 1890s, ragtime was all the rage in the whorehouses and barrooms of the Mississippi River area, played by pianists who were usually black, self-trained, and unable to read Western music. Tom Turpin, James Scott, Eubie Blake, and Scott Joplin emerged as both composers and performers, and by the early twentieth century sheet music was spreading the new music to homes that otherwise would not have been able to participate in the development of the new form. Pianists taught themselves how to write down what they were trying to do or found assistants to help them, and soon daughters of the respectable white middle class could, in all innocence, be enthusiasts of a black art form.

Joplin became the most visible composer of ragtime. The son of a laborer and a domestic servant, he nevertheless grew up in a musical environment. His father played the violin, while his mother played the banjo and sang. During their time as slaves they had played not only for themselves and their community, but also for whites. Scott thus had ample opportunity to hear waltzes, schottisches, and quadrilles as well as cakewalks. He also heard much black church music, and in all probability learned effects from the habit blacks had of clapping their hands, often in a syncopated way, while they sang spirituals. The family of course was very poor, but seized whatever circumstances it could. Scott, for example, did much of his early practicing on pianos in the homes of white folks while his mother cleaned them.

The rise to fame was slow. Joplin played at first for black churches, schools, dance halls, but he yearned both socially and musically for acceptance in the respectable white world. The barriers proved all but insuperable for the man if not the music. He studied what European music he could; he got as far from home as the Chicago World's Fair; but he was doomed for most of his life to performances in saloons and whorehouses where the attention of patrons was all too often not on the music. In 1899 his "Maple Leaf Rag" appeared, to become his most popular piece and a staple of the craze for ragtime that began shortly thereafter. But Joplin profited little from his originality. Whites ran the music business and refused to pay more than token sums for the use of black songs. Wounded financially, Joplin also felt inferior socially; he wanted above all to achieve white respect for black talent, and he was sure that only in formal, European art forms would this be forthcoming. He labored away on larger works, most obviously the opera *Treemonisha*, but never managed to master any form except that one so closely associated with his name. His life thus provided, in its way, a rather sad paradigm for much ethnic achievement in America: untutored originality leading to popular success, but that success being emotionally unsatisfying. Ethnic artists wanted to be respected American artists, not realizing that the new things that they had to say were often incompatible with conventional white forms. In deemphasizing their roots, they gave up precisely what they had to offer. Ragtime was simply not compatible in any significant way with European opera, and any attempt to marry Europe, Africa, and America in this way was doomed to failure. Europeans quickly recognized the originality and cleverly adapted it for use especially in the ballet, but it took years before "respectable" black opinion was willing to express pride in these important racial contributions to the culture of the world.

PART IV

A NATIONAL CULTURE
1901–1941

Chapter 10

The Reunion with Europe, 1901–1941

As America entered the twentieth century its creative life seemed hopelessly divided. On the one hand, progressives and pragmatists in effect said to their young: adjust and improve a worthy democratic culture. Write about the possibilities of the one country on earth that seems to offer hope for all mankind. Do so in a language that average citizens can understand, whether that language be in words, pictures, music, stone, or on a stage. On the other hand, a growing number of expatriates said to their young: America is a philistine, provincial land. The legacies of a narrow puritanism are too constricting either for you or your language. If you don't want to go into some area of business, the place is hopeless and derivative. Go to Europe, get some culture, become cosmopolitan. The politically disinherited, chiefly blacks, agreed with both sides for their own reasons. They found life in America unsupportive, but they did not have the opportunities to go abroad for any kind of freedom: a person has to have an economic base to enjoy political freedom, and the luxury of travel to broaden cultural horizons follows only later. Blacks had to stay at home and develop alternative means of expression: to become, in effect, internal emigrés rather than external ones.

The emphasis here should be not on most of the issues that have dominated American cultural history through the nineteenth century but on a new concept: the languages of difference. While progressives and pragmatists were developing a democratic language, a language of sameness, of democracy, of community, the growing ranks of what became known as modernists were developing the languages of modernism: languages of difference, of aristocracy, and of exile. Because American democracy did not nourish them, they left it either for Europe, if they could afford it, or for the underground if they could not. They learned to speak cubism, futurism, fauvism, Orphism, and imagism, and they did it to the chief language that did not end in *ism*: to jazz, that language of outgroups that synthesized the major heritages of American blacks and spoke freshly to all those eager for something genuine and new. Modernism, cosmopolitanism, and Europe went together, and did so until the forces of politics and war drove artists back to America during the 1930s. By then, the country was far more open to receive them than it had been in 1900. The National Culture, thus, proved inhospitable only for two generations. The language of democracy and the languages of modernism spoke to each other after all; they just needed an extended period of mutual study. After 1945, America proved cosmopolitan enough to speak sensibly to Europe; Europe in turn had learned some important truths about democracy and was willing to listen, and indeed to talk back as soon as it could get itself rebuilt.

The story of the American reunion with Europe thus begins with Gertrude Stein, a highly improbable figure on the world cultural stage, who took up many of the goals of Henry James, the ideals of William James, and the artistic alienation of James Whistler, and just after the turn of the century went to Paris and set up a salon that proved legendary in its success in introducing talented Americans to their European counterparts. The story continues with the many writers she influenced with her peculiar ideas of prose style, and then shifts to her chief rival, the poet Ezra Pound, who accomplished in London much the same thing for poets. It then shifts its focus to examine the intellectual migration from Europe to America—a subject scholars have only recently begun examining, so complex are the issues, disciplines, and languages involved. The goals for all of these cultural travelers, no matter how different they might seem on the surface, remained the same: the freedom to exercise the imagination, to create as the spirit dictated, and not to accept the impositions of society, whether they be impositions of religion, of economic ideas, or of arbitrary governments. The long-term result for America was the establishment of a cosmopolitan culture, where people from a countless variety of backgrounds could create largely as they wished without having to have their works approved by anyone. However chaotic the result might have seemed, it was preferable to the alternatives that came close to destroying European civilization entirely.

II

Gertrude Stein (1874–1946) and her brother Leo (1872–1947) grew up in the family of a prominent Jewish businessman whose affairs took him across the Western world. She never knew the stern theology, the boring Sundays, and the hostility to aesthetic perception which other Americans absorbed. She never concerned herself with the survival of the fittest or the disappearance of God. Instead, she grew up traveling in America, Austria, France, and England. Pampered by indulgent parents, she experienced two foreign languages and three foreign cultures before she was five years old, and only then settled in a stable home in Oakland, California. She could thus assume a proprietary attitude toward all of America and not worry too much about any one place; and she could assume the importance of Europe without having to worry about its corrupting effect on American manners and morals. As an adult, she consistently maintained the position that, for a creative person, life in a foreign culture was essential. For her, as for James and Whistler, Paris was an obvious choice, and she remained there far more devotedly than either of them for most of her adult life. In part due to her presence and influence, indeed, much of American culture during the years before and after World War I existed in Paris, as if undergoing an apprenticeship in a school of advanced aesthetics.

Gertrude and Leo Stein both absorbed the best of the traditional culture before expatriating themselves. Both worked closely with William James during their period of study in Cambridge in the 1890s and emerged with feelings of reverence toward that extraordinary intelligence. Gertrude in particular immersed herself in physiological psychology and was involved in several significant experiments while still a student. James took her seriously as a possible professional in the field, and she went on to the Johns Hopkins Medical School. There she seemed to be one of several women who were achieving places for themselves in professions that were opening up to them for the first time in American life. But she did not have the drive and the discipline to finish her degree. After beginning well she became bored, her work deteriorated, and she left. By the outward standards of the Protestant Ethic, she was a failure; unconcerned, she went off to Europe to experiment with her writing and to absorb the new styles of painting.

The medical training had not been wasted. From it she took both important ideas and stimulating experiences. From James in particular she took ideas about the stream of consciousness, about habit and the way unconscious drives expressed themselves in speech and behavior. From her medical training she took memories of her period as a midwife, when she traveled frequently into the poor black districts of Baltimore to deliver babies and absorb cultures foreign to her own. She soon put these influences to use, most successfully in the "Melanctha" section of *Three Lives* (1909), where a black woman and her lover try to work out their differences and communicate effectively. Leo carried many of these same interests into serious study of psychoanalysis and a life spent in study of Freud's theories; Gertrude tried to establish new verb forms, new speech patterns, and new fictions that would enable one consciousness to study the workings of another. Never as successful in any one work of art as Henry James, she nevertheless not only began the study of blacks in serious American fiction, she also gathered around her a group of painters and writers who shared her goals and who in time went beyond her in their own achievements.

Leo Stein was fascinated by the work of Flaubert, and Gertrude modeled

Three Lives in many ways on *Trois Contes*, and especially on "Un Coeur Simple," the story of a lower-class woman living on the edge of insanity. For Stein as for James, Flaubert was a pioneer in the development of a modernist aesthetic, seemingly realistic and traditional in his art, yet modern in his obsessions with form and his explorations of consciousness. Melanctha, like Félicité, existed chiefly in her relationships; she had her attachments, her loves and hatreds with a few people around her, and thus seemed not so much a real person as an object defined in space by other objects that were also defined in space. Cubism had not yet achieved an aesthetic to deal with this sort of sensibility, but Stein was already experimenting with a sense of the multiple perspectives that existed upon any person or object and trying to fashion a prose that would do in literature what her friend Pablo Picasso did in painting. Dialogue became central in such a situation, as the means by which a consciousness tried to establish itself; dialogue was the way a person communicated, and it was also the way a person discovered a perception of self through the perceptions of someone else. Dialogue in some sense became the verbal means for establishing the multiple perspectives of cubism.

In "Melanctha" and in her other experiments, Stein thus tried to use dialogue to establish these multiple perspectives on consciousness—with mixed results. Writers from Sherwood Anderson to Richard Wright became fascinated by her attempts to write in a continuous present. She maintained that the present was essentially timeless, in a sense parallel to the concepts of Freud. Nothing was ever lost on her characters, and their histories, memories, dreams, fears, and perceptions all intruded into their conversation and consciousness. The unconscious, preconscious, and conscious merged, often with chaotic results. She explained her work not by references to Freud or James, but by references to Cézanne. She pointed to his apples and his chairs and insisted that these objects catalyzed her writing. Every writer had the privilege of explaining how she began, but in this case knowledge about Cézanne did not help much. Stein may have been concerned with apples, but her consciousness of those apples has been the focus of subsequent scholarship.

Stein was soon at work on the enormous novel eventually published as *The Making of Americans*. It proved unreadable for all but the most devoted, but like occasional works in the history of literature, it was important for what it represented and for the influence it had on writers who probably never read more than a few pages of it. Shapeless and unfocused, it was an attempt to tell the story of America through the experience of Stein's own family, but it collapsed in large part because Stein was interested only in herself, her own perceptions, and how she became the person she was. Like most modernists, she had lost interest in the larger world and tended to subsume everything to the consciousness of the present moment. Yet as so often happened, an older art form—here the form of the traditional Victorian three-volume novel—was the form with which the author was most familiar; this new material was poured into the old, worn-out forms, and like new wine in old wineskins it burst its container. Henry James managed to make an effective transition, and European novelists were soon far more effective than any Americans in working out the formal implications of modernism, but in this case Stein's failure was worth noting because it demonstrated so conclusively what was happening. The form of Flaubert could not contain the apples of Cézanne nor the perspectives of Picasso.

Much of what Stein wrote impressed readers as nonsense, but in places she was capable of brief statements that summed up her ideas clearly. Instead of Cézanne's apples, she substituted the concept of the noun and the earthy quality of potatoes. Stay true to the noun, she told people, stay true to the real object. Even as she tried to recreate the flow of consciousness, she thought the writer should "forget grammar and think about potatoes." Writers should not worry about conventional ways of meaning and perceiving, but should observe, as it were, one potato after another, for such repetitions of objects were what a functioning consciousness perceived. This meant repeating perceptions over and over again, and Stein's repetitions soon became her hallmark. In several works, with minor variations, appeared the line, "a rose is a rose is a rose is a rose," and it became her most famous. For her, the roses were like potatoes, or the apples of Cézanne, but for average readers they were merely a ludicrous outburst from a strange woman who had left America to live abroad a life that might not bear close examination. She snorted. For her the language was wearing out and she was trying to make it new. Her strange repetitions made people think about language and realize a new vitality for the noun. She told audiences that their questions were proof that she had succeeded: they not only remembered her sentences, they quoted them correctly. She was no fool, she said, and she knew people didn't go around repeating themselves all the time. But she insisted that "in that line the rose is red for the first time in English poetry for a hundred years."

III

Of the many writers, painters, and musicians who acknowledged Stein's influence, Ernest Hemingway stood out for both originality and achievement. For his generation, World War I had worn out the language; what for Stein had been an excess of Victorian rhetoric and an inability to express the flux of the conscious present was for Hemingway's generation a massive fraud: as the narrator of *A Farewell to Arms* summed it up, he "was always embarrassed by the words sacred, glorious, and sacrifice and the expression in vain." He associated them with war proclamations which stressed the patriotic virtues of acts which seemed utterly senseless to the common soldiers involved. Stein's hatred of clichés became Hemingway's hatred of abstractions; both took refuge in the close examination of the concrete as the means for expressing consciousness. "There were many words that you could not stand to hear and finally only the names of places had dignity. Certain numbers were the same way and certain dates and these with the names of places were all you could say and have them mean anything." All abstract words like "glory" or "honor" or "courage" were "obscene beside the concrete names of villages, the numbers of roads, the names of rivers. . . ." The war had blown up everything but roses and potatoes.

Like many writers of his generation, Hemingway grew up in a traditional Protestant home and rebelled against it. His parents were members of the upper-middle class in a Chicago suburb, and they did everything possible to bring up their children in a morality that ignored unconscious drives, sexuality, and precise concrete expression. The war had liberated the young from this sort of repressive prissiness, but war could not supply a style. War could make long Victorian novels impossible, it could prevent the discussion of ideals, it could make the political process seem contemptible, but it could not teach young writers the means of coping with the pain and emptiness which resulted from physical violence and the loss of meaning. Stein's lessons, and indeed her comforting physical presence in Paris, seemed to bring together the lessons which writers needed. Jews had avoided the arid wasteland of Protestant prohibition; Jews understood wars and other disasters; Jews had not corrupted the American mind with abstractions. Stein in effect became the Jewish mother of the next generation of American writers, whether Protestant like Hemingway or Roman Catholic like F. Scott Fitzgerald. Her epitaph about the young people of the 1920s, that they were all a "lost generation," was at the front of *The Sun Also Rises*, and supplied them with a sort of negative identity when all else had failed.

Many of the modernists felt most comfortable as symbolists, unable to name their topics directly but preferring to evoke them through the representation of other objects. They also missed the comfort of the old beliefs even as they rejected their content, and in Hemingway these conflicts came together in ways that evoked traditions that were well established in American writing. Hawthorne and Emerson had known all about dying religions and the need to transcend narrow moral prohibitions, and no one had worked more effectively in a natural landscape devoid of a just God than Melville. Hemingway's work was suffused with the symbols of the religions he could not accept, both the Protestantism of his parents and the Roman Catholicism of the Spain he loved. In his earliest stories of the Michigan woods, the concrete details of hunting and fishing became the external events, the potatoes which the writer observed as his central character calmed his shattered nerves by walking, observing, putting up his tent, casting his bait, or absorbing Indian life. In the Europe of the first novels, such images persisted and continued to suggest the rituals of a dead religion. In the Spanish bullfight, with its elaborate ritual of danger, courage, and death, Hemingway found an influential substitute for the sacrifice of Christ in the Holy Communion service. Modern man had to make his own substitutes for religion, and the bullfight, or the hunting expedition, or a fight between boxers, became symbolic of what had happened to the consciousness of Western man. The style Gertrude Stein had so much difficulty using herself seemed in the hands of her disciples the natural speech of people for whom ideals were dead, nouns were the only reality, and rituals in nature the last refuge of wounded modern man.

IV

The vogue of Hemingway, his friends and enemies, and the general popularity of a phrase like "the lost generation," can leave the impression that the most important American contributions to modernism were in prose: the novel, short story, and journalism. In some contexts this was true enough, as young people imitated the speech and assimilated the ideas in *The Sun Also Rises* and the Michigan short stories. Well into the 1950s, promising young writers were still going to Paris and trying to be young Hemingways, even as the old one deteriorated into a suicidal alcoholic whose work painfully parodied itself. Professors kept it alive in distant lands, perhaps because Hemingway's vocabulary and sentence structure made him a relatively easy master of a hard but vital language for students to study. A very few pages went a very long way.

But while Hemingway will always have devoted male followers, one of his friends and correspondents has turned out to be the more important influence. Ezra Pound has become the dominant figure in the literary and cultural history of the period after about 1909. Arriving unknown in London, he quickly made friends with such major figures as poet William Butler Yeats and editor Ford Madox Hueffer, and effectively took over their salons and influenced the younger poets in ways more substantial and more significant for the internal history of literature than anything Hemingway and the Stein salon managed to accomplish. While the popular anecdotes came out of Paris and preempted attention, a linguistic revolution was coming out of London between 1909 and the outbreak of the war in Europe in the summer of 1914. In this context, Hemingway was one of Pound's disciples in prose, and he knew it. And Pound, in turn, was so much a disciple of Walt Whitman that he wrote a famous poem about the relationship.

For a few brief years, modernism in poetry led a geographically confusing life between three great cities, with Pound's adaptations of Whitman's precedents providing a unifying thread. In America, in Chicago, Harriet Monroe began to publish *Poetry*, with Pound as her chief European talent scout. In a remarkably short time, Pound, T. S. Eliot, William Carlos Williams, and Robert Frost were all publishing there, and young subscribers all over the country could see between two covers something of what was happening in London. The older meters began to die out, and free verse became something of a hallmark of liberation. The new topics, which Whitman had pioneered—sex, the city, poverty, suffering—were taken for granted, and a new emphasis developed on the most recent problems of civilization, such as the impact of technology and the deadening impact of mass existence. Above all, the young developed a belief in experimentation for its own sake. They wanted to speak a new language in both matter and manner, and anything "new" seemed self-justifying.

In London, the French ideas about art that Henry James and Whistler had discovered were making headway among a small group. Most of the British public was unaware of the threat to their most cherished notions about art, and assumed that figures like Oscar Wilde were simply publicity hounds with erotic tastes that went well beyond what the law would tolerate. But Wilde, Whistler, and their entourages were actually the first scouts of a large literary and cultural movement that would eliminate most of the conventionally accepted figures active at the time from the history books. In their distrust of nature, in their belief in form and their disbelief in a comforting deity, they were undermining the old verities even though their own works were not yet of long-term significance. The drawings of Aubrey Beardsley, the plays of Wilde and George Bernard Shaw, and the earliest poetry of William Butler Yeats were all harbingers of the future.

But the future was in France, a France not discussed in the Stein salon. French literature arrived in London in 1899 with the publication of Arthur Symons' little book, *The Symbolist Movement in Literature*. English-language writers had known something of the new developments in Paris, but Symons brought them all together in a journalistic way and gave English the word *symbolism* with which to describe what was happening. What had seemed merely a period of decadence in English culture, the "yellow nineties," was proving to be a period full of possibilities. In time, English-language writers especially in anthropology and literary criticism would add notions to those already in the air. A young American like T. S. Eliot, for example, could discover the work of Jules Laforgue in Symon's book, pillage James G. Frazer's *The Golden Bough*, season with concepts from Jessie Weston's *From Ritual to Romance*, and produce by 1922 *The Waste Land*, the poem which more than any other work summed up what the modernists were trying to do. Not since the Transcendentalists had imported German romanticism through the writings of Coleridge and Carlyle had the literature of both sides of the Atlantic been in such close relationships both to other countries and to ideas from other disciplines.

For American poetry, the key movement was Imagism. In 1912, Ezra Pound,

Hilda Doolittle, and Richard Aldington had their famous teashop conversation in Kensington that resulted in the publication of *Des Imagistes: An Anthology* in 1914. It was characteristic of Pound that he organized his friends into something that had a name and a platform that could attract attention to itself and help along the careers of all of them. It was also characteristic that he brought in a pseudo-French title, to add a certain panache to the whole affair as well as to indicate the persistent debt which all of them felt to French literature. Amy Lowell arrived from Boston, to add her wealth and social status to a movement skeptical of both, and for a brief period Imagism seemed the wave of the future. In 1915, Aldington gave it its most succinct summary as a platform for new verse; poetry had six great essentials: it should use the language of common speech and insist on exact words and not merely decorative ones; it should create new rhythms, of which free verse should be one; it should allow a poet freedom in the choice of his subject; it should present an image, rendering particulars rather than generalities; it should produce hard, clear poetry; and it should strive for concentration. As its best, Imagist verse did those things, but Pound himself soon tired of it and went on to other and more exciting experiments, and Amy Lowell elbowed out most of the competition and led the movement down paths that were distinctly less original.

On the surface, Pound seemed about as far from Walt Whitman as a person could get, but in fact he represented in important ways the confluence of French, English, and American literary traditions and the resulting birth of modernism as a recognizable climate of creativity. Although born in Idaho, he had grown up in a Philadelphia suburb and had attended the University of Pennsylvania. Long engaged to Hilda Doolittle, he was also friendly with William Carlos Williams, and these university relationships continued to shape American poetry for the next five decades. Pound specialized in late Medieval and early Renaissance romance languages, and for some time seemed to be on the conventional path into a life of scholarship in these areas. Little was of interest to him in America, and he used his graduate fellowship money to go to Europe and to begin the course of reading that so influenced his verse. His early prose discussed this material creatively and his early poetry imitated it to the point at times of loose translation. But Pound evolved swiftly; he found the arguments of T. E. Hulme and the platform of Imagism persuasive, and was soon producing a hard, clear, classical verse that was clearly modernistic in its implications. But unlike the British, he was an American for whom Walt Whitman was at least as important as any French writer. The solitary singer, the free man in the American landscape, the speaker of democratic rhythms, was too important to forget, and Pound made his famous "Pact" with his predecessor: like a son he had quarreled with his father, but the time had come to make friends. "It was you who broke the new wood,/ Now is the time for carving./ We have one sap and one root—/ Let there be commerce between us."

For his generation, Whitman had been well-read. He loved Italian opera, studied ancient history, and was an amateur expert on astronomy. Pound proved to be even more curious. In addition to the French literary interests expected in someone of his academic background, he soon felt a fascination for the Orient in many of its aspects. He went through the manuscripts of the American Orientalist Ernest Fenollosa and thought he discerned lessons for Imagism in written Chinese. Each character was, for Pound, a separate image, unsullied by connecting material, and thus each Chinese word was an Imagist poem. Modern scholars of Chinese deny it, but for Pound the fascination was a useful device. An excellent critic and translator, he seemed at times in his early work too close to his sources, too derivative even in his innovations. Study of the Orient helped him to distance himself from Western culture—the culture which did not reward his academic or his literary efforts, and with which he quarreled throughout his long life. To be creative, American conservatives often had to quarrel with their true past—the past of puritanism, empiricism, and democratic liberalism—and choose a past in which they could live free. While conventional liberal artists could be satisfied with political freedom, and work like Vachel Lindsay toward the apotheosis of Lincoln or the election of Bryan, modernists had to free the mind from mundane concerns and find their voices in the timeless world of great art. Pound found more to admire in French, Provençal, and Chinese art than he did in American and British art, and through such study liberated himself as much as he could from the expectations of a culture that had little regard for poets.

His great disciple in art was T. S. Eliot. Pound specialized in discovering geniuses for Harriet Monroe and other editors, and in Eliot he found a student worthy of his attention. Also a graduate student in flight from the normal career progress of a young professor, Eliot had come to France to study at the Sorbonne. The outbreak of the war drove him to England, and there he found a religion and a cultural tradition which appealed to him far more than the New England Unitarianism of his St. Louis childhood. But where Pound went to the Orient, Eliot went into anthropology, myth, and religion; in addition to the wealth of material in *The Golden Bough*, he also read modernist prose carefully, and in Joyce's *Ulysses* found the inspiration that fused his learning into an appropriate form. The novel was appearing gradually as he wrote *The Waste Land*, and in 1923 he reviewed the complete work in words that applied as much to his poem as they did to the novel. *Ulysses* was "the most important expression which the present age has found" and its "mythical method" had great importance for art. By this term, Eliot meant "manipulating a continuous parallel between contemporaneity and antiquity." With Joyce, this meant the parallels between the life of Leopold Bloom in contemporary Dublin and the life of Ulysses long ago. This method was "a way of controlling, of ordering, of giving shape and significance to the immense panorama of futility and anarchy which is contemporary history." He then argued that psychology, ethnology, and *The Golden Bough* "have concurred to make possible what was impossible a few years ago. Instead of narrative method we may now use the mythical method. It is, I seriously believe, a step toward making the modern world possible in art."

So it proved. Eliot's first draft of *The Waste Land* was original enough, clearly a personal expression along the Whitman pattern of his recent experiences in Europe. But under Pound's editorial hand the poem became a showcase of modernist technique. It shifted continuously from the present of London to various periods in the past; it seemed to have no consistent plot or narrative voice. Like a modern painter or film maker, Eliot experimented with montage techniques, pasting one medium so to speak on top of another. He took on the modern city with the ruthlessness of a Dos Passos or a Döblin, the dull boredom as well as the noise and the dirt. Bits of dialogue wandered in and out between arcane material from classical mythology, and the concept of the stream of consciousness suddenly seemed central to American literature. Pound's editing sharpened contrasts, focused on images, and made for a poem that seemed to impress and bewilder people at the same time. But those who read it couldn't seem to get it out of their minds.

V

The work of Pound and Eliot represented something of a high point of achievement for American cosmopolitanism. Here were Americans who had taken their ideas to Europe, absorbed European influences, and created work influential on literate people irrespective of where they lived. Even as they did so, political circumstances in Europe were creating a situation in which creative Europeans could no longer function. America the philistine looked increasingly attractive to refugees from Hitler and Stalin; its culture might seem thin, but its borders were open to the talented, and fruitful careers were possible there. An European intellectual and cultural migration soon took place which dwarfed the earlier American one, and the consequences for both American history and the history of the world were far more serious.

Migrants arrived in four areas of cultural achievement. In the hard sciences, the key area proved to be physics. During the years immediately after World War I, physics was already in the process of becoming internationalized, and Americans played a small but significant role in this process. Journal articles in German and English circulated throughout Europe and America, and a number of European centers became internationally known for bringing important scientists together. Work on quantum theory, the major concern of these years, proceeded with the cooperation of men ranging from Leipzig and Berlin in the east to Cambridge in the west, and there were centers of innovation in the smaller countries as well. Many Americans came in contact with this thought at places like Ernest Rutherford's Cavendish laboratory at Cambridge, and American money, supplied chiefly through the various agencies of the Rockefeller Foundation, brought significant numbers of Europeans to America to pursue their work. It was a propitious time, since America had finally reached something like scientific maturity and had the beginnings of academic and institutional resources necessary to assist these scholars and to profit from their presence.

Given these early contacts, scientists could also profit from a special clause in the American immigration laws. The country was no longer as hospitable to immigrants as it had been, but clause 4d of the National Origin Act allowed clergymen, teachers in higher education, and their families to enter America without having to qualify for the quotas allotted to their countries of origin. Once in America, they found that the language of science was international enough so that linguistic problems were not so great as they otherwise might have been. They found as well that American university structures were far freer and more open than those in Europe. In Europe, the chair professor could dominate research in his field, and need not communicate with his associates. In America, a scientist found that his status and dignity suffered from the more democratic and indiscriminate atmosphere, but his mind profited. Departments were larger and relations between separate departments closer. Money was more available for equipment, travel, and publication; graduate students offered creative stimulation within the field, and colleagues from outside fields offered new perspectives and searching questions. Coupled with the disruptions caused by emigration, the impact on the best minds was extraordinarily stimulating.

Between 1927 and 1933, conditions in Germany deteriorated visibly. Many scientists preferred to ignore the rising anti-Semitism and the success of the Nazi party, but did so at their peril. In 1933, organizations began forming to assist displaced scholars, the first being the Academic Assistance Council in England. The leading emigré force in the Council was Leo Szilard, the energetic Hungarian physicist who later played such a major role in American nuclear development. The leading symbol for the group was Albert Einstein, already world-famous and as a Jew the perfect figure for obtaining publicity for the plight of those scholars who were losing their positions all over Germany. England, however, did not have the academic or financial resources to absorb more than a few of the needy men, and America became the refuge of last resort. The Emergency Committee in Aid of Displaced German Scholars organized in May 1933, later to substitute the word *foreign* for *German*. The key institution was the University in Exile founded in New York at the New School for Social Research. Alvin Johnson, a founder of the school and editor of the *Encyclopedia of the Social Sciences*, had corresponded with or met many prominent German academics in the course of his work. When he read of the

Nazi decrees dismissing so many of the men he knew and respected, he raised money quickly and privately to set up an organization that would enable German scholars to continue working together as well as cushion the shocks of their arrival in a new country and their searches for permanent places in other institutions.

Many of the results of this emigration were intangible. It is always hard to measure the influence of the ideas of a gifted teacher. Even so, the arrival of roughly one hundred of the most eminent physicists produced in what had been Germany and Austria-Hungary, plus a scattering from Italy and elsewhere, measurably remade the map of American physics and had obvious impact on the entire world. A few examples suffice only to suggest the range of this achievement. At the Institute for Advanced Study in Princeton, New Jersey, the most eminent figure in 1933 may have been Albert Einstein, but the most influential proved to be a thirty-year-old Hungarian, John von Neumann. Einstein's creative work was over, but von Neumann was at the beginning of possibly the most distinguished career in recent American science. His most important practical invention was the modern electronic computer. Mathematicians as far back as Blaise Pascal had experimented with calculators, but von Neumann was the man who devised a general logical code that was able to deal with all problems in such a way that the computer did not have to be reset each time a problem was solved. He eventually made possible the construction of large computers that could solve an infinite number of problems and store the results for future use. In the opinion of his fellow workers, the modern computer that is so central to current government and business practice might never have been developed without von Neumann's work; at best, its development would have been delayed at least a decade.

Von Neumann was also deeply involved in the research into nuclear fission that proved to be the most spectacular contribution that the emigrés made. As Laura Fermi has told the story, between 1920 and 1927 Eugene Wigner, George Gamow, Felix Bloch, Hans Bethe, Edward Teller, and Victor Weisskopf all experimented with nuclear fission before their emigration to America. They arrived to find colleagues well prepared by the international contacts of the 1920s to profit from their insights and institutions well equipped with the large, powerful accelerating machines and other apparatus necessary for genuinely advanced experimentation. Men who had worked alone or in small groups found themselves working in large teams around each machine, and the advance of knowledge quickened remarkably because of the coming together of men from such diverse backgrounds who could work together with the most modern equipment. Leo Szilard came to America in 1937, with Enrico Fermi from Italy and Niels Bohr from Denmark close on his heels. Bohr brought the news that German scientists had discovered the fission of uranium. At this point physics became politics: the thought of Hitler having a functional atomic bomb was one of the most terrifying imaginable to a group of talented refugees. It motivated them to the extraordinary efforts of the next six years.

Szilard was a key mover in the group. A friend of Lewis L. Strauss, the future chairman of the Atomic Energy Commission, Szilard wrote Strauss of the fears the group had, meanwhile consulting hurriedly with Edward Teller, Eugene Wigner, and Enrico Fermi. Thus three Hungarians and an Italian began the process that led to the atomic bombs that were dropped on Japan in 1945. They wrote an urgent letter to President Roosevelt, bearing the prestigious signature of Albert Einstein, to inform the president of the danger that could threaten the country. The response of the government was predictably slow and uncomprehending, but the beginning of the large-scale European war and the increasing danger of American involvement soon facilitated action. An Advisory Committee on Uranium was established, and then a National Defense Research Committee, which included several scientists. Soon a secret scientific laboratory was established at Los Alamos, New Mexico, specifically to develop an atomic bomb. The group included von Neumann, J. Robert Oppenheimer, Teller, and Emilio Segrè, with Bohr and others visiting frequently.

The success of the atomic project, and the impact of the atom on world history, is too well known to require narration. But perhaps two aspects of the project need underlining to illustrate the cosmopolitan forces at work within American science. The men most deeply involved were mostly aliens and some were technically enemy aliens: Germans, Austrians, or Italians whose countries were at war with the United States. Yet America was so open that even these figures could quickly win places at major institutes and universities and be included in highly secret government projects. America was not without its own anti-Semitism and xenophobia, nor was the government without grave doubts at times about the loyalty of its most vital employees. In one of the more amusing examples of what could result from this difficult situation, Hans Bethe did highly technical work on the armor plating that reinforced the hulls and decks of warships and then applied theories of elasticity and shock waves to what he learned. The results were so important to the American navy that it classified them as secret; Bethe did not have security clearance, and so he was not allowed to consult his own paper in its subsequent drafts.

Of more enduring importance was the way European talent combined with characteristic American methods of procedure. In Europe, the individual talent and training of a physicist was often first-rate, but the culture did not encourage the immediate application of new research. There was no tradition of constant experimentation and use that had become traditional with American capitalism. Already weakened by emigration, European countries in the 1930s and 1940s were in no condition to do much with the ideas their remaining experts generated. Yet in America, the gap was at the most six years from the Einstein letter to the dropping of the first functional bomb, materially hastening the end of the war with Japan. The phase of production really began only in 1943. Science and government had long been close in Europe, but not in America; the migration of the scientists and the demands of war had exerted such pressure that an American tradition could change, and the culture absorb such an extraordinary collection of talented people.

Unlike the refugee scholars in the natural sciences, who spoke the international language of science and who possessed skills that were often immediately useful, the hundreds of trained social scientists who came to America in the 1930s faced severe problems of employment and language. Approximately five thousand American Ph.D.s were unemployed in 1933, money in university budgets was scarce, and learning to lecture in English was a severe psychological strain. The problems facing Hans Morgenthau upon his arrival were not unusual. Already a promising political scientist with two books and several years of teaching experience, he was informed by a girl at the agency designed to assist scholarly refugees that his chosen field was glutted with applicants and he should look for work as an elevator boy. His wife went to a Jewish employment organization and was told that she was too old at thirty-one even to apply for a sales-clerking job. He soon found work teaching nights at Brooklyn College, paid by the hour like a janitor; she worked at Macy's. Their living quarters were so inadequate that Irma Morgenthau showed up at work one day covered with bites from bedbugs; she was asked to stay home until her appearance improved. Hans Morgenthau's students at Brooklyn College taught him English and the couple fled to Kansas City, where Hans found university work. In time, he became one of the great figures of American political science at the University of Chicago, and came to world attention in the 1960s as a critic of American foreign policy in Vietnam.

The major impact of the migration on the social sciences was on sociology and psychology. In sociology, the impact was chiefly upon two sharply conflicting areas which continue to dominate American sociological discussion. The career of Paul Lazarsfeld represented the coming to America of the "research institute" model for research in sociology and the methodological style such institutes demanded. At the time he was a student, European training emphasized the study of philosophy and detached speculation about society. Lazarsfeld resisted this trend and when he arrived in America he found an important group of scholars beginning to insist on fieldwork, the study of personal documents, and the measurement of public opinion. His earlier work on the unemployed in the Austrian village of Marienthal had brought him to the attention of the Rockefeller Foundation, and he arrived in America in 1933 on a grant from that institution. Circumstances in Austria deteriorated seriously, and with the help of Robert Lynd at Columbia University Lazarsfeld participated in several projects in New York and neighboring New Jersey, investigating chiefly the radio, public opinion, and effective advertising. Odd as it may sound, he found his early experience in studying political activity in Vienna useful in analyzing American advertising, referring many years later to "the methodological equivalence of socialist voting and the buying of soap." Of particular importance for the future structure of American universities, he also found what he called "partly a psychological substitute for political activities" in the development of research institutes. Using experience derived from his Socialist party and youth-movement days, Lazarsfeld developed an organization that attached itself to a university but that independently negotiated contracts and pursued its research independent of any university faculty. Key members of the institute would have professorial status, and the institute would provide salaries and experience for young doctoral candidates and they performed functions for each contracted project. Unknown in the 1930s, such institutes now sometimes generate the majority of an American university's budget. Modern social science research is no longer conceivable without them.

Such work is also fraught with academic and institutional danger. One of the most influential critics of Lazarsfeld's innovations was the German emigré sociologist Theodor W. Adorno. A key member of the Marxist Institut für Sozialforschung in Frankfurt, Adorno arrived in America in 1938 to join the exiled institute in New York and to work on some of the same projects that involved Lazarsfeld. A man of great independence who prided himself on his ability to "transcend mere adjustment," Adorno compared his journey to work each day with Kafka's Nature Theater of Oklahoma, and he has recorded his astonishment at finding himself working in an unoccupied brewery under conditions that would "scarcely have been conceivable by the lights of the European academic community." A man of relentlessly Hegelian cast of mind, Adorno was mystified by the American emphasis on practicality and application. He soon became an enemy of many of the implications of the Lazarsfeld approach. To go from theory and ideology to data was the only responsible academic mode of procedure for Adorno; to allow data and projects to deter-mine research meant that the scholar abandoned his integrity and hired himself out to anyone willing to finance him. Science-oriented researchers prided themselves on the value neutrality of their work. Adorno scoffed, and insisted that merely choosing to work on such topics was a value judgment.

As a sociologist of music, he was also insistent on the value of culture and the inability of "science" to measure or evaluate that which was genuinely important in a given society. Adorno's decade in America led directly to his massive study of anti-Semitism and the potentially fascist character, *The Authoritarian Personality*, one of the seminal works of American sociology. It also led to an increasing acceptance, in the 1960s and after, of his criticisms of contracted, science-oriented research: students and radicals during the Vietnam War sud-denly found their universities and professors hopelessly compromised by years of service on government- and foundation-sponsored research, much of it now being used to fight an unpopular war in Asia, or to subvert radical governments in Africa and Latin America.

The impact of the emigration on psychology came earlier and proved even greater. American psychology had been an outpost of German influence from the time William James studied with Wilhelm Wundt in Leipzig until Freud came to America for his Clark University lectures in 1909. But for the next twenty years or so, American psychology was dominated by the behaviorism of John B. Watson. Anything philosophical, functionalist, or introspective went out of fashion, and experiments with animals, conditioned reflexes, and visible external behavior in general became the normal modes of procedure. Psychology became American and provincial, hostile both to general theory and to research on mental activity. In Germany, by contrast, the work of Max Wertheimer, Kurt Koffka, and Wolfgang Köhler had attacked earlier emphases on the perception of sensory elements. They replaced this empiricism with an emphasis on the Gestalt, or the entire unit of function. They insisted that meaningful activity could not be separated into stimuli and responses. It must be examined as a whole; a whole could not be divided into its parts without destroying what was important about it. The most famous research in the school occurred as a wartime accident: Köhler went to the Canary Islands to study chimpanzees, and the war forced him to remain in Africa for six years, with remarkable theoretical results. Köhler then came to America to enjoy a wide influence for his many publications and to catalyze several unforeseen applications of Gestalt theory. Through the work especially of Wertheimer and his student Catherine Stern, the methodology of the school was applied to elementary education in mathematics and the sciences, causing a change in pedagogy so great that even parents with Ph.D.s soon had trouble understanding the work their children began to bring home. Through Rudolph Arnheim, a student of Wertheim in Berlin, the psychology of art came to America and Gestaltist concepts have dominated that new field ever since.

Despite this influence, the Gestaltists had nowhere near the impact on the larger arena of American culture that psychoanalysis in its various forms had. The aging Sigmund Freud in Vienna relied increasingly on only a very few figures in the 1930s: chiefly his daughter Anna, and Heinz Hartmann. During the 1930s these two worked out the basis for what is now known as ego psychology, pushing Freudian investigation into the study of the entire human personality in its normal social contexts and changing the focus of Freudian analysis from early childhood toward adolescence and adulthood. Hartmann himself stopped for several years in Paris and Switzerland and did not reach America until 1941, but his basic interests came to the New World much earlier with the migration of Erik Erikson, the key younger man in the ego psychology group. Of mixed Danish, Jewish, and German background, Erikson had lived for several years as a wandering art student before settling in Vienna to teach at an experimental school for the children of parents who were either studying psychoanalysis or being psychoanalyzed for their own private problems. Erikson received his own analysis from Anna Freud and further confused his own sense of national identity by marrying a student of modern dance who was half-Canadian, half-American. The rise of Hitler meant open hostility to anything touching the "Jewish" profession of psychoanalysis. In effect, the entire field emigrated and Erikson arrived in Boston in 1933.

Erikson soon brought two key interests into American psychoanalytic practice. Through his friendships with anthropologists like Margaret Mead, Ruth Benedict, Gregory Bateson, and Scudder Mekeel, he became fascinated by research into Sioux Indian cultures. Through this work he began to see that he had to study entire cultures, and not simply the sick individuals who were the usual focus of psychoanalytic work. Customs, religions, and relationships were appropriate subjects for research, and Erikson had a particular interest in the socialization of the child: how he grows up, adapts himself to the needs of family and society, and becomes an adult. Second, Erikson slowly came to realize that psychoanalysis had erred in seeing a person as merely the sum of his problems, as an entity somehow to be cured. Erikson wished to transcend disease as the focus of attention; the metaphor he often used was that of a war correspondent trying to study "war" only by examining the front-line trenches. Just as war included all of society and much invisible activity, so the person included much behavior that was in no way sick. By 1950, Erikson had followed this interest to *Childhood and Society*, the influential book that developed Freud's three phases of the life cycle of the child into the eight phases of the normal adult. Many of his corollary theories made him into an American culture hero, especially influential during the campaign for black rights in the 1950s and the battle for educational reform in the 1960s. His subsequent books, *Young Man Luther* and *Gandhi's Truth*, both had a major impact on the methodology of historical writing as well as in the sophistication of psychoanalytic theory applied to adults.

As with any migration, the influence was not entirely one-way. The European scholars learned much from America even when they disliked the culture and preferred to return to Europe after the war. Adorno has written of how he stopped taking things for granted in America, and was in a way deprovincialized. The European emphasis on philosophy and theory broke down at least in part in the face of American empiricism and utilitarianism. European reverence for all that was scholarly and intellectual found difficulty surviving in a country so militantly egalitarian. Democratic forms had penetrated the whole of life in America, he wrote, while in Germany they were little more than the "formal rules of the game." Even so stubborn and resistant a man as Adorno could exult in the American sense that things were infinitely possible, and he especially admired the American resistance to fascism. Like Thomas Mann and a few

the humanities, the emigrés were most influential on academic philosophy.
ng the 1920s, the *Wiener Kreis* (or Vienna Circle) in Austria formulated its
k on metaphysics. Developing scientific ideas formulated originally by
nann von Helmholtz, Ernst Mach, and Albert Einstein and influenced by a
ber of more contemporary scientists and mathematicians, the *Wiener Kreis*
ulated the ideas now known in English as Logical Positivism. The leader for
period was Moritz Schlick, a man with an American wife and a fluent
mand of English. No one in the circle was familiar with American philoso-
, but in 1929 Schlick was a visiting professor at Stanford University, and the
t year Herbert Feigl visited Harvard. The two men made many friends, one
he most important being Charles A. Strong, a retired professor of philosophy
l psychology at Columbia who was also a son-in-law of John D. Rockefeller.
ong himself was fascinated by Einstein's theory of relativity and its philosoph-
l consequences and Rockefeller money was to be a significant factor in
inging philosophers to America and helping them find permanent places.

The Harvard connection became especially significant. Feigl found there the
ost original American theorist of physics, Percy W. Bridgman, whose *Logic of
odern Physics* (1927) was not only a classic of scientific thought but a book
aving much in common with Viennese patterns of thinking. Clarence I. Lewis,
lfred North Whitehead, and Suzanne K. Langer were there as well, and
V. V. O. Quine was only the most brilliant among the graduate students. Feigl
nd the rest did not know the work of Charles Sanders Peirce at the time, but
hey profited from the seminal work Peirce and William James had done in the
Cambridge area. Emphasizing a functionalist approach, these philosophers
stressed that you should never ask about the theory or metaphysics of meaning
of a concept, you should ask only about the rules according to which the function
is used. Philosophers elsewhere, especially those with strong religious feelings,
objected, but the work of the *Wiener Kreis* proved to be especially influential on
American psychology. Men like E. G. Boring, E. C. Tolman, C. L. Hill, and B. F.
Skinner gave the Viennese ideas a warm reception and carried their influence
far from their original sources.

It is a mistake, however, to dwell merely on professional contacts and technical influences. No one will ever measure the total impact of the intellectual
migration on American life; one can only suggest it with examples. The case of
Vassar College provides one. Vassar took onto its faculty the German art historian Richard Krautheimer, a specialist in early Christian archeology. For the
government, he gave invaluable advice during the war on the important monu-
ments in Rome that ought to be saved from destruction, and it is through his
influence that Rome emerged from the bombing virtually intact from an arche-
ological point of view. In his classes, Krautheimer had Phyllis Bronfman Lambert, heiress to the Seagram whiskey fortune and already on the path to a career
with Mies van der Rohe. When her father began to plan another architectural

others, Adorno chose to return to Germany; they perhap:
as much as they had brought over a decade earlier.

In the arts, the immigrants made the greatest impact
though German innovators had been creating modern "fun
for some years, as far as Americans were concerned the :
movement in the field was the publication of Le Corbusier'
ture (1922), translated into English in 1928. In it, Le Corl
neoclassical columns, pediments, and entablatures that litte
landscape. Instead, he asked architects to look at pure mod
liners, airplanes, cars, skeletal factories, cylindrical grain ele\
that emerged would be humane, objective, and functional. I
seum of Modern Art staged an important show that pictured t
ture and gave it its name. Published as *The International Style* b
Hitchcock and Philip Johnson, the catalog laid down the prin
erned much of the best American architecture for the next
building should display the true character of its construction and
of its intended function. Instead of the solid mass apparent in
there should be the effect of volume; the symbol of a new building
a brick but an open box. Buildings should seem regular and stanc
avoid all unnecessary decoration.

These ideas took root in America through the direct influence
After spending three years in England, Walter Gropius, the famous
the German Bauhaus, came to America in 1937 and an influen
Harvard. He soon brought Marcel Breuer to join him. Mies van der
to the Midwest, and two other former Bauhaus teachers later joined
Illinois Institute of Technology. Having the resources of one of the wo
universities, Gropius quickly made Cambridge, Massachusetts, the wo\
for the exchange of modern ideas on architecture. Through his fi
Architects Collaborative (TAC), he established a modernist, collectivi
which put into influential structures the ideas that had been gener:
Europe for three decades. Mies' opportunities were only somewhat less
Henry Heald, the president of IIT, commissioned him to design a co.
campus. The result, plus subsequent structures built in Chicago nearby,
Mies world-famous. America played its role as well: it not only supplie
institutional and financial support which had been so lacking in Germany, i
supplied ideas developed from the traditional balloon-frame housing of
England, which were particularly influential on Gropius and Breuer; and n
modern technology vital to making functionalist ideas possible: new kind
tinted glass, surfacing material, sealants, and mechanical equipment. As witl
many aspects of the emigration, it was this unpredictable combination of Eu
pean ideology and training and American support, willingness to experimei
and utilitarian invention that made these innovations possible.

horror for the New York skyline to be the headquarters for Seagram Distillers, Mrs. Lambert was able to change his mind and have him select Mies as his architect. Mies produced one of the most beautiful and publicized structures of modern architecture. No one will ever know how many other examples of indirect cultural transmission took place unobserved by historians.

In countless ways, then, the intellectual migration of the 1930s marked the end of American provincialism and the emergence of America as a cosmopolitan, modern culture. Americans had been seeking out Europe on its own turf for generations, paying homage to the old and established. The need for such pilgrimages was largely over by the late 1920s, as Americans by that time had found their true voices—whether in the novels of Ernest Hemingway or in the music of Aaron Copland. By then the tide was reversing, and Europeans found that expertise was not enough; that political stability, tolerance, openness to change, and a democratic pluralism were essential to true innovation. By the end of World War II, with most Americans still at home and many Europeans choosing to remain in their adopted country, young people growing up could take cosmopolitanism for granted. For better or for worse, they were citizens of the world who happened to be Americans.

Chapter 11

The Indigenous Arts, 1901–1941

Yet American democracy was not all arid prairie. For many highly educated individuals, the pressures of Victorian culture could seem stifling, and escape the only way to find the freedom from convention that creativity required. Others did not agree. Black culture developed with little consciousness of Europe. The children of immigrants found European inspiration at home and were usually too cut off from higher education to find gentility of any kind much of a threat. A few major artists rebelled against European conventions for reasons of their own. After World War I, the cultivated European modernists and the self-trained American folk artists took more and more from each other's traditions. As American literature and music gained an audience in Europe, and as European modernists began to flee to the West, advanced artists with the full benefit of European exposure began to rediscover their own country. As the mature careers of such figures as Aaron Copland and William Faulkner indicated, an artist could pick and choose from both European and American materials by the late 1920s and feel comfortable with such new freedoms by the mid-1930s. This assimilation laid the groundwork for the cosmopolitan culture that emerged after World War II.

II

Various innovations in black music developed all along the Mississippi River in the 1880s and 1890s, but the place which proved the most fruitful was the city of New Orleans. The unique environment there fostered cultural experiments that could not have taken place anywhere else in America. By 1917 those developments had come together to form jazz, and with the migration of blacks in search of more rewarding employment opportunities than they could hope to find in the South, the new art form spread rapidly north to Chicago and New York.

New Orleans was, first of all, the one urban area in the country where neither

British nor Protestant values were predominant. It was a city French and continental in its cultural tone, and blacks were a part of this. They had often moved there from Caribbean islands, spoke languages derived from French and Spanish, and when they achieved economic success turned to Paris as the place for holidays or the education of children. Roman Catholicism was the dominant religion, and that meant that Protestant ideas about fun, sin, morality, and music never controlled the ruling classes. People were free to enjoy music especially, and few Sundays in the city were complete without band concerts, dances, and musical performances either in the city itself or out on Lake Pontchartrain.

Second, blacks in New Orleans enjoyed better social conditions than anywhere else in the country. Slavery had been relatively easy there, and even before emancipation a skilled lower class of masons, carpenters, and blacksmiths had developed, making the economic transition to freedom far easier. Housing in the city was never rigidly segregated, and for a generation many black children even had the chance to attend integrated schools—a practice which only the restrictive laws of the 1890s eliminated. The music and the easy racial atmosphere often went together: New Orleans was probably the only place in the country where black musicians were commonly the music teachers of middle-class white girls. Indeed, racial intermixing on less exalted levels was also common, and many young white males were in the habit of keeping mulatto mistresses, formally set up in separate houses after agreement with the mothers of the girls. The children of such relationships soon formed an identifiable class of black French creoles who often attended the same schools as the white children of the same fathers. An abnormally large number of talented jazz musicians emerged from this group.

Third, New Orleans had a large but informal system of black club life that attempted to unify the community and secure it against disaster. Even American whites had few agencies to help them in time of sickness or sudden death, and for blacks, with their limited financial resources, the situation was even more serious. Black clubs thus served as voluntary insurance companies as well as social institutions, and joined the churches in sponsoring asylums, schools, and fund drives. One of their special activities was the funeral: every member could rest assured that he would leave the earth with a long funeral march to the cemetery, and that his surviving brothers would then burst into a series of lively tunes to speed him on his way. Generations of young people who have danced to "When the Saints Go Marching In" have largely forgotten the origins of the tune in the New Orleans funeral ceremony.

Fourth, New Orleans benefited from its location as the chief port of the entire South. As such, sailors from all over the world arrived and departed, bringing not only their tunes but their instruments. After the end of the Spanish-American War, their numbers included troops as well, trying to get home from Cuba or from military camps on the nearby mainland. These soldiers often played instruments and some were in military bands, and when they needed some ready cash they proved willing to pawn their instruments in the city. Black children thus had a far better market in which to buy instruments than children elsewhere: many of course made their own, and many were handed down from talented parents, but as jazz developed it absorbed whatever instruments were most available, and thus many of the early jazz bands resembled military bands in their instrumentation. Brass predominated, with cornet and trombone often the most audible, and it took years before jazz musicians perfected the saxophone or replaced the cornet with the more European sound of the trumpet.

Finally and inevitably, New Orleans and its whorehouse district deserve mention. Named Storyville after the politician who sponsored the appropriate legislation, the district brought together black musicians as well as those engaged in less exalted professions. The sumptuous decor of the houses usually included a piano, where ragtime proved to be the most popular form, and nearby were the cabarets where small bands could entertain customers and facilitate the purchase of profitable drinks. By about 4:00 A.M. the houses closed, and then the musicians and singers gathered on their own time. Both ragtime and Dixieland jazz grew in this somewhat fetid atmosphere, and often tunes that originated on slave plantations or in churches metamorphosed into the new art forms.

The greatest of the musicians to emerge from Storyville was Louis Armstrong. Born between 1898 and 1900, he was the son of a day laborer and a prostitute. He never had much of a family life, appropriate food, clothing, education, or discipline and learned what he could from the sordid scenes that surrounded him. As he sold coal or delivered newspapers he was surrounded by music. Although unable to read a note, he intuited the rhythmic sense of what was going on. An incident involving a .38 revolver put him in a home for black orphans, and while there he picked up some of the rudiments of jazz performance on the tambourine, drums, and also horn. When he emerged at age sixteen, he supported himself by playing with pick-up groups and quickly attracted the attention of those entrepreneurs who ran the cabarets.

The pressures of war closed Storyville in 1917, causing economic disruption among musicians as well as prostitutes. After playing on the floating establishments that went up and down the Mississippi, Armstrong moved on to Chicago, where he and a number of other New Orleans players were soon bringing the new rhythms to the heart of the urban North. The advent of national prohibition helped corrupt many aspects of national life, and one key development was the nightclub with close connections to the gangster world. Musicians who cooperated with the prevailing social conditions found steady work and decent wages, and no veteran of Storyville could spend too long regretting the supremacy of hoodlums like Al Capone. Jazz thrived in this social underworld, and white musicians joined blacks in one of the few areas of American life where color mattered far less than talent. Armstrong's talent with cornet and then trumpet was a legend while he was still in his twenties, and while a member of the band of Joseph "King" Oliver he all but blew the competition out of the city. He also found a certain marital and musical stability in his alliance with Oliver's piano player, Lillian Hardin; she became Armstrong's wife, and in the process taught him European harmonics. The shift from cornet to trumpet proved to be the musical symbol of his evolution: the respected instrument of Europe replaced the military instrument of the Spanish-American War bands just as more conventionally European arrangements were replacing the unwritten spontaneities of Storyville.

Throughout the 1920s, usually in collaboration with a talented manager named Fletcher Henderson, Armstrong achieved a following among young musicians that has rarely been matched in American history. He was not only the first black to accomplish this, he accomplished it at the same time that the sophistication of the phonograph record made mass distribution possible. Where the early rags had to be written down or else recorded definitively on piano rolls, by the middle 1920s Dixieland jazz could go out over the radios and the phonographs of the land to show talented youths what the musical possibilities really sounded like. Groups like the Hot Fives and the Hot Sevens, on records like those from Okeh, were symbols of liberation in a "jazz age," separating the taste of the young from the taste of the old. Color seemed irrelevant. The sound of a trumpet or a piano was inherently color-blind, and white youths were as enthusiastic as black youths in their devotion to Armstrong, Earl Hines and Jelly Roll Morton—all black—as well as to Bix Beiderbecke, Benny Goodman, and the growing numbers of white musicians who soon deserved equal billing.

Armstrong became almost as much a popular entertainer as a trumpeter. His lips gave him trouble, and he became a singer and actor in a large number of Hollywood roles, all of them asking him essentially to play himself. Jazz, too, entered the mainstream of American life. Words like *the blues* and *ragtime* lost much of their technical meaning, and even musicians were capable of saying things about their music that were demonstrably incorrect. By the late 1920s, jazz was a part of New York culture, and thus at the center of American creativity. Ironically enough, many black cultural leaders scorned the music as lower-class and debasing, even as whites left fashionable parties in Greenwich Village and took their taxicabs north to Harlem for nights on the town. Such were the contradictions of American life in the 1930s that those whites frequently entered the heart of black America to sit in segregated splendor. The jazzmen were all black, and the audiences all white. Not until the late 1930s did Benny Goodman and Lionel Hampton pioneer in the presentation of integrated jazz bands playing to anyone who wanted to pay his money and come. By then the music was called swing, and little remained of its idiosyncratic origins in some of the more disreputable institutions of the lower Mississippi.

III

The assimilation of the blues into conventional musical awareness provided an excellent example of both the absorptive power of the predominant culture and the inability of minority idiosyncrasy to survive for more than about two generations. With its technical origins in Africa and its social origins in slave songs, black churches, and the casual noises of existence in the lower class, the musical form had many distinctive elements in its early years. The blues generally had a slow beat expressive of the need to work in appropriate rhythms for the picking of cotton or the towing of barges and used the call-and-response pattern common in church music and in music where many of the singers did not know the words or have much musical skill. Improvised at first, the words dealt with the miseries of everyday life: the faithlessness of women, the omnipresence of the boll weevil, the cruelty of straw bosses, the oppressiveness of the heat. The human voice had no trouble hitting blue notes, and some of the original qualities of this American art form remained in the recordings from the late 1920s and early 1930s, when folklorists finally got around to preserving the work of Charley Patton, Blind Lemon Jefferson, Robert Johnson, and others. Unlike most Western folk music, the accompaniment, usually a guitar, provided more than mere rhythmic and harmonic background to the lyrics, serving instead as a second voice. In a manner reminiscent of the older call-and-response pattern of the spiritual, the instrumental accompaniment constantly interacts with, expands upon, and answers the vocal line. These early guitarists would bend the strings in order to achieve blue notes, or slide a knife, straight razor, or bottleneck along the strings to produce a slurred, whining tone that approximated the human voice. These original blues followed a simple pattern, with two lines repeated, followed by a third that developed the idea in a new direction. The pattern might then be repeated with different lines, and then the singer might go on with an appropriate narrative in a straightforward exposition of the causes and consequences of the song.

By the mid-1920s the blues had entered a second phase, often called city blues. This style was characterized by its standardized form, with regular beginnings and endings and two or more instruments in the accompaniment. It was dominated by female singers—Bessie Smith, Ma Rainey, Ida Cox, and Alberta Hunter, among others. Probably the most famous of all the blues singers was Bessie Smith, the "Empress of the Blues," and her version of Handy's "St. Louis

Blues" the single best example of blues in this more sophisticated stage of development.

Smith used the earlier lyric pattern, and her voice took its own rhythms and hit its own notes, but the accompanying instruments seemed to be playing in a far more conventional "Western" fashion, as if the African pentatonic style lodged in the black voice while the European diatonic took refuge in the instrumentation. The shouts and falsettos persisted also, although they too became formalized as time went on, far cries indeed from the street songs and the field hollars of slavery. But songs that become popular take on a life of their own; and besides, no one, especially no white person, could possibly imitate Bessie Smith. The black dialect tended to smooth out, the chord structures to become conventionalized, and in time "St. Louis Blues" became one more piece of jazz that musicians wrote down, practiced, and then worked out their own innovations upon.

The composer who did most to assimilate jazz into the mainstream of American culture was George Gershwin. The son of Russian-Jewish immigrants with no special musical talent, Gershwin grew up in the great cultural melting pot of New York, absorbing black jazz along with dozens of other available styles. The little training he had was European, but Gershwin was remarkably lazy and refused any sort of professional discipline for long. He had one of the greatest senses of melody in the history of American culture, yet never mastered more than the most elementary notions of harmony and counterpoint. At fifteen he dropped out of school and put his ears to work on Tin Pan Alley, the commercial center of the American popular music business, where young pianists could make a living demonstrating sheet music to customers on tinny-sounding pianos. He began to write his own songs, and almost without thinking he picked up black music along with all the other musics around him. Black life fascinated him. A frequent visitor to Harlem, he never seemed bothered by questions of race. He was capable of great sensitivity toward individual blacks and admiration for their music on one day, and on the next equally capable of taking seriously projects for blackface extravaganzas that would make a sensitive liberal blush for shame. Like many new Americans, Gershwin simply did not know; the Civil War meant no more to him than the French and Indian War. He was a musician, and musicians took their inspiration where they found it.

Gershwin began his public career in the musical theater, involved with figures like Jerome Kern, Victor Herbert, Florenz Ziegfeld, and P. G. Wodehouse. By 1919, when he was scarcely twenty-one, he had his first relatively successful musical, and continued into the 1920s, finding teachers and assistants when he needed them, his remarkable originality masking his technical incompetence. During one abortive project for a show based on black musical forms, he became acquainted with Paul Whiteman, a bandleader with a flair for publicity who was determined to win for jazz a respectable audience. Whiteman's arranger was Ferde Grofé, one of the most gifted men in the business, and the three men soon made musical history. Whiteman arranged for a concert that would feature the new music and commissioned Gershwin to produce a blues rhapsody to be the centerpiece of the occasion. Gershwin readily agreed; although he had never written anything more complicated than a song, he soon produced a two-piano version that strung together songlike melodies. Technically well harmonized and melodically effective, they made jazzy rhythms into something that any conventionally trained musician could master with a little practice. But the piece had no structure and no sense of development whatever. It also lacked orchestration, since Gershwin did not know how to orchestrate, but Grofé got to work and in remarkably short time the *Rhapsody in Blue* (1924) was ready for public consumption.

The work was a great success and went on to become one of the symbolic pieces of the decade. White audiences had no trouble with it, whether in formal orchestral garb, in piano solo versions, or in Whiteman's own dance-band version. Black jazz had become a white trick, the adjective *jazzy* something one did to a conventional sound to make it sound different—hit a blue note, syncopate the rhythm, allow the clarinets a rousing glissando, permit the trumpets a section played with mutes. The innovation proved so respectable that Gershwin went on to write his *Concerto in F*, the change in name from rhapsody to concerto indicating silently that the blues had been bleached beyond hope of recovery and had become about as controversial as the polka. An excellent piece in its own way, the concerto soon took an honored place in world music, but it was a place next to Stravinsky's experiments with ragtime, Debussy's experiments with the cakewalk, and the attempts by Maurice Ravel and Darius Milhaud to exalt the primitive components of French modernism. American blacks did not write such compositions, and real jazz headed underground and persisted in the ghettoes of New York and Kansas City. Coleman Hawkins, Lester Young, Charlie Parker, and John Coltrane produced work that proved far more difficult to assimilate.

Gershwin and those like him hardly noticed. He fastened onto one of the best-sellers of the 1920s, DuBose Heyward's *Porgy*, and in the years shortly before his death worked out one of the greatest of all American contributions to the musical theater. The story of the crippled black beggar in Charleston could easily have been made into a hopelessly sentimental piece of vaudeville minstrelsy, but Gershwin managed to turn his defects into virtues. He went to Charleston to study blacks in situ, then retired to an island where the inhabitants spoke Gullah to write the music. The result was not much in the way of structure and needed considerable revision before it seemed stageable at all, but the tunes swept the world, and appeared over the years in every conceivable sort of arrangement—few of which deserved the word *jazz*. American culture had done its job; the result was indeed art. But it was not black art. Blacks played the characters and even the instruments, but whites wrote the songs, managed the production, and took the vast bulk of the profits. That was the way the cultural melting pot worked.

IV

Among the predominant white communities, the indigenous arts also began to flourish, far less dependent on European inspiration than they had been throughout the first two and one-half centuries of American history. James Fenimore Cooper and Nathaniel Hawthorne had been able to create works of art out of themes from the American past, but both had been in awe of European culture and fearful that the American past had been too brief and too lacking in incident for sustained creativity. By the end of the nineteenth century, this feeling was no longer so widespread. Artists were growing up who could look back to the Revolution, abolitionism, Transcendentalism, slavery, and the Civil War, and find more than enough inspiration and a number of appropriate role models. They were not unaware of Europe, but they no longer felt the kind of desperate need for it that Henry James or James Whistler felt. Their work thus became quite as indigenous as that of the New Orleans jazz musicians.

In classical music, the towering figure who emerged was a man totally neglected during the time of his major compositions. To his friends and neighbors, Charles E. Ives was a successful life insurance executive, remembered to this day for his contributions to the art of estate planning. His friends knew of his musical interest, but saw little in it beyond the playing of pieces informally at home or at college and occasional stints as church organist in various Protestant churches in the greater New York area. For most educated Americans, the chief musical presence in the country was Edward MacDowell: trained in Europe in the tradition of Franz Liszt, and the closest America could come to the romantic nationalism of an Edvard Grieg or an Antonin Dvořák. His two piano concertos are European in any formal sense of the term, and even his piano solos, based though many are on American Indian tunes, have had all the thematic and rhythmic vigor refined out of them.

Ives was different. He felt comfortable as an American. He did not receive his training in Europe, and did not regret it. Instead, he worked closely with his father George, a Danbury, Connecticut, bandmaster with all sorts of unorthodox ideas about form, rhythm, and harmony. George Ives, for example, was entranced by musical accidents of the kind that happened to any citizen who listened to the sounds of his home and town. He would sit in the front room of his house, listening to his wife sing a hymn in the kitchen, to the children playing their pianos in neighboring houses, and to the passers-by as they whistled. To any trained European, such sonic clashes, with their different rhythms and accidental disharmonies, were noise and not music, but to both George and Charles Ives they were American music—accidental, creative compositions which should inspire a truly talented composer. One of Charles' earliest memories was of a rainy day when his father became obsessed with the ringing of a church bell nearby. Every few minutes he would rush out into the rain, listen carefully, and then come in soaking wet to try to duplicate the sound on the piano. He never quite succeeded, because the tone of the bell lay between two of the notes on the piano—an instrument that could play tones and half-tones but not quarter-tones. Years later, Charles Ives was still experimenting with quarter-tones, and left compositions which utilized them for the inspiration of young musicians unaware of their origin in the noise of a damp New England day.

Another experiment of which George was fond was that of having singers divide up into groups, singing not only different songs, but in different keys. He might have three or four going at once, often arranged so that the audience would hear the songs loudly or faintly, one acting as a kind of strange echo or reflection of another. Europeans were familiar with antiphonal singing and with rounds, but George's experiments would have struck them as professionally incompetent noise. But to Charles, this nonconformity was a liberating experience. "Father thought that man as a rule did not use the faculties that the Creator had given him hard enough," he recalled later. When he was about ten years old, George "would occasionally have us sing a tune like 'Swanee River' in E-flat while he accompanied us in the key of C. This was to stretch our ears and strengthen our musical minds. . . ." Charles did not think that his father had "the possibility of polytonality in composition in mind" when he did this, at least not in the modern sense of the term. Rather, he "wanted to encourage the use of the ears and mind to think for themselves and be more independent. . . ." That was just the sort of rebellious insubordination that any self-respecting European conservatory would have stamped out. A good German wrote fugues and mastered the sonata form, he did not waste his time with Negro songs and two keys playing at once.

Charles Ives did not lack competent training, however. He went to Yale College to study under Horatio Parker, a competent pedagogue whose own training had been traditionally Central European. Ives and his professor clashed repeatedly but the experience was fruitful, and to the end of his compositional life Ives preferred to think of his works, no matter how unconventional they might sound, as sonatas, symphonies, quartets, and the like. Only rarely did he invent new terms for his new forms and sonorities, as in his "orchestral sets." Indeed, in many ways he resembled a European radical like Richard Strauss, roughly his contemporary: a master of traditional forms, yet constantly experimenting with new sonorities and trying to expand conventional notions of form.

Strauss wrote "tone poems" that were essentially programmatic, telling the stories of Don Juan or Till Eulenspiegel to audiences presumably familiar with the prose versions. Ives wrote his compositions as program music about America: his memories of Danbury, legends of the revolution or the Civil War, evocations of Emerson, Hawthorne, or Thoreau. In this way his work was as American as Strauss' was German.

Few Americans understood him. He wrote steadily from the middle 1890s, when he was a student, until World War I, when poor health and professional discouragement combined to dry up his inspiration. Because no one wished to publish or play the music, it remained unknown, and its composer received none of the criticism and encouragement which would have made him refine his concepts, complete his works, and exercise an influence over the young. Ives simply piled up his music, rough drafts, revisions, and rerevisions, into chaotic heaps that neither he nor anyone else could master easily. The problem for musicologists has thus been extraordinary, as texts had to be extracted, completed, and printed without help from a man too discouraged and ill to remember what he had been trying to say. By the end of the 1930s, a few devoted professionals had begun the arduous process of bringing this music to the public, and by the late 1940s something of an Ives vogue was developing. Europeans, newly conscious of America, suddenly found that this obscure yankee had experimented with every form of musical modernism that was technologically possible when he was composing. The polyrhythms and polytonalities, arhythmic and atonal music, aleatoric or chance compositions, prepared pianos, and the use of blocks of wood to play chord clusters—all were there, and even so august and austere a figure as Arnold Schönberg was willing, in time, to pay homage to the indigenous creativity of at least one American composer.

V

Like Charles Ives, Frank Lloyd Wright was deeply influenced by indigenous ideas and family memories. He too read widely in the American Transcendentalists, and took ideas about art, morality, nature, and God from the writings of Emerson, Thoreau, and Horatio Greenough. He too received his training from American masters—from Dankmar Adler, Louis Sullivan, and other pioneers of the skyscraper in the Chicago area at the end of the nineteenth century. He too grew up securely within the bounds of an American religion: in his case the Unitarianism of his preacher father and his mother's influential clan. Both men created works of fine art that preached moral values to Americans—who frequently did not understand a word of what was being said to them. Wright received more recognition than Ives while still a young man, but then went into an eclipse of reputation. Only in the 1930s did Wright emerge as the greatest American architect, with influence from Germany to Japan, often on other architects whose work he openly condemned. By the 1950s, both men were living legends in American culture, hopelessly out of date themselves, yet continuously alive in the minds of later generations of creative people.

Such parallels are never perfect, however; Wright was far more conscious of European ideas than Ives, and in time he proved exceptionally sensitive to innovations from India and Japan. His mother insisted that she had willed his future as an architect during her pregnancy, and one benefit of such a domineering parent was that Wright received his early education in the famous method of Friedrich Froebel. To the end of his life, Wright recalled "the strips of colored paper, glazed and 'matt,' remarkably soft brilliant colors." He loved "the geometric byplay of those charming checkerboard color combinations," "the structural figures to be made with peas and small straight sticks," and "the slender constructions, the joinings accented by the little green-pea globes." Through the use of the "smooth shapely maple blocks with which to build," he acquired a sense which never left his fingers, of "form becoming *feeling*." To another child, it might all have been as formative as a conventional coloring book or birthday-gift erector set, but to Wright such training in the nursery set him on his path. Emerson had already told Americans that natural objects corresponded to spiritual ideas, and for Wright the lesson transferred easily into mathematics, especially geometry. "In outline the square was significant of integrity; the circle—infinity; the triangle-aspiration; all with which to 'design' significant new forms. In the third dimension, the smooth maple blocks became the cube, the sphere and the tetrahedron; all mine to 'play' with." Even in kindergarten, it seemed, Wright proved capable of mixing European and American ideas in ways so unorthodox that they simply had to be American.

Wright spent his early years in Wisconsin, but went to Chicago for his training. He had little college education, but instead learned, apprentice fashion, from Adler, Sullivan, and the other architects then active in the rapidly growing city. William Le Baron Jenney and Henry Hobson Richardson had already established the existence of the skyscraper; the development of new steel technology and the elevator, requirements of modern business for more space, and the cramping effects of massive city growth all encouraged the development of tall buildings. The firm of Adler & Sullivan were pioneers in taking such urban necessity and making an art form out of it. In Wright's later accounts, Louis Sullivan was the *Lieber Meister* who most influenced him, although scholars agree that the influence was more personal than stylistic. But Sullivan was a great reader of Whitman and other American Renaissance writers, and he shared with them a vision of art that was both democratic and integrated with nature. To later eyes, few structures were less integrated with nature than the modern skyscraper, but that was not the way Sullivan saw it.

Perhaps the key concept explaining the position of these architects was the old romantic notion of functionalism. To a functionalist, architecture had to reflect moral and ethical ideas and teach them to new generations. Buildings had to be honest. Forms had to function in the ways that they seemed to function. A building should express its purpose and that of its age. Materials should be used with integrity.

Brought up on Froebel, Wright also absorbed the work of John Ruskin, William Morris, and the British Arts and Crafts movement. Eager to rid the minds of his readers of the sheer clutter of most Victorian buildings, Ruskin tried hard to force people to see nature and art directly rather than through anecdote or moral lesson. Nature for Ruskin as for Emerson was closely tied to God, understanding it was a moral act, and improved aesthetic perception among the democratic masses was the key to the growth of a better society. Above all, Ruskin wanted his artists to be happy citizens, and he was all too inclined to value a work of art in direct proportion to the amount of enjoyment it created in the hearts of those who built it. William Morris carried many of these notions even further, embracing socialism and founding businesses that tried to provide opportunities for skilled workmen to integrate creativity, religion, and politics. He designed typefaces and chairs, textiles and stained glass, and an extraordinary number of wallpaper designs that had organic names like Daisy, Fruit, and Pomegranate. By the end of the nineteenth century, British Arts and Crafts reformers like Walter Crane and Charles Ashbee were visiting Chicago, bringing the legacies of Ruskin and Morris to places like Hull-House. Jane Addams and Ellen Starr were only two of many reformers who found these ideas attractive and Frank Lloyd Wright one of many young reformers who presented his ideas to Hull-House audiences. In this complex manner did social reform and architectural theory come together, just as did indigenous American and imported European ideas.

But Wright did not swallow anyone's ideas whole, and in one of his most famous talks, delivered at Hull-House in 1901, he first paid homage to the tradition of Ruskin and Morris but then established his distance from it. The tradition their names represented "miscalculated the machine"; one could understand why they hated the machine, but the hatred was obsolete by the twentieth century. For Wright, "the Machine is Intellect mastering the drudgery of earth that the plastic art may live; that the margin of leisure and strength by which man's life upon the earth can be made beautiful, may immeasurably widen; its function ultimately to emancipate human expression!" They all shared a devotion to democratic ideals, but the duty of the modern architect was to use the machine to create a beautiful environment. The machine was "the tool which frees human labor, lengthens and broadens the life of the simplest man," and by so doing so becomes "the basis of the Democracy upon which we insist."

Without buildings, these ideas meant little. Wright was extraordinarily vivid in what he wanted to do to the landscape. The old houses that Americans lived in had to go because they *"lied* about everything." They "had no sense of Unity at all nor any such sense of space as should belong to a free man among a free people in a free country." Unthinking architects stuck buildings upon hills with no sense for the landscape, their structures boxes "cut full of holes to let in light and air," or else "clumsy gabled" chunks of "roofed masonry" which any decent carpenter could have put up without much thought.

> The buildings standing around there on the Chicago Prairies were all tall and all tight. Chimneys were lean and taller still—sooty fingers threatening the sky. And beside them, sticking up almost as high, were the dormers. Dormers were elaborate devices—cunning little buildings complete in themselves—stuck on to the main roofslopes to let the help poke their heads out of the attic for air. Invariably the damp, sticky clay of the prairie was dug out for a basement under the whole house and the rubble stone-walls of this dank basement always stuck above the ground a foot or so—and blinked through half-windows.

Walls in these structures tended to be "be-corniced or fancy-bracketed up at the top into the tall, purposely, profusely complicated roof." This roof, in turn, was "ridged and topped, swanked and gabled to madness before they would allow it to be either watershed or shelter." The outside of the structure "was bedeviled," "mixed to puzzle-pieces with corner-boards, panel-boards, window-frames, corner-blocks, plinth-blocks, rosettes, fantails, and jiggerwork in general."

Wright engineered a wholesale assault on these crimes against taste. He disposed of the attic and basement. He lowered the ceilings and eliminated dormers. He knocked down many of the interior walls, permitting privacy chiefly in bedrooms and utility areas. He emphasized only a central fireplace, so that a warmly united family could remain together, and not be separated each person in his own room. Families in a Wright home were expected to like each other's company, and only screens in a large central space divided affairs off from one another. He introduced broad roofs that sloped gently if at all. He liked windows in horizontal bands, under comforting eaves. Light and air became parts of the design, and casement windows allowed a more intimate relationship to the out-of-doors. He even insisted on designing his own furniture so that it would be compatible with his housing designs—a practice that led to countless stories of how uncomfortable it was to adapt one's frame to a sup- posedly organic aesthetic.

Wright's homes became the most famous and influential examples of the Prairie Style of American architecture. Other architects deserved mention as well: George G. Elmslie and William Gray Purcell; the husband-and-wife team of Walter Burley Griffin and Marion Mahony; Barry Byrne; and Hugh M. G. Garden. Griffin and Mahony carried the ideas as far away as Canberra, Australia, while Byrne became one of the most successful architects of churches in his generation. The Prairie Style thus began with a certain type of residential structure, but its ideas permeated the architectural world, influencing countries and styles that outwardly seem to have no relation to it. In this sense, an indigenous American aesthetic had influence far beyond any previous artistic creation arising from the New World.

VI

Ives and Wright represented an extraordinary flowering of Protestant culture in America, as if two hundred and fifty years of cultural life immersed in religious values had suddenly justified itself by producing remarkable artists of world stature. But Protestantism had severe limits as an inspiration for the arts: it was too inhibiting, too programmatic in its assumptions, too dogmatic in its tone, to be continuously productive of major artists. Instead, America had the advantage of its immigrants, and of new European ideas that could be absorbed by native Americans. Artists from non-Protestant environments were coming of age even as Ives and Wright created their major works—artists who began the slow process of making America into a cosmopolitan, modern culture.

The preeminent artist growing up in America who illustrated these trends, was Eugene O'Neill. His childhood circumstances alone set him off from everything that Ives and Wright could take for granted. He was a son of the theater; his father was a master of melodrama, known everywhere for his repetitious portrayal of the title role in *The Count of Monte Cristo.* Family life customarily included hotels, restaurants, railroad trains, and alcoholic binges. It did not include Sunday schools, the Protestant Ethic, or much concern about social acceptability. The O'Neill world was mentally disturbing: what was normal for Eugene was all but unknown to most American boys. Not only was his father a rake as well as an actor, his mother was an abject neurotic, unable to cope with her husband's behavior. A hypochondriac and invalid, she escaped into a dreamworld of drugs rather than cope with reality. Theatergoers can sample the contours of the resulting family life in the painfully autobiographical play *Long Day's Journey Into Night.* Finally, the family was not Anglo-Saxon and Protestant, but Irish and Roman Catholic: lower-class on Eugene's father's side, "lace curtain" on his mother's. Such people normally had a hard time socially in America, in some areas ranking below Negroes in social acceptability. Adjustment to American society was difficult under the best of circumstances, and both Eugene and his brother took frequent refuge in alcohol as a means of surviving in a land of disapproving Protestants.

Such an intelligence did not read conventional American books; it scarcely knew what they were. O'Neill was thus free to sample whatever came into his hands, and one institution in New York City proved crucial to his cultural growth. Benjamin Tucker was a minor American intellectual force, but a significant spokesman for a gentle variety of anarchism and individualism; he ran the Unique Book Shop, and stocked it with many of the works of the most modern and modernist figures then active in Europe. Tucker once described himself as "an atheist, a materialist, an evolutionist, a prohibitionist, a free trader, a champion of the legal eight-hour day, a woman suffragist, an enemy of marriage, and a believer in sexual freedom." He and his bookshop were the most important influences on O'Neill: American in themselves but European and modernistic in impact.

The German philosopher Friedrich Nietzsche was the preeminent deity of the bookshop, and books like *Thus Spake Zarathustra* and *The Birth of Tragedy* proved so influential on the young man that when asked, in 1928, if he had a literary idol, O'Neill replied: "The answer to that is in one word—Nietzsche." For the son of a household bathed in dreams, histrionics, alcohol, and drugs, Nietzsche's rhapsodic tones, his almost hysterical affirmations, his stress on a pagan acceptance of life and on the eternal recurrence of certain patterns could only have seemed autobiographical commonsense. Just as the enemy for Nietzsche was the stultification of orderly, middle-class life and its conventions, so for O'Neill the enemy was often American bourgeois Protestantism with its lack of place for someone of his background and talents. And of course both Nietzsche and O'Neill had a deep reverence for things Greek; it is odd to think of Greek theatrical influence mediated through German philosophy, but that is in fact one major vehicle through which it obtained its power over American playwrights.

Three European playwrights also had a crucial impact. George Bernard Shaw had influence through works, like *Mrs. Warren's Profession*, that violated Victorian proprieties and introduced new and sometimes outrageous themes to the stage. More important was Shaw's work as a critic: *The Quintessence of Ibsenism* was one of O'Neill's favorite books at the Tucker bookshop, and so great was his infatuation that O'Neill managed to attend at least ten performances of *Hedda Gabler* while he was in college. Ibsen was a key means through which O'Neill got rid of the melodramatic theater of his father and came to see the theater as a place where he could portray his social and intellectual revolt against much that was accepted in the modern world. Most important of all was August Strindberg, the Swedish playwright whose views on women and the family were fully as warped as O'Neill's. "Strindberg still remains among the most modern of moderns, the greatest interpreter in the theatre of the characteristic spiritual conflicts which constitute the drama—the blood—of our lives today," O'Neill wrote in 1924. Only through his "supernaturalism" may we "express in the theatre what we comprehend intuitively of that self-defeating, self-obsession which is the discount we moderns have to pay for the loan of life." Strindberg was the dramatist who "knew and suffered with our struggle years before many of us were born," and who "expressed it by intensifying the method of his time and by foreshadowing both in content and form the methods to come. All that is artistically enduring in what we loosely call 'Expressionism'—all that is artistically valid and sound theatre—can be clearly traced back to" *The Dream Play, There Are Crimes and Crimes*, and *The Spook Sonata*.

Outside the theater, two other writers helped O'Neill arrive at a modernist aesthetic. Like Joseph Conrad, O'Neill was in the habit of running off to sea whenever life became too much for him, and for both men life on a boat took on symbolic and formal properties: life as journey, floating as aimlessness, the deck as dramatic stage, the horizon as the future. Life for both men seems to have been without religious or philosophical meaning, and could take on meaning only when men came in contact with each other or with nature. Conrad clearly helped the younger man put all this into words and forms, and O'Neill throughout his life retained an almost neurotic affection for the sea: swimming in it, writing about it, redecorating his houses to resemble cabins—even down to the small round windows that he designed to resemble portholes.

The last major influence was the psychoanalyst Carl Jung. Audiences and critics were always finding Freudian influences in these plays about perversion, repression, and the unconscious, and doubtless O'Neill did pick up much of Freud out of the air of New York intellectual life. But O'Neill denied that Freud was a direct or important influence on his work, and perhaps should be taken at his word. There were many differences between the mystical Protestant Jung and the secular Jewish Freud, and O'Neill temperamentally had far more in common with Jung. O'Neill had inclinations toward a Roman Catholic mysticism, and his family life had been full of the dreams and memories of which Jung had made so much. Both men yearned for some kind of universal order and sought to conceptualize it through groups of symbols that frequently mystified the uninitiated. Jung would talk of "archetypes" or "psychological" truths, while O'Neill preferred the everyday vocabulary of "Fate," "mystery" and "the biological past," but the parallels seem clear. Both men assumed that a person's unconscious drives ruled his conscious behavior, and that this unconscious was somehow collective. Both playwright and psychoanalyst were expressing in manageable forms the unconscious mindsets of the masses of people. For both men, salvation of sorts came from overcoming the sin of pride to achieve genuine knowledge of the self.

O'Neill began to find the forms and platforms he needed in the four years between 1913 and American entry into World War I in 1917. He became involved with a group of radical artists: Communist John Reed and his companion Louise Bryant; modernist painter Charles Demuth; sculptor William Zorach; and the theatrical team of George Cram Cook and Susan Glaspell, desperately eager to revive Greek civilization and its standards through a reinvigoration of the American drama. Several drama groups in Greenwich Village groped toward a new aesthetic, but the most fecund ground seemed to be in the summer colony of Provincetown, on Cape Cod. There, in a renovated fishhouse, with high tides flowing under the boards and people sitting on chairs they had brought themselves, a select few watched one of O'Neill's best early works, now known as *Bound East for Cardiff*, the Conradian work that began modern drama in America. The group soon moved to the city, and for the next several years O'Neill was able to experiment with plays in a situation rather similar to that of the Intimate Theater August Strindberg had run in Stockholm. By 1920 the apprentice days were over, and *Beyond the Horizon* opened on Broadway, a public success.

The greatest career in the history of American theater quickly developed; a Nobel Prize in 1936 certified the international nature of the achievement. O'Neill experimented with psychoanalytical forms, with atavism and Greek tragedy. He went far beyond Shaw in the shocking nature of his topics and rivaled Joyce in his probings of the unconscious. He played with masks and pioneered in writing decent roles for Negroes. In so doing, he proved that indigenous American material could in fact be adapted to the modern world, and could assimilate successfully the most mature discoveries of the modern European stage. Some Americans had to go to Europe to learn about modernism; some learned from Europeans in America. O'Neill learned on his own, through books, trials and errors. His work heralded the arrival of a new maturity in American creative achievement.

VII

The generation that matured creatively between the end of World War I and the beginning of World War II made the final transitions necessary for America to be a genuinely cosmopolitan culture. Earlier Americans had had to go abroad to meet their peers and be creative in a nurturing environment; they needed foreign academic training to complete a professional preparation that met the highest standards. A few became permanent expatriates, returning rarely if at all to the United States. Even where adequate, European-quality training was available, as at some of the graduate departments of the Johns Hopkins or at Harvard, the infrastructure of American culture was not truly able to absorb most of the products. The taste of the public was not sophisticated; review media were weak; too few colleges, museums, and concert halls were open to anything innovative.

By the 1920s and 1930s, this situation was fast ending. On the one hand, European scholars began their migrations in the face of postwar impoverishment, redrawn national borders, and political upheaval. Few countries could absorb many emigrés at any productive level even in times of peace, and with the imposition of dictatorships in Central Europe during the 1930s, more and more scholars and artists sought security in America. American students after World War II could take such resources for granted, and by the late 1940s no pianist, ballet dancer, scholar of Russian history, or museum curator had to feel in any way inferior, in terms of training or available resources, to anyone in Europe. On the other hand, Americans had gone to Europe in such vast numbers between the wars that European standards could be taken for granted in many areas even without having the European migrants immediately at hand. One reason European physicists could have such an impact during World War II was that American physics had become so good during the twenty preceding years. What seemed exotic in 1919 seemed commonplace in 1945.

The difference is almost too clear when the careers of Charles Ives and Aaron Copland are juxtaposed. Ives, the totally indigenous yankee suspicious of Europe, learning from his European-trained teacher but scornful of much that he represented, faced a totally hostile audience and lapsed into creative silence around the time of World War I. Copland, by contrast, was a cosmopolite who sampled the best European training, discovered various means of coping with American conditions, and emerged after World War II as a perfect example of the new American nation: a citizen of the world, recognizably American, with both a sophisticated and a popular audience.

Copland's cosmopolitanism emerges in two different ways from his own writings. He worked, first of all, within a consciously European musical context. Where Ives looked back at folk songs, band music, Transcendentalist essays, and other such examples of indigenous Americana, Copland wrote as if unaware of such materials. Instead, he pictured himself as a rebel against late nineteenth-century romanticism, especially the bloated German romanticism associated with the operas of Richard Wagner and the tone poems of Richard Strauss. He identified instead with composers in Russia and in France who criticized this devotion to artistic self-expression and preferred to use *their* folk material as a guide for the development of new musical forms. Folk material came in rhythms and forms which had not ossified in the music conservatories, and thus seemed ideal for pioneering work. "Here at its very inception is a basic difference between romantic and modern music," Copland said. "The German romanticist was highly subjective and personal in the expression of his emotions." A modern composer, by contrast, "seeks a more universal ideal. He tends to be more objective and impersonal in his music." The emotional climate of the modern world was different. "Romanticism, especially in its later stages, now seems overexpressive, bombastic self-pitying, long-winded. The tempo of modern times calls for a music that is more matter-of-fact, more concise—and especially, less patently emotional."

Nothing could sound more European and professional; such a manner of discourse, improbable before World War I and unremarkable after World War II, assumed that musicians in America were musicians before they were Americans, just as doctors might assume that they were men of science before they were men of "American" science. But Copland did not ignore America, either. If European composers like Béla Bartók and Zoltán Kodály could experiment with Hungarian folk music, he could experiment with American folk music—and the greatest of American folk music for his generation was jazz. Jazz had had an enormous vogue in Europe after 1908: Claude Debussy, Maurice Ravel, Igor Stravinsky, and Erik Satie had all experimented with it, and so when Copland took it up seriously, it seems open to question whether he did so as an indigenous American mining his nation's heritage or as a trendy European student, eager to participate in a new fad. By the 1920s it hardly mattered, and the question never really came up.

He was a highly conscious if not always accurate analyst: What interested composers "was not so much the spirit, whatever it symbolized, as the more technical side of jazz—the rhythm, melody, harmony, timbre through which that spirit was expressed." Jazz might be a folk music, and it might be American, but it had technical aspects that were more professionally compelling. "From the composer's viewpoint, jazz had only two expressions: either it was the well-known 'blues' mood, or the wild, abandoned, almost hysterical and grotesque mood so dear to the youth of all ages." Copland insisted that these two moods encompassed "the whole gamut of jazz emotion," and that "any serious composer who attempted to work within these two moods would sooner or later become aware of their severe limitations." But he also admitted that "the technical procedures of jazz had much wider implications, since these were not necessarily restricted to the two moods but might be applied to any number of different musical styles." In this frame of mind, Copland wrote his *Piano Concerto* and his *Organ Symphony*, key efforts to unite jazz and classical, American, and European materials.

Copland also worked biographically in a context vital for understanding his art and its place in American cosmopolitanism. He was no small-town yankee Protestant like Ives, but a big-city Jew. Ives could take all of America for granted; Copland could take nothing for granted. "I was born on a street in Brooklyn that can only be described as drab. It had none of the garish color of the ghetto, none of the charm of the old New England thoroughfare, or even the rawness of a pioneer street. It was simply drab." He received no encouragement from his family, and when he wanted to find a music teacher he had to look for one himself—at the age of thirteen. Even years later, he would write that "it fills me with mild wonder each time I realize that a musician was born on that street. Music was the last thing anyone would have connected with it. In fact, no one had ever connected music with my family or with my street. The idea was entirely original with me."

But Copland found a way out. His family was no help, his government felt no obligation to nourish the arts, but occasional wealthy foundations provided an opportunity unknown in other countries. Supported chiefly by the Guggenheim Foundation, he went several times to Europe. He found a young, little-known harmony teacher, Nadia Boulanger, and their sessions were such a success that Copland became the first in an extraordinary line of young American composers who found their own, American voices, through work with this Frenchwoman. Insofar as anyone helped American classical music mature, it was Boulanger, and some of Copland's earliest experiments in capturing an American idiom were written at her encouragement. America was itself not yet receptive to such compositions, but Copland nevertheless persevered both with his writing and with performance. In collaboration with another young experimentalist, Roger Sessions, he helped sponsor the Copland–Sessions Concerts, and so between 1928 and 1931 at least some avant-garde New Yorkers could get a taste of the sophisticated union of Europe and America that would mark the art of the future.

Life was never smooth for creative artists in America, and Copland's art does not have obvious linear developments from one "phase" to another. He tried experiments; some worked and some did not. Some achieved a limited audience acceptance and some scarcely any. Jazz provided inspiration for only a few years; European atonalism proved briefly attractive. But no sensitive American could live through the depression of the 1930s without rethinking the relationship between the artist and society: here were people starving, with legitimate political and social demands; and here were artists, from music to literature, cutting themselves off and indulging in precious experimentation, chiefly for the benefit of each other. The situation was musically and politically unacceptable, and just as writers like John Dos Passos and John Steinbeck were developing a new, socially conscious collective art form in literature, so Copland set himself the task of developing a form appropriate for the mass audiences that he knew were available. American society needed a new music, a music that would use the mass media—film and radio especially—to communicate in ways never before possible. The isolated, experimental artistic mentality of the 1920s was gone, and in its place came the composer for the masses. "What the radio has done, in the final analysis, has been to bring to the surface this need to communicate one's music to the widest possible audience." This might look like opportunism, but in fact it stemmed from "a healthy desire in every artist to find his deepest feelings reflected in his fellowman. It is not without its political implications," for it also stems partly "from that same need to reaffirm the democratic ideal that already fills our literature, our stage, and our screen." His generation of composers were "the men who must embody new communal ideals in a new communal music."

In this mood, Copland produced the works that have made him one of the most respected and popular musicians in the world. Taking myths and legends from the American past, from *Billy the Kid* to *Appalachian Spring*, he produced work after work that won popular respect both as music and as dance. The themes and rhythms were as complex as anything produced in the Paris of Stravinsky and Ravel, and yet they were accessible even to untutored audiences who wished little more than a tune to hum and stamp their foot to. The campfire dances, shootouts, and wedding ceremonies were all events Americans recognized as their own, yet the scores demanded a great deal from musicians and commanded the respect of the pedagogues. Europe and America had come together, and America had finally achieved a cosmopolitan art that could be performed successfully anywhere.

VIII

In a less obvious but more profound way, William Faulkner provided the best example of the growing together of the European and American emphases. He also synthesized the earlier sectional attitudes that were becoming less important for Americans in general. He was not only the modernist writer of indigenous materials, he was the Southern writer who best embodied in art the closing of the West and the emergence of a genuinely national culture. Readers around the world, starting with the French, soon regarded him as the best American writer. For reasons many find hard to verbalize, his difficult style and inarticulate characters transcended national borders and the boundaries of language. His very lack of answers on the race issue also seemed attractive; many problems have no solutions, which the rest of the world had long discovered to its sorrow. Racial prejudice became the most important issue in the world in the postcolonial era, and Faulkner's emphases on the tragic inevitability of conflict, and the ability of minorities to endure, found not only a Nobel Prize but an audience among students with no particular training in literature. Several stories became films, although the more complex works have thus far resisted such popularization.

The last word on Faulkner will never come in, but the mixed nature of his achievement still invites comment. Faulkner wrote well in many places, showing tragic insight and deadpan comedy of a kind that must seem odd in the far corners of the globe. But he also wrote badly. He misused words, persisting in the use of obsolete romanticisms in English usage in a way that weirdly paralleled the way the South held onto old social customs. His pronouns were the despair of grammarians, whole pages going by based on a *he* that had no obvious antecedent. Many characters had the same name, and some with the same name were not even of the same sex. Plots had no consistent narrative or sense of time. Characters, especially women, often seemed to live on the level of animals; sex and violence always lurked in the next chapter, then lingered in memories for a century. Feelings of incest and bestiality were not unknown; at least one famous male character clearly had feelings for a cow that commonly belonged elsewhere, and several were retarded even by the low standards of backward rural areas. Educated, urban readers found the early Faulkner something of a freak show, and many thought that each successive work lowered the tone of an American novel that was already too low. Religious opposition was extreme, unmollified by Faulkner's ostentatious use of Christian symbolism. Only in the violent world that emerged from World War II did he come to seem almost normal, as if all this murky prose were in some way just the way life was, and find the critics that he needed for full acceptability.

Faulkner was notoriously inarticulate about his life and art, retreating to alcohol at the least excuse and demanding that readers read and stop asking personal questions. But in one letter of November 1944 he made a relatively clear statement of what he most often had in mind. "I am telling the same story over and over, which is myself and the world," he wrote Malcolm Cowley, who was putting together *The Portable Faulkner.* Thomas Wolfe, then a Southern writer of exaggerated reputation, "was trying to say everything, get everything, the world plus 'I' or filtered through 'I' or the effort of 'I' to embrace the world in which he was born and walked a little while and then lay down again, into one volume." Faulkner was trying "to go a step further," and he was sure that taking this extra step was what confused people when they found his style opaque. "I'm trying to say it all in one sentence, between one Cap and one period," as if it were all to go, so to speak, "on one pinhead. I don't know how to do it. All I know to do is to keep on trying in a new way." He was inclined to think, at that relatively late stage in his career, that "my material, the South, is not very important to me. I just happen to know it, and dont have time in one life to learn another one and write at the same time." He was sure that it did not much matter what part of the earth a writer chose, for one place was much like another, "the same frantic steeplechase toward nothing everywhere and man stinks the same stink no matter where in time." All life was personal, in other words, and the minute always in some way participated in the universal. Put into the form of a slogan, Faulkner was always writing about the personal experience of the timeless and trying to say everything at once.

Faulkner was born in a small Mississippi town in 1897, and like Hemingway and Copland grew up with the century. In 1902 the family settled in the university town of Oxford, a long drive south of Memphis. The writer's father was a lower-middle-class office worker who drank a good deal but eventually managed to find a minor post at the university. Family life was unhappy, lived on the fringes of respectability, with downward mobility a real possibility. The writer grew up with no strong male role models and thus sought them in the history of his region.

Like most of the South, the Faulkners seemed to have more of a past than a future. Nothing seemed promising; everything grand or tragic had happened years earlier, before, during, or just after the Civil War. For the writer, the ancestor of choice was his great-grandfather, Col. W. C. Falkner, C.S.A., the family name being without a *u* in those days, and C.S.A. standing for Confederate States of America, the locally preferred name for the South during the war. Colonel Falkner was author of one of the many romances of the Old South, *The White Rose of Memphis*, and his ability to unite the myths of region and family with a talent for writing held great significance for Faulkner. He did not, however, swallow the myths of those earlier generations whole. He valued them as myths and thus far more glorious than mere realities. Faulkner's private letters clearly show that he regarded the Old South as violent, lazy, and illiterate, with only a small elite separating the entire area from barbarism. The slave population generated music of beauty and importance, and people individually were capable of admirable behavior, but the place was a cultural desert.

He was clear about this and drew obvious lessons from it. The South was too busy in many ways to be creative and had no traditions either for making art or preserving it, he wrote Cowley early in 1946. "For all their equipment for leisure (slavery, unearned wealth) their lives were curiously completely physical, violent, despite their physical laziness." When they were not doing anything like hunting or farming, "they slept or talked. They talked too much, I think. Oratory was the first art; Confederate generals would hold up attacks while they made speeches to their troops. Apart from that, 'art' was really no manly business. It was a polite painting of china by gentlewomen." Southerners often had education and owned libraries, but they contained mostly classic works and other people's speeches. "The negroes invented the songs and their songs were not topical nor even dated in the sense we mean. So there was no literate middleclass to produce a literature." This lack of any middle class permeated the sociology of his novels, because he knew that, when a Sutpen or a Snopes emerged from the lower class, they did not enter the middle class so much as try and fail to become barons. The only art they had was the tradition of "old songs from 15th–16th century England and Scotland, passed from mouth to mouth because generations couldn't write to record them." Only with the writer's own generation had enough time passed and enough of a middle class emerged to start recording the life of the region in permanent form. Here the South did better than the North, because it lost the war. "The only clean thing about War is losing it."

Elsewhere, Faulkner also made clear his identification of a loose equation between the North, progress, and machinery, and the South, stasis, and the humane community. The North will bring capitalism and mass production to the South, in the process disrupting the sense of community, of humans dealing with humans, that was integral to the oral traditions of the South. The machines were usually cars, sometimes airplanes, and any hunter for symbols in these novels could easily begin by watching how the machines disturbed, injured, and killed characters. Only blacks, who could not afford cars let alone planes, retained the stoic sense of dignity of lives lived among those who ate, drank, and breathed rather than among those that consumed oil and gas.

As a teenager, Faulkner struck many as disconnected and lazy. He wandered unhappily in and out of high school, sampled a course or two at the university, and completed nothing measurable. The indolence was deceptive, as it often was in the South. He was reading the Bible and a good deal of nineteenth-century British and French poetry. Much of his early writing imitated this verse: the emotions of young lovers, fauns cavorting in sylvan nature, and the dreams of lost innocence. His own poetry was terrible stuff, but useful for understanding the early fiction. Faulkner took about a decade to get this sort of thing out of his head, and did not write much of importance in prose until he stopped writing poetry. As an old man, he referred to himself as "a failed poet," and the phrase was apt as well as ironic. He was very much a failed poet, although by then he had managed to accomplish something far more significant.

Faulkner wanted to serve in World War I but never saw action. He wandered off to Greenwich Village for several months, as if trying to become a trendy modernist aesthete, but did only one thing worth noting: he met a bookstore owner named Elizabeth Prall, who went on to marry writer Sherwood Anderson. After several years as one of the world's worst postmasters back in Oxford, Faulkner joined the Andersons and several minor writers to work for the New Orleans *Double Dealer*, a literary journal that was encouraging unknown Southerners in the creation of art. Tulane University was nearby, with its faculty and library, and books kept coming in for review. Faulkner thus had a chance to discover Oscar Wilde and George Moore and to review contemporary works by such writers as Robert Frost and Conrad Aiken. He probably heard about the work of James Joyce and Joseph Conrad, but little evidence survives to support studies of literary influence. He certainly did not read such major thinkers as Freud and Frazer; Faulkner was not an intellectual in any sense of the term.

He listened instead. In this he imitated Anderson, a writer who also wrote about stories rather than events: written short stories or novels about oral tales, tales of men who talked about their Civil War memories or made up the memories they preferred, tales repeated over and over with embellishments. The fact of myth, the reality of tale-telling, is the focus here, the modern way of persisting in the habit of Old South oratory. It was as if the oral traditions of both black and white Americans had gone underground during the Civil War, only to reappear in the 1920s to supply a new mode of discourse that outwardly seemed to resemble the stream of consciousness in the work of Joyce or Proust, but which was intrinsically different.

Anderson was also the man who, Faulkner recalled many years later, gave him the best advice he ever got. He did not have to write on cosmic or even American themes, whatever they were. He had to recognize that he too had a place from which he had come, a place that he possessed imaginatively, and that in doing it justice, he was also doing justice to his country. "You have to have somewhere to start from: then you begin to learn," was the way he remembered Anderson talking. "It dont matter where it was, just so you remember it and aint ashamed of it." One place was as good as another. "You're a country boy; all you know is that little patch up there in Mississippi where you started from. But that's all right too. It's America too."

At first Faulkner didn't absorb the message. He wrote his bad poetry and two bad novels. He went to Paris in the 1920s the way everyone else did but met no one of importance, either French or American. He wandered about, grew a beard, drank a great deal, and wrote. He appears nowhere in the memoirs of others and wrote nothing about it himself. He returned to Oxford and remained there, with occasional stints in Hollywood, for the rest of his career. He had found his patch, he named it Yoknapatawpha County, and he wrote a novel called *Flags in the Dust*. It appeared in print as written only in 1973, but as *Sartoris* it appeared in 1929 and began the major phase of his work, which lasted from about 1929 through the publication of the stories in *Go Down, Moses* in 1942.

Many of the realities of Faulkner's "small patch" are already evident in *Flags*. Nothing much ever happens directly; everything seems to have happened already, in another time or place. What is present is the reality of words: the memories, myths, and tales of the Civil War that has been over for about sixty years at the time of the novel. The words are also of blacks, who are less important here than they soon will be; of failed relationships, for much of Faulkner's work will be about the way people fail to connect in family and community; and of modernity and modernization, usually in the form of auto-mobiles, airplanes, or some other type of machinery. Two men named Bayard Sartoris, grandfather and grandson, and two wars, the Civil War and World War I, imply connections between times past and present, and an even older Bayard Sartoris lingers in the memory of the grandfather. An undertone of satire, even farce, keeps the book from sentimentality: the oldest of the three Bayards reportedly died of an excessive desire to obtain some anchovies, his recklessness in their pursuit slyly implying that perhaps motives less than grand were behind much Southern behavior during the unpleasantness of 1861–1865. Grandfather Bayard dies of a heart attack due to young Bayard's bad driving. Bayard himself dies in a plane crash. Anchovies, cars, planes, tied together by the sheer triviality of the initiating acts that caused the deaths and by the odd notion that death is always incidental, often quixotic, and not of much importance to anyone but the deceased. So much for the traditions of Southern gentility.

The Sound and the Fury (1929) followed almost immediately. For many critics, it is one of the author's two or three most important works, ranking with "The Bear" and *Absalom, Absalom!* This is the first truly experimental work Faulkner wrote; he felt that his earlier work had been derivative, which it was, and that he had had to think too much of publishers and marketplace, to which the mutilation of *Flags* into *Sartoris* testified. So Faulkner wrote to please himself. He was certainly aware of Joyce and Proust and other experimenters in both English and French, but by and large was most directly a product of Southern oratory and Sherwood Anderson's encouragement to exploit the talk of his local area.

The talk of *The Sound and the Fury* was often of incest and suicide. Most of the book takes place on Easter Weekend 1928, with important events occurring on 2 June 1910. Minds wander back and forth, recalling earlier events or their results. One of the four sections is largely the stream of consciousness of the idiot Benjy, obsessed by his sister Caddy and little girls in general; this is the sort of thing that got Faulkner his unpleasant reputation in respectable circles. A second section takes place in the mind of Quentin Compson, a student incapable of dealing with his or his sister's sexuality; he plays incessantly with the theme of time as he goes through the day of his suicide. A third is in the words of greedy, manipulative brother Jason. One climax in the novel comes when a second Quentin, the girl who is Caddy's illegitimate daughter, takes revenge on Jason and steals from him money he is in turn stealing from her, so that she can run off with the pitchman from a road show. The final section, written in straightforward narrative fashion, focuses on the black servant Dilsey, who somehow manages to keep this unattractive family functioning, and endures, like the South itself.

From a modernist perspective, the four points of view of what are essentially the same events, the stress on sex and violence, the role of the idiot, the pervasiveness of greed and exploitation, and the manipulations of time are what made the book seem so seminal to other writers. Like *Ulysses* or *Remembrance of Things Past*, it seemed to put fiction on an entirely new plane, where conventional narrative disappeared along with conventional time, conventional values, and any common sense of what was real. What critics overlooked was the kinship Faulkner also had with another type of modernism that paralleled his own even more closely: that of Thomas Mann. The early Mann of *Buddenbrooks* had studied both a family and a culture in decay, as children failed to inherit family commercial skills and preferred to spend their time cultivating aesthetic sensibilities. The later Mann, of *The Magic Mountain* and "Death in Venice," was using an elaborate irony to adumbrate the atmosphere of madness and sexual nonconformity that seemed all but pervasive in modern Europe. Faulkner was not as sui generis as Americans seemed to think.

Faulkner continued his experiments in *As I Lay Dying*, a collection of voices heard round a body as it heads for burial. It must have seemed an even more daring experiment, but remains essentially pointless. *Sanctuary* was melodrama, with much to be said for it in terms of its exploitation of the materials of popular culture and its genres. But neither work measured up either to its predecessor or its two successors. *Light in August* (1932) is the novel that fools the most readers. They underrate it because on its surface it seems conventional, as if a writer could not be an artist unless he were constantly expanding the techniques of narration and exploding a reader's sense of form. They do less than justice to a work that remains great even though it makes sense.

Ever since Pound and Stein, modernism had been above all things a climate of creativity in which artists who felt they had no decent place within their own cultures developed a new language in which to express themselves. They were educated outcasts, internal or actual emigrés, those who because of taste, race, language, or sexual orientation could not fit in. *Light in August* is the work in which Faulkner assimilated the technical innovations of modernism while thematically bringing a cast of outcaste characters together to reenact the most basic act of Southern violence, or "reality" concerning outcaste status: the lynching of a male, presumably but not obviously black, for a crime that seems to be the rape and murder of a white woman. In this as in most great modernist works, in actual fact no one really knows the actual facts.

The novel appears to have several plots that do not hang together but are all about marginality, about people who do not and cannot fit in, in the archetypal modernist predicament. Lena Grove is pregnant out of wedlock. Joanna Burden is a yankee who cares too much for blacks ever to fit into Southern society. In wildly different ways they don't measure up to the local moral code.

The chief male characters don't either. Gail Hightower is a study in how words can preempt action. Hightower is Christian, abstract, and impotent; he failed to satisfy his wife, she strayed, and the Ku Klux Klan punished him for their connubial dysfunction. Finally, Joe Christmas: outsider as scapegoat, black when he wants to be, white when he wants to be, one of the most isolated characters in all literature. Looking like a tramp, rootless, incapable of seeming comfortable anywhere, he has on his face a look that makes a fellow workman want to run him through a planer. He seems to have been a foundling, and most people assume that he is a white baby that someone abandoned. He himself assumes that he has some black blood, for people call him black when he does something wrong. With Christmas, blackness is a state of the soul, some deep flaw like original sin, that seems to have little connection to race. Adopted by an unpleasant white family that tries to beat Christianity into him, he learns to behave in ways that will hurt his parents' feelings; what will hurt them most is knowledge they had brought up a black son.

In adulthood, Christmas lives in such a way as to force the reader not to sympathize. Given the symbolism of his name and initials, some readers assume he is somehow a Christ figure, as if Faulkner were Graham Greene with a drawl.

But this is one of many examples where Faulkner merely toys with Christian symbolism without doing much with it. A psychic outlaw, Christmas seeks out sex with white women in order to disgust them later with the knowledge that they had just shared a bed with a black; he positively seeks physical retribution, and almost kills a woman when she doesn't seem to care. Eventually Christmas finds the Burden house, sets up as a bootlegger, becomes Burden's lover, and balks only when she tries to rehabilitate him and give him normal adult respon- sibilities of management and money. He cannot face the notion that his black- ness is irrelevant.

This tale of outsiders contains some stream of consciousness, but focusing on that device has caused readers to neglect the importance of the work as a tale about tales. Not only do most of the events happen offstage, with a focus on what people say about events and not on what actually happened, but the central "fact" of the novel turns out to be a tale as well. Christmas' black blood was a made-up tale like all the others. He was really the illegitimate son of a poor girl who became infatuated with a circus hand who reputedly had some Mexican blood. The blackness is thus all assumption, all internal, all a misunderstanding. Once again, race is a figment of the American imagination, a tale that its citizens made up to embody their human flaws. Southerners were Americans in that all were guilty. Slavery was truly the original sin, and segregation and violence its inevitable offspring.

After *Light in August*, *Absalom, Absalom!* (1936) was a reversion both to experiment in technique and to opacity in style. This single work contains so much of Faulkner's greatness and so many of his flaws that critics inevitably pick it apart, a pointless exercise for a history book. But insofar as any one book could sum up the problems of a section, *Absalom* summed up the South and made it America.

Faulkner did the same for the West in "The Bear," which achieved final form in the stories collected in *Go Down, Moses*. This is an adventure story of the closing of the Southwestern frontier. It has many of the elements of the slave issue, but in its essence it is the West of innocent nature before the coming of civilization that is the scene of the hunt. Ike McCaslin grows from age ten to age sixteen in the first three parts of the work, from innocence to a certain level of experience. Each year the men go off to hunt Old Ben, the legendary great bear who rules the forests, and each year the hunt marks off time for the boy. Ike learns the myths and the rituals, above all to respect nature. But the woods change, and Old Ben starts killing domestic farm animals and otherwise getting out of line, and so one hunter trains up a mean dog, Lion, to finish the hunt. In time, dog and men do the job. Then, part four seems to be a reversion to the old Faulkner style of opaque murmurings about race and greed, and part five a brief look at the same woods after progress and the logging companies have obliter- ated all that made the area meaningful.

"The Bear" brought all of Faulkner together. It has aesthetic remnants from his early days, with the story becoming a King Arthur tale of a search for a Holy Grail, with high motives and low characters combining in a quest myth. It has scenes that seem borrowed from the John Keats of "Ode on a Grecian Urn" (1820), with the killing of Old Ben a frieze that encapsulated the meaning of the West the way the Keats urn encapsulated the meaning of Greece. It has a modernist sense of time: the years of the main part of the story seem to be from 1877 to 1883, with Ike discovering family scandals after he turns twenty-one in 1888, but they in turn go back three generations. It employs the dialogic method, the tale of tales, beginning with Ike listening to the older hunters speak in the opening paragraphs and continuing with the journal entries of Uncle Buck and Uncle Buddy that detail the corruptions on which family life had been based. Finally, and regrettably, it strives for biblical profundity. Ike has his carpenter's tools, he believes in Christian stewardship, and he seems to be intended as a Christ figure. It is also no accident that the wisest person in the book is an Indian of mixed blood from slaves who also probably has white blood as well. The point is that no one really knows and the three major varieties of America are mixed together.

Faulkner did not have any solution to sectional or racial problems, let alone theological ones. He knew that civilization had closed the West and that the Civil War had defeated the South. He knew that the society he loved was corrupt at its core. What he was saying is not the liberal exhortation to reform, but the conservative understanding that communities all cohere in some way. They have to, to give meaning to the tale and to the lives of the tellers. People, races, and communities were all in America together, and his role was to illuminate the picture, to put the frieze on the urn, and leave it to others to find solutions.

PART V

A COSMOPOLITAN CULTURE
1941–present

Chapter 12

The Recovery of American Ideals, 1954–1965

Because of the stress on moral reform, the changes progressives encouraged never went very far. They had what they thought was a viable system, and they wanted to perfect it: to encourage more meaningful competition, to put good men in office, to inform consumers honestly about what they were purchasing, and all the other reforms that received so much publicity but made so little difference in the long run. Society did not become more moral; first it went to war and then it wallowed in a decade of fiscal excess.

The Depression began to settle in late in 1929, becoming serious early in the 1930s. The Republican president Herbert Hoover had been a capable progressive administrator; despite his great abilities, he proved too inflexible to deal with the crises that surrounded him, and his stiff appearance and unbending public announcements cost him public confidence. His successor, Democrat Franklin D. Roosevelt, had also been a progressive and few anticipated that he would do much that was materially different from Hoover. But Roosevelt was flexible and experimental, and his wife Eleanor provided added impetus. Like Jane Addams and Alice Hamilton, she had been something of a product of the social-settlement movement, and she was warm and spontaneous in her sympathies with the poor and the immigrant. The two Roosevelts helped initiate a New Deal that instituted secular, welfare-state reform for the first time in America.

In contrast to the regulatory measures of the progressives, the New Dealers enacted measures that really made a difference in how the masses lived their lives. They took a much firmer grip on the economy, abandoned the gold standard, and restricted business practices on an unprecedented scale. They created massive job projects, putting people back to work even when there was no obvious work to do. They enacted the first social security program, so that old people could have a minimum income during their retirement years. They enacted a labor relations measure that exempted labor from laws which had proved restrictive and gave unions a permanent place in the American system. The president made a point of bringing a woman into his cabinet, appointing Jews and Catholics to high positions, and in general making the sons and daughters of recent immigrants feel important within a system once exclusively Protestant and predominantly Anglo-Saxon. The first lady opened the White House doors to groups never previously invited there, traveled indefatigably, and even wrote a newspaper column, breaking traditions of propriety less gregarious predecessors had set. She became a folk hero to large portions of the population, and an example of everything that was wrong with the country to a few.

II

But for all its commonsense experimentalism, the New Deal was inadequate in its reconstruction of American life. Roosevelt tried and mostly failed, and only the economic impact of World War II revived the economy for any sustained period of time. The New Deal also failed in another area that one could term qualitative, the area of civil rights. The New Deal was too mired in poverty and unemployment to have much time for blacks and other minorities. Eleanor Roosevelt could invite them to the White House and speak to their conventions, but her husband had too many Southern congressmen whose votes he needed for more important reform measures. The black population prospered a bit during the 1930s because they were poor and the New Deal tried to help all poor people; but as blacks they remained at the bottom. Other minority groups saw their most talented sons and daughters rise to influence; blacks managed little more than the grudging appointment of an occasional officer in the segregated army. They were on their own with precious few resources beyond a century and a half of American ideals, none of which seemed to apply to them. The recovery of those ideals was the great task of the third wave of twentieth-century reform, which reached its crest only with the Civil Rights Bill of 1964.

At the end of the Civil War in 1865, the Thirteenth Amendment to the Constitution asserted that "Neither slavery nor involuntary servitude, except as a punishment for crime whereof the party shall have been duly convicted, shall exist within the United States, or any place subject to their jurisdiction." Slavery in law was thus over, but no one knew what would happen to the blacks who were suddenly free. No one had planned for their freedom. The emphasis had been upon freeing the democracy from the sin of slavery, and the amendment did this. But it did not educate blacks, find them jobs, build them houses, or give them the vote. And it left them in the hands of bitter white men who regarded them as hopeless inferiors, incapable of citizenship.

For a brief time, the blacks had friends in power in Washington. Known as Radical Republicans, these legislators were not free of racism themselves; being politicians they also had political and economic motives for their acts which were not entirely altruistic. Nevertheless they cared more for blacks than other groups, and when Southern whites indicated their intention of reducing the newly freed slaves to something resembling peonage, they enacted yet further methods of protecting blacks. The Freedmen's Bureau Bill and the first Civil Rights Act asserted that the national government would protect them if the states refused to do so, and explicitly granted them the rights to make and enforce contracts; buy, sell, and own real and personal property; sue in the courts and give evidence; and have the full benefit of all laws and proceedings for the security of their persons and property. By law, blacks were equal to whites.

The Fourteenth Amendment made this protection a permanent part of the American Constitution. Its enactment was an attempt to prevent some future Congress from repealing black rights. It granted the rights of citizenship to everyone born or naturalized in the United States, and said that no state could in any way limit the privileges of citizenship, or "deprive any person of life, liberty, or property, without due process of law; nor deny to any person within its jurisdiction the equal protection of the laws." Southern states had to accept these amendments in order to return to the Union. Two subsequent measures which aided blacks were the Fifteenth Amendment and the Civil Rights Act of 1875. The amendment protected the right of blacks to vote, and the act guaranteed to all people "the full and equal enjoyment of the accommodations . . . of inns, public conveyances on land or water, theaters and other places of public amusement." It also granted rights of jury service.

Insofar as the law could, the law did grant equality. But reality was very different. Most blacks lived where they had been freed and knew no other life. They had no money, education, property, or power. For a while, Northern white attention protected them from Southern white wrath and exploitation, but by 1877 the war was legally over and life back to "normal." Southern whites regained control, and Northern whites—who were often fully as racist even if they had not approved of slavery—lost interest. Few people could sustain moral indignation for very long, and most citizens wanted to get back to settling the country, expanding the economy, and making money.

The courts reflected this waning zeal. Many decisions could be cited to demonstrate the gradual loss of black rights. Two in particular returned to the states virtually all the power of determining who could vote, and denied that suffrage was a necessary attribute of citizenship. In effect, this allowed whites in all states to prevent blacks from voting, and meant that no court would support any blacks who complained about it. The most famous of all these decisions was *Plessy v. Ferguson* (1896), a case originating in Louisiana which dealt with the right of blacks to travel in unsegregated railroad cars. The majority argued that the Fourteenth Amendment conveyed no such right, and that segregation was compatible with democratic liberties. No law could abolish distinctions of color, and no law could force people to mingle if they did not want to. Such segregation laws did not in any way imply inferiority, just the desire of whites to travel, eat, and socialize among their own kind. This decision became the major legal support for one law after another that separated the races in many states, not only in the South, and denied blacks the equality they should have won with the Thirteenth, Fourteenth, and Fifteenth amendments.

The most educated blacks soon began a counterattack, sure that in time the American legal system would yet again reflect American ideals. The NAACP, the organization W. E. B. DuBois and a number of liberal whites had founded in 1909, was the most obvious institutional response. Another, which in time proved equally important, was the slow rise to excellence of the Howard University Law School in Washington, D.C. The preeminent black educational institution in the country, the school remained impoverished in both money and talent until it began to improve in the 1930s. A few gifted administrators and legal talents made it a center for civil rights information, and began to train young lawyers who could lead the fight in the courts against segregation. The most eminent of these young men was Thurgood Marshall; in his astonishing career he overcame all the barriers of prejudice to rise to the Supreme Court itself, an example both of the inequalities of the American system and the ability of gifted people to change that system and make it work better.

The Howard lawyers and the NAACP decided that education was the area in which segregation was legally the most vulnerable. The law permitted separate schools only if they were equal, and this opened up an obvious line of attack. Only a few blacks wanted training in advanced subjects: pharmacy, law, medicine, architecture, and so on. Community feelings were relatively weak, since few students were involved, and they were of advanced age. Proving that separate schools were not equal would not be hard, because equipment for a dental school or books for a law library would be resources easy to document, and if the number of machines or of books were obviously unequal, that would be enough. It was possible to pass off some fraud of an elementary school as separate but equal, even if it lacked school buses, toilet facilities, or science equipment, but only the most hopelessly bigoted juries could decide that separate graduate and professional schools were equal to those of the best state universities.

The other consideration was financial. Separate elementary and secondary schools could run inexpensively for the substantial numbers of black children involved, but setting up acceptable postgraduate institutions for only a few blacks was a ludicrous proposition. Preposterous sums for buildings, faculties, books, and equipment would be required, merely to keep a few adults from sitting next to whites. If justice were possible within the American system, then integration at this level seemed the place to begin.

By the late 1930s, Marshall and his associates began to win small victories. In Maryland and Missouri, blacks won token admissions to law schools. Resistance continued, but it seemed clear that blacks could win such cases if they were patient and willing to bear the expense. Several states meanwhile thought they could solve their problems by paying out-of-state tuition to blacks so they could study in an integrated environment. By the early 1950s, at least a few states were actually making substantial contributions toward the establishment of black schools, hoping to keep the courts away by making a genuine effort to be equal within a segregation system. It proved to be a case of too little, too late.

In other areas of society, blacks made small gains. Franklin D. Roosevelt's Executive Order 8802 used the wartime defense build-up as a means of forcing employers to hire workers without regard to their race, and in the armed forces a compromise form of integration evolved, where black units and white units coexisted, and where black officers up to a certain level were permitted to command black troops. But military resistance was very great, Southern officers were often in important positions, and only severe presidential pressure could force change. President Harry S. Truman took a major step in this direction once the war was safely won, and so troops fought on an integrated basis for the first time in Korea (1950–1953). This military experience was a socially valuable precedent, for it brought together men still of an impressionable age, made them train and fight together, and then sent them back to civilian life with memories of an acceptable, integrated racial environment. In the long run, such experiences helped open up white housing and jobs to blacks.

In labor unions and in polling booths, progress was slower. Union members often were of the same ethnic group, memberships often passed from one generation of a family to another, and no outsiders of any color were especially welcomed. Unions had had a long fight in America to win their places in the sun, and were unwilling to share their gains with blacks. In voting, the issue was more general. Blacks had the legal right to vote, but lived in areas where whites refused to acknowledge that right. The result was a series of ingenious laws that effectively excluded blacks from genuine participation in the political system. White primaries often selected the candidates; literacy and comprehension tests, unfairly administered, eliminated blacks foolish enough to attempt to vote. Payment of poll taxes often eliminated the poor, and most blacks were poor. The record was a sorry one.

But in education, the legal situation remained promising, and if education could be integrated it seemed possible that the rest of society would follow. A number of cases developed slowly in the postwar years, the crucial one going into the history books as *Sweatt v. Painter*. This case involved the efforts of a mailman to enroll in the University of Texas Law School, the preeminent institution in the Southwest. The university refused him, and the state quickly set up an academic joke of a law school for blacks in a few rented rooms in Houston. It did not have a faculty, library or student body, but nevertheless the local courts declared that it offered separate but equal facilities for blacks and that therefore there was no need to enroll them in the white state law school. Sweatt kept up his campaign, and in 1947 the authorities opened a somewhat more respectable institution in Austin for black law students. Lower court decisions were adverse, and so Thurgood Marshall took the case to the Supreme Court, where he won in 1950. But the decision was a narrow one, and it did not overrule *Plessy*; segregation was still the law of the land.

The language of the *Sweatt* decision, however, was important. For the first time, it admitted intangible considerations into the discussion of segregation. To count books and bathrooms, or compare teachers' salaries, missed the point. The University of Texas Law School "possesses to a far greater degree those qualities which are incapable of objective measurement but which make for greatness in a law school." These qualities included "reputation of the faculty, experience of the administration, position and influence of the alumni, standing in the community, traditions and prestige." The majority found it "difficult to believe that one who had a free choice between these law schools would consider the question close."

It was an important victory, but not a major breakthrough. The Supreme Court in those days was a mediocre group that seemed unlikely to unify on any issue, let alone a decision that would end segregation in the public schools. But a number of new cases were developing that seemed promising, and Marshall was determined to press forward when the court changed and the cases seemed appropriate. After years of misfortune, luck finally was with the blacks. The chief justice died unexpectedly, and his replacement was former Governor Earl Warren of California, a politician of considerable ability whose civil liberties record on the whole seemed friendly to the black cause. Warren had no great academic or legal talent, but he was sympathetic to the underdog, and above all, he had the tact to bring the feuding justices together. He took his time, adjusted his arguments, and in 1954 came down with a unanimous decision that rewrote American law on the issue of segregation in education.

Oliver Brown et al v. Board of Education of Topeka, usually abbreviated *Brown v. Board of Education,* came out of Kansas, a Midwestern state which practiced limited segregation. Brown himself was mild-mannered and unassertive, and hardly a leader of social change, but he was upset because his daughter had problems in getting to a distant black school, even though a white school was close by their home. His case soon far transcended this minor issue, and it accumulated social science data which challenged the whole framework of segregated schooling. Following the lead of Swedish sociologist Gunnar Myrdal and black sociologist Kenneth Clark, the court accepted the argument that intangibles were important, that education was central to citizenship, and that psychological damage was an unacceptable risk. Segregation deprived minority children of equal educational opportunities and retarded their mental development. "To separate them from others of similar age and qualifications solely because of their race generates a feeling of inferiority as to their status in the community that may affect their hearts and minds in a way unlikely ever to be undone."

The decision disturbed the South. In border states, compliance came easily. But in Virginia and the deep South, resistance seemed total. The law of the land had changed, but whites refused to accept it. The court insisted that states introduce integration with "all deliberate speed," but many whites seemed to define "deliberate" as sometime after they themselves were dead. In many areas, nothing really changed.

Behind the gentilities of legal discourse, however, a social revolution was underway that gave black America a leader of world stature. Martin Luther King, Jr., needed federal legal protection for his campaigns against segregation, but the courts needed him if their decrees were to have any impact on a racist culture.

III

In the years since the civil rights revolution, scholars have worked hard to write King's biography and to outline in detail the problems he and his allies faced in their struggle. The story has become increasingly complicated, much to the sorrow both of those who admire King and those who would like to think that the American government, its legal system, and those white politicians who seemed to be leading the revolution, were all worthy of respect. All that seems to remain is the achievement itself: civil rights worked, whatever its flawed origins. Of all the achievements of the 1960s, civil rights laws have stood the test of time and public acceptance best. They have not remade the world, but they have eliminated legal blemishes that had become intolerable.

Martin Luther King, Jr., was the product of the black upper-middle class in Atlanta. His grandfather had founded the Ebenezer Baptist Church, and his father was its pastor when King emerged to national prominence. The family survived the Depression reasonably well, and young Martin grew up with at least a few white friends. By the standards of black America, he was neither poor nor underprivileged, and good schooling was also available. But still, the lines were there, and King found them painful. One day, as he told the story, the son of a white grocer who had been his playmate told him that he could not play with him any more. "I never will forget what a great shock this was to me." He asked his parents what it was all about. "We were at the dinner table when the situation was discussed, and here, for the first time, I was made aware of the existence of a race problem. I had never been conscious of it before."

By white standards, King did not have a good education; he never did spell very well, his grammar was poor, and he was not an outstanding student at Morehouse College, perhaps the best of the black colleges. He also had severe theological and vocational doubts. He had an almost hereditary lien on his father's pastorate, yet he had great trouble accepting the fundamentalist ideas that the Baptist Church insisted upon for its leaders. He finally decided that Christianity had great truths about myth, ethics, and morals at its core and that he could accept a broad-based type of faith. He continued to have trouble reconciling Christian attitudes in theory with the practice that he encountered in the white community. The question always remained in his mind, he said, "how could I love a race of people who hated me and who had been responsible for breaking me up with one of my best childhood friends? This was a great question in my mind for a number of years," one he could not conquer until he came to know white students through several groups that bridged the various college campuses in Atlanta.

King finally committed himself to the ministry and attended Crozer Seminary in Pennsylvania. There he had an intense love affair with a white girl of German immigrant origin that nearly led to marriage. His friends all liked the girl but no one could picture her as the wife of a black leader in the segregated South. He had to choose between his family and his career on the one hand or his personal preferences for a wife on the other, and it took him months of painful indecision before he broke off the relationship. One of his friends, interviewed years later, felt that King "was a man of a broken heart—he never recovered," and this may well be true. The experience not only brought home many of the realities of race relations, it may well have caused a certain cynicism about marriage and the permanance of sexual bonds. His marriage to Coretta Scott appears not to have been a happy one, and biographies now leave the impression that he married chiefly out of a career commitment. Certainly the glare of publicity as well as the slanderous rumors government investigators generated made any normal family life impossible. King's behavior became a major issue when the FBI and other enemies used his activities as pretexts for invading his civil liberties and defaming the legal efforts at ending segregation.

Although journalists later made much of the presumed inspiration of Mahatma Gandhi for many of King's attitudes, in fact he drew most of his ideas from white domestic sources. One was Walter Rauschenbusch, the leading theologian of the Progressive Era and one of the most distinguished teachers the Baptist church ever produced. In two books, *Christianity and the Social Crisis* (1907) and *Christianizing the Social Order* (1912), Rauschenbusch had adapted the liberal and radical thought of the nineteenth century to church purposes, and reworked theology into a way of doing good works in the world. Rauschenbusch was very much a liberal progressive, optimistic about the nature of man as well as the possibilities of working within the system. Such attitudes did not survive the First World War any better in the church than in society, and Rauschenbusch's name and influence went into eclipse, but not before helping to inspire the leading political theologian of the interwar years, Reinhold Niebuhr.

After years of ministering to a poor congregation in Detroit, Niebuhr emerged into public spotlight with *Moral Man and Immoral Society* (1932), an unsparing attack on the inadequacies of the progressive outlook. He was especially critical of the secular liberalism of John Dewey, and insisted repeatedly on the role of sin in personal life and the importance of power in public life. He warned about confusing the two realms and against any effort to apply personal ethics to public issues. King became a follower of Niebuhr's ideas and referred to his books throughout his life. Niebuhr sharpened his sense of sin, of the corrupt nature of human beings and social institutions, and the need to be realistic about political and social power. Christian love was not enough, and waiting for progress silly.

A third influence, less known outside church circles, was Edgar S. Brightman. King read his works at Crozer and chose the Boston University Graduate School for his Ph.D. because Brightman was there. The professor was an advocate of "personalism" in theological studies, the idea that the human personality was the standard measure of value in the world. King took this to mean that all personalities were of equal value and worth nurturing. The connection to his later civil rights campaigns remains obvious.

Unfortunately, the enormous amount of attention that world fame generated led to a close scholarly reexamination of King's writings. A team of black scholars led by Clayborne Carson discovered that King plagiarized large sections of his doctoral dissertation and was sloppy in giving proper credit to sources that he had obviously used. Never a good student, perhaps still depressed by his Crozer love affair, under pressure to marry a proper wife, finish his degree, and take on church responsibilities, King committed what for scholars was an academic crime. Indeed, he seems never to have held scholarly attitudes toward writing and publishing at all, and to have assumed a preacher's habit of quotation from the Bible or any other relevant text was a matter of course. His later publications, most obviously *Stride Toward Freedom*, also borrow heavily from such books as Paul Ramsay's *Basic Christian Ethics* and Anders Nygren's *Agape and Eros*.

Like King's marital problems, his habit of borrowing words had no outward impact on the civil rights revolution while it was under way. That began on 1 December 1955 when a dignified, soft-spoken black woman with tired feet refused to give up her seat to a white passenger in Montgomery, Alabama. Rosa Parks knew the law; so did every black in the city. A black who wanted to ride the bus paid the required fare at the front, left the bus, walked to the rear, got on again, and sat in the back if there was room. Whites got on in front and had the front seats reserved for them. Parks had been seated on the borderline between the sections, and city law required her to move if a white person wanted the seat. She refused even under threat of arrest. She was the fourth woman to defy the rules that year, but her case sparked the revolt. Blacks in Montgomery were tired in more places than their feet. They did not like the segregated schools, segregated restaurants, segregated swimming pools, or segregated toilets. They were tired of rude treatment and police harassment. They did not like the lack of good jobs. They did not like the violence that was always in the air.

Brown v. Board of Education had heartened blacks. It gave them a sense of a decent future, at least for their children. The NAACP was the chief vehicle of black protest, and Rosa Parks had been an NAACP secretary. Her pastor was the Reverend Mr. Ralph Abernathy, and one of Abernathy's most promising younger colleagues was King. The leaders of the black community caucused, decided on a bus boycott to protest segregation and Parks' arrest, and elected King the leader of the movement. The early years of the xerox revolution were underway, and the group managed to run off forty thousand copies of their boycott statement at a local college. Eighteen black taxicab companies, countless volunteer drivers, and a great many tired feet all joined to keep the buses empty and economic pressure on a bus company, most of whose riders were black. The goals were minimal: courteous treatment by bus drivers; first-come, first-served seating, blacks at the rear, whites at the front; and the employment of black drivers on routes which served the black areas of the city.

At best, the white response was a polite refusal. At worst, white extremists bombed King's home, fired black employees, canceled black insurance policies, and arrested blacks on preposterous charges. King and many other leaders were themselves arrested, served brief periods in jail, and won their cases only on appeal to federal courts—a pattern which repeated itself relentlessly for the next decade. In time, a superior court invalidated city segregation laws, and the Supreme Court affirmed its decision. But the courts were only a sideshow; they were not telegenic. Montgomery generated many pictures, in the form of photographs and future demonstrations that had even greater visual impact.

King's greatest trial came in Birmingham. Birmingham seemed "trapped for decades in a Rip Van Winkle slumber," he wrote. It was "a city whose fathers had apparently never heard of Abraham Lincoln, Thomas Jefferson, the Bill of Rights, the Preamble to the Constitution, the Thirteenth, Fourteenth and Fifteenth amendments or the 1954 decision of the United States Supreme Court outlawing segregation in the public schools." One key demand was for integration of lunch counters; blacks found their exclusion from lunch counters in stores where they often spent great amounts of money especially humiliating. "Food is not only a necessity but a symbol, and our lunch-counter campaign had not only a practical but a symbolic importance." White moderates, as was their custom, decried black extremism and demanded civility—which in effect meant the abandonment of protest and the acceptance of permanently inferior status. King invoked his ancestors: Jesus, Amos, Paul, Martin Luther, John Bunyan, Abraham Lincoln, and Thomas Jefferson were all disruptive, and all had every justification for overturning an unjust government. "One day the South will know that when these disinherited children of God sat down at lunch counters, they were in reality standing up for what is best in the American dream and for the most sacred values in our Judaeo-Christian heritage, thereby bringing our nation back to those great wells of democracy which were dug deep by the founding fathers in their formulation of the Constitution and the Declaration of Independence." White Birmingham responded by bombing seventeen black churches, endangering the lives of countless demonstrators and innocent by-standers, and putting pressure hoses and police dogs on anyone who threatened the status quo, whether black or white. The pictures of the ensuing violence inflamed world opinion far beyond anything that had happened in Montgomery.

The inhumanity of the white response defeated its own goals. President John F. Kennedy sent a new and broad civil rights bill to Congress; Northern busi-nessmen with Birmingham interests put pressure on local businessmen to end their opposition. Shame played some role, not to mention the horror caused by the blast which killed four little girls innocently attending a black church. In August 1963 King led a massive march on Washington; a quarter of a million people, about 35 percent white, gathered nonviolently to express their support for the decent acceptance of blacks within the American system of values. King's address has gone down in history as perhaps the most famous ever given in modern America. In tones redolent with the rhythms of black music, both religious and secular, he told the world that he had a dream. The architects of American democracy had created a nation for every man, black as well as white: everyone had a right to life, liberty, and the pursuit of happiness.

Even though great difficulties remained before achieving these goals, "I still have a dream. It is a dream deeply rooted in the American dream that one day this nation will rise up and live out the true meaning of its creed—we hold these truths to be self-evident, that all men are created equal." One day, he proph-esied, on the hills of Georgia the sons of slaveholders and the sons of slaves would be able to sit down together as brothers. Even in Mississippi, "a state sweltering with the heat of injustice," an oasis of freedom would develop. He wanted his four children to live in a nation where their character would be important, not the color of their skin. As the words of one of the most famous American songs had it, all Americans could repeat: "My country 'tis of thee; sweet land of liberty; of thee I sing; land where my fathers died; land of the pilgrim's pride; from every mountainside, let freedom ring." And when that day came, then all of God's children, "black men and white men, Jews and Gentiles,

Catholics and Protestants—will be able to join hands and to sing in the words of the old Negro spiritual: "Free at last, free at last; thank God Almighty, we are free at last.' "

IV

King's activities made him into a symbol of American commitment to civil rights and an example of personal heroism. He won a Nobel Prize at age thirty-five, and by the time of his assassination was one of the most admired Americans in the world. But the personal and political triumphs he could celebrate should not overshadow the larger issues involving race and its place in a capitalist democracy as it fought for the moral leadership of the world, against a communism that denied its religious, economic, and political principles.

Inside the nation, King's forces faced Democratic administrations that seemed supportive, and a law-enforcement apparatus that was supposed to be even-handed in its recognition of black rights. In fact, the Kennedy family was ambivalent throughout the black revolution, and when it did become concerned, its attitudes were based more on fears about the American image abroad than on any strong commitment to racial equality. The president and his brother, Attorney General Robert Kennedy, did not regard civil rights as all that important, and neither wished to offend powerful Southern members of their own party. Continuing the New Deal tradition, they assumed that legislation that helped poor people in general would help blacks and other minorities along the way, and that no one could reasonably expect more. Both Kennedys regarded the freedom rides and demonstrations as generative of bad publicity, distracting voters and provoking antiblack backlash that could easily translate into anti-Democratic votes.

The major focus of the Kennedy administration was on foreign policy. In this area the president regarded King as offending peoples that America wanted as allies in the fight against communism. On one occasion, Robert Kennedy placed civil rights at the center of foreign policy rather than domestic policy. Rights for blacks were a part of the postcolonial fight for the rights of subject peoples everywhere; both Kennedys and King agreed on this. But whereas King saw this relation as requiring more demonstrations and stricter laws, Robert Kennedy declared: "We, the American people must avoid another Little Rock or another New Orleans," referring to incidents that had happened before Birmingham. "We cannot afford them. . . . Such incidents hurt our country in the eyes of the world." When blacks won civil rights victories without violence, it would "without question aid and assist the fight against Communist political infiltration and guerilla warfare." When Birmingham then dominated the news, the Kennedys noted that intelligence reports from the Soviet Union reported 1420 anti-U.S.

news reports that used the violence there to hurt America. Despite their subsequent reputation as civil rights pioneers, the Kennedys regarded the issue as less important than the Cold War and were moderate about what its goals should be.

One important related issue was the involvement of the Federal Bureau of Investigation (FBI) in harassing King and undermining all efforts of blacks to achieve equality. Here the leading figure was the long-time director of the FBI, J. Edgar Hoover, a man whom Kennedy reappointed. Hoover was antiblack, anti-Communist, and antiradical; in recent scholarship he comes across as almost a cartoon figure. At the time, however, he wielded great power, in part because he maintained extensive files on presidents and other leaders that could damage their careers. In a characteristic maneuver, early in the 1960s Hoover warned that key advisors of King were Communists or former Communists or sexual deviates.

The charges were technically true. The chief target was Stanley Levison, who had long been a contributor to Communist party activities. He was also an important figure around King and the Southern Christian Leadership Conference. Another was Jack O'Dell, who never hid his Communist past and said repeatedly that the Communists in America had fought for the Negro when no one else was paying them attention. This was true. What was untrue was the relevance of the matter to the demonstrations. Neither Levison nor O'Dell were currently party members and both were genuinely committed to King's goals. King's response was apropos: So what?, he asked.

The sexual issue was also plausible but even less relevant, especially coming from an FBI director whose closest companion was a male and who was widely believed to be a latent if not an overt homosexual. The chief target at first was Bayard Rustin, a homosexual who had had several problems with the law about his private activities. Increasingly, however, the target was King himself. Thwarted in his college love affair, married to a woman with whom he found relations difficult, constantly away from home, King lived a life that invited rumors. In addition, he was charismatic, and attractive women made deviation from the standards of Baptist propriety all too easy. The matter grew exceptionally unpleasant in its mixture of the public and the private.

The issue compromised everyone in the end. In his pursuit of Communists, Hoover had the full support of the administration, and he used this issue to get the written permission of the attorney general to wiretap telephones. In fact, the whole matter was preposterous. The American Communist party by the early 1960s was little more than a collection of FBI agents. Government spies were at times more numerous than believers after the disillusionment following Nikita Khrushchev's anti-Stalinist campaign of the 1950s. But Hoover was obsessed by Reds, blacks, and beds, and the wiretaps enabled him to compile dossiers on King's private life as well as the civil rights movement. He and the FBI made

King and close associates miserable; they planted disinformation, spread rumors, and did all they could to smear the civil rights movement. It is not a pretty story, and the reputation of the Kennedys has sunk lower with each new history book. Hoover's reputation could hardly be lower and seems unlikely ever to recover.

President Kennedy was assassinated in 1963, enabling his successor Lyndon Johnson to use his death as a weapon in the battle for civil rights. Given the similarities in their domestic goals, Johnson and King should have been allies. In fact, they hated each other. Johnson became obsessed with the war in Vietnam and could not abide opposition to a crusade he thought holy. King opposed him, becoming one of the most visible Americans to do so. "The war in Vietnam is but a symptom of a far deeper malady within the American spirit," he said in a major speech, and he demanded "a radical revolution in values." That was what conventional politicians and law enforcement officials feared.

V

As King's activities continued to provoke violent demonstrations and the government opposed him with indefensible tactics, the country went through a cultural revolution. As a shorthand designation, *the sixties* now refers to this sharp shift in values. Antiwar activity and civil rights activity were only the two most obvious, photographable aspects of a change that struck deep into the generation of students who came of age after 1960.

They were the children of the baby boom. Their parents had survived the Depression and fought World War II, while birthrates declined and most prognosticators anticipated a renewed depression in the later 1940s. Instead, America experienced inflation and a higher birthrate. Soldiers came home and bred families with three or four children, all of whom needed schooling, clothes, food, and so on during the 1950s. These children knew only "Eisenhower prosperity" and could hardly imagine depression or war. They took a great deal for granted, feeling entitled to comforts and privileges their parents had only yearned for. Many quietly accepted their good fortune, but others seemed bored, and oppressed by prosperity.

Discontent took a number of forms. In comic books, rock-and-roll music, films starring James Dean or Marlon Brando, and in the poetry and prose of underground writers, a "beat generation" emerged. Although unaware of much history, they looked back chiefly to outsiders, like the Henry Thoreau of *Walden* and a life lived at a subsistence level, in accord with nature. Jack Kerouac in *On the Road* and Allen Ginsberg in "Howl" provided fiction and poetry that became emblematic of this type of dissent. More recently, they looked to California guru Henry Miller, the bard of male sexual athleticism. His *The Air-Conditioned*

Nightmare was reprinted during this period, and its title summed up the scorn the Beats seemed to have for the achievements of capitalism. Pictures of Elvis Presley decorated the walls of the rooms of countless teenage girls, and an increasing number of their brothers became familiar with the drug culture celebrated by William Burroughs—heir to the Burroughs Business Machine fortune, but becoming better known for such works as *Naked Lunch* and the surrealistic mentality that accompanied hallucinogens.

The black revolution was thus only in part an agitation for civil rights, led by a Nobel Prize-winner who believed in nonviolent resistance. It was also a blow against conformity and complacency, a provocation to violence that could help a generation bored to psychic death to reaffirm its sense of worth. Blacks spoke their own language, and so music was important; they did not accept capitalism, so left-wing theory was important. They had few places in the universities, so they were corrupt handmaidens of the status quo. Blacks led a freer, more authentic sexual life, which young white males and at least a few of the females wished to emulate. They knew the ecstacy of drugs. The 1960s tied all these together, and tied them in turn to the movement against the Vietnam War. Neither American culture nor its politics would ever be quite the same again.

Chapter 13

The Primacy of Foreign Policy, 1941–1977

American foreign policy was not an important subject in the history of the world during the nineteenth century. America seemed to have few interests outside its own borders, and no military force capable of demanding respect for its flag. Pioneers headed south and west, expanding the nation relentlessly and occasionally infringing on the territories of Spain, Canada, and Mexico. American democrats often voiced a sympathy for their brothers in Latin America or Europe. American ships occasionally touched on Japan, China, and India. But by and large, America was not a matter of much concern in London or the lesser capitals of the world. Foreign policy remained under the influence of the ideas of John Quincy Adams, content to remain free of entanglement with countries that were far away. The term that covers the period is *isolationism*, essentially the notion that the country should develop itself in isolation from the wars and monarchies that disrupted the rest of the world.

Insofar as any single event ended American isolation, it was the Japanese attack on Pearl Harbor, Hawaii, on 7 December 1941. The Germans declared war shortly thereafter, and so the country found itself fighting in both Asia and Europe; economically it was the only Western nation capable of providing vital war materials to its allies. With astonishing rapidity, the economy shifted to a war basis, and the military assumed the size and importance that it has since retained in the economy. Yet much of the innocence of isolationist thought remained deep in the American character. Popular books like Ambassador Joseph E. Davies' *Mission to Moscow* and Republican presidential candidate Wendell Willkie's *One World* seemed determined to gloss over both the behavior of Joseph Stalin and the need for force in order to survive in the modern world. Hundreds of thousands of readers seemed to assume that victory, good will, and a United Nations would usher in a millennium. Such vacuities were perhaps useful in arousing public opinion to favor war sacrifices, but they produced little intelligent thought and in the long run led to disillusionment and a hunt for those who had "betrayed" the cause.

On the whole, Americans had derived their culture from Europe, and Europe retained its centrality to American thinking even though Japan was the nation that provoked American participation in the war. At first, the primary focus of attention was on Germany, and all other considerations were secondary to the defeat of the Nazis. This meant an alliance not only with Great Britain and the Free French, but also with the Soviet Union. In time, the Soviet relationship became central to most American thought on foreign policy. President Roosevelt, never a clear or systematic thinker on such matters, preferred to deal with Stalin directly, or through trusted emissaries like Harry Hopkins who were normally willing to overlook Soviet attitudes and activities that were totalitarian in their implications. Such figures hoped that Russian communism was mellowing, that the brutalities of collectivization were over, and that the Moscow trials had not been the travesty of justice that in fact they were. They stressed the great sacrifice that Russia had made to defeat Hitler: roughly sixteen times as many dead as suffered by the West. Roosevelt was sure he could deal with Stalin, and he was personally sympathetic to Russia's anticolonialist attitudes toward the third world.

But Roosevelt died in 1945, and his successor, Harry S. Truman, lacked his experience and subtlety. Often unjustly attacked in office, then unjustly praised by later scholars, Truman was a mediocre politician who inherited a job he did not merit. Under him, a number of foreign policy experts emerged who changed the course of American policy to make it far more hostile to Russian ambitions. Names like Dean Acheson, George F. Kennan, and Dean Rusk rose to visibility, and as a group controlled the foreign policy of the country for the next two generations, regardless of which political party was in power. Kennan soon changed his mind and became a sharp dissenter from standard policy; the failures of Vietnam caused severe splits among the once-united foreign policy intelligentsia; and the brief reign of Henry Kissinger added important new elements to American thinking. But, basically, foreign policy became bipartisan, interventionist, and militantly anti-Soviet. In a few brief years, America had gone from excessive isolationism to excessive interventionism; the faith in Christianity, capitalism, and democracy of course remained.

The change in orientation to the Soviets began in Moscow toward the end of the war. Ambassador W. Averell Harriman and his top advisor George F. Kennan were far more suspicious of Soviet intentions than President Roosevelt. They knew of Stalin's paranoia; they also knew that Russia had been invaded from the West twice in thirty years, and that nothing America could do would prevent Stalin from a wholesale rearrangement of his western borders, a forcible transplantation of populations, and the establishment of puppet states along vulnerable borders. Many American politicians, led by the president, seemed to talk as if free elections were likely in Eastern Europe, when in fact those areas had never been truly democratic. Their monarchies and elites had great contempt for both democracy and for the Russians, and so encouraging thoughts of free elections and expecting the Russians to keep out were both counterproductive. Harriman and Kennan advocated a greater realism in dealing with the Soviets: America should understand Russia's problems and its history, and should avoid wishful thinking that would only interfere with a sensible policy in the area.

Roosevelt ignored their warnings but Truman did not. As the Russians moved into Poland, Czechoslovakia, Hungary, and so on, Truman increasingly sought the advice of hardline anti-Communists like Dean Acheson, who became his secretary of state in 1949. By his own account, Truman was unconscionably rude to Russian diplomats. He proved insensitive to Russian history or the legitimate necessities of Russian foreign policy. He believed his own propaganda and thus found it impossible to deal with a world in which right and wrong were never absolute. Under secretaries of state Acheson, Dulles, and Rusk, America rebuilt its military force and demonstrated its willingness to intervene almost anywhere in the world where it felt its interests threatened. The North Atlantic Treaty Organization and the South East Asia Treaty Organization testified to deep American military involvement wherever Russian influence seemed dangerous. Both the Korean War and the Vietnam War resulted.

Behind this intervention and its failures lay one obvious problem: most of the world did not share America's faith in Christianity, capitalism, and democracy. Most of the third world was too poor to worry about freedom of the ballot, of speech, or of the press. Food was their chief need; if they could also be free of heavy taxes, able to exercise their religion in peace, and be assured of civil order, the rest hardly mattered. To many of these people, the values of tradition, of family, of their own religion and culture were far more important than secular or competitive Western values. To them, the West often meant unemployment, inflation, war, mechanization, pollution, and the disruption of the family. Even in highly developed countries, the goal of equality seemed preferable to the evils that they saw in capitalism, the corruption that seemed to go along with democracy, and the bigotries that accompanied a foreign religion. Americans found this hostility to their way of life all but incomprehensible. As a nation founded by people fleeing wars and autocracies, they were sure that they understood these things better than anyone else. During the nineteenth century, many peoples had listened. After 1945, many more did not. Participation in two world wars had cost the country much of its innocence, but it took a long series of failed interventions to bring the point home to many of those involved.

II

The "hot war" against Germany ended officially in the early summer of 1945, but even before the guns fell silent the "cold war" against the Soviet Union had begun. President Roosevelt and Harry Hopkins had tried hard to cooperate with Marshal Stalin, but second-level officials did not share Roosevelt's optimism. For a brief period between 1944 and 1947, the chief advocate of a firmer line against Soviet expansionism was George F. Kennan; a famous long telegram from Moscow in 1944 and an article on "The Sources of Soviet Conduct" published anonymously in 1947 were the key texts in which he advocated greater pessimism and realism in dealing with the Soviets. Kennan argued that Stalin was determined to secure his western borders and that America could do nothing about it. But American interests were legitimately involved with the freedom of states farther to the west, and America had every right to work peacefully to secure some kind of democratic autonomy for Finland, Austria, Czechoslovakia, Yugoslavia, and Greece. War was not a viable alternative, but many peaceful means were available to keep the Soviets from too aggressive a push into the area. The word Kennan used was *containment*: America should work politically to contain the Soviets within acceptable perimeters. Their borders would be safe, but they would not control most of Europe.

Kennan's ideas had taken shape under Roosevelt, but they came to world attention under Truman. Washington changed remarkably between 1944 and 1947, and the new administration seized on the word, and Kennan's genuine authority, to fashion a policy far more belligerent and severe than anything he could have anticipated. President Truman and a number of his advisors, not to mention many of their successors, had a great faith in that new weapon, the atomic bomb. With the bomb, they were sure, they could threaten the Russians and moderate their conduct. But the Russians seemed to pay little attention to the bomb, for under the circumstances it was an inherently unusable weapon. If the Russians seized power in Poland, did you bomb Warsaw, thus killing thousands of the innocent Poles you were presumably trying to save? Did you actually bomb Moscow, Leningrad, or Kiev the way you had bombed Hiroshima and Nagasaki? But that would start a massive new war, not end one, and likewise destroy civilians without necessarily disturbing Russian military power or changing its foreign policy. Americans had yet to learn about the impotence of great power in the modern world.

Bomb or no bomb, the Russians took over Eastern Europe between 1945 and 1948. Winston Churchill came to America to warn that an "iron curtain" had fallen between freedom and totalitarianism, and hardliners in Washington began scaring themselves and the country with visions of implacable hordes of

Russians slowly marching west. In fact, that sort of behavior was not the Russian style. Just once had Russia tried such tactics, in the Winter War against Finland. The damage had been so great that the experiment was unlikely to be repeated. In fact, Russia had suffered more from World War II than anyone else and was understandably reluctant to try war again. The Russians preferred political subversion and *coups d'état,* and subsequently proved in both Finland and Austria that under certain circumstances they might even withdraw from territory they controlled, if proper safeguards for neutrality were guaranteed. Kennan himself pointed all this out, over and over again. He insisted that even in revolutionary situations like those in Greece, China, and Vietnam, Russia made little effort to intervene, and indeed that in China most of the intervention was on the side of the Kuomintang, the same side that the United States was supporting. Stalin was far more worried about secure borders than he was interested in spreading communism. To escalate this concern into a cold war was a needless misreading of circumstances.

Indeed, if any power was intervening in world affairs far from its own borders, it was the United States. The end of the war had brought the end of British and French hegemony in Africa and Asia, although it took another generation for many whites to recognize the fact. The British and the French simply could not afford the expense in money or manpower of maintaining their empires, and they made desperate attempts to make the United States change its traditional attitude of sympathy toward new nations, and instead take over the role of colonial policeman. When America reluctantly accepted this role, most obviously in Vietnam, it lost its moral authority in the eyes of many third world leaders. For them, the issue was colonialism; for Americans, the issue was the containment of communism. As President Truman defined the issue for himself and his successors early in 1947, the world was divided sharply into two camps, one free and open in its institutions, one closed and repressive. The policy of the United States should be "to support free people who are resisting attempted subjugation by armed minorities or by outside pressures."

To anyone familiar with American history, the speech was redolent with the assumption that capitalism, Christianity, and democracy were superior to all other economic, religious, and political systems and that no sensible person could deny it. The obvious context was Eastern European, the obvious reference to Russia. But the language was general and seemed to apply to Africa, Asia, and Latin America. When so applied, it seemed ludicrous to many people of good will. Their world was not divided between the followers of John Locke and those of Karl Marx; to assume that it was was simply another example of Western colonialist presumption.

Thus was the pattern set: he who was not with America must be against it. Truman and Acheson pushed through the NATO alliance, intervened in Korea, and built up an enormous military force within the country. They took language that had once had relevance to specific circumstances in Eastern Europe and applied it to the world. They scared the American people with visions of little Hitlers and Stalins popping up around the world, unless America intervened to stop a series of "Munichs." Like so many generals, they continued to fight the last war rather than reformulate ideas appropriate for the current one. And when their own best advisors, like George Kennan, pointed out the misunderstandings, they found themselves on the sidelines.

III

Not the least of the ironies of recent American foreign policy has been that the focus of most activity has turned out to be Asia rather than Europe. Once their satellites were in place, the Soviets made no further aggressive moves in Europe. On several occasions, Berlin seemed likely to provoke a military confrontation. On separate occasions, Hungary, Czechoslovakia, and Poland provoked the use of Soviet force to correct deviations from the Russian party line. But the sort of overt aggression practiced by the Nazis never occurred.

Asia proved to be the testing ground for American policy, but Americans could never develop a consistent attitude toward Asians. China provided a continuing example. During the nineteenth century, Chinese laborers had entered the American West to act as cheap labor on the railroads and in the mining camps. Their presence seemed to aggravate race prejudice to an extreme degree, to the point where the Chinese Exclusion Act treated them as if they belonged in the same immigration category as imbeciles, paupers, and prostitutes and were thus unworthy of citizenship or further immigration quotas. Yet at the same time, China as a distant nation had not only great cultural prestige, it also proved the most popular area for Christian missionary endeavor. Every year, young evangelicals went forth to convert the heathen, cure them of their debilitating diseases, and educate them "up" to Western standards. A novelist like Pearl Buck could win wide popularity and a Nobel Prize for novels portraying the quiet heroism of Chinese peasants as they survived poverty, famine, and flood without losing their essential humanity. Americans never seemed able to choose between heathen coolies and potential Christian converts, and this dualism has forever marked American diplomatic responses to events in the area.

American diplomatic interest in Asia went back to Secretary of State John Hay's efforts, at the turn of the twentieth century, to obtain economic privileges in China for American citizens equivalent to those enjoyed by more overtly colonialist powers. But nothing of much consequence affected American attitudes until 1937, when the Japanese established a puppet state in Manchuria. By then it was becoming clear to almost everyone in America that the Japanese were dangerously expansionist, and that China and all of Southeast Asia were in military danger—a danger that could harm American interests in the oil, rubber, and other resources in the area. It seemed necessary to find allies willing to fight the Japanese, and the Americans found their man in Generalissimo Chiang Kai-shek.

Chiang had been just another heathen warlord in his early career, living with concubines and allying himself to any power, including the Soviets, willing to help him. But when he realized the immense potential involved in American aid in the fight against communism, he renounced his concubines and married Mei-ling Soong, an American-educated Methodist whose family was one of the economically most powerful in China. Chiang learned to speak the language of capitalism, Christianity, and democracy; he was genuinely anti-Communist; and besides, America had no one else to turn to. So effective was the propaganda of his Kuomintang party in America that virtually no one publicly pointed out that Chiang was in fact a hopelessly corrupt military dictator without a democratic cell in his vigorous body.

One can visualize the way American ambivalence toward China worked its way into foreign policy through the difficult relationship between Henry Luce and Theodore White, two of the best-known journalists of the century. Luce had been born in China, the son of Presbyterian missionaries, and he grew up without ever doubting the validity of his family religion, the efficacy of capitalism, or the superiority of American democracy. After an expensive private education, he founded *Time* magazine and quickly built it into the centerpiece of a powerful communications empire. He remained throughout his life convinced that Chiang and his wife were the best friends America had in China, and he lost no opportunity to give them favorable publicity in his magazines. He was also politically powerful, and few politicians were willing openly to antagonize him on an issue, like China, that seemed peripheral to their own interests.

During the 1930s and early 1940s, however, China had on its soil a group of talented young diplomats who spoke Chinese, knew the culture intimately, and refused to find merit in the vacuous pronouncements of the Kuomintang. Known as the Old China Hands, John Patton Davies, John Stuart Service, and John Carter Vincent were part of the best traditions of American diplomacy, and the reports they sent back to Washington remain to this day the core of any historical treatment of the subject. Allied with them in their attitudes were a number of talented young journalists, of whom Theodore White became the best known. Trained at Harvard by John K. Fairbank, long the doyen of Chinese studies in America, White went to China as a correspondent for *Time* and threw himself into a study of the culture. He was also devoted to Henry Luce, and it was with a kind of horror that he discovered that his carefully prepared reports, sent to his employer, appeared in print only after censorship and revision. Only after the war, in *Thunder Out of China*, could White get his story across, but by then it was too late. The words of himself and the Old China Hands were distorted or ignored, and Chiang went down to the defeat which his incompetence so richly merited.

What White and the others had been reporting was that Chiang and his armies were alienating their people with taxes and torture. Starvation and venality went hand in hand, and since America and democracy had allied themselves with the Kuomintang, they too suffered from popular hatred. By contrast, Mao and the Communist Chinese lived austerely and behaved well. They seemed to represent both order and an effective opposing force to the invading Japanese. Considerations of ideology were largely irrelevant to a people who had been first invaded, then starved and finally taxed into peonage. To Americans conditioned to think of communism, Russia, aggression, totalitarianism, and atheism as being essentially interchangeable terms, this attitude was incomprehensible: to a comfortable middle-class culture, freedom to work, worship, and vote was of supreme importance. Few people in the third world shared these concerns. Their work was harsh whatever the regime in power, no one permitted them a meaningful vote, and no one cared much what they believed anyway. Of the two alternatives the Kuomintang was a known evil, the Communists an unknown possibility. Most chose the latter and the country went Communist in 1949.

American voters were unprepared for a Communist China. The propaganda of the Luce magazines and their allies had prevented any realistic assessment of conditions in China and the rhetoric of the Truman administration had made people incapable of clear thought on the subject of communism. Inept diplomats had misinformed both Roosevelt and Truman; competent ones had been ignored, maligned, and even fired. Led by Senator Joseph R. McCarthy, a noisy clique of congressmen kept up a steady stream of accusations against anyone who had ever tried to deal with, or even understand, communism. The best experts left the State Department, and with them went any competence in the formulation of Asian policy for a full generation.

IV

Like Theodore White, George F. Kennan found that telling his employer truths it did not want to hear was a fruitless endeavor. Neither *Time* nor the American government fired its discontented employee, but in each case he left for the intellectual freedom to report the truth as he saw fit.

Kennan had joined the Foreign Service in 1925, studied Russian, and served all over Central and Eastern Europe. In his two volumes of memoirs he mentions Geneva, Hamburg, Tallinn, and Riga as well as Moscow. He also married a Norwegian woman, thus equipping himself in the most personal way for a cosmopolitan life, cut off from the provincialisms of his isolationist country. His early pages show him in disapproval of the "histrionic futility" of much American policy, with its empty gesturing, lack of intellectual substance, and posturing for public relations effects. On the other hand, he recalls a fine group of experts at the American Embassy in Moscow in the middle 1930s, one fully capable of keeping Washington accurately informed of what was going on.

As World War II approached, Kennan served in Washington, Prague, Berlin, Lisbon, and London. He became increasingly critical of the poor administrative policies that President Roosevelt tolerated, and especially condemned "the basic elements of the unrealism that prevailed in the entire approach of FDR to the problems of Eastern Europe." He was especially critical of the way in which American diplomats handled the early negotiations for the formation of the United Nations. Woodrow Wilson had bungled similar negotiations a generation earlier, and Roosevelt was determined not to repeat the errors. Instead, he made different ones. He pressured the reluctant Russians to join the United Nations in such a way as to make their mere participation a key American goal, something that could be bargained over. Somehow it seemed an admission that Americans could not govern the postwar world by themselves; they needed Russian cooperation. Such a stance "was bound to fortify their [the Russians'] belief in the strength of their own position and to increase the severity and greediness of their asking price for the very collaboration we were anxious to have."

The establishment of the UN was intimately tied to Russian plans in Eastern Europe. Russia planned to annex parts of Poland and to compensate the Poles with parts of Germany. Wholesale deportations of population, as well as the establishment of satellite states, were inevitable. Yet American leaders continued their traditional sentimentalism about "democracy" and the "self-determination of nations," pandering to the immigrant populations that provided voting blocs in many states. The dangers of overinvolvement, impotence, and disillusionment were great. It was not the establishment of the UN that was the problem so much as the expectation that it would do very much that Americans could approve. Woodrow Wilson had raised similar hopes in 1919, with disastrous results. Everything that America wanted in Europe depended on Stalin's cooperation, and it was clear to Kennan that Stalin was not going to cooperate. United States policy was "based on a dangerous misreading of the personality, the intentions, and the political situation of the Soviet leadership."

In trying to make his points, Kennan produced the Long Telegram of 1944 and the anonymous article on containment in 1947, in the process becoming an important ideological force in the formulation of American policy. But he soon realized that too many people in power misread his work. He wanted to accept the idea of spheres of influence and the fact of Russian dominance over Eastern Europe. He advocated political moves that would minimize Communist influence in other European governments. He did not think the Russians were going to send troops across borders, nor did he like the American tendency constantly to universalize policies and issues. Just because one policy might be appropriate for Poland did not make it appropriate for Italy. Greece might merit American support in suppressing internal revolutionaries, but that did not justify an American intervention in China. Americans, he wrote, "obviously dislike to discriminate. We like to find some general governing norm to which, in each instance, appeal can be taken." By the same token, Americans like "to attribute a universal significance to decisions we have already found it necessary, for limited and parochial reasons, to take." America could not simply fight World War I to punish aggression or save England, it had to see itself making "the *world* (nothing else) 'safe for democracy.' " We could not fight the Japanese because they attacked us; "we did not feel comfortable until we had wrapped our military effort in the wholly universalistic—and largely meaningless—generalities of the Atlantic Charter." The country that preferred its religious, economic, and social system above all others anywhere felt an odd compulsion "to divide the world neatly into Communist and 'free world' components, to avoid recognition of specific differences among countries on either side, and to search for general formulas to govern our relations with the one or the other."

Kennan insisted, long after the publication of his article in 1947, that his readers had misunderstood him in three ways. He had been addressing the use of Soviet power within the Soviet Union, and not its actions in Eastern Europe; he had been discussing the political containment of a political threat, not the military containment of a military threat; and he had failed to limit his words in time and space—the time being the immediate aftermath of a world war, and the space being the Russian border area to its west. To his way of thinking, only five regions in the world possessed the means for conducting modern warfare: the United States, the United Kingdom, the Rhine Valley and adjacent areas, the U.S.S.R., and Japan. The Soviets controlled one of these areas, and American policy should prevent them from ever controlling a second. *Containment* was the word that described such a policy.

In 1950, Kennan went on a long leave at the Institute for Advanced Study, the first of many absences from power that resulted in much important scholarship but less influence in the State Department. He warned against any attempt to invade China or restore Chiang. He refused to agree that the Korean invasion was part of a long-term Russian plan to conquer the world: it was Korea in 1950, not Austria in 1938, and analysts had to make proper distinctions. He warned his friend, Secretary of State Dean Acheson, about trying to take over from the French in Vietnam. These areas were not among the key five, and Russia was not all that directly involved. He could not get his points across to the people who mattered, and like Theodore White he began to write books as a private citizen to evade the constraints of his job. Those books, like White's, were influential, but not enough to prevent the disastrous mistakes of the next decades of American foreign policy.

V

If any statesman represented American policy to the world in the early decades of the twentieth century, it was Woodrow Wilson: his Presbyterian moralizing, his sense of America's mission to a corrupt Europe, his self-righteousness, his noble defense of democracy, his sloganeering about such abstractions as the "self-determination of nations," "freedom of the seas," and making "the world safe for democracy": all these, both the admirable and the infuriating, were part of Wilson's legacy. Wilson had gone from the heights of popularity at the start of the Versailles Conference in 1919 to the depths of obscurity after he bungled the effort to achieve Senate ratification of the resulting treaty. After World War II, his greatest disciple was Secretary of State John Foster Dulles, a man with many of Wilson's character traits, a man who had himself been present in Paris during the peace negotiations but a man determined to avoid Wilson's mistakes. Just as many of his fellow diplomats were obsessed with the Munich analogy and determined never to give in to aggressive dictators, so Dulles was obsessed with the Versailles analogy: the world would disintegrate into chaos and war if America did not involve itself in the policing of it everywhere.

Cold War rhetoric was already needlessly inflammatory when he took office in 1953: NATO was in existence, rearming Western Europe; the Berlin airlift was a recent memory; the Korean War was bleeding American resources and patience. Instead of calming things down, Dulles resorted to a rhetoric of confrontation: newspapers and magazines talked about the need for "an agonizing reappraisal" of American policy, ending containment and beginning the job of rolling back communism, at least to the Russian border; about the need for a policy of "massive retaliation" with nuclear weapons if America were attacked; and of his willingness to go to the "brink of war" to establish the firmness of American policy. Critics began to warn about Dulles' "brinksmanship" and to decry the "pactomania" of his efforts to conclude pacts of military assistance with countries around the world. Such a public stance rather did Dulles and the Eisenhower administration an ill service. Dulles may well have been a peculiarly irritating statesman whom foreigners often resented, but he was also an able and intelligent man—fluent in French, widely traveled, and more aware of foreign responsibilities than most Americans. In fact, under his administration, the Korean War ended, arms expenditures were kept at reasonable levels, and words replaced troops as instruments of intervention on most occasions. Both he and President Eisenhower deserved credit for the moderate actions of the administration.

Despite this moderation, Eisenhower demonstrated in his memoirs that he had the same views of Southeast Asia that other foreign policy statesmen of both parties shared. He insisted that the war was a war for freedom against slavery, and not a war to preserve French colonialism. He talked of the rights of small nations to free elections and good government, yet admitted that Vietnamese leaders friendly to the West were incompetent and that in a free election Ho Chi Minh would have won. He indicated that he only heard of Vietnam because he was the NATO commander and was unable to get full French cooperation in Europe because the French were sending their resources to Vietnam: once more, European priorities were skewing analyses of Asian problems. He endorsed the "domino theory," with its assumption that if one more Asian country went Communist, then each of its neighbors was likely to follow, like a row of dominoes, each causing the fall of the one next to it. Thus a Viet Minh victory would endanger Thailand, Burma, Malaya, East Pakistan, and Indonesia. And in a letter of 4 April 1954 to British prime minister Winston Churchill, he spoke of "the imposition on Southeast Asia of the political system of Communist Russia and its Chinese Communist ally," and drew yet again on the Munich analogy: "If I may refer again to history; we failed to halt Hirohito, Mussolini and Hitler by not acting in unity and in time. That marked the beginning of many years of stark tragedy and desperate peril. May it not be that our nations have learned something from that lesson?" They had indeed learned all too much and were once again identifying an Asian leader with Hitler, seeing Communist-supported nationalism as Nazi-dominated international aggression. But as the available historical record now shows clearly, both Mao and Ho, during and immediately after World War II, were more than cordial to America and eager to cooperate with it in freeing Asia of imperialism. American obtuseness, not Russian expansionism, led to two generations of conflict in the area.

The arrival in power of the Democrats in 1961 gave many observers the impression that a major change had occurred. Only in the superficial sense of the arrival of a new generation was this the case. Eisenhower and Dulles had formed their ideas under Woodrow Wilson and the debates surrounding World War I, modifying them a bit with the events of World War II. President John F. Kennedy and his secretary of state, Dean Rusk, were products of World War II and the Cold War; they thought of themselves more as pragmatists and realists than as idealists. The real contrast was in a reversal of emphases: where Dulles had escalated the rhetoric of anti-Communism to new heights, and staunchly supported American notions of religion, politics, and capitalism around the world, Kennedy seemed to have a wry good humor about these subjects. He refused to fret about socialism or neutralism either in politics or in international relations, and as a rather secularized Roman Catholic he could never share Dulles' evangelical zeal. He seemed genuinely to understand and to want better relations with third-world countries. Yet in practice, Kennedy clearly thought

Eisenhower and Dulles had been dreary in thought and too cautious in action. With the full support of Rusk, another Presbyterian moralist of the Dulles variety, Kennedy wanted a more interventionist foreign policy, one based on a vast superiority in conventional weapons. Instead of "massive retaliation," America would emphasize "flexible response."

In practice this change meant the start of the greatest arms race in history. Under Eisenhower, America had held arms superiority over the Soviet Union, but not to the extent that it could destroy Russian power at first strike. The Russians seemed content with this. But under Kennedy, a vast expansion of armaments occurred that quite needlessly provoked the Russians into a buildup of their own—one which then, of course, justified still further American buildups. One of the many ironies that resulted was that, with the vast increase in weapons on both sides, neither side was as safe as it had been earlier. Quite aside from the needless expense and the psychological stress involved, more weapons meant less protection. Another casualty was diplomatic. Where the Russians always knew where they stood with Dulles, they could never figure Kennedy and his advisors out: they talked about peace and détente but prepared for war. The Russians came to the conclusion that they could not be trusted.

The great burden of this policy fell on Asia, but it had its impact in Europe as well. Nothing demonstrated this quite as well as Kennedy's German policy, with his famous insistence that he was a Berliner. The Russians and East Germans were putting great pressure on Berlin in 1961, and Kennedy consulted Dean Acheson and other hardliners of the Cold War. The advice he received was, in summary: don't negotiate. He picked the president of Finland, of all people, to explain his position to. The Soviets had in fact withdrawn from their occupations of both Finland and Austria, in exchange for the pledged neutrality of those two countries, thus demonstrating an enlightened self-interest that in no way threatened any defensible American position. Soviet policy, Kennedy told Urho Kekkonen, "is designed to neutralize West Germany as a first step in the neutralization of Western Europe. That is what makes the present situation so dangerous. West Germany is the key as to whether Western Europe will be free." It was a revealing and preposterous remark. It implied that Finland, Austria, and Yugoslavia were not free because they were neutral. To be free was to be allied to the United States. To give in on Berlin would weaken Germany, a weak Germany might fall into neutrality and thus lack of freedom, and all Europe might be threatened. It was the sort of logic that cost America its reputation as the disinterested leader of the free world.

The key testing ground for Kennedy's policy, and that of President Lyndon B. Johnson who inherited it, proved to be Vietnam. It was not an area where America had much legitimate interest; it had minor economic and military significance. America had not signed the Geneva accords of 1954, which had terminated the French colonial war there, and had no real specialists available who could sort out the complex issues that surrounded the political and social problems of the area. The north was a dictatorship under the Communist rule of Ho Chi Minh; the south was a dictatorship under the Roman Catholic minority of Ngo Dinh Diem. Both areas contained large numbers of people who had originated in the other. Neither side had ever enjoyed democratic freedom. In Asian eyes, the most important issue was the elimination of Western colonialist forces from a Vietnamese nation that should be unified. The north sought the aid of China and Russia to help rid the south of French and Americans; the south sought the help of Americans, Australians, and Koreans to help rid its territory of Communists, whether Vietnamese, Chinese, or Russian. The majority Buddhist population in the south played no formal role at all.

Rusk did not see it that way. As the former undersecretary of the air force, Townsend Hoopes later wrote: "In his always articulate, sometimes eloquent, formulations, Asia seemed to be Europe, China was either Stalinist Russia or Hitler Germany, and SEATO was either NATO or the Grand Alliance of World War II." President Kennedy was rather contemptuous of the northern forces, and seemed certain that American guerillas in cooperation with southern forces could contain the situation. But in actuality, Vietnam was hardly on his mind at all; like Rusk, he too was thinking about Europe. Embarrassed by Khrushchev's visible contempt for a young and inexperienced president, shamed by the fiasco of the Bay of Pigs invasion of Cuba, Kennedy felt that he needed to prove his courage and the strength of American resolve. Vietnam was the next crisis that came, and so for world-political reasons, he felt he had to intervene.

When Johnson became president, he inherited Kennedy's advisors, men he seemed to hold in great respect. Inexperienced in foreign affairs, ill-informed about Asia, he apparently believed much of his administration's own propaganda about democracy in Vietnam and the dangers of Communist invasion. The whole situation seemed preposterous to Asian experts in many American universities and most foreign countries: Southeast Asia had never been a democracy in any Western sense of the term, and any attempt to install it by force smacked of both hypocrisy and imperialism. Communist Vietnamese could hardly be called invaders of the south, since at least at the start of the war most of them had been Southeast Asians operating within their own country. But Washington insisted on equating revolutionary nationalism with international communism, a pattern that it has repeated with numbing consistency elsewhere in the third world. Johnson seized on a trivial incident in the Tonkin Gulf and received from Congress the authority to respond in any way he found suitable. The Vietnam War was the result—a great disaster both to the people of Vietnam and to American foreign policy.

Johnson honestly felt that he had no alternative. As he told biographer Doris Kearns in 1965, if he had abandoned Kennedy's commitment to Vietnam and "let the Communists take over," then he "would be seen as a coward" and his "nation would be seen as an appeaser," and he and his nation "would both find it impossible to accomplish anything for anybody on the entire globe." Everything he had ever learned about history told him that had he "got out of Vietnam and let Ho Chi Minh run through the streets of Saigon," then he would be doing "exactly what Chamberlain did in World War II." He would be "giving a big fat reward to aggression." He was convinced that if America let communism win in South Vietnam, "there would follow in this country an endless national debate— a mean and destructive debate—that would shatter my Presidency, kill my administration and damage our democracy." He could never forget that President Truman and Secretary of State Acheson "had lost effectiveness from the day the Communists took over China." He knew what miseries the country had endured in the years that followed, and thought them nothing compared to what "might happen if we lost Vietnam."

Just exactly who gave Vietnam to Johnson, thus enabling him to lose it, will remain forever obscure; the phrase alone demonstrates all too clearly the way too many American minds were accustomed to working throughout the world. But the statement is deeply enlightening; virtually everything it states is demonstrably incorrect. Johnson was clearly thinking of World War II and the loss of China, misunderstanding the lessons of both. Neither Mao nor Ho had been even remotely a Hitler; Chinese Communists had never invaded China, and North Vietnam could hardly invade its own country, regardless of what the French had agreed to in Geneva. Ho's desire to rid his country of the French and the Americans bore small resemblance indeed to Mao's efforts to rid his country of the Kuomintang, although perhaps his efforts to defeat the Japanese would be a closer parallel. Neither China nor Vietnam produced much of a parallel for Hitler's invasions of Austria, Czechoslovakia, Poland, or Russia. Even the reference by implication to the Korean War was hopelessly faulty, for no mass army had crossed any recognizable boundary, and nothing in Korea would prepare American soldiers for the war against civilian villagers that met them in Vietnam. The Vietnam War as a war had no precedents, and so parallels were always misleading. Instead, it was one of many examples of faulty American analysis of the third world: whether it was the Eisenhower administration intervening in Guatemala and Iran, or the Reagan administration meddling in El Salvador and its neighbors, the scenario seemed all too familiar: the forces of property and dictatorship were identified with stability and democracy; the forces of the poor and the revolutionary were identified with Communist aggression and Russian expansionism. No one ever learned. Capitalism, Christianity, and democracy, American style, were simply not exportable to most of the world. Trying to export them resulted in government tyranny, unchristian behavior, and undemocratic governments. Good intentions produced lamentable results.

VI

The creation of foreign policy in America was the duty of a group that resembled an extended family: the relatives, in-laws, and close friends of policymakers succeeded each other with comforting predictability. Fosters, Lansings, and Dulleses had been hovering around the State Department since the nineteenth century, the Achesons were related to the Bundys by marriage, and if blood did not tell, then attachment to Harvard or Yale seemed to make up the difference. Few people questioned the basic assumptions of the Acheson–Dulles–Rusk years, however much they might squabble about tone or terminology.

But change did occur occasionally at State, long after it had affected other areas in the country. Jews and Catholics, often the sons of European immigrants, had entered the cabinet and the Supreme Court, as had Negroes. The evangelical moralism that had dominated the country through the administration of Herbert Hoover no longer seemed entirely to dominate the making of foreign policy by the 1960s, and by the 1970s, two figures were known throughout the country for their ability to influence presidents who otherwise sounded as moralistic as their predecessors. Henry Kissinger brought the accent of German Jewry to the White House and to countless television audiences, looking and sounding quite unlike any of his predecessors as secretary of state. Zbigniew Brzezinski was Polish Roman Catholic by background, an odd figure indeed to be the chief foreign policy advisor to a Georgia Baptist president like Jimmy Carter. Both men subsequently published memoirs of their time in office.

Only Henry Kissinger reached the highest diplomatic office in the land, and only he produced books that have some pretense to being contributions to the philosophy of diplomacy. His two volumes of memoirs demonstrate both how different he was from his predecessors and yet how similar he was in many important ways. Just as America seemed able to absorb multitudes into its political and cultural life, making them seem in time much like more established settlers, so the State Department seemed able to digest a Kissinger and make him sound and think like those around him. He prided himself on his new ways of thinking, but he was only partially correct.

Kissinger remained obsessed with Russia and with Europe. Regardless of many pages devoted to China or West Asia, behind his analyses was always some suspicion that the Russians were either behind the problems or somehow planning to profit from them. At the core of Soviet strategy, he insisted, was a "ruthless opportunism," and he countered it with his own version of American responsibility to maintain a balance of power. "To expect the Soviet leaders to restrain themselves from exploiting circumstances they conceive to be favorable is to misread history. To foreclose Soviet opportunities is to define the limits of

Soviet aims." The steady stream of advice runs through the books: Soviets never change; you can't trust them at all. You have to keep them constantly in mind, talk to them often, make sure they know that you know what they are doing, and subordinate all other policies to that of containing them.

From this basic stance, Kissinger drew three principles: of *concreteness*, by which he meant that all negotiations must be specific, on well-prepared programs, and not some vague moralistic effusion; of *restraint*, always meeting a Soviet challenge with a response appropriate to the challenge, and not talking about massive retaliation or the brink of war unless it were truly necessary; and finally his most famous term, *linkage*—everything around the world was related. Events in China were somehow related to events in Latin America. Food was related to oil. You could not divide up foreign policy into neat categories, and, say, sell wheat to the Soviets while cutting off oil, unless you had consciously traded something for something else. If the Soviets cooperated in Vietnam, you could let them have a reward in Turkey. Everything was linked. To carry out such a policy, Kissinger established a close and long-term relationship with Anatoly Dobrynin, the Soviet ambassador in Washington. The two men kept up what was called "the channel," through which passed countless pieces of information in an effort to prevent misunderstandings and to work out linkages.

One of the weirder fantasies of the Kennedy–Johnson years was that America should rearm to the point where it could carry on two and one-half wars; that is, fight effectively major wars against Russia and China while remaining capable of a smaller adventure, perhaps in Angola or Guatemala. Given this precedent, Kissinger in office seemed something of a moderating voice, happy to settle for one and one-half wars. He was willing to deal with both Russians and Chinese, and his diplomacy with both countries was successful by any fair standard of judgment. He never indulged in the sanctimonious moralities of the Dulles days nor the hypocrisies of the Kennedy regime, talking peace while escalating the arms race. He says that he wanted "to give up the obsession with a Communist monolith," and to learn to treat Russia, China, Vietnam, and Cuba as separate countries, not necessarily cooperating in all their activities. However far he may have fallen short of such goals, he was at least aware enough of the problems to articulate them.

But the other side of this realistic coin was a mind formed in Europe and scarred permanently by the events of Nazi anti-Semitism and the role of America as the rescuer of Jewish immigrants like Kissinger himself. Kissinger may not have shared Dulles' moralism, but his sense for the European balance of power often produced a position that was indistinguishable from it. Some of the most illuminating pages of the memoirs are those where Kissinger describes the origins of his vision of America. "The principles of America's honor and America's responsibility were not empty phrases to me." He had been prepared for them by childhood in Fürth, a suburb of Nuremberg, one of the centers of Nazi support in the 1930s. He and his family endured constant discrimination and threats; his father lost his teaching job, friends shunned them on the street, and Henry had had to attend a segregated school. "Through this period America acquired a wondrous quality for me. When I was a boy it was a dream, an incredible place where tolerance was natural and personal freedom un-challenged." Even when he later knew at first hand about America's failures and problems, he could never forget that in America, at least, Jewish boys like himself did not have to cross the street to avoid getting beaten up. He could never indulge in the hypercriticism with which young people, born in America and not knowing about life elsewhere, attacked their nation during the Vietnam years. The blemishes were certainly there, but "they could not obscure for me its greatness, its idealism, its humanity, and its embodiment of mankind's hopes."

He thus felt the turmoil of the Vietnam debates deeply. He had not agreed with or participated in many of the decisions that had led to American interven-tion, but felt "that my appointment to high office entailed a responsibility to help end the war in a way compatible with American self-respect and the stake that all men and women of goodwill had in America's strength and purpose." He felt it imperative that America leave the war in good order and without humiliation. His adopted country, after all, had not entered the war out of some monstrous conspiracy, but rather out of "a naive idealism that wanted to set right all the world's ills and believed American goodwill supplied its own efficacy." On his own visits to Vietnam as a professor, he had been most impressed by the nameless Americans who as individuals had been helping individual Vietnamese toward a better life. That was his war, not the indefensible genocide of the radical imagination. He insisted on the view of the war "as a genuine tragedy. No one had a monopoly on anguish."

The argument was in many ways well put and believable. This vision of America has long been shared by many Europeans of older generations. Amer-ica had saved the British and the French from the Germans twice; it saved at least some Jews from the Nazis; it had given a new home to many fleeing Stalin. It had helped in the establishment of Israel. This was the America that held the allegiance of so many Jews during and after World War II. It could not be the country of radical attack, committing genocide on innocent Asians fighting against colonialism. Once again, the argument had returned to Kennan's insights about the application of European precedents to new Asian circumstances, only this time the problem was more a matter of mood and memory than one of antiquated doctrine. Almost as if he had never examined his own presupposi-tions, Kissinger argues essentially that the world is still divided between the forces of light and the forces of darkness, that Russian aggression is everywhere, that American values and its economic and political system all go together, and that, given free choice, the vast majority of people everywhere would choose to live in the American way. Once again, critics are faced with a man who argues, in essence, that because American motives are pure, American actions are defensible and the results worth fighting for.

Kissinger thus missed one of the greatest lessons of recent diplomacy: that people who mean well do some of the greatest damage in the world, and that purity of heart has been the justification for many of the worst horrors in human history, from the Inquisition to the Iranian revolution. It never occurs to him, at least in print, that most Vietnamese might not want to live like Americans and that the South Vietnamese government seemed an international disgrace to neutral observers as well as to a majority of its own citizens. The contours of his policies, and their results, thus all too often proved indistinguishable from those of his predecessors.

Yet when Kissinger dealt with China and Russia, his tone changed and his results were far more impressive. His own president, Richard M. Nixon, had been one of the worst critics of any intelligent policy toward China in the late 1940s and 1950s, and it was one of the great surprises of the 1970s that his administration reversed more than thirty years of incompetence in dealing with mainland China. Kissinger deserved much of the credit for this shift, and when his memoirs shift into their fascinating passages on Mao and Chou En-lai, a new world of language and analysis opens up. He seems to attack the very naiveté he himself demonstrates on Vietnam, and the doctrines of national self-interest and the balance of power reappear. "Americans are comfortable with an idealistic tradition that espouses great causes, such as making the world safe for democracy, or human rights," but have proven quite "inhospitable to an approach based on the calculation of the national interest and relationships of power." The Nixon administration wished to educate the voters in the requirements of the balance of power, and "this implied a diplomacy in which our weight had to be available to the weaker side even in a conflict among Communist states whose domestic practices were deplored." In other words, America should help China if Russia attacked it. John Foster Dulles would have called it trifling with one's immortal soul and muttered in *Life* about the danger of pacts with the devil. Kissinger survived what little opposition actually materialized, and opened relations with China.

Kissinger did relatively well in dealing with the Soviet Union also. He did not indulge in moralistic phrase-making, but instead talked to the Soviets in terms of power and predictability. "The Nixon Administration's hard-headed geopolitical approach to East–West relations, though not easily grasped at home, was in fact effective with the Soviet leaders." They had no objections to manipulating the moralistic phobias of Western leaders, but in fact "they really do not know how to deal with a sentimental foreign policy." Trying to understand Russian problems sympathetically, "as if foreign policy were like personal relations," could never succeed. In fact, Nixon shared many character traits with Russian leaders—dour, mistrustful men all. "He knew that there was no substitute for posing calibrated risks that would make aggression appear unattractive; he strove mightily to preserve the balance of power." Kissinger and Nixon by and large succeeded. They made détente a reality.

Chapter 14

A Culture of Outsiders, 1943–1958

While the controversies over black civil rights and the Vietnam War dominated the headlines, creative artists were remaking all of American culture. The puritan heritage that had so dominated the attitudes toward capitalism and democracy faded, as competing religions and ethnic groups achieved a more equal place in society. As they did so, the wave of talented immigrants found jobs more worthy of their accomplishments. Students who went to college in the 1950s and 1960s had far more opportunities to encounter challenging ideas in all areas of knowledge than ever before, and in a broad range of activities, from technology and marketing to agriculture and art, America seemed preeminent in the world. By the 1970s, this situation was changing as the world recovered from its military and political debacles. By the 1990s, with the Soviet Union metamorphosed into the Commonwealth of Independent States and Europe about to become a unitary trading competitor, everything seemed very different. Even the news began daily with reports of the Japanese stock market rather than the one in New York.

Nothing illustrates the absorptive qualities of the American scene after 1945 like asking a simple question: in the world of arts and letters, who were the major figures of, say, 1955? Opinions will always vary on such questions, but in the world of painting, for example, the two dominant names were Jackson Pollock and Willem de Kooning; in literature, Ralph Ellison, Vladimir Nabokov, and Saul Bellow. All were outsiders from the traditional areas of American creativity. Pollock was from a poor family without conventional religion; de Kooning was a Dutch immigrant of highly dubious legal status; Ellison was a black, Nabokov an immigrant of Russian origin, British education, and recent residence in Germany and France; and Bellow was a Canadian Jew. Puritanism was irrelevant except as a subject for satire, and capitalism very nearly so. But democracy was taking on new meanings all the time.

Explaining such a situation requires a return to the very different art scene of the days just before the outbreak of World War I.

II

As of New Year's Day 1913, there was really only one place on American soil where a student could get any idea of the best recent work in art. A young photographer of German background, Alfred Stieglitz, had set up the 291 Gallery to help educate American taste up to European standards. Neither his parents nor his wife approved of his efforts, and the general public ignored him. But he persevered, giving small shows to experimental artists and publishing relevant material in *Camera Work*. At least one writer for this publication, Marius De Zayas, was thoroughly contemporary in his tastes, and so the 291 circle was not entirely unprepared for the arrival, on 14 January 1913, of the French artist Francis Picabia. The famous Armory Show was about to begin, and Picabia had come to see the fun. He took a look around, and informed Americans that art had always been a "synthesis of the beliefs of all people," that in America "all beliefs exist here together," and that therefore the creation of art in America was impossible. De Zayas agreed. Their efforts, and those of their successors, proved them wrong within two generations.

As any art history book will point out, the Armory Show was the notorious beginning of modern art in the American public consciousness. Stieglitz had communicated only to an élite, but with this show, art became news. The most famous of all the works shown was by another Frenchman, Marcel Duchamp: "Nude Descending a Staircase" sounded delightfully risqué, yet when viewed offered not titillation but a cubist experiment in multiple perspectives. Moralistic Americans seemed not to know whether they should be outraged at having to look at a French nude or outraged because when they looked they could see nothing human in the picture. Provincial and insecure, uncomfortable before the foreign, most Americans shared the views of former president Theodore Roosevelt, who wrote a famous column on the exhibition.

For him, the European modernists were "extremists" whose work implied "death and not life, and retrogression instead of development." Roosevelt thought Americans erred "in treating most of these pictures seriously." He found little to endorse in the cubists, the futurists, and the "near-Impressionists." "The Cubists are entitled to the serious attention of all who find enjoyment in the colored pictures of the Sunday newspapers." As for the painting whose title he translated as "A naked man going downstairs," Roosevelt wrote that he had "a really good Navajo rug" in his bathroom which was a far more successful example of cubist theory. He had contempt for the futurists and could see no way in which their work was any more advanced than "the later work of the paleolithic artists of the French and Spanish caves." The sculptures also irritated him, not to mention the publicity which they received. "Why a deformed pelvis should be called 'sincere,' or a tibia of giraffe-like length 'precious' is a question of pathological rather than artistic significance." His was a classic bourgeois stance. Nature gave artists their forms, and artists should follow nature's example. The distortion of nature somehow seemed abnormal and certainly unamerican.

This publicity helped make Duchamp the other important European figure to begin the cosmopolitanization of American taste in art. He proved a difficult mentor. He seemed to hate the old, the classical, or anything implying good taste in art. He declared that the art of Europe was finished and that "America is the only country of the art of the future." To achieve success Americans should stop imitating Europeans. As for himself as a European, he sometimes behaved as if decreasing creativity were an artistic obligation. In time, he gave up art for chess, but even his jokes and silences seemed to have enormous implications for the history of art. He claimed to be more interested in ideas and the mind than in painting, and there is no reason to doubt him. His one great achievement, in terms both of publicity and art history, was the discovery of the "readymade," any found object he deigned to notice, proclaim to be art, and sign. The first of these, the *Bicycle Wheel* of 1913, was precisely that, a found wheel from a bicycle. As art, it had a common subject matter, it engaged the participation of the observer, it was quite random, and it had an obvious relation to reality. All these aspects, expressed in words, had independent influence in the history of art, and critics have analyzed them closely. But at the time, few could cope with such innovations. Duchamp soon achieved even further notoriety with his *Fountain*, the found urinal he submitted with a straight face to an exhibition. America in 1917 might be willing to fight for France, but Gallic ideas of art seemed to leave something to be desired.

During the years after World War I, American and European artists remained aware of each other. A number of Europeans, of whom Arshile Gorky seemed most important at the time, settled permanently in America; a number of Americans, of whom Man Ray seemed most important, went in the other direction, settling chiefly in France. A few American institutions displayed European works, and with the establishment of the Museum of Modern Art, or MOMA, in 1929, visitors to New York could be aware of many of the most fruitful developments across the Atlantic. For the founders of MOMA, modern art began with Cézanne, Gauguin, Seurat, and Van Gogh and continued through "The School of Paris," "Cubism and Abstract Art," "Fantastic Art, Dada and Surrealism," and "Bauhaus 1919–1928," to list its best-known exhibitions. During the 1930s and early 1940s, European enthusiasms were evident in shows like "African Negro Art," "Prehistoric Rock Pictures in Europe and Africa," "Twenty Centuries of Mexican Art," "Indian Art of the U.S.," and "Ancestral Sources of Modern Painting."

As at least one of these shows indicated, America received cosmopolitan influences from the south as well as from the east. Three Mexican muralists—

David Alfaro Siqueiros, José Clemente Orozco, and Diego Rivera—who had risen to prominence in the 1920s, became key influences in New York in the 1930s. All were committed leftists who painted large-scale murals with obvious political content and representational techniques. Some California painters like Philip Guston and Jackson Pollock had known of Mexican work from an early age, but only during the Depression did the Mexicans make a strong impact on the larger art world. Their major works included the murals which Orozco did for the New School in 1930–1931 and for Dartmouth College in New Hampshire in 1932–1934. Rivera had a large show at MOMA in 1931–1932 and achieved national celebrity in 1933 when he painted the head of Lenin into a mural located in that monument to capitalism, Rockefeller Center. Siqueiros actually lived in New York City during 1936–1937.

But the Mexicans, whatever their technical skills, were revolutionary, collectivist painters. Toward the end of the 1930s such political currents became less popular: the New Deal ran out of steam, the Stalin purges became common knowledge, and in time the Hitler–Stalin Pact completed the disillusionment of all but the hardiest fellow travelers. America was ripe for another vogue, and it arrived, a bit belatedly, in the same manner as cubism a generation earlier. Surrealism came over on a boat from France.

Surrealism had been all the rage in Paris in the 1920s, the last of the modernist "-isms" that remade modern art: cubism, fauvism, futurism, and so on. It had contained a substantial literary content and was deeply influenced by the psychologies of Sigmund Freud and Carl Jung. A few Americans were on the fringes of the movement; Matthew Josephson actually entitled his autobiography *Life Among the Surrealists,* but in fact American awareness of the experiments involved had to await the MOMA show of 1936. Even then, only an immigrant like Arshile Gorky seemed genuinely sympathetic. But in 1939 the surrealists began their flight from Nazi persecution and in time made their way to New York. The long list of names included André Breton, Marc Chagall, Salvador Dali, Max Ernst, Fernand Léger, Jacques Lipchitz, André Masson, Piet Mondrian, and Yves Tanguy; New Yorkers, always overly impressed by anything Parisian, suddenly paid attention. In doing so they began the processes that led to abstract expressionism and made New York City the capital of world art by the late 1940s. The process of assimilation had its symbolic formalization when Max Ernst married heiress Peggy Guggenheim, and her museum, Art of This Century, began to give shows in 1942 for her husband and his friends.

III

Jackson Pollock was a child of the West. Born in 1912 in Wyoming to a family involved in ranching, dairy, and fruit farming, he had moved frequently before settling down in Southern California. His was not, however, a typically provincial cultural background. His family always had a tendency toward pantheism and an interest in mysticism, and Pollock long retained an interest in Asian religions, especially Buddhism and the teachings of the Indian philosopher Krishnamurti. As an art student, he was also much drawn to the Mexican muralists and admired Diego Rivera for both artistic and political reasons.

In 1930 he moved to New York, to study at the Art Students League. He worked, oddly enough, with American Scene painter Thomas Hart Benton, at a time when Benton was deeply involved in studying Renaissance art principles. In the long run, as Pollock himself insisted, his "work with Benton was important as something against which to react very strongly," but he was fascinated by the Renaissance and turned out many student sketches in that style. Both men were hard-drinking "he-men" from the hinterlands, and at least for a while there was an obvious affinity between them which seemed very odd in terms of their later careers.

From Benton Pollock moved on to experience two of the key cosmopolitan influences then prevalent in the city. He renewed his adolescent attachment for Mexican mural art, this time by working in the workshop that David Siqueiros was running at Union Square. The attraction of the place was not one of style, but of an atmosphere of experimentation. As Axel Horn, one of the students, later recalled, Siqueiros was a man of enormous energy who was stimulating to be around. He encouraged new creative tools, such as the use of lacquer, which "opened up enormous possibilities in the application of color." The students "sprayed through stencils and friskets, embedded wood, metal, sand and paper. We used it in thin glazes or built it up into thick globs. We poured it, dripped it, spattered it, hurled it at the picture surface." Lacquer dried almost immediately, yet could be removed easily. What emerged was a series of "accidental effects," and Siqueiros soon came up with a theory of "controlled accidents." While art historians still dwell on the social art of the Mexicans and examine their political impact during a radical decade, it seems entirely possible that they should receive more attention for their contributions to experimental modernism. In particular, the stress on the spontaneous act and the unplanned effect had great relevance for later developments in painting and had their corollaries in the other arts of the time, most obviously the musical experiments of John Cage.

The important influence was that of surrealism. The movement had begun during World War I, when the French poet Guillaume Apollinaire wished to explain the ways in which the work of Marc Chagall and Giorgio de Chirico went beyond realism. The next few years were those of the primacy of Dada, with its stress on gratuitous acts, accidents, collages, photos, three-dimensional objects, found art, and the like. The connections between painting and writing were close, and the leading spokesman for surrealism in the 1920s was the writer

André Breton. He grew bored with Dada and became deeply interested in a more philosophical approach to creativity that would be based on ideas of the subconscious and irrational. In 1924, he came out with his famous Surrealist Manifesto. Surrealism was "pure psychic automatism, by which an attempt is made to express, either verbally in writing or in any other manner, the true process of thought." It was "thought's dictation, in the absence of all control by the reason and every aesthetic or moral preoccupation being absent." The movement was based "on the belief in a higher reality of certain hitherto neglected forms of association, in the omnipotence of the dream, in the disinterested play of thought." It had a tendency to substitute itself for other physical mechanisms and "to substitute itself for them in the solution of life's principal problems." Thus defined, it has obvious affinities for psychoanalysis.

The 1936 MOMA show, the arrival of so many surrealists in New York, and the opening of Art of This Century all made leading artists belatedly aware of a movement that was exhausted in Europe. The process by which Pollock assimilated American scene painting, Renaissance principles, Mexican mural art and its accidents, and surrealism is not all that clear, but his lifelong interest in mystical religions provides a unifying strand. Always interested in the mental and unseen, open to influences unknown to most of his countrymen, Pollock had long been aware of the work of Carl Jung and other psychoanalysts; Jung's interest in archetypes especially appealed to him, and the roles of accident and memory in painting are clearly relevant to any Jungian cast of mind. The combination of this intellectual stance with his choice of marital partner helps make his evolution explicable. At one of the Guggenheim exhibitions he met and soon married artist Lee Krasner, the American-born daughter of a Russian-Jewish emigré family. Fluent in Russian, Yiddish, Hebrew, and English, Krasner added to her cosmopolitan qualities with studies at the famous school that German painter Hans Hofmann ran in New York. European ideas and languages were a part of her daily life, and it is almost as if Pollock confirmed his new international role by his alliance with her.

At some point between 1943 and 1947, Pollock became "Jack the Dripper," the nickname he acquired because of his new style of "action painting"—although this term did not come into common use until 1949. Many of the experiments of the Siqueiros workshop were there: spilled and dripped paint, puddled and spattered paint. Pollock felt cramped by small tidy canvases on easels and preferred instead massive ones he could lay on the floor and walk around. Indeed, their size seems to have been limited only by the size of his workshop; transporting and hanging Pollock works have been a headache for museum directors ever since. The visual effect of the works, though often striking, seemed to take second place to the feeling, actions and intentions of the painter; in effect the art which the viewer saw years later in a museum was actually more of a psychological self-portrait than any attempt to convey an image. Even the equipment changed: easels, palettes, and brushes gave way to sticks, trowels, and knives, and the paint was mixed with sand, broken glass, and other foreign matter.

IV

Lee Krasner was not the only person Pollock met at Peggy Guggenheim's shows. With his introduction to Willem de Kooning he discovered his great counterpart in the art history of New York, the European who brought his world to the city, struggled to find his own American voice, and ultimately shared with Pollock the avant-garde leadership of the years around 1950. Born in Holland in 1904, de Kooning had come out of a lower-middle-class environment and a rigorous apprenticeship to a firm of Rotterdam commercial artists and decorators. In America at the time it was customary to think of the artist as a man cut off from his society, only rarely useful to industry or daily life. But in Holland such was not the case; art was useful, democratic, and a part of normal life. De Kooning thus became professionally competent in carpentry, design, house painting, and portraiture—the sort of polymath who actually could design his own house from foundation to furniture.

But he was dissatisfied with prospects at home and made repeated, sometimes illegal attempts to get to America. He knew something of the writing of Whitman and the building of Wright, but little else about American culture, and his impulses seem to have been economic rather than artistic. "I didn't expect that there were any artists here," he told an interviewer many years later. "We never heard in Holland that there were artists in America. There was still the feeling that this was where an individual could get places and become well off, if he worked hard; while art, naturally, was in Europe." Certainly it seemed to be after his arrival. De Kooning found outlets for his real skills nonexistent, became a house painter and odd-job man, and worked himself into American society very slowly. But over the years he visited the museums and galleries of the city and came to meet influential people. He seems also to have developed something of a psychological block about finishing his works, and few survive from this period.

His European predilections always stayed at the back of his mind. Italian futurism and especially Russian constructivism were important; he publicly recalled his debts to Lissitzsky, Rodchenko, Tatlin, Gabo, and Kandinsky. But of all the modernist movements, he liked "Cubism the most. It had that wonderful unsure atmosphere of reflection—a poetic frame where something could be possible, where an artist could practise his intention." Instead of wanting to get rid of the past, "it added something to it." De Kooning, like many others, then paid his debt to "that one-man movement, Marcel Duchamp—for me a truly modern movement because it implies that each artist can do what he thinks he ought to do—a movement for each person and open for everybody."

Where Pollock turned to dripping and splattering, de Kooning remained faithful at least in theory to nature as the source of his painting. But the two men shared the drift toward abstraction, toward the concept of the canvas as theater. "Painting isn't just the visual thing that reaches your retina—it's what is behind it and in it." He was not especially interested in "abstracting," in "taking things out or reducing painting to design, form, line and color." He painted in the manner he did because he could not keep out "drama, anger, pain, love, a figure, a horse, my ideas about space." Through the eyes of the viewer it becomes once again "an emotion or an idea. It doesn't matter if it's different from mine as long as it comes from the painting which has its own integrity and intensity."

By 1952 abstract expressionism seemed triumphant to the most knowledgeable painters, although the general public remained cool for many years. In that year, de Kooning's most outspoken supporter, Harold Rosenberg, published one of his most famous essays, in the process defining what had happened. "At a certain moment the canvas began to appear to one American painter after another as an arena in which to act—rather than as a space in which to reproduce, re-design, analyze or 'express' an object, actual or imagined." In effect the canvas became "an event" instead of "a picture." No longer did the painter approach his easel "with an image in his mind; he went up to it with material in his hand to do something to that other piece of material in front of him." Suggesting "Abstract-Expressionist" as one obvious name for all this, Rosenburg emphasized that what counted was "its special motive for extinguishing the object, which is not the same as in other abstract or Expressionist phases of modern art." Thus, a modern painting was "an act . . . inseparable from the biography of the artist," a "moment" in his life. Europe and America had come together to produce a new kind of art that was in its turn creating new theories about art. In the days of Alfred Stieglitz, the very thought would have been a joke. America had become a cosmopolitan culture, and its artists were originating instead of absorbing.

Innovative work was soon common and art critics now call its creators the New York School. Neither a single style nor a single school, the New York School was a loose community of artists and their friends in allied arts who saw each other constantly in the early 1950s, in an area roughly defined by 8th and 12th Streets, and First through Sixth Avenues. The area was full of galleries, bars, restaurants, and schools as well as residences, and even when its inhabitants left they often went to the same place—Black Mountain College in North Carolina being one famous example. Merely to list the names of those who became most famous shows how cosmopolitan the New York School really was: Arshile Gorky had been born in Armenia, Mark Rothko in Russia, and Claes Oldenburg in Sweden. Both Josef Albers and Hans Hofmann, the most influential teachers, were from Germany. Even the Americans were from all over: like Pollock, Philip Guston and Robert Motherwell were from California; Robert Rauschenberg was from Texas and Jasper Johns from Georgia. New York City had become a state of mind, an attitude toward art, and a home for those born somewhere else. It was the first place in America of which this was true, but as the decades went by such creative cosmopolitanism became less and less unusual throughout the country.

V

Ralph Ellison was the first black writer successfully to capture the underdog experience in literature. Frederick Douglass, Booker T. Washington, and W. E. B. DuBois had done their shares, but during the generations after the Civil War few listened outside their own community. The quality of writing in fiction or verse was mediocre and derivative. Other ethnic groups did no better. White, Anglo-Saxon Protestants ruled literature, and blacks wanting to read about themselves had to do so in the works of Mark Twain or William Faulkner. An occasional Theodore Dreiser or James T. Farrell emerged to represent a slightly different ethnic mix, but for blacks only the minor products of the Harlem Renaissance made even a slight mark on the larger culture. For Americans of Chinese or Spanish origin, there was next to nothing.

Ellison showed how an ethnic group could produce a man of art. He had grown up in an Oklahoma family well aware of literature and politics. His father had been so enamored of Emerson that he named his son Ralph Waldo; his mother was a supporter of Socialist leader Eugene V. Debs and an active campaigner against state segregation laws. For young blacks in the early decades of the twentieth century, only athletics and entertainment offered much in the way of advancement into the middle class, and Ellison eagerly immersed himself in music. He took up the trumpet and the soprano sax, and found his friends and role models among the jazz musicians of Oklahoma City. King Oliver, Ida Cox, and the Old Blue Devils Band were for him what presidents and explorers were for white boys. At the same time he studied European classical music, and when he went off to Tuskegee Institute in 1933, his great ambition was to compose a symphony that in some way would sum up the black experience in America. Richard Wagner had produced a symphony at twenty-six; Antonin Dvořák had written a "New World Symphony" based in part on black music. Ellison wanted a place beside them.

Tuskegee actually provided him with competent musical training, but his true talents turned out to be in literature. Through Hazel Harrison, the European-trained teacher of piano, he discovered the work of Alain Locke and the ferment surrounding the Harlem Renaissance and Locke's edited volume, *The New*

Negro, which was one of the key vehicles acquainting readers with its achievements. Interested in a number of the arts as well as philosophy, Ellison found it difficult to concentrate exclusively on any one; in time he left college to go to New York to study sculpture. He soon abandoned it for writing, largely under the influence and encouragement of Richard Wright, whose *Native Son* was soon the first black-written best-seller in America. Through Wright Ellison discovered the prefaces of Henry James, the novels of Joseph Conrad and Fedor Dostoyevsky, and the criticism of Joseph Warren Beach. He was soon deep in the literature of modern life, and in time discovered the work of French radical André Malraux. *Man's Fate* was perhaps the most successful work of art produced by a radical in the 1930s, and when Ellison heard Malraux appeal for support for the Spanish Loyalists at the same party where the black blues singer Leadbelly performed, something seemed to click. "It is such accidents, such fortuitous meetings, which count for so much in our lives," he recalled later.

In order to publish *Invisible Man* (1952), Ellison had to conquer many obstacles, not the least of which was conventional white expectations of what a talented black writer should say. The "greatest difficulty for a Negro writer was the problem of revealing what he truly felt, rather than serving up what Negroes were supposed to feel, and were encouraged to feel." But where most black writers, including Richard Wright, never really transcended this problem, Ellison not only did so, he did so by turning it into one of the themes of his art. Ellison not only used the counterpoint between appearance and reality, he also refused to give in to the social scientific habit of quantifying and generalizing about status. "I felt it important to explore the full range of American Negro humanity and to affirm those qualities which are of value beyond any question of segregation, economics or previous condition of servitude."

Ellison wanted to capture the essence of American life in all its diversity; he was in no way restricting himself to blacks as a subject, to any conventional notion of the novel form, or any particular style of writing. He was also deeply concerned with language and the artistic validity of any style in which he might write. "Our speech I found resounding with an alive language swirling with over three hundred years of American living, a mixture of the folk, the Biblical, the scientific and the political." It could be slangy, academic, or poetic—depending on the occasion. "As for the rather rigid concepts of reality which informed a number of the worlds which impressed me and to which I owe a great deal, I was forced to conclude that reality was far more mysterious and uncertain, and more exciting." It was also more promising for the artist. "To attempt to express that American experience which has carried one back and forth and up and down the land and across, and across again the great river . . . from contact with slavery to contact with a world of advanced scholarship, art and science, is simply to burst such neatly understated forms of the novel asunder."

Many critical terms apply to *Invisible Man.* It is a quest for identity, a *bildungsroman* about the growing up and education of a young man, and a novel of initiation, full of rites and rituals as the hero moves from one stage to the next. It is also a symphony, integrating black folk themes and language into an established European art form, after the manner of Dvořák. It is full of movements, in both the musical and the mobile senses of the term. The author has a prelude, states themes, elaborates them, does variations upon them, has interludes and even occasional dances, and comes to a riotous climax. Meanwhile the Invisible Man moves from South to North, from visibility to invisibility, from innocence to experience, from cliché to his own speech, from aboveground to underground, from gentility to outlawry, from a man unaware of violence and politics to a man well-versed in both. As a symphony of black identity, it concerns a not-human boy who is what everyone wants him to be, and how he changed into a human adult who will not adjust to capitalism, communism, racism, or convention. Ellison was well over twenty-six when he wrote it, but then the work plays better than the tripe Wagner turned out so young.

In the early pages of the novel, many of the themes of American cultural history, and the black place in it, become aspects of a highly symbolic world of light, music, puns, and history—material that could never have had a place in earlier American literature. A simple statement of "fact" becomes emblematic of hundreds of years of subordination and discrimination: "I live rent-free in a building rented strictly to whites, in a section of the basement that was shut off and forgotten during the nineteenth century"; his home is like the place where a bear hibernates. It all seems matter-of-fact until the reader understands that all blacks have been living in the basement of American culture since emancipation, rent-free but forgotten. The bear becomes the Brer Bear of countless folk tales, always in combat with the white Brer Rabbits who keep setting traps for him. Throughout the novel the narrator will be the poor black bear trying to get out of the traps laid by whites, or blacks who have adjusted too well to white demands.

But America is cosmopolitan, and the Invisible Man is a good American: "Though invisible, I am in the great American tradition of tinkers. That made me kin to Ford, Edison and Franklin," all of whom were white self-improvers whose words will be parodied on succeeding pages. But blacks also have another American hero, Louis Armstrong, and suddenly American cultural history has been integrated, trumpets blaring. The Invisible Man has five recordings of Armstrong's music; above all, he likes to play the Fats Waller blues tune "What Did I Do, To Be So Black and Blue?" And he likes to hear it especially when smoking "grass" and eating his favorite dessert.

Things become more complex. *Black and blue* is the slang expression for internal bleeding—what happens when a wound has caused an injury but the skin has not been broken. But of course blacks, being black, do not become black and blue because such injuries are invisible unless they appear beneath white skin. When blacks suffer, in other words, when they are beaten, no one can see their wounds. Only the external blood is visible. But the meaning of *blue* in the black and musical communities is hardly confined to wounds; blue notes and the blues have been well-known terms for close to a century, musical equivalents in some ways to the wounds suffered internally by slaves or oppressed freemen. Thus, in a seeming reverie, we get an underhistory of American culture: the woe, internal bleeding, invisible wounds, jazz music; the bear's den in a segregated building, where a truly enterprising young man, a black Edison in a way, can tap into the power lines of white capitalism and draw for his own use an enormous amount of power. A shocking tale, to be sure, but then the book is full of puns, too.

Then there is that dessert: vanilla ice cream and sloe gin. Sloe is the rather blackish fruit of the blackthorn, but when used to flavor gin it turns the resulting beverage red. As the reader watches the consumption of this treat, musing about the role of color in American culture, the whole nation takes on a slightly different hue. You mix the black berry with the white or pale gin, you add blue notes and internal bleeding and you suddenly find yourself consuming a new America: the red, the white, the blue—and the black. The book that follows is cosmopolitan with a vengeance.

VI

The world of Vladimir Nabokov was about as far from that of the young Ralph Ellison as it was possible to get. He was born in St. Petersburg, the son of an eminent jurist and his wealthy wife. The family was highly educated, politically liberal, and fluent in English. Their son grew up trilingual, speaking the English of his governess, the French of the aristocracy, and the Russian of the larger population. Subsequent studies in England and long residence in Germany only confirmed what anyone would suspect from such a person: a cosmopolitanism in the original sense of that term, a man who inhabited the cosmos, who could survive almost everywhere—and incidentally transform that anywhere into art. The revolution forced Nabokov out of Russia; he never liked Cambridge or Berlin. The approach of World War II made France seem perilous, and so provincial America acquired him, *faute de mieux*. It was not a precise match, but then it never is. Nabokov went through many of the painful maladjustments that emigrés experienced, although his linguistic and literary abilities ensured that he always had some kind of job.

Marginality, exile, deracination—these are among the great themes of the recent novel. Nabokov had been uprooted from four different countries, and it is hardly any wonder that his characters sometimes seem unreal, their impulses obscure, their logic irrational. His social class had been exterminated, and his father assassinated—by mistake, as it turned out—so it is hardly any wonder that death, accident, and random violence suddenly emerge from his pages, but only in America did he stay long enough and feel welcome enough to get the feel of place in his work in a more than superficial way. But it was a very special kind of encounter complicated by his origins and the linguistic complexity of his multinational European experience. The experience of deracination and random violence appears in the behavior of his characters at the same time that simultaneous knowledge of three languages made them think and talk in ways that seem entirely new in American literature. The logic and rhythms from one language enter another, just as past experiences invade the consciousness as it perceives the American reality. The sense of never being understood, both literally and figuratively—of always being a politely tolerated guest—permeates many of the books. This sense of multicultural displacement is one of the most important elements in the modern novel in many languages, just as it is in demography—the writer, so to speak, as displaced person. It thus seems almost logical for a writer to try to transcend time and death as well as logic.

America has a central role for such artists. A New World, a "virgin land," a place of refuge from the wars of Europe both in legend and in fact, America becomes a playground of the imagination, a place where anything can happen and usually does. America, far more than Lolita or illicit love, is the theme of Nabokov's greatest book—a book that restored his wealth to the point where he could uproot himself once again and move to Switzerland. *Lolita* is clearly a novel about a European expatriate who conceives an ungovernable passion for a twelve-year-old American nymphet. Reviewers at the time had trouble deciding whether old Europe was debauching young America, or whether in fact it was America that was doing the seduction—but either way, the clash of cultures provides the central tension in the work. If Humbert represents modern Europe, then it is mad and perverted; if Lolita represents America, it is physically attractive, shallow, and deeply corrupt. Obviously Europe and America are both far more than this, but this is where the reader must start.

Lolita receives Humbert as readily as America received Nabokov: willingly but coldly, her mind on other things. She and the landscape then tend to merge, as the illicit couple travel around America. Much of the book is a highly imaginative recreation of the American landscape, based on Nabokov's extensive lecturing around the country. The land, alas, gave up its virtues to visitors just as readily; to a European used to the tidy parks and organized recreation areas of Germany, the American landscape was both overwhelming in uncontrolled natural beauty and hideous in its visible exploitation. "Now and then, in the vastness of those plains, huge trees would advance toward us to cluster self-consciously by the roadside and provide a bit of humanitarian shade above a picnic table, with sun flecks, flattened paper cups, samaras and discarded ice-cream sticks littering the brown ground." Lolita would wander off to the public facilities, fascinated chiefly by the inventive toilet signs; "while lost in an artist's dream, I would stare at the honest brightness of the gasolene paraphernalia against the splendid green of oaks, or at a distant hill scrambling out—scarred but still untamed—from the wilderness of agriculture that was trying to swallow it."

This was not simply the case of one more European, fleeing for his life, achieving freedom only to complain about the lack of cultural and governmental amenities. It was rather the sad and ironical commentary of an intelligence always doomed to think in vast, sublime dreams, only to have to face up to sordid, time-bound realities. Even the sexual scenes participate in this poignant juxtaposition, as when a few pages later Humbert had to "register" his "disappointment" at the "lyrical, epic, tragic but never Arcadian American wilds." They certainly were "heart-rendingly beautiful," with "a quality of wide-eyed, unsung, innocent surrender that my lacquered, toy-bright Swiss villages and exhaustively lauded Alps no longer possess." Many lovers had indulged their mates and tamed that landscape, but in America "the open-air lover will not find it easy." "Poisonous plants burn his sweetheart's buttocks, nameless insects sting his; sharp items of the forest floor prick his knees, insects hers." All around one can imagine the rustling of snakes and the possibility of dragons—"while the crablike seeds of ferocious flowers cling, in a hideous green crust, to gartered black sock and sloppy white sock alike." It is never easy to adjust to a new country.

But if there is less to Lolita than meets the eye, there is more to America. Nabokov's central concern is with the creative imagination as it attempts to transcend time and death. The concept of the "nymphet" depends on the desire of an aging man to conquer time, to keep his imagination and even his body young, and to deny anything unpleasant that interferes. America becomes "the future" for both Humbert and Nabokov, as it has been for so many earlier immigrants, while Europe has always been "the past," stultified by tradition, corrupted by greed, politics, and war. Nymphets are those girls, between the ages of nine and fourteen, who have an indefinable sex appeal for much older men. The age gap is important, but the fleshly aspect is merely emblematic: "It is a question of focal adjustment, of a certain distance that the inner eye thrills to surmount, and a certain contrast that the mind perceives with a gasp of perverse delight. . . . Ah, leave me alone in my pubescent park, in my mossy garden. Let them play around me forever. Never grow up." Not the least of Lolita's attractions is that she reminds Humbert of an earlier love; "the twenty-five years I had lived since then, tapered to a palpitating point, and vanished."

Thus, in their strange ways, the visions of Ellison and Nabokov came together. Two outsiders, condemned always to feel foreign in middle America, were each trying to find his voice through analysis of the culture. Even a generation earlier, writing of such quality could never have come from such marginal groups as blacks or immigrants. Yet here it was, both *Lolita* and *Invisible Man* being popular and critical successes, giving to better-established Americans a new sense of what their country was all about. America proved still to be a new land, even three centuries and a half after its birth, and both writers found existence there a complex fate. Both also wished to transcend the past, and to use the "newness" of the land to start life afresh.

VI

The career of Saul Bellow offers yet another version of American cosmopolitanism after the war. He was born and grew up in a Montreal slum, in a strictly orthodox Jewish family where Yiddish was more common than English, and where French was the language of the dominant majority of the city. The family moved to Chicago when he was nine, and he moved through local schools, the University of Chicago, and nearby Northwestern. He thus had no real need to feel "foreign" as an adult, and certainly the psychological center of his fiction for many years was Chicago, both literally and as a "type" city for the life of urban America. Like Ralph Ellison and many other young writers, he stayed alive during the Depression in part through work with the WPA writers' project, and also managed a brief stint of college teaching. But his literary generation was the first to experience the possibility of actually being "rooted" in the immigrant American experience. In the New York area, many of the intellectual migrants had grouped themselves around the New School, *Partisan Review*, and related institutions, and so a young writer of the 1940s could easily identify his peculiar ethnic background with the meaning of America. In time, President Kennedy would make it a cliché that America was a nation of immigrants, but long before he did so, much of the America which was culturally active was the collection of immigrant intellectuals in New York City and their native-born associates. Around *Partisan Review*, the key names included Philip Rahv, William Phillips, Lionel Trilling, Delmore Schwartz, Isaac Rosenfeld, and Paul Goodman. Theirs was a world of radical politics, Freudian and Gestaltist psychology, Sartrian existentialism, and above all else, modernist literature. These figures adopted Bellow as one of the most promising of their younger writers, and their influence permeates his work: the plot of *Dangling Man* seems to parallel that of Sartre's *Nausea*; that of *The Victim* resembles that of Dostoyevsky's *The Eternal Husband*; and Delmore Schwartz himself inspired *Humboldt's Gift*. The immigrant experience had taken root so quickly that aspects of it already were coming to seem "typically American."

Many writers took one look at the postwar world and evolved what critics now call, awkwardly, the "post-modernist" novel. Building on the innovations of modernism—the stream of consciousness of James Joyce, the sexual liberation of D. H. Lawrence, the timeless memories of Marcel Proust, the ironies of Thomas Mann—the post-modernists carried modernism to extremes. Plots and logic fragmented; rationality became itself deceptive; love became hatred; peace was war by other means; narrators were unreliable while liars sometimes told the truth; drugs became a key to wisdom; science fiction and the mystery novel became respectable genres, often hard to distinguish from mainstream fiction. Normal sexuality seemed a quaint aberration, while homosexuality, rape, and mutilation came to seem conventional to experienced viewers of the literary scene. To anyone familiar with the typical literature of America before the war it seemed preposterous, foreign, unassimilable. Dreiser may have associated sex with power, and Faulkner may have used the corncob in ways no farmer would approve, but such behavior was clearly exceptional, horribly unusual, not to be expected. After 1945, it was expected. All of it. Nothing was impossible in fiction.

Bellow observed it all, but almost alone among respected writers, he retained conventional attitudes toward plot, character, and setting. Herzog might write letters to dead people, but then the epistolary novel was hardly a recent innovation. Augie March traveled over America, Mexico, and Europe like an American Tom Jones. Henderson invaded Africa like some enormous Don Quixote, yet another half-mad idealist trying to find something noble in a world given over to crass materialism. The striking thing about Bellow's plots is how old-fashioned they really are. Yet the world that his characters see is the post-modern world—chaotic, ugly, hypocritical, deceptive, sexually anarchic, irrational; psychoanalysis seems to be central both to plots and characters, and there are modish references to Dostoyevsky and Sartre. This juxtaposition of old-style plot and new-style world has become Bellow's trademark, and one reason for his widespread acceptance. Readers have more to hang on to than they do in many other recent novels.

Thus the ironies in his career abound: the Canadian Jew as Great American Novelist; the post-modernist writer who uses hackneyed conventions; and, even odder in some ways, the writer nurtured by the New Deal radicalism and Trotskyist critics turning out so belligerently conservative in all of his recognizable political attitudes. Because of his friends and supporters, Bellow for some years passed as a writer vaguely on the left despite the apolitical quality of most of his work. But the events of the Vietnam years affected him as they did so many older intellectuals and writers, and the implicit conservatism of his vision became insistent. Where previously private problems of guilt, marriage, and job satisfaction seemed central, a book like *Mr. Sammler's Planet* (1970) glared at a world that had, as the saying went, gone to "pot." The central character, a half-blind, embittered refugee from Nazism, has become full of loathing for his adopted country. Its apologists talked of the "greening of America" where he could only see the trashing of America. Sammler had seen his world collapse once, and he was not sure but that it was about to collapse again. Liberalism was not enough, and he smelled decay everywhere. It was a bad book, but a very American attitude. Bellow had become so absorbed into American culture that he had come to sound like the grumpiest white Protestant industrialists, furious in their clubs about the servants, the politicians, and the sexual morals prevalent in their old age.

Bellow will not be remembered for these late works. He will instead be valued for his more exuberant work, in particular *The Adventures of Augie March* and *Henderson the Rain King*. His work of the 1940s had been too close to its European models and he had felt, as he remarked later, very constrained in his writing at that time. But he soon managed to fight free of the elitism that he sensed among the writers and critics in the modernist tradition. He could never feel comfortable as a mandarin, and he still felt awkward within the larger American society; university professors had made it clear to him that as the son of Russian Jews he would never "have the right *feeling* for Anglo-Saxon tradition, for English words." But by the early 1950s, Bellow's roots were solidly in American ground. Augie March is an outsider adjusting to America, a boy of uncertain parentage and immigrant culture trying to find his identity and his proper relationship to his country. From the days of Natty Bumppo, Ishmael, and Huckleberry Finn, American males had been going out into the world to seek experiences in the unknown, finding their characters and their country in the process. So Augie ventures forth, trying jobs, girl friends, and mother figures—he even samples that American profession, a life of crime—but somehow survives it all. By the end, like so many Americans, he finds some notion of who he is as an American while living abroad, and the book ends with a brief evocation of American history:

> Look at me, going everywhere! Why, I am a sort of Columbus of those near-at-hand and believe you can come to them in this immediate *terra incognita* that spreads out in every gaze. I may well be a flop at this line of endeavor. Columbus too thought he was a flop, probably, when they sent him back in chains. Which didn't prove there was no America.

Augie is the young man out to shape himself as an American; Henderson is the American out of shape, trying to untwist his psyche after enduring too many of the pressures of civilization. He feels overwhelmed by the pressures of parents, wives, children, farm, money, drunkenness, even his music lessons and his teeth. On the one hand, his soul screams out "No, No, get back, curse you, let me alone!," while on the other, the "ceaseless voice" in his heart says "I want, I want." He may be a Protestant pig farmer, ridiculous in his twenty-two-inch neck size and his green shorts, but he is in fact Bellow's Yiddish version of the problems of modern life, piling *angst* upon trivial detail, exploding with wrath and imagination, and so American in his ludicrousness that he is almost an embarrassment to critics looking for sober experiments and philosophical commitments.

Augie covers Mexico and Europe; Henderson takes on Africa—in the modern world, no place is safe from Americans finding themselves. He has developed a "pressure in the chest" that periodically bothers him, the objective correlative of the pressures of civilization, most of which seem to attack Americans first. They have to get things off their chests before they can function, experience a kind of emotional heart attack before they can be free adults. Most of Bellow's heroes camp out in seedy hotels, summer houses, or boarding houses, trying to take stock of their unrewarding lives. Henderson, being as Protestant as anyone in the State Department, wants to reorganize an African kingdom. The project is no more mad than anything else in the modern world, and as he mutters to his readers, "Of course, in an age of madness, to expect to be untouched by madness is a form of madness, but the pursuit of sanity can be a form of madness, too."

Following the precedents of Joseph Conrad, he trades the heart of one darkness for another. He wants to leave civilization and penetrate deep into the interior. He sheds his baggage, symbolically and in fact, but things still go awry. He meets children but scares them unintentionally; he sees a girl who reminds him of his own daughter and fails to cope with her just as totally as he failed to cope with his daughter. In the heart of Africa, he meets a man who upsets him by talking in English, "the great imperial language of today, taking its turn after Greek and Latin and so on"—he understands its presence, yet cannot imagine it. He finds a cistern full of frogs that the superstitious natives refuse to use; to help them out he tries to blow up the frogs and succeeds in destroying the whole water supply. The pattern is all too clear: not only does he fail to get away from the pressures of civilization, he also brings its irrational death and destruction with him.

In the end, it is the imagination that triumphs—Henderson's, Bellow's, and America's. Dream, myth, and adventure all turn out to be part of the creative process, and civilization is in some way the totality of its achievements. Men will never conquer death or desire, but through art they can at least try to win dominion over themselves. The American artist, in short, suffers from the same problems as his counterparts around the world. For over three centuries American geography, religion, and politics have convinced American artists that life in the New World was different. Time defeated this great deception, and the accidents of war and migration in time fused the nations of the world into a country called the United States of America. A cosmopolitan country now faced the problems of men everywhere, and readers everywhere valued those American writers who could make art out of the pain.

And so, in the middle of Africa, an American could harangue his native friend, with the words "Americans are supposed to be dumb but they are willing to go into this. It isn't just me. You have to think about white Protestantism and the Constitution and the Civil War and capitalism and winning the West." All these physical tasks were over when modern man was born, and so he was left the biggest task of all: "to encounter death." Something had to be done. "Millions of Americans have gone forth since the war to redeem the present and discover the future." He knew that people were trying to do the same things he was "in India and in China and South America and all over the place." It was the destiny of his generation of Americans "to go out in the world and try to find the wisdom of life. Why the hell do you think I'm out here, anyway?"

It was a good question, and it made Americans akin to thinking people the world over. A peculiar past was ending but a common future was beginning.

Chapter 15

The Conservative Hegemony, 1969–1992

The period from the 1930s through 1968 seemed dominated by the words *survive* and *absorb*. Americans had somehow to survive the Depression and absorb the numerous displaced people who wished to make new careers in the Western Hemisphere. They had to survive the war and absorb a whole new range of imperial responsibilities, from the expense of a large defense department at home to the need to understand and pacify distant peoples engaged in brutal but only dimly understood wars abroad. Americans then tried to survive the Cold War and absorb the fruits of a resilient capitalism as it found new strength during the 1950s. Then, just when things seemed to be working out, they had to survive the rebellious children of the baby boom and absorb their radical discontent with the status quo. The shocks never seemed to end, and when enemies without seemed quiet, enemies within became demanding.

While few Americans noticed, the rest of the world caught up. Europe recovered its economic clout by the 1960s, and by the 1990s was emerging as a genuine equal in the wars for international markets. Japan was already a rival for both, its excess funds buying companies all over the world. Smaller economies, in Korea, Taiwan, Hong Kong, and Singapore were suddenly competitive in certain areas, from shipbuilding to children's clothing. The Soviet Union collapsed entirely from internal incompetence and proved almost as threatening in its disintegrative weakness as it had in united health. At times, the world seemed like Versailles all over again, every small people demanding national independence and acting violently whether or not they won that status. Bitter small wars broke out in the former Soviet Union and the former Yugoslavia, but most Americans resisted the old tendency to intervene. Only in the case of the Iraqi invasion of oil-rich Kuwait did America intervene, and even then only with substantial international cooperation. Omnipotence was a thing of the past, and the United Nations assumed real importance, something it rarely had before the 1990s.

In the perspective of history, the year 1968 seems pivotal. It seemed so at the time, with street demonstrations and assassinations dominating the headlines, and it seems so a generation later, if not quite in the same way. At the time, anarchy threatened and many people genuinely felt that the country was about to fall apart. In fact, although in the short term, public pressure forced an end to the war in Vietnam, the truly important long-range result of 1968 was the arrival of a new conservative climate of opinion in the country that dominated its politics and fostered the emergence of a conservative intellectual establishment that would have seemed preposterous a few years earlier. It questioned all aspects of the welfare state that had seemed to be emerging from the 1930s through the middle 1960s. It fostered as well a climate of creativity that spread throughout the culture. While certain artists persisted in older tendencies, new artists emerged who found virtues in well-established forms. Tonality and melody reappeared in music, nature in painting; decoration in architecture was no longer a crime, and at least a few distinguished novels came out with plot, character, and setting.

The most convenient way to organize recent American cultural life is to visualize a dominant conservatism, with remnants of three other past climates still producing important work and presumably ever ready to win fresh supporters and emerge in new ways should the circumstances warrant. A few radicals kept alive the spirit of "the sixties," and a few post-modernists reigned in university literature departments. Far more numerous were the liberals: grown flabby with success, they had no real policies to advocate when Johnson's Great Society collapsed. Secular from birth, they had no way of dealing with the religious and moral issues that enraged voters. Bred to civil libertarianism and sensitive on matters of race and ethnicity, they had painful trouble dealing with abortion, child pornography, drug addiction, unmarried motherhood, and all the rest of the unsolvable problems of modern urban life, so visibly tied to racial minorities and persistent poverty.

II

Conservatism had been a respectable minority position throughout the early years of the twentieth century. It had dominated the Supreme Court, from the social Darwinism of Oliver Wendell Holmes, Jr., to the administrative reformism of William Howard Taft, however much such thinkers might have differed among themselves on specific cases. It united the South, split though it was between the advocates of industrialization (The New South) and a persistent agrarianism (The Southern Agrarians). It was fashionable in many university English departments, as they developed a New Criticism that had much in common with Southern agrarianism and a New Humanism that saw literary study as the core of any defense of humanistic learning in the face of Dewey's pragmatism and its persistent efforts at introducing an adjustment psychology and a vocational emphasis. It held the allegiance of numerous literary giants: Edith Wharton and Willa Cather had never been anything other than conservatives as mature artists, while Ezra Pound and T. S. Eliot gravitated in that direction once they found their mature, modernist voices as poets. And most businessmen, despite cultural illiteracy, seemed to be conservative by instinct.

But by 1950 conservatism was in disarray. The Democrats had been enacting liberal measures under the New Deal and were still promoting a Fair Deal, with the New Frontier and the Great Society still to come. Secularism seemed established, and if educated people went to church they did so the way they took vitamins: it was good for you, and the brand did not matter. So few intellectuals expressed specifically conservative views that Lionel Trilling, the best-known liberal in literary studies, could publish a book in which he dismissed such attitudes out of hand. "In the United States at this time liberalism is not only the dominant but even the sole intellectual tradition," he wrote in *The Liberal Imagination*. "For it is the plain fact that nowadays there are no conservative or reactionary ideas in general circulation." He could detect certain vestiges in the provinces, but outside ecclesiastical circles he thought that conservatives did not "express themselves in ideas but only in action or in irritable mental gestures which seem to resemble ideas."

This smugness was widespread; liberalism had been in academic and political power for so long that it assumed the right to govern both word and deed, and its advocates talked only to each other and did not deign to notice genuine opposition. But liberalism was vulnerable in several ways: to charges of corruption, in the Truman administration especially, as a machine politician rewarded too many of his faithful friends and paid too little attention to what they did; to charges of procommunism, because of past liberal-left alliances, based on economics during the Depression and then the exigencies of war, which required the refurbishing of the image of the Soviet Union as an anti-Nazi ally; and to charges of inefficiency and needless bureaucracy, all but inevitable after almost twenty years of relentlessly building up the power of the federal government to wage war on poverty at home and the Axis abroad. All the charges had some merit, but not a great deal. Their lack of intellectual substance was also a measure of conservative desperation. Conservatives sensed what they were against but had few clear notions of what they were for.

This negativism always remained a factor, but over the next thirty years conservatives developed specific issues that they could focus on: economic theory, exemplified by the ideas of Milton Friedman and the Chicago economists who shared his views; civil rights; education; deregulation; reform of the legal system; and the revitalization of conservative Protestantism. They also developed a respectable journal to discuss them in and telegenic journalists to present their cases to larger audiences. In *National Review* and its editor, William F. Buckley, Jr., they found something of a St. George, out to slay the dragons of liberalism and secularism. He pictured himself as sitting athwart history, telling it to stop where it was—and, to as great an extent as was possible for one man to accomplish such a feat, he did so.

III

No figure did more to change the dominant climate from liberalism to conservatism than journalist William F. Buckley, Jr. (b. 1925). Having never been a real part of America when young, he seemed unaffected by its enthusiasms. His story is a true oddity in cultural history, for he became so influential in large part not because he was representative but because he was not. He came on the scene alone, found allies in strange places, and somehow wielded the results into a magazine, a political campaign, a popular television show, and seats at the right hands of the mighty, most definitely including presidents.

Buckley's father had been a Texas oilman in Mexico, successful until the revolution led to his expulsion. Young William was raised to hate revolutionaries of all sorts and to love the Roman Catholic Church insofar as it taught cooperation with capitalism and the protection of private property. The entire family deplored the New Deal at home and all talk of intervention abroad. Educated privately, by Spanish-speaking maids when young, French-speaking tutors in the early teen years, and in preparatory schools, the ten siblings outwardly shared few of the characteristics of American democratic life. They were also fearsomely outspoken, and when William attended Yale College after World War II and disliked its liberalism and secularism, he fought back. In *God and Man at Yale* (1951) he asked the alumni to reclaim their school for capitalism and Christianity, infuriating the faculty and administration with his open contempt for the values of academic freedom. The outrage continued when he and his brother-in-law, Brent Bozell, published *McCarthy and his Enemies* (1954). Most vocal academics despised Senator Joseph R. McCarthy of Wisconsin, in his campaign against Communist influence in Washington, but for Buckley the senator was doing what had to be done, identifying the malign ideas and influences in American life and uprooting them.

A quick study rather than an intellectual, Buckley carried his family prejudices with him when he founded *National Review* in 1955. A journal designed expressly to oppose the liberal *New Republic, National Review* tried to bring together all the antiliberals of the 1950s: religious conservatives, isolationists, ex-Communists, procapitalists, Southern Bourbons. Its masthead even included six Jews, as if to emphasize that the New Right was open to believers of all responsible faiths.

For thirty-five years the biggest issue in the magazine was anti-Communism. Such former Communists as Willmoore Kendall, Max Eastman, and Frank S. Meyer brought the same sectarian zeal to the right that they had to the left, and it meshed fairly well with the Roman Catholic Falange sympathies of the extended Buckley family. To such people, the New Deal had been a step down the road to socialism, and both liberals and socialists were endangering all Western values. The magazine supported Senator McCarthy, an expanded Pentagon and intervention in Eastern Europe when such countries as Hungary or Czechoslovakia rebelled against Soviet hegemony. Most of the staff thought of capitalism and private property as prerequisites of true democracy. All the words and associations of early American history were there, sounding odd in the secular, liberal environment that seemed so dominant.

Since most Democrats and liberals by this time professed a strong anti-Communism, other issues helped to define conservative policies. Race was important in the early years. The Buckleys had been segregationists, given to making caustic jokes about blacks. Editorials took the general position that most blacks were not educationally qualified for full citizenship and that the South should regulate its own affairs, not only in politics but also in such areas as schooling, transportation, marriage, and the office. The slogan "You can't legislate morality" was one many unideological Americans agreed on. But as time went on and liberal demands became law, both *National Review* and its editor adapted. Bozell was a strong influence here, more tolerant on race if less so on theology. Increasingly, this conservative acceptance of liberal initiatives became a national consensus, and so conservative candidates profited accordingly.

Other issues included how to improve schooling, how to interpret the Constitution, how to deal with censorship, how to regulate abortion, how to lessen the tax burden. As conservatism evolved, Buckley did also. At first, he had seemed like an intellectual whose long words and sarcastic tongue could have little appeal to middle America. This image began to change during the presidential campaign of Senator Barry Goldwater in the years leading up to 1964. Although he had numerous doubts about Goldwater's intelligence and suitability for the presidency, Buckley and his journal supported him against so obvious a New Deal liberal as President Johnson. But even as liberalism was enjoying its final victories, Buckley campaigned quixotically for Mayor of New York. He never expected to win—his famous reply to the question What would you do if elected? was Demand a recount!—but he wanted publicity for his views and got it. He won far more votes than expected, and their core seemed to be working-class Democrats, such as union members, police and fire officials, who thought that the civil rights revolution had gone too far but were unwilling to vote for the small-town capitalism that the Republican party seemed to embody. He became a media star and took advantage of his fame by launching *Firing Line*, a television interview show that caught on, as week after week he taunted liberal victims or launched conservative initiatives. As time went on, his intellectual credentials seemed thinner and thinner, while his fame as a journalist spread. He wrote a series of best-selling novels, based in part on his CIA experience, and other volumes equally trivial. He became a public personality, like a movie star, and when movie star Ronald Reagan moved into the White House, his victory seemed complete.

IV

Just as William F. Buckley, Jr., seemed to moderate his views as he expanded his influence, so conservatism as a whole found that it had to appeal to the large center of the electorate if it wished to exercise power. Ideology was all very well in universities and on talk shows, but the true goal of any pressure group is to change policies and practices. Ideologues themselves rarely exercise power directly and are usually not good administrators anyway. Buckley may have kept a wary eye on Washington, but his attention tended to be on the controls of his yacht—something he wrote about with more affection than he could summon up for politicians.

The great cliché of the 1980s was that a Reagan revolution remade American government. President Ronald Reagan, the Great Communicator, restored dignity to the presidency, brought conservative principles to power, kept military might preeminent, made morality again fashionable, made the tax system fairer, and so on. As with most slogans, this one had some truth. Ronald Reagan had almost mesmeric control over the electorate and did change the nature of much political debate. He spent enormous sums on military hardware, revamped the tax system, and appointed conservative judges to toughen up the administration of the law. But what seemed much more significant during the decade after his departure from office was the way in which the Republicans accommodated themselves to decades of Democratic rule. Bureaucracy in the modern world learned long ago how to protect itself against electoral whims, and bureaucrats protect their jobs regardless of election results. What triumphed, as the title of the best memoir of the Reagan years had it, was politics, not conservatism.

The author of *The Triumph of Politics*, David Stockman, served as Director of the Budget during the first Reagan term, 1981–1985. He was not only the youngest visible member of the administration, he was the most intellectual and ideological, and thus provides the best view of the actual experience of conservatism as it exercised power under a popular president. The picture of President Reagan that emerges from Stockman's book is enough to bewilder anyone who takes democratic politics seriously, but it is one that other memoirs confirm. Reagan was something of a hero to Stockman, so much so that he had trouble addressing the president at all. Stockman soon found him "too kind, gentle, and sentimental" to lead the revolution that was supposed to be going on in his name. At first impression, Reagan seemed to be giving a "miserable" performance, to be unprepared for responsibility and ill-informed about every important issue. His words were usually "filled with woolly platitudes," and Stockman "felt kind of sorry for the guy." Reagan "was more ancient ideologically than he was in years. I considered him a cranky obscurantist whose political base was barnacled with every kook and fringe group that inhabited the vasty deep of American politics."

Despite—or perhaps because of—his deficiencies, Reagan gathered force; like other skeptical conservatives, Stockman fell into line because he had nowhere else to go. Although the presidency could inspire awe, it never seemed to make Reagan either intelligent or effective. He governed by anecdote. He agreed to suggestions he clearly did not understand. His staffers misled him repeatedly, confusing him to win agreement. The budget was the special problem of the director: "The problem was that the President did not have great depth of understanding about the tax code. The complexities, intricacies, and mysteries involved in the tax breaks that the Congress wanted were simply beyond him." He seemed to be incapable of understanding "the link between the federal tax structure and the budget. He could not grasp that to fiddle significantly with the former was to change the numbers in the latter—and for the worse." After several years of service, Stockman concluded with an audible sigh of exasperation that the president was a "terminal optimist" and an embarrassment to all of his competent appointees. "What do you do when your President ignores all the palpable, relevant facts and wanders in circles. I could not bear to watch this good and decent man go on in this embarrassing way. I buried my head in my plate" and departed from further involvement.

Stockman's book concentrates on three issues. The first is social security, a vital American substitute for much of what constituted socialism and the welfare state in Europe. Most countries pay pensions out of current tax revenues. The American prejudice against "socialism" was such that President Roosevelt had insisted on a pay-as-you-go policy that withheld money from paychecks and then made an appearance of paying back their own money to retirees later. Doing things in this manner quieted consciences and with subsequent tinkering seemed to work. But politicians could not leave it alone. Since it was popular, they could amend it to make the changes they advocated take on the aura of popularity. Stockman was blistering in his criticisms.

"No single issue was as critical to the success of the Reagan Revolution as Social Security reform." It was eating up one-third of the entire domestic budget. It only seemed to be a paying back of wages withheld earlier. "The truth was that the politicians had sweetened nearly everyone's earned pension with extra dollars for dependents, low earnings, and numerous other concepts of 'need' that had nothing to do with what a worker had put into the fund." Behind this tinkering was a liberal desire to redistribute wealth. "Some workers got back 90 cents on each dollar of taxes and some got as low as 15 cents for most of what they'd put into the fund. This was supposed to help the poor." Dependents' benefits were especially arbitrary and potentially costly, depending on whether a wage-earner had a dependent spouse or minor children. "Another gusher of cost was the open-ended and lax disability benefit program." Much of what Stockman said in his critique was perfectly correct, both as fact and as conservative doctrine, but politically irrelevant. The politicians wanted to tinker with benefits and people loved to get them. Any truly conservative approach would have cost votes and lost the power to do anything at all; Stockman never had a chance, and social security lumbered into the 1990s as bloated, illogical, and expensive as ever.

The other two issues are intimately related: the huge budget deficit and the military bills that caused it. The story was both very complicated and quite simple. It involved arcane budgetary projections through computers that were inaccurately programmed, leading Stockman to issue figures that were misleading, but which no one wanted to admit were misleading. They in turn misled the president, who deeply wanted both a huge increase in Pentagon spending and a smaller federal budget. Reaganite rhetoric had been bitterly anti-Communist and anti-Washington for a long time: it demanded more military security for far less money, or so it seemed, for the message said to lower taxes while spending whatever it took to beef up the military. Reagan never seemed to understand that most of the federal budget was enacted into legal obligations that could not be changed—debt payments, salaries, social security obligations—without more upheaval than Congress would stand. The real question was simple: Would higher taxes or higher debts pay for all the military expansion?

The Reagan in Stockman's book had neither force of character nor intelligence. He could neither enforce discipline nor think clearly, and as a result his secretary of defense, Caspar Weinberger, became the villain of the piece, the man who refused to compromise and who intentionally confused Reagan into supporting an expansion which in turn made any initiatives elsewhere financially impossible. The description of how the debate proceeded remains something of a classic for conservatism in power but disarray: Weinberger came to the most important meeting with "a blown-up cartoon. It showed three soldiers. One was a pygmy who carried no rifle," who represented the budget of Democratic predecessor Jimmy Carter. "The second was a four-eyed wimp who looked like Woody Allen, carrying a tiny rifle," presumably to represent the Stockman budget limits. "Finally, there was G.I. Joe himself, 190 pounds of fighting man, all decked out in helmet and flak jacket and pointing an M-60 machine gun," presumably to fire away for the Weinberger request. "It was so intellectually disreputable, so demeaning, that I could hardly bring myself to believe that a

Harvard-educated cabinet officer could have brought this to the President of the United States. Did he think the White House was on Sesame Street?" Apparently so. The resulting debts are still there, preempting social programs a full decade later.

As it always is in politics, the verdict on the conservative years was that it won, but in winning, conservatism had to make so many compromises as to make anyone concerned with intellectual or moral issues wonder at the price of victory. The 1980s seemed to confirm, in America as in Europe, that the welfare state had about reached its limits. In Britain, Germany, France, and Scandinavia, the situations were not all that different, and, while no one was looking, the Eastern European countries suddenly began to opt for what they thought of as capitalism. The Soviet Union became the Commonwealth of Independent States, East Germany joined West, Marxism became passé, and Austrian economics voguish. It was not so much that the American Way had triumphed, or even some supranational conservatism, but that a phase of history had ended. Voters everywhere seemed too worried about making a living and keeping some kind of humane system going to indulge in ideology.

V

Radicalism is not a subject that often seems important in American history. It helped provoke the Revolution and the Civil War, but it usually existed more in the minds of conservatives than in any large-scale threat to the status quo. Students like to romanticize radicals, but in America they often have a hard time finding many. When they do, the individuals often turn out to have been foreigners, or those who lived almost entirely alone.

The 1960s were an exceptional decade in many ways, and not the least of these was that from about 1964 to 1969 it generated a genuine radicalism. The liberal hopes of a Martin Luther King and a Lyndon Johnson did not go far enough to satisfy minority groups, at the same time that, coincidentally, other serious issues also came to maturity. The left split violently on the results of these pressures. The mainstream supported President Johnson not only on the issues of civil rights and his War on Poverty, but also on his fighting of the war in Vietnam. Others found the gains in civil rights and on poverty inadequate and not always concerned with the truly important issues, and they were totally at odds with the government on the war. The results over the long run were a strengthening of conservatism, as the only effective bulwark against radicalism; a weakening of liberalism, as it spent a generation wringing its hands about what it had done both at home and abroad; and the spreading of radical fragments throughout the culture, often in ways the next generation did not recognize. Radicalism in the 1960s seemed to flare and die quickly, but it also pushed the culture along various roads far faster than would otherwise have been the case.

In addition to civil rights and the war, issues treated in detail in other chapters, radicals focused especially on the private and personal areas of human life. Pampered and comfortable by comparison to their parents, the college-age young had the leisure to pursue private agendas, and only a series of invasive experiences mobilized them into the potentially violent demonstrators of 1968. Insofar as one concept can bring together the concerns of this generation, it would be *consciousness*.

Having a decent level of material satisfaction, the young had the time to be bored and to seek for nonmaterial satisfactions. They often used it to attack the very capitalism that provided them with their leisure time. They professed to dislike the boredom of lives spent rising early, working hard, saving money, and planning for a distant future. The 1950s had been notorious for sobriety, reticence, formal clothing, styles of speech, and the sheer seriousness with which the young took themselves. As this superficial level of criticism became clichéd, deeper levels received attention. With some of the young, this meant a critique of capitalism as a theory of the mindless pursuit of greed. For many, the religious side became important, as materialism seemed soulless. Since in America work always existed in a religious context, a rebellion against both seemed appropriate. Anyone who expressed high ideals that questioned authority could win a following, and thus Martin Luther King, Jr., or a number of lesser figures could achieve prominence in a brief period of time.

Consciousness became important as the positive side of this implied critique of conventional economic and religious ideas. Material wealth dulled consciousness, and this was bad. Conventional religion was too comfortable, and that was bad. Something interior had to replace what the conventional institutions of society found valuable, and for the young this became a stress on consciousness, on heightened awareness of anything that transcended the boring realities that seemed to dominate life at home and school. And since America seemed to offer few alternatives, they began to look abroad for ideas and heroes, and at home to explore new possibilities. Sometimes this meant the applied idealism of a Gandhi; other times it meant the doctrines of otherworldliness associated with Buddhism. On occasion during the 1960s, the quest for meaning became so varied and anarchic that each individual seemed to have a separate source of authority or meaning, but nevertheless common threads did run through a great variety of quests.

Drugs were the means through which a growing number of individuals sought to heighten consciousness, escape boredom, and transcend the material and spiritual insufficiencies of their day. William James had tried a drug briefly; cultural radicals in Greenwich Village had followed his example before World War I. But outside a few isolated groups, such as black jazz musicians, drugs had never been much of a factor in American life before World War II. But over the years chemists had worked on the most common drug, the Indian religious substance known as peyote and its active ingredient, mescaline; and with the active ingredient in sacred mushrooms, psilocybin. By the late 1930s, Dr. Albert Hoffman of the reputable Swiss drug company, Sandoz Chemical Works, had synthesized something called diethylamide of lysergic acid, a colorless, odorless, tasteless, and seemingly useless compound that he called LSD. He had been looking for a drug that would stimulate breathing, and then for a drug that would help in treating schizophrenia, and Sandoz was distributing the drug for this purpose during the 1950s.

No one outside professional medical circles paid much attention until the British novelist, Aldous Huxley, who had settled in California, took mescaline in 1953 and wrote up the results as a profound mystical experience in *The Doors of Perception*. He specifically advocated the use of drugs for religious and spiritual purposes, as means of transcending the spiritually oppressive atmosphere of the postwar world. His ideas came to the attention of the director of the Kaiser Foundation Hospital in Oakland, Timothy Leary, who had stumbled on mushrooms which stimulated visions during a trip to Mexico. He quit his post and went to Harvard to pursue serious research interests, and in short order was experimenting with both friends and students. One of these was the poet Allen Ginsberg; never one to hide his enthusiasms under a rug, Ginsberg spread the word about his wonderful religious visions. Meanwhile, the Harvard administration took a dim view of teachers who experimented with unproven drugs on their students and severed Leary and a colleague from their positions. He went on to a bizarre if charismatic fame, his most famous moment coming in 1967, when, dressed totally in white and with flowers in his hair, he told twenty thousand rapt followers: "Turn on to the scene, tune in to what is happening, and drop out—of high school, college, grad school, junior executive—and follow me, the hard way." Shortened to the slogan, "Turn on, tune in and drop out," it became a mantra that served in lieu of a philosophy for many of the less thoughtful of the decade.

Drug experiences frightened the older generation, infuriated the police, and made for colorful anecdotes, but they represented more than just an aberrant social custom. Although American Indians were the original source of the ideas around peyote, Asian Indians and Japanese were soon receiving attention as well. Hindu mysticism and Zen Buddhism attracted a number of Americans, both as pilgrims and as proselytizers of the ideas. Led by poet Gary Snyder and former Episcopal priest Alan Watts, many students sampled the ideas of Asia, often reaching conclusions that Asians rejected. When nirvana, or personal extinction, proved to be a selflessness that Americans found difficult to achieve, they threw themselves instead into the more appealing notion of spontaneity, of living out one's passions, of following one whim after another. Sexual activity seemed to be one area of existence of special appeal; it certainly broke down barriers, gave pleasure, and seemed instinctual and thus less formal and institutional.

Several writers seemed to keep typewriters with them at all times, writing down experiences as soon as the ecstasy level permitted. If Ginsberg became the best-known poet, Jack Kerouac and Ken Kesey were the best-known writers. Kerouac reportedly had a vast supply of teletype paper that went through his machine in one long paragraph, 120 feet of it becoming *On the Road*. Although several publishers turned it down, it became a best-seller, the bible of young rebels who always wanted to be heading on to the next stimulating encounter, whether with God, a vision, a song, or an enthusiastic sexual partner. Kerouac himself was more into God and alcohol than sex and drugs; his *The Dharma Bums* explicitly linked the young rebels to Zen Buddhism. Kesey was into the connections between drugs and madness. Presumably the mad were merely those who could not adjust to capitalism and boredom, and so madness became not only a metaphor for creative maladjustment but a language of criticism and a valid response that "normal" people should take seriously. *One Flew Over the Cuckoo's Nest* (1962) became a popular film starring Jack Nicholson; more than any other single work, it brought together the themes of cultural radicalism as they developed independent of the more public issues of civil rights and war. Conservative journalist Tom Wolfe assured a small but permanent fame for the whole business when he published *The Electric Kool-Aid Acid Test* (1968). Kesey's Merry Pranksters, his Day-glo bus, the LSD, and the exotic costumes— all were such good copy that common citizens could be forgiven if they overlooked the serious ideas that were sometimes at issue.

At first, in fact, civil rights and the war were liberal issues, not radical ones. The New Left, as radicalism came to be called, did not start as anything political. The surviving records indicate that meaningful lives, utopian communes, new types of family structure, new modes of transmitting knowledge were all more central than public issues. Their inspiration was not Marx or Bakunin, but Thoreau and Whitman. They were interested in personal development and in society only as it consisted of improved individual units. But as the cultural issues spread beyond the small bands of artists and religious seekers, larger issues such as the Cuban missile crisis or the civil rights crusade kept intruding. The Free Speech Movement at the University of California, Berkeley, helped to tie issues together—the right to talk about civil rights, student rights, war protestors' rights and women's rights, joining all those issues in ways that reminded thoughtful observers of the spread of abolitionism. Most of the young seemed to be attached to colleges, and they were soon identifying those institutions with others: large corporations, the military, and the government. The connections were indeed close, as universities had military recruitment divisions functioning on campus, businesses donated money and hired graduates, the military threatened students with the draft, and the government restricted both public and private behavior in ways that seemed unnecessary.

Early in 1965, President Johnson escalated the war in Vietnam with the infusion of massive American military forces in all areas. In so doing he galvanized the campuses, activating youth who had earlier been content to cultivate inner space or worry about course requirements. Students who had spent their summers organizing black voters in the South, or otherwise gaining political experience, suddenly found hordes of new activists eager to oppose the war and willing to look anew at other issues. In mid-April, many marched on Washington, to hear Students for a Democratic Society (SDS) president Paul Potter declare that the war had "provided the razor, the terrifying sharp cutting edge that has finally severed the last vestige of illusion that morality and democracy are the guiding principles of American democracy." He had to agree with Senator Wayne Morse of Oregon, one of only two senators to vote against the Tonkin Gulf Resolution, that "the United States may well be the greatest threat to peace in the world today." He flatly denied that the United States was defending freedom, as the president insisted. It was killing Vietnamese, not freeing them, and in the process curtailing freedom in America. Fighting the war "has led to even more vigorous governmental efforts to control information, manipulate the press and pressure and persuade the public through distorted or downright dishonest documents." It sounded like a radical fantasy at the time, but scholarship has confirmed that things were quite as bad as the radicals imagined.

All the themes of the New Left were coming together, and from 1965 through the 1968 elections, radicalism throve under the pressure. Hordes of students who otherwise would scarcely have drawn a rebellious breath were out demonstrating, to save themselves if not the Vietnamese. Many of their universities were co-opted into the war machine, sending faculty to Washington, supporting Reserve Officers Training Corps (ROTC) activities, and accepting Pentagon or other contracts for military-relevant research. Civil rights for blacks were involved, for blacks supplied a disproportionate number of military recruits, who were expected to fight and die for freedoms they did not yet have at home. Liberalism was now the enemy, for this was a liberal war, waged for liberal principles, led by two liberal presidents and platoons of bureaucrats who thought of themselves as good liberals. White middle-class students found that even freedoms they had long assumed to be sacrosanct, from experimental sex to drugs to hair to clothing, were suddenly under attack as unpatriotic, immoral, irresponsible and unhygienic. And of course capitalism remained an enemy, for it was supplying the war machine all too efficiently. The war was clearly being fought at home as well as abroad, and over all aspects of what America meant: its morality, its economic system, its politics. The sound was familiar: Christianity, capitalism, democracy.

VI

The most talented writer to emerge from the ambiance of the 1960s has been T. Coraghessan Boyle. He first attracted a following with short stories that dwelt on the stereotypes, clichés, and culture heroes of the day, not only satirizing them but also pushing them past all conventional logic. The stories seemed to provide antic answers to absurd questions: If people were really descended from apes, could the two species enjoy meaningful relationships even now? Would not the ultimate act of post-modernism be to choose Idi Amin as a husband? What would a child be like if genetic engineering arranged for him to gestate in the womb of a sow? What must life have been like for Carry Nation's husband? No area of literature, from Norse epics to children's dog stories seemed immune to hyperbole, and no geographic area out of bounds. Boyle showed up in Red China one minute, Tasmania the next. His work left the distinct impression of an author with an impressive gift for language who had consumed a bit more LSD than the literary world required.

Boyle caught his wind in the novel quickly. Both *Water Music* (1982) and *Budding Prospects* (1984) deserve far more critical attention than they have received. The latter especially captures the ambiance of the 1960s better than any competitor. But even with these significant achievements, Boyle did not seem a candidate for major status until *World's End* (1987), a work of fiction with a complete vision of American history that transcends the usual clichés about both fiction and history. Coming originally from Peekskill, New York, Boyle based his work on several historical events that were crucial to the area and its portrayal in literature, especially the writings of Washington Irving. The book thus exists within time, yet with constant violations of chronology and the logical sequences that *history* as a word suggests. It is also spatial. The Hudson River is a central focus, with its boats both real and imaginary, and at times a character seems capable of approaching a specific boat at a specific time, only to discover that he is off by centuries and confused about place as well. Even though political fiction has been notoriously resistant to post-modernist devices, Boyle proves comfortable in using them to subvert themselves. In this work, characters suffer "an attack of history" and become "sick with history," as if it were typhoid obtained from drinking the Hudson water. Even as the younger generation gyrates away at its interminable parties, the novel insists that even bad faith is hereditary. Indeed, it organizes the secret history of Peekskill: acts of betrayal in the late seventeenth century prove to be types of similar acts in the middle twentieth century. A Wouter becomes a Walter as both betray their class and their family, and always a member of an exploited tribe or class is ready to betray it to the exploiters. Space seems to be in league with time: the World's

End of the title is a ship's graveyard where countless boats have gone down, yet no body ever recovered.

Marcel Proust taught generations of readers to think of madeleines as keys to memory; Boyle replaces them with the potato pancakes of his mother and the chemically treated flesh of a liverwurst sandwich. Food, one of the delights of sixties radicalism, is also pollution, and the pollution covers past behavior as well as food best left undigested. *World's End* exists chiefly on three time planes: the period from 1663 to 1692, during which the Dutch patroons expropriate Indian lands by fraud, with the collusion of dishonest tribal history-tellers, and then pass on the traditions of exploitation to the British; the period from about 1946 through 1949, covering the activities of left-wingers at the start of the Cold War, and the vicious ways in which local patriots repressed them; and the late 1960s, chiefly a year or two on either side of 1968, the height of the radical revolt against Vietnam, the police, conventional sexual mores, and of course capitalism. Names, memories, tales, and grievances commingle as Indians and ancestors pass along the fragments of the past. Truman Van Brunt tries to write it all down in the manuscript of *Colonial Shame: Betrayal and Death in Van Wartville*, but of course he is another dishonest chronicler. No voice in the modern novel is reliable, nor is any memory. The madeleine, the potato pancakes, and the chemical liverwurst all lie, even as in toto they convey the truth: of bad faith, dishonesty, betrayal, and exploitation.

As befits a work that toys with post-modernism even while rejecting most of its pretensions, *World's End* plays with its characters, its references and influences. It both uses and spoofs psychological criticism, with the USS *Anima* a boat that rocks invaders back on Jungian dreams and propels them forward into repetitiously destructive behavior patterns. Walter Van Brunt is always modeling himself on existentialist heroes, from actor James Dean to Camus' Meursault and Gide's Lafcadio. He is especially likely to think of them when he is betraying his wife or otherwise behaving despicably. Puns litter the landscape, often highly allusive ones: characters are constantly losing their feet, acquiring artificial limbs, and then trying to walk in someone else's footsteps; "watch your step" becomes almost a leitmotif, with death or exile the punishment for not so doing. Sing Sing, the jail for the last of the Mohonks of the twentieth century, acquired its name from the Sint Sinks, a long-extinct tribe; white men can't even get Indian names straight when they are exterminating them. The Indians sometimes get their revenge, however, seducing Dutch women and the wives of modern exploiters, giving the infant heir to the property brown skin and green eyes that seem impervious to three hundred years of bleaching. And the hippies! Boyle never can resist spoofing those who might seem his natural allies: their clothing, their smell, their faithlessness, their inability to get even the simplest of ideas straight. Walter encounters the prize specimen as he sips warm Cold Duck at a party: the works of J. R. R. Tolkien are clearly an analysis of the politics of the Vietnam War: "*Clearly*, man—I mean how could Tolkien make it any clearer without slapping you in the face with it?—Smaug's just a stand-in for Nixon, right? . . . Napalm, brother, that's what Tolkien's talking about."

Behind the persiflage lies a serious point of view: the crucial act of betrayal in this corner of the modern world occurs when Truman Van Brunt betrays the left in its efforts to put on political concerts shortly after the onset of the Cold War. The Cold War had begun in 1946 with Winston Churchill's Iron Curtain speech in Fulton, Missouri, had become exacerbated with the early negotiations concerning the United Nations, was entering a glacial phase during which most of Eastern Europe fell under Russian control, and would reach a real crisis point with the Berlin airlift of 1948–1949. The Democrats who had ruled in Washington since 1933 split over how to deal with the Russians, and former Vice President Henry Wallace formed a Progressive party to contest the 1948 elections against a president also named Truman. Although Wallace was not himself a Communist, his party picked up the support of many sympathizers, and by the time the votes were cast seemed to be little more than a front for communism both at home and abroad. Among the supporters of the Progressives was the famous actor and singer Paul Robeson. One of the best-known blacks in America, Robeson had long held close associations both with the Soviet Union and with native American Communists. He was not himself a member of the party.

As the major artist of the political left, Robeson was giving numerous concerts for the cause, and one of these was scheduled for Peekskill, New York, on 27 August 1949, under the sponsorship of People's Artists, Inc., an agency with close ties to the left. Proceeds were earmarked for the Harlem chapter of the Civil Rights Congress. Under the stress of the Cold War abroad and an increasingly hostile atmosphere toward anything even vaguely reformist at home, the local American Legion and other such patriotic groups made an uproar. In local eyes, such concerts were invasions by outsiders from that suburb of Moscow, New York City: urban, Jewish, leftist, and probably deviant sexually—such assumptions were hardly the invention of the 1960s. The night of the concert, trucks and cars barred traffic, thugs committed violent acts against both participants and spectators, and the police did nothing to stop the carnage. In Robeson's eyes, the fiasco was a direct attack on him and on blacks generally; issues of foreign policy and anti-Semitism were presumably secondary. A barrage of public statements subsequently filled the press. No resident of Peekskill could have remained unaware of it all.

Boyle recreates the atmosphere with accuracy. Black rights, however, were not important to his book; Indian rights were. He therefore rearranged details to suit his themes, while retaining the framework of the actual historical events. This is the event for Truman Van Brunt's betrayal of his family and his former political allegiance, the act which replicates the betrayals of the seventeenth century. Only one Indian remains to observe events; now the leftists are the Indians, betrayed by those historians they trusted, just as Wasamapah had betrayed the Kitchawanks. *World's End* thus becomes that anomaly, a novel post-modernist in structure yet self-subverted by the history it details, in which the capitalist right, with the help of the Trumans of the world, expropriated the Indians of the seventeenth century and then the workers of the twentieth. The cultural children of the 1960s then betray their radical heritage through mind-less self-indulgence. The book is thus just as hard on the left of Boyle's young adulthood as on the right. No one emerges looking very appealing. But the last of the Kitchawanks has impregnated the wife of the last of the male Van Warts, and as the book ends, history takes its revenge with the birth of yet another brown-skinned, green-eyed baby, Indian in at least a few of his genes, the presumptive heir to the entire Van Wart estate.

VII

In contrast to the world of radicalism, which always seemed obsessed by history and the politically relevant, that of the post-modernists mistrusted both history and relevance. At times, this distinction became blurred, as various post-modernists seemed to be using Marxist and post-Marxist writers to make severe attacks on the curricula of the American university. This appearance remains deceptive. Post-modernists were true heirs of the modernists, and in America modernism was usually apolitical or antipolitical. After World War II, a few highly politicized Europeans became fashionable in post-modernist circles, as names like Saussure, Derrida, Foucault, and Barthes became common intellectual currency even as they lost the attention of European intellectuals. This set of influences, although important in a restricted academic setting, had less impact on genuinely creative Americans. What it did was reinforce attitudes prominent elsewhere in the culture, helping forge a post-modernist stance that by the 1990s was having a considerable impact on legal studies and ethics as well as poetry and the novel.

Post-modernism as a term always came in for attack; no one seemed to be happy with it, and no two critics agreed on a clear, interdisciplinary definition. Indeed, to bemused outsiders who could penetrate the jargon, the chief contention appeared to be that critics had become more important than writers and painters. In the uglification of the language that resulted, post-modernism privileged criticism and foregrounded the critic as it impacted departments of literature, philosophy, and sociology. Nevertheless, the painters kept on produc-ing items that could be displayed, or at least photographed and then displayed; writers kept on producing novels, stories, and poems; and so on through archi-tecture, music, and related areas of human creativity. Post-modernism was thus a rather incoherent stance, a generalized climate of discontent with the state of things as they were: with the politics of the 1960s, with inherited traditions in the arts, with social and philosophical concepts. Over the long run of three decades, from roughly 1960 to roughly 1990, it comprised innumerable internal feuds and seeming contradictions, but on the whole, post-modernists advocated mistrust of the language and the products of language; skepticism about the ability of any statement to be "true" in any meaningful sense; a preference for the critic over the artist, with the corollary belief that criticism was the newest and greatest of the fine arts. It also included an instinct for the minimal: the least invasion of the artist into the work of art; a preference for the simplest, most mundane subjects and materials for art; and a leveling of the popular, the "inartistic," to the same plane as the elitist or "artistic."

Improbable as it seems, the most important American in the evolution of modernism into post-modernism was not a poet, like Ezra Pound, or a prose experimentalist like Gertrude Stein, but a musician named John Cage. Cage was a Californian by birth, the son of an engineer who devoted much of his time to inventions. While his father worked on submarines, John played with pianos; he seemed to have a fascination for them—*talent* is not quite the right word—and he tinkered endlessly, often disturbing relatives and puzzling teachers. An erratically brilliant student, he discovered Stein's writings in college, and when they confirmed his general impression that most formal learning was nonsense, and especially that history was nonsense, he quit, began writing poetry, and headed off for France. He studied a little architecture and a little painting, and a little bit more music, but he was always erratic in his interests and his skills, and never had the proper background for anything advanced. He liked the works of Bach, Scriabin, and Stravinsky the most. But he refused to undertake serious study of music or anything else. His attitude, he wrote later, "was that one could do all these things—writing, painting, even dancing—without technical training. It didn't occur to me that one had to study composition. The trouble was that the music I wrote sounded extremely displeasing to my own ear when I played it."

Family and fiscal life being unsettled during the Depression, Cage survived as he could, chiefly by giving lectures on modern painting and music, about which he still knew little. He managed to find a teacher, Richard Bühlig, who was familiar with the music of Arnold Schönberg, and under his often exasperated direction, Cage even worked out his own tonal system, one that used two twenty-five-tone ranges, one low and one high but sharing the middle; "no single tone in the shared range was to be repeated until all twenty-five had been used," Calvin Tomkins has reported. Such a system at least gave the impression that Cage was learning to structure his work, however much it resembled Schönberg's own atonal or serial system. Notoriously prickly, Schönberg was not much impressed, and later told an interviewer that Cage was "not a composer, but an inventor—of genius." His father's son, so to speak, and a shrewd analysis. For the rest of his career, Cage proved to be an inventor more than a composer, someone more original than talented.

His very aberrations became central to post-modernism. Here was someone who could never master systems, so he preached an art without system. He could never master the history of music, so he found the idea of a continuous present appealing. He had trouble understanding what teachers were trying to communicate to him, and could only rarely make himself understood; perhaps art should not be about communication at all. Earnest souls all around him thought art should organize life into meaningful patterns, but he couldn't see meaningful patterns in life or art, so he found himself comfortable with the assumption that art shouldn't make anything meaningful or systematic. He wondered if he had much of a self to express in art, so perhaps other artists were not all that different, and critics should stop talking about art as expression, too. Life seemed unpredictable, indeterminate, throwing up materials like the sea threw up flotsam. Maybe art should be like life, a chance creation made out of accidental discoveries. Stein had made much of play in her writings; perhaps "purposeless play" was the true heart of music; perhaps art and life should be identical.

Cage seemed to be composing in a contextual vacuum, the ultimate solipsist of the arts. In fact, he had antecedents. Charles Ives had worked in some of these areas of discovered sound, vernacular discourse, and chance composition, although Cage took a while discovering such a historical ancestor. But he did know the written work of Henry Cowell, author of *New Musical Resources*, a statement of musical modernism, and *Toward a New Music*, the work of Mexican composer Carlos Chavez. Such works taught him how to achieve new sounds from old instruments, and new compositional techniques that altered conventional senses of time and tonality. Another immigrant, Edgard Varèse, had several lessons to teach about percussion and timbre. By about 1938, Cage was ready to perform on what he called the "prepared piano," an instrument that had been tortured through mistuning and the insertion of bits of paper, wood, felt, or whatever else was at hand. He says he tried ashtrays, pie plates, and screws, and fondly recalled seeing Cowell use a large darning egg at one of his own concerts. Anything that worked was fine: "I soon had a whole gamut of new sounds, which was just what I needed. The piano had become, in effect, a percussion orchestra under the control of a single player."

In his serendipitous way, Cage discovered Oriental philosophy at about the same time. A friend had once suggested to him that every inanimate object possessed a spiritual life of sorts, one that could be released if it were made to sound. Cage was entranced, perhaps by the religious implications, perhaps by the sheer illogic of the whole idea. During World War II he discovered Asian Indian music through one of his students, and Oriental philosophy through the writings of Zen Buddhist Dr. Daisetz T. Suzuki. Inner man and outer object seemed to be speaking to each other in what Cage took to be a divinely inspired language. His music, he decided, should have as its purpose, giving to people a greater sense of their own being. It should imitate the way nature operated, not the way it appeared. Nature seemed to him to be chancy, indeterminate in its operations, and so his music should be the same. He then discovered the *I Ching, or Book of Changes*, and his development ended. By tossing sticks or throwing coins, he could compose music totally the product of chance. As objects expressed their inner spirit through the sounds, he could compose as the world functioned, entirely at random; and as he worked out the "logical" consequences, no two performances ever need be the same.

By 1952, Cage was testing the outer edges of both experimentation and audience tolerance, even in New York City, long thought to be capable of tolerating anything, no matter how preposterous, so long as it seemed trendy and bore the label *experimental*. Columbia University featured a Cage performance in its McMillin Theater in that year of a specially commissioned work, *Imaginary Landscape*. Outdoing himself for the occasion, Cage spaced twelve "Golden Throat" RCA radio sets across a stage, each with two "performers." Late in the evening the piece finally had its turn, and random selection, vernacular tones, and audience effects all had their day. For four somewhat bewildered minutes, the avant-garde audience watched and listened as the performers searched the dials looking for sublime effects. To no avail; they had waited too long, and most stations had gone off the air. With rare exceptions, only static, a kind of white noise, came forth, random enough, sublime in its way perhaps, but not especially stimulating musically.

Undeterred by mere fiasco, Cage also that year turned out his *4'33"*. Pianist David Tudor performed it at Woodstock, not far from the city. It consisted of three movements of complete silence from the pianist, who opened the keyboard three times, and closed it three times, as a helpful, old-fashioned way of orienting anyone who felt lost. The audience heard chiefly the sound of wind in the trees during the first movement, a patter of raindrops during the second, and a goodly amount of grumbling during the third. As composer and conductor Pierre Boulez said later about the totality of Cage's career, "I love John's mind, but I don't like what it thinks."

Cage experimented with chance and nirvana, frequently braving European audiences no more enraptured than New York ones. By 1958, his reputation was sufficient to stage a major retrospective at Town Hall. Sure of a media event if not an artistic breakthrough, a large audience of both partisans and scoffers turned out to see dancer Merce Cunningham turn himself into a conductor and then into a human chronometer, which was what *Concert for Piano and Orchestra* required. The idea was to imitate a clock, an odd choice since the entire inspiration for the piece was otherwise arbitrary; a chronometer seems too logical and scientific for Cage's psyche. "The only thing I was being consistent to in this piece was that I did not need to be consistent." The audience was soon participating enthusiastically as well, as it so often did during Cage performances. When the recorded version appeared two years later, critic and fellow composer Virgil Thomson was in a genial mood; it had been "a jolly good row and a good show," he wrote. "What with the same man playing two tubas at once, a trombone player using only his instrument's mouthpiece, a violinist sawing away across his knees, and the soloist David Tudor crawling around on the floor and thumping his piano from below, for all the world like a 1905 motorist, the Town Hall spectacle . . . was one of cartoon comedy." Both orchestra and audience seemed to be having a good deal of fun.

Cage developed complex notational innovations guaranteed to drive conventional musicians to extremes of speech and behavior; he wrote poetry and prose that has the same effect on absorbers of print—*readers* would be too precise a term for those who consume his publications. Repeatedly Cage found his justifications in the workings either of nature or the teachings of Buddhism. Both were common concerns among cultural radicals of the 1950s, and were unconsciously laying the groundwork for what critics soon labeled postmodernism. The term that perhaps summed it up most usefully for outsiders was *field of awareness*, or *field theory*. "The whole notion of an indeterminate, interrelated field of awareness, which man cannot possibly enter or comprehend with his conscious mind alone, strikes Cage more and more as one of the keys to an understanding of our time," Calvin Tomkins has noted. Cage "is more and more certain that the methods he has chosen to use in his work—chance, indeterminacy, and theater—are in tune with the underlying temper of modern life."

Just as the 1950s, behind the facade of Eisenhower prosperity, nurtured beat literature and occasional radical discontent with the politics of prosperity, so it nurtured radical art, and no place was more seminal in this than the college in North Carolina that had so attracted the painters of the New York School. At Black Mountain, Cage had friends on the faculty, especially composer Lou Harrison, even then known for his interest in Oriental ideas in music. Cage visited in 1952, his visit coinciding with the presence of such other experimental artists as Merce Cunningham in dance, Robert Rauschenberg in painting, and Charles Olson in poetry. One of Cage's more fruitful ideas was to stage a "concerted action" in the main dining room: with a musical score composed by chance, with "dancers" moving about the stage as they wished, with Cage himself reading a lecture from the top of one stepladder, with Olson reading poems from another, with David Tudor playing the piano, with Rauschenberg playing 78 rpm records—the chaos caused a sensation of sorts. What anyone could have "learned" from such goings-on remains problematic, for what survived was more a general sense of creative, interdisciplinary openness to experiment than anything specific. Given the close connection of many of the college artists with New York City, the word spread there quickly, and the event went down in cultural history as the first "happening," the first spontaneous outburst of what became a staple activity during the 1960s.

Black Mountain has had its historian, but no one has yet traced out the long-range cultural consequences of this frenetic spontaneity for all the arts. Cunningham, for example, became an especially close friend of and collaborator with Cage. His choreography became known around the world as the cutting edge of modernity in dance: it treated the stage as what seemed to be an open field, it separated music from dance, and it separated the whole sense of "time" in both dance and music from what normal audiences would call the "beat." Both Cage and Cunningham thought of time the way a radio announcer did: five minutes for the news, one minute for an advertisement, fifteen minutes for a soap opera episode, etc.—time was duration, not beat. Music and motion had to begin and end together, but were on their own in between. Nothing "meant" anything; a dance did not have a moral, a plot, or points of reference. It was merely a self-contained, self-referential happening. Like Cage, Cunningham believed in chance to the point of having the movements of his dancers determined by the toss of a coin.

On the walls during that first happening were several paintings by Robert Rauschenberg: white on white, abstract presentations that bore an obvious relationship to the white noise of the radios, or of the audience, during the silences of the Cage concerts. This was a relationship that bore collaborative fruit for some years, as well as indicating that a unified climate of creativity was developing that in time included all the arts. Painting, however, was where the action was for a while, and Rauschenberg's career the best available example of how new cultural attitudes were developing that replaced abstract expressionism as the major voice of American artistic experimentalism.

Like John Cage, Rauschenberg was someone who always seemed a lonely outsider, all but incapable of fitting into conventional cultural categories. Born in a depressing town on the Gulf Coast of Texas, the grandson of a German immigrant and his Cherokee wife, Rauschenberg grew up in a fanatically religious home where the Church of Christ forbade almost any activity a boy could think of. Hunting and fishing were the only permissible refuges from a concentration on sin, but the boy was so near-sighted that he couldn't fire a gun with much accuracy and he never had much gift for catching fish. He focused instead on animals; one of his many pets, a nanny goat, may well have been the source for one of his most famous works of art. The boy at first wanted to be a preacher, but soon gave that up. He was never much good at school, but thought a career as a veterinarian might prove rewarding. He went to the University of Texas, but balked when his anatomy instructor demanded that he dissect a live frog; he'd had several as pets. After he set his designated specimen loose in some protective bushes, the dean suspended him. World War II was on, and he headed off for the navy. Never the sort to look for trouble, he informed his superiors that he had no intention of ever shooting anybody, and he soon found himself on hospital duty. He spent most of his tour of duty at Camp Pendleton, California, working with psychiatric cases. "This is where I learned how little difference there is between sanity and insanity and realized that a combination is essential," he remarked later. "Actually I always liked the patients best before they were cured, before they became boring and adjusted." He channeled most of his spare time into the making of drawings. He decided to become a painter when he wandered into the Huntington Library, saw several classic British portraits, and could think of nothing better in life than a career doing such things. He retained an affection for Joshua Reynolds' *Sarah Siddons as the Tragic Muse* for life.

Always a bit naive and suggestible, he'd heard that Paris was the place for young American artists to go. That had been true after the First World War but not after the Second, but he didn't know that and went anyway. He didn't speak any French and had little training, and received no encouragement from the Académie Julian, that graveyard of so many aspiring provincial artists lost in Paris legend. He assimilated as much art as he could at the Louvre and at local galleries. Most of it made little sense to him, and he went a bit overboard in his enthusiasm for all things artistic. "I was so incredibly excessive," he told Calvin Tomkins later. "I'd even stopped using brushes in my work; I loved the medium so much I was painting with my hands, trying to get as involved as I could with the act of painting. What came out were mostly messes." His girlfriend wanted to go to Black Mountain College because of the experimental art being taught there. Josef Albers, the expert on color from the Bauhaus was there; even *Time* magazine thought he might be the greatest art teacher in America.

Even now, Black Mountain sounds enticing. In addition to Cage and Cunningham, it had or would attract Buckminster Fuller, the de Koonings, Franz Kline, and Paul Goodman; the poetry was so plentiful and of such quality that it remains in the literary histories as an entire school, the Black Mountain School, with Charles Olson only the most eminent. But Rauschenberg managed never to fit in with anything he could possibly have planned; certainly no one as undisciplinable as he was likely to get along with Albers, a humorless German authoritarian who had little sympathy for the bohemian life-style of those around him. Rauschenberg later claimed that he learned a good deal from his teacher, but Albers himself treated his student with contempt and soon departed for the last stage of his controversial career at Yale. Rauschenberg found a new and different teacher in John Cage.

Unaware of many of the fashionable currents dominating the New York scene, by 1951 Rauschenberg was reducing his palette to bare minima; in particular, he was experimenting with all-white paintings, some of large size.

These were minimalist in every sense of the word: they used the minimal available color, the minimal imagery, and they expressed as little of the personality of the artist as seemed possible. What they did instead was change with the changing daylight, reflect passing shadows, and invite onlookers to see anything in them that they might wish to see. Without knowing it, Rauschenberg had indeed found the visual equivalent of Cage's silences, of art as in some way an occasion for better experiencing daily life.

Rauschenberg met Cage in 1951, and Cage first came to Black Mountain the next year. He loved his friend's white paintings, describing them as "airports for lights, shadows, and particles" in a 1961 essay. The appreciation was mutual and remained so for a long time. "I didn't know then whether the way I was thinking was crazy or not," the painter said later. "The fact that John was so celebratedly intelligent gave me confidence he didn't even know I needed." Cage agreed. "There was from the beginning a sense of absolute identification, or utter agreement, between us." The first happening soon followed, and much of what became post-modernism in the visual arts.

Rauschenberg's life always seemed full of zigs and zags, as aimless as anything in the art of the 1950s. He married a fellow artist but eventually decided that he was bisexual. He went to Europe with his friend Cy Twombly but could not adjust to Rome any better than he had to Paris; he came home while Twombly remained. He read up on Gertrude Stein, and was always asking expatriates for anecdotes about her, but showed little inclination for a life led on the edges of salons. He dabbled in photography and thought for a while of abandoning paintings for pictures. He took up several of the crazes of the day. Collages fascinated him; he juxtaposed fragments of glass or fabric, adding parts of umbrellas or flashing lightbulbs to change the pace. The Imagists had experimented seriously by putting disparate objects together in words, and now he wanted to place the actual objects together, without connectives or logic. He carried his lust for silences even further and erased a de Kooning drawing —it took him a month and forty erasers. He labeled it with simple accuracy: ERASED DE KOONING DRAWING   ROBERT RAUSCHENBERG   1953. He liked the result but decided that he would not do it again.

VIII

The world that Rauschenberg, Cage, and Cunningham inhabited, along with such allies as the Black Mountain poets, clearly shared many values, none of them much in vogue in the New York City art world. In the 1950s, that was the world of Hans Hofmann's New York School, of Jackson Pollock, Willem de Kooning, abstract expressionism, and the cold war of American creativity as it protected the avant-garde from Communist takeovers. But the ego of the artist, the angst-ridden, existentialist world of Harold Rosenberg's criticism, was fast losing its creative energy. "As far as I'm concerned, Expressionist esthetics— theories about a special relationship between the artist, his materials, and his audience—are pure Hollywood, the stuff of which coffee-table art books are made," critic Amy Goldin wrote. By 1968, she had enough of a secure vantage point to hoot at the whole business. "The painter as yoyo artist, sending SELF out to the end of the line and then retrieving it, miraculously loaded with transcendence, by a tricky flick of the wrist." The audience meanwhile would be sullen and yearning, and repeating "Sock it to me." Eyes glazed from looking into the void, the artist would leap off the precipice into a canvas. If he made it, "Orgasms all around. Happy, Happy." She reviewed the core assumptions of an expressionist esthetic and termed them "silly."

Against such maximalist gestures, minimalism seemed plausible. Rauschen- berg and his friends were approaching by one path, but other, very different artists, were also on the way. Critic Brian O'Doherty later wrote about those artists who specialized in the "vernacular glance," a way of seeing that "doesn't recognize categories of the beautiful and ugly. It's just interested in what's there." Jasper Johns, a friend of Rauschenberg for many years, made his mark with an American flag painted in encaustic, a difficult technique that required the artist to mix his pigment with hot wax to build up an exceptionally rich surface. He moved on to paint targets, numerals, and letters, objects all vernacu- lar enough but not the sort that appealed to Rauschenberg. He found them too negative, too enclosed, for his Texas exuberance to feel comfortable with. Other artists became minimalist in different ways: Morris Louis and Kenneth Noland developed "color-field abstraction," producing a decorative art that left many observers in that horrible circumstance known as silence. It looked "nice" but hardly told a story, or expressed an ego, or even generated happenings worthy of anecdotal repetition. It was so minimal that critics were reduced to distinguish- ing between those fields which seemed organic and those which seemed geo- metric or simply undifferentiated. Frank Stella soon emerged from the "nonexpressionists" as the artist to reckon with: he wanted no human content in his works and specialized in black stripes. It didn't hurt that he was married for a time to Barbara Rose, one of the leading art historians of the period. Some stripes were more equal than others in an undifferentiated field.

Many observers with no customary connection to the fine-art scene were bewildered by the plethora of seemingly inexplicable new works. They could have learned the basics from an old master who reemerged during the 1950s and 1960s, Marcel Duchamp. The media discovery of the 1913 Armory Show, the Frenchman had seemed then to be a leading cubist. But he had tired quickly of cubism and gone on to the choosing of "readymades," the coffee grinders, hatracks, shovels, and the famous urinal, "Fountain" (1917). He had also be- come fascinated with the creation of art in the fourth dimension and had spent the intervening decades designing works capable of participating in this new territory of the imagination. Publicly, he proclaimed that he was not interested in what he called retinal art, art that merely pleased the eye; he was interested in a conceptual art, an art that was in service to the mind. Always playful and eager to provoke the philistine, he also claimed to be more interested in breathing and in chess than in painting. "Je suis respirateur," he repeated to interviewers, who seemed increasingly fascinated by the spectacle of an artist who seemed to be such a major influence and yet who never seemed to be practicing an art. But what Duchamp had done was to place objects in the foreground of discourse and to speak of important levels of understanding that no one could expect to understand at first viewing. It was a recipe for, first, an exaltation of the object, and then its becoming evanescent, as concerns of the mind became more important than what a viewer could see before him at a gallery.

Emblematically enough, Duchamp not only maintained his close connections to America and its artists, he became a citizen in 1954, as if to foreshadow the bondage which much American post-modernist thinking would pay to French precedents. As his own fame grew, the concerns he had set in motion before America entered World War I went their merry ways. He had stressed objects of everyday existence; the whims of the artist; the necessity of shocking viewers; the role of *blague*, the joke, and all its satirical relatives in making people think about art. He had worried about the fourth dimension and about its correlative, how to reduce a three-dimensional world into two; he had been an elitist of a peculiarly French variety, professedly in service to mass taste and eager to incorporate kitsch into an art world that had become too proper, too rarified. And although an artist, he was not a publicly productive one; people hung on his every critical exhalation, on his theory rather than on his practice. Art, indeed, seemed almost to get in the way of criticism. Art in service to the mind in practice meant paying attention to the products of the mind no matter what arrived in the galleries.

Robert Rauschenberg was a born Duchampian. The spontaneity of happenings, the erasing of a drawing by a master, the possibilities cast by shadows on a white-on-white painting, the collaboration with artists such as Cage and Cunningham, who liked experimenting with time sequences and saw no need for music and dancer to share a common beat: all the signs were there. As Rauschenberg, Jasper Johns, and other artists moved away from the existentialist egomania of abstract expressionism, they carried on in a Duchampian manner.

Consider the goat. Always a pet-lover, Rauschenberg came across a long-haired Angora goat one day in 1955; the animal was sitting, stuffed, in the window of a secondhand furniture store. Its fleece was matted and one side of its face bashed in, but the painter worked away, trying among other things to cover the injuries with paint; he wanted the animal for a work of art. He dawdled over the problem for five years, mounting it in various positions and against different backdrops. At one point it acquired a spare tire—a real one—around its middle, presumably the realization of a common slang term for putting on weight. It was certainly putting on paint, and must have weighed a bit. Eventually, with the help of suggestions from Jasper Johns, Rauschenberg made a flat platform to be a pasture for his goat and added various elements of collage and garish color. He had found his object; it was common enough, and it certainly seemed to be in service to the mind—perhaps as the mind recalled its youth, or perhaps just as a reminder that goats had to pull their weight under the ecological burden of waste products from the automotive industry. The possibilities were unlimited. He called it "Monogram" (1959).

Realism came to a conceptual climax of sorts in the great vogue for pop art that swept New York and the gossip columns of the art world during the early 1960s. The Kennedys were in the White House; Martin Luther King, Jr., was on the march; and "the people" were "in" as a category. Nothing could seem more democratic than Campbell's Soup cans or massive blow-ups of cartoon situations, and for a brief moment, names like Andy Warhol and Roy Lichtenstein had what Warhol whimsically but accurately labeled their "fifteen minutes" of fame. Other artists, such as Alex Katz and Philip Pearlstein, reasserted the validity of paint and actually painted realistic pictures of recognizable people, although rarely in poses anyone would have found flattering. Realism was in, one way or another, but at some point between the assassination of President John F. Kennedy late in 1963 and the escalation of the war in Vietnam in the spring of 1965, it seemed to wither away. What was left was an artistic minimalism, or conceptualism, in which neither real people nor recognizable locations played any role at all. Art became devoid of representation, nonrepresentational rather than merely abstract, for *abstract* implied something prior in nature that could be abstracted from. The new art, the art of Frank Stella, Mark Rothko, Ad Reinhardt, and Barnett Newman, had been around, one way or another, for some time; but the 1960s was its vogue period. It was often monochromatic, geometric, two-dimensional. Insofar as it embodied ideas—it certainly didn't seem to embody anything else—it rejected the outside world completely, from civil rights to agitation on either side of the war issue. Post-modernism was truly apolitical at this time and in these genres; it would not long stay that way.

The radical outbursts of 1968 affected almost every area of the culture. Whether creative people were political or not, they perceived that American life would never be quite the same again. The impact of the violent summer in Chicago especially was like that of a major war: it sped events up, it excited opposition, it made certain attitudes seem obsolete.

One trend that hastened on its way into the museums was the persistence of one type of modernism into a post-modernist vision. In the eyes of such leading critics as Clement Greenberg and Barbara Rose, the best of current work continued the formalist side of modernism: conceptualism, or minimalism, with

Frank Stella as perhaps the leading practitioner. But although their opinions always retained the respect of the artistic community, they became increasingly irrelevant, the voices of history, as in Rose's textbook, *American Art Since 1900*, rather than of current New York gallery practice.

A more influential trend all but abandoned painting. In the writings of Harold Rosenberg and Lucy Lippard, the objects in nature that "normally" inspired the artist were becoming "anxious" and in danger of disappearance. Rosenberg published *The Anxious Object* (1966), and two years later, Lippard published the article version of "The Dematerialization of Art," in which she assumed that all art had become conceptual and that "matter is denied." What was replacing it, to make a complex story rather simpler than it probably should be, was the photograph of an event, or perhaps some scene where the meaning was a verbal addendum to whatever incidental objects might be in place. As Susan Sontag, who became for some the major analyst of this transformation, put it in *On Photography* (1978): "A Modernist would have to rewrite Pater's dictum that all art aspires to the condition of music. Now all art aspires to the condition of photography."

The shift may have started with the happenings of Black Mountain College and New York City after 1952. It may have started with Jean Tinguely's notorious self-destructing "Homage to New York," which produced a much-republished photograph during its hilariously malfunctioning single day of life, 16 March 1960, at the Museum of Modern Art—although the words of *New Yorker* writer Calvin Tomkins were at least as important in helping the event achieve its immortality. Whatever its provenance, the elevation of photography to privileged status helped define the 1970s and 1980s as a unified, postmodern period in the visual arts. Seeing the museum or the gallery as large, sterile cubes, artists headed outdoors or at the very least turned the indoors into a performance area. Newly liberated women exalted their bodies and their freedoms, while men made patterns in the ice, built jetties into lakes, or "wrapped" bridges and coastlines. The ice might melt, the Great Salt Lake rise and obliterate a jetty, and the artist himself might dismantle his wrappings before legal authorities did it for him, but the result always became one or more photographs commemorating the achievement. Such photos reduced a three-dimensional experience into a two-dimensional one, easily reproduced; any viewer could have a framed version of the event. That made the event essentially timeless, always both past and present, and infinitely variable, meaning something different to each viewer in each viewing situation.

As such, photography fitted in most closely with the new poetry of John Ashbery, the new novel of John Barth, and the new deconstructive criticism, all of them assuming the adjective *post-modern*. For all their variety, such work all seemed intentionally "undecidable," "indeterminate," "contingent," "multiplicitous," and "polyvocal," to borrow or adapt the most popular critical buzzwords for what was happening. Whereas works of art had been icons or precious objects to critics in the 1950s and before, now they suffered an acute decline in status. Art was no longer either precious or separate from daily life and experience; the perceptions of the viewer were more important. The viewer could make anything out of a work of art; this was a privilege. Nothing in the work was stable, no meaning good for more than the immediate moment. Indeed, any art that threatened to become permanent was in itself threatening; thus the event, the performance, the moment, became everything; take its picture and move on. The performer even replaced the poet as verse became oral, read aloud in preference to being written. The political paranoia so obvious in public life under presidents Nixon and Johnson had become a suspicion of all creativity, of all invocations of "Truth," "principles," and "standards."

Issues of the imagination went to the very core of the public life of the period, as fiction and fact often seemed to trade places not only in the media but also in the White House. "Where does Nixon's fictional self-creation end and the historical figure begin? Can such a distinction be made about a man who watches the movie *Patton* for the third or fourth time and then orders an invasion of Cambodia meant to destroy the Vietcong Pentagon, which he told us was there, but which has never been found?" asked Richard Poirier in *The Performing Self* (1971). "Why should literature be considered the primary source of fictions, when fictions are produced at every press conference?" Surely secretaries of state Rusk and Kissinger or secretary of defense Robert McNamara were more successful "mothers of invention" than anyone supposedly devoting a life to painting or music. "What can I invent that the Kennedys haven't actually accomplished?" But then, surely such men were really only pictures on a television screen, no more real, or three-dimensional, than the war itself.

IX

Any number of works of art, from one of Cristo's wrapped public structures to a John Ashbery poem, could serve as specific examples of these post-modern attitudes. But the critical voices of deconstruction reigned supreme, and none attracted so much attention as that of Paul de Man of Yale University. His rise and fall provide a convenient set of parameters for a type of thought that had little use for parameters, not to mention biography.

At first, deconstruction appeared to have nothing much to do with conceptualism, minimalism, or the other popular terms of the later twentieth century. Most cultural historians trace it back to the work of Ferdinand de Saussure, a linguist at the University of Geneva whose work achieved its most famous form with the lectures that students reworked into the posthumous volume *Course in*

General Linguistics (1916). It soon attracted broad attention and was seminal in the development of both semiotics and general linguistics. At the core of the work was the assumption that language was not the orderly progression of meaning that it had seemed to be during the nineteenth century. Instead, it was a system of signs with only an arbitrary relationship to meaning or to any object in nature. Each language had its own words for house, tree, run, walk, anger, or joy, and no one should postulate anything necessary about the relation of such words to what they purported to describe. The signs in language deserved study as a complete system, or in terms of their relationship to each other. Hot, in other words, meant nothing except in relation to cold. At this point the words *signifier* and *signified* came into use: a signifier was the sound or look of a word as a word; a signified was the assumed meaning or referent. Semiology, the science of the study of signs, became the focus of attention, and language a presumptive model for other sign systems. A later pioneer like Jacques Lacan, for example, could argue that the unconscious was structured in the same way language was.

This view had a slowly broadening impact on anthropology, philosophy, and literary criticism, usually under the rubric of structuralism. Americans were slower than Europeans to respond, however, and not until the 1960s did the time seem ripe to introduce structuralist ideas to a broader American audience. The Johns Hopkins University sponsored a conference in 1966 that its organizers intended to spread structuralism into all of the human sciences, and invited Jacques Derrida as an appropriate closing speaker. All seemed to go well until Derrida arose to report that structuralism was finished: it lacked any substantive center; in place of the unified structure that Saussure had assumed, Derrida saw only chaos, or play. In other words, nothing anchored meaning: language, he argued, "invaded the universal problematic," "everything became discourse," and no "transcendental signified" was certifiably present "outside a system of differences." In other words, critics should focus directly on language, and assume that nothing existed outside language. In place of Truth, postmoderns had only interpretations. Once the news had registered, critics assumed that no text had a stable meaning, and no two readers assimilated the same work. One reader's opinion was as good as another's.

In a profession where the editing of texts had been a favorite exercise for doctoral students, where literary history sometimes dominated entire departments, and where the New Critics had for a generation and more insisted on works of art as precious objects or verbal icons, such a stance was unacceptable. It was relativism run amok, and indeed it picked up the support of such relativist philosophers as Richard Rorty, the most extreme of the descendants of John Dewey. It seemed to mock religion, metaphysics, and art in about equal measure and made literary criticism all too often sound like bad translations from the French. It made the reader more important than the writer and the critic more important than anyone. It seemed to paralyze many aspiring critics; after they proved they could deconstruct a few texts, they had little else to do. Writing was unstable, reading infinitely variable, meaning illusory; no two critics could or should agree. All they could do was make dazzling displays, much like peacocks flashing their plumage.

Deconstruction had its most visible impact at Yale, with stiff competition coming from Cornell, Johns Hopkins, and then Duke. It developed swiftly, hitting its crest in 1979. Derrida's *Of Grammatology* appeared in English in 1976, other works soon following. In 1979, both the collaborative volume *Deconstruction and Criticism* and Paul de Man's *Allegories of Reading* appeared, with Geoffrey Hartman's *Saving the Text* (1981) and Richard Rorty's *Consequences of Pragmatism* (1982) close behind. Jonathan Culler brought out *On Deconstruction* in 1982, and de Man republished *Blindness and Insight* (originally 1971) in 1983. An impressive number of articles in specialized journals demonstrated the immediate absorption of the critical principles these works contained.

Paul de Man stood at the center of the storm, revered by friends, colleagues, and literature teachers. A presumptive refugee from the chaos of Nazi-occupied Belgium, he had married an American student, won an appointment to the prestigious Society of Fellows at Harvard, and landed at the top of the profession by becoming chair of both the French and the comparative literature departments at Yale. Between 1971 and his death late in 1983, de Man published rapidly, applying poststructuralist attitudes to critical theory and specific texts. His chief allies were Geoffrey Hartman, J. Hillis Miller, and—for a time— Harold Bloom, with Derrida himself enjoying a series of visiting appointments.

De Man's sudden death provoked an outburst of devoted memorializing, capped by Barbara Johnson's assertion at a 1984 memorial service: "In a profession full of fakeness, he was real." Unfortunately for these believers in the disjunction between the signifier and the signified, adulation also provoked research, even into the very history and biography that de Man had tried so hard to eliminate from critical vocabularies. A young Belgian scholar, Ortwin de Graef, uncovered 180 articles that de Man had written during the Second World War inside occupied Belgium. All appeared to be collaborationist in tone, and a number were explicitly anti-Semitic. Subsequent research turned up the information that Paul had been the nephew of the leading Belgian quisling, Hendrik de Man, and a propagandist for the Nazi point of view. He had also had a common-law wife and three children, and pursued a career as a publisher toward the end of the war and during the first three years of the peace. As the inconvenient data appeared, de Man turned out not only to have been a fascist but also a deserter of his wife, an evader of any responsibility for the expenses of his three sons, and a business fraud who had left a string of angry creditors when he emigrated to the United States. As charming as he was deceitful, he had managed to find visiting appointments, only to skip out on his rent and deface or steal the contents of at least one faculty home he sublet. Eminent scholars and writers nevertheless helped him on his way, unaware of his politics or his personal aberrations.

When the news broke, shock spread everywhere. To enemies of deconstruction, the revelations only too obviously subverted the very ideas that de Man and other poststructuralists had been preaching. The misguided efforts of Derrida in particular to defend his friend only made matters worse. In a larger sense, however, poststructuralism as an approach lived on in countless ways in several disciplines, most notoriously in the Critical Legal Studies movement based at the Harvard Law School. In some form, it reached receptive students who already knew that politicians lied, that advertisements were detached from any truth about the objects they tried to sell, and that the visual images the media projected were signifiers no one could depend on. Businessmen and politicians had absorbed the lessons of deconstruction even if they had trouble spelling the word.

X

To most of those who observed from a distance, all three of these climates appeared almost irrelevant to broad national concerns. Conservatism seemed an isolated collection of malcontents, growing old and out of touch, almost as if its few visible leaders were straw men who had trouble becoming animated enough to be of use in a debate. Radicalism long appeared to be little more than the Beat movement in literature, only occasionally redeemed by exotic behavior, clothing, and attacks on large institutions. Few suspected that radicals could have much impact on either race relations or the course of the Vietnam War, and many remained convinced that radicals only made matters worse on these issues. Post-modernism did not really develop outside the fine arts until the 1970s, and never managed to seem significant to the larger public. Liberalism reigned supreme.

Liberalism dominated academia fully as much as it dominated political discourse. John Kenneth Galbraith wrote best-sellers in economics extolling the public sector and attacking the greed as well as the incompetence of many capitalists. John Rawls reasserted liberal ideals in philosophy and Robert Dahl did the same in political theory: each gave the distinct impression that most decent people agreed with their core assumptions and that all they really needed to do was clarify fine points. In public policy, Walt Rostow all but asserted the right of American economic and political assumptions to rule activity everywhere in the world; since he worked at the White House, he was in a position to use both foreign aid and military troops to do so. Historians were especially visible: Kenneth Stampp reexamined slavery to demonstrate the reality of what blacks had lived through as a people and to assert that "innately, Negroes *are*, after all, only white men with black skins, nothing more, nothing less," while C. Vann Woodward insisted that segregation had not always been the law or the custom of the land, North or South.

Perhaps the most visible academic liberal was Arthur M. Schlesinger, Jr., professor of history at Harvard, a special assistant to President Kennedy, and then a scholar on the graduate faculty of the City University of New York. Making his early reputation with books on the age of President Andrew Jackson, Schlesinger also staked out a place for himself on the anti-Communist left with the articles collected in *The Vital Center* (1949). Following the theologian Reinhold Niebuhr, he insisted on the importance of the totalitarian threat from the Soviet Union and the need to intervene in Europe with such assistance as that proposed in the Marshall Plan. At home, he pushed hard for an expanded public role for the state in the spirit of presidents Roosevelt and Truman. He was thus in an excellent position to assume a visible place in the campaign of John F. Kennedy for president. When Kennedy won, Schlesinger accepted a position in the White House, which he used to take notes, make friends, and otherwise prepare himself for the role he played over the next thirty years: court historian to Camelot, extolling its virtues, excoriating its enemies, and protecting the memory of the Kennedy family first and liberalism second.

No contemporary book demonstrates the liberal infatuation with the Kennedys quite so openly as Schlesinger's second collection of essays, published in 1962. The introduction to *The Politics of Hope* was smug. It dismissed the Eisenhower years as materialistic, moralistic, and unimaginative and hostile to intellectual life, idealism, and even wit. "We have awakened as from a trance," he proclaimed; self-righteousness is no longer in control of the State Department. Instead, the Peace Corps was sending hundreds of idealistic young people out into the underdeveloped world. The life of the mind had achieved a type of liberation. Government was in the process of supporting the arts. Satire was popping up in cabarets, and "wit has become respectable; it is even presidential now." It surely said something about the self-image of liberal intellectuals that they could honestly feel that a sense of humor was part of the definition of liberalism. It was not a mistake that anyone would make even six years later.

Schlesinger participated chiefly in areas of foreign policy, and these inevitably became the focus of his memoir, *A Thousand Days* (1965). He then worked for Kennedy's brother Robert, and so was in position to write *Robert Kennedy and his Times* (1978) after the younger Kennedy was assassinated in 1968. The two volumes are among the most important sources for anyone charting the disintegration of American liberalism during the 1960s and 1970s.

Read as memoir and even mea culpa, these two volumes are not entirely uncritical of the Kennedys nor of the author himself; he learned some hard lessons. They do, however, make a detached observer wonder why the two men are worthy of so much respect as illustrious leaders of liberalism if in fact they were so slow to comprehend both the folly of the interventions in Vietnam and the importance of the civil rights agitations until both were out of control. Again and again, Schlesinger analyzes the dilemma President Kennedy faced over Laos and Vietnam: Secretary of State John Foster Dulles and the Eisenhower administration had begun low-level commitments to Southeast Asia, and there-fore American prestige had been committed, the argument began. A new president could not look weak in his dealings with the Communist threat, and therefore could not back out of a potentially lethal situation. Constantly quoting the president's skeptical remarks, pointing out his full realization of how the French had become mired down, Schlesinger follows Kennedy step by step not toward a valid policy but toward a genuine confusion. Kennedy did not know what policy to pursue or how to lead the American people to any sensible solution. On the left of the Cambridge liberals who made most of the serious policy decisions, John Kenneth Galbraith usually counseled restraint and with-drawal, the least intervention possible. As ambassador to India, he actually knew something about Asia, but his remarks were apparently too well-informed and witty to be taken seriously by the State Department. They preferred the ideas of the right wing of liberalism, for whom Walt Rostow, recently of MIT, was the chief spokesman. Rostow was infatuated with counterinsurgency movements of all kinds, and when not misusing the Munich analogy he could always be counted upon for irrelevant references to conditions in Malaya or the Philip-pines. With allies such as General Maxwell Taylor and former Harvard dean McGeorge Bundy, Rostow most frequently prevailed. Galbraith returned to Harvard, to become one of the few eminent liberals with little to repent on matters of foreign policy.

In his volume on President Kennedy, in print before public opinion finally turned against the war, Schlesinger painted the picture of a president trapped by history. The interventions in Vietnam were justified in this book because there were no alternatives; public opinion did not permit withdrawal. Everyone's eye was really on Moscow and everyone's memory on Munich. Neither Kennedy nor Schlesinger questioned the importance of Vietnam to American defense nor the close connections between Hanoi and Moscow. Unfortunately, both positions were palpable nonsense: Vietnam was not important and had little connection to the Soviet Union. The questions remain: If Kennedy was such a gifted leader, why didn't he lead? If liberals understood foreign policy so well, why did they misunderstand Asia so persistently, and with such devastating results? Even so notorious a tory as General Douglas MacArthur had warned repeatedly about the folly of another Asian war. Why did so few liberals listen?

By the time he published his biography of Robert Kennedy, Schlesinger had long since repented. He remained unwilling to give any credit to the Tafts who had warned against such interventions, or the Eisenhowers who had decided that interventions would cost too much in terms of both funding and international friendships. But Schlesinger had come to agree with them and had joined his friend Galbraith as spokesmen for antiwar liberalism. Unfortunately, history had played one of its cosmic little jokes and handed the job of making peace over to President Nixon and Secretary of State Kissinger, neither of whom had clean hands on the subject. Schlesinger thus found himself bending into ungainly postures in trying to justify both President Kennedy's actions and Robert Kennedy's need to convert from staunch interventionist to equally staunch opponent. Too good a historian to twist the factual record, Schlesinger nevertheless insisted that President Kennedy's most probable intention at the time of his death was to pull the troops out as soon as the 1964 elections were over. This analysis did little to enhance the president's reputation for either courage or leadership; it also clashed with the preponderance of the evidence that other commentators cited. It became, instead, one all-too-authoritative source for film director Oliver Stone in his notorious cinema fantasy *J.F.K.*, which made a hero out of a president who had never been especially insightful or heroic, and made his assassination into a plot by pro-war schemers eager to prevent a withdrawal.

The second great issue that split political liberalism was civil rights. Given the background of the Kennedy brothers, their initial apathy on the subject was understandable. Their father, ambassador to England Joseph P. Kennedy, had been one of the most conservative Democrats during the years between the world wars, and no one growing up in the Irish strongholds of the Boston area would ever hear much that taught respect for civil liberties in general or minority rights for blacks in particular. The Democratic party had long been sharply divided on the issues, conservative Southerners balancing out liberal Northerners. Neither President Roosevelt nor President Kennedy could afford to split his party on black issues, and the stresses of both hot and cold wars meant that civil liberties often suffered. The Japanese went into internment camps, religious objectors to war service went to jail, and when Republican senator Joseph R. McCarthy went on his rampage against suspected Communists in the early 1950s, he found support from many Democrats, including his good friend former ambassador Kennedy. Kennedy, indeed, lobbied successfully to put his son Robert on McCarthy's staff as assistant counsel. The whole episode haunted Robert Kennedy for the rest of his life, as few on his left were willing to forgive this lapse. Indeed, he remained a personal friend of Senator McCarthy long after leaving the committee position, even though he came to dislike strongly many of the things McCarthy did. Neither John nor Robert Kennedy was an obvious liberal at the start of his career; they were merely opportunistic public servants who were the victims of their inheritance.

This background continued to affect both brothers for life. McCarthy died of acute alcoholism and political irrelevance, but the figure of FBI Director J. Edgar Hoover became a constant aggravation throughout the 1960s. Hoover too was a friend of Joe Kennedy, and neither brother made any effort to replace him. But as Dr. Martin Luther King, Jr., stepped up his campaign for civil rights, the Kennedys both found themselves trapped by their own ambivalence about blacks and by Hoover's devious intransigence. Here too, by the time they were in power, the Kennedys had come to liberal positions but felt themselves constricted by precedents and political circumstances. Public opinion was no more friendly to broad advances in black rights than it was to a withdrawal of troops from Asia, and Kennedy wanted to win reelection before doing much in a visible way for the cause. Once again, his reputation for leadership evaporated when examined on a significant issue. Robert Kennedy did no better, and was capable of hot opposition to King's initiatives. He also was the administrative figure who gave in and authorized the wiretaps Hoover wanted on King and other leaders of the movement.

Once again, to his biographer's relief, Robert Kennedy changed under pressure. Out of office, he came to see the black point of view, moving from a conservative liberalism to a liberalism on the fringes of radicalism. Few true radicals would ever trust a Kennedy, for historical rather than contemporary reasons, but during the last years of his short life, Robert Kennedy unquestionably qualified. He belatedly but firmly came out against the war and in favor of black rights and became a major threat to the war liberalism of President Johnson.

Liberalism disintegrated under these strains. President Johnson deserved the most credit for civil rights advances, but he also deserved the most blame for the escalation of the war. Because most of his key advisors were holdovers from the Kennedy years, liberalism received little but blame all around: on war issues, because the war was proving a disaster, and on civil rights, because blacks were rioting for yet more attention from the government. The Kennedy brothers, so ambivalent and indecisive on these issues while in power, profited enormously in death. All those who found President Johnson an unacceptable leader were free to fantasize about what President Kennedy would have done, or what a President Robert Kennedy might have achieved. Martyrdom lent enchantment to their images, with historians like Schlesinger providing what seemed to be authoritative guides. Time and other historians have long since had second thoughts on many of these issues, and the reputation of the Kennedys will always be problematic at best. The new president, Democrat Bill Clinton, had almost to disown the very word *liberalism* in order to get elected in 1992, and if he were to succeed better than his liberal predecessors, it seemed clear that he would have to develop new programs to fit the old label.

XI

As with most climates, liberalism was far more than just a series of political actions and their results. One of the neighbors of the Kennedy clan when they were at home in Hyannisport was the writer William Styron, who settled into a summer home on Martha's Vineyard in 1964, only a short sail away. Relations were cordial if not close, and in terms of overt behavior, Styron was a supporter of Kennedy-style liberalism. He had long supported causes usually identified with the left of center: he opposed capital punishment for criminals and sometimes worked to assist specific offenders; he opposed infringements on academic freedom and civil liberties; he opposed the war in Vietnam, and supported Senator Eugene McCarthy in his quixotic effort to displace President Johnson in the early months of 1968; he was a long-time supporter of equal rights for blacks; he added his name to manifestos that denounced the oppression of writers in dictatorships such as those in the Soviet Union and fascist Spain; he attended the 1968 Democratic convention, although at other times he indicated a general aversion to politics. He was married to Rose Burgunder, a Jewish activist with Amnesty International.

Because he came from Virginia and often used the stream of consciousness or other means of evoking a central, self-analytical consciousness, Styron regularly faced critics who typecast his works as grandchildren of William Faulkner, and there was some justice in this. *Lie Down in Darkness* (1951) was a study of a decaying Southern family, soaked in alcohol and bad faith, with an errant child running off to sexual liberation, compulsions, and suicide; full of time shifts and tales told about other tales, with only the loosest of relationships to ascertainable "facts," it alluded frequently to *The Sound and the Fury*, *Sanctuary*, and *Absalom, Absalom!*. But a little of this sort of criticism went a long way. Even among Southern writers, Robert Penn Warren was clearly more central, with *All the King's Men* more directly relevant to Styron's early work than anything by Faulkner. But the whole stress on the South when writing about novelists after the war was trite; the category was a leftover from earlier days. It needed reexamination and discarding as largely irrelevant to a country that was outgrowing any lingering sense of regional identity. Styron had also read his Conrad and Flaubert, his Melville and Fitzgerald, and knew a decent amount about both the prose and verse of seventeenth-century England.

After a long stay in Europe and the production of two lesser works, Styron began work on a project he had been mulling over for many years. Coming himself from that part of Virginia where Nat Turner led a famous slave rebellion, and having himself personally profited from a family inheritance that had originated with slave ownership, Styron had become obsessed with the subject of slavery and his own rather vicarious involvement in it. As a white liberal, a friend of black writer James Baldwin, and a strong supporter of the civil rights revolution of the 1960s, he felt a call to devote one major novel to the cause. Begun in 1961, at the start of President Kennedy's New Frontier, *The Confessions of Nat Turner* was in the shops in September 1967, as the bitterness over civil rights approached its height. Greeted warmly by most white liberal critics, it sold well, won two major book-club adoptions, and won its author the 1968 Pulitzer Prize. It also won him the undying enmity of most black radicals who wrote on the subject, for he had dared to trample on what they regarded as exclusively black material.

When all the controversy boiled itself down, the basic problem with the book remained the same liberal one that Kenneth Stampp had faced when he dared to write about the black experience of slavery. By openly treating blacks as if they were whites, of assuming a white ability to speak like and for black people, white liberals were well-meaning trespassers. To black radicals, they were stealing black words and black souls just as their ancestors had stolen black bodies. Whether novelists or historians, blacks had been ignoring Nat Turner in print for 135 years or so; most of them seemed hardly aware of Turner until Styron showed them what they were neglecting. No matter; Turner was theirs, and they savaged Styron for the very crime of thinking Turner to be, more or less, much like himself.

Aside from a speaking voice that simply did not sound like that of a slave, the real trouble with the book as a historical meditation was its inability to face a central problem in analyzing the black experience. The most impressive speculative essay ever written on the psychology of slavery was Stanley Elkins' *Slavery* (1959, 1968), a work that caused as much controversy within the historical guild as *Nat Turner* with the larger public. Elkins had used recent scholarship on the experience of Nazi prison-camp inmates, mostly Jews, to examine the problem of infantilization, of how the prisoners had come to identify with their guards and the system that was oppressing them. Applied to slavery, Elkins suggested that the character of "Sambo," the happy-go-lucky, childlike slave, was a predecessor of such inmates. A total system of exploitation had produced mutations of character regardless of race, and analysts had to face such possibilities directly and avoid the clichés of racial discrimination. Styron had read the first edition of Elkins' work and praised it, but he seemed unaware of the dilemma it placed him in. On the one hand, he wanted a Nat Turner who was much like William Styron and fellow slaves who were just whites with black skins. On the other hand, Styron had to portray a system of total exploitation that infantilized and brutalized its subjects to the point where they would slaughter women and children to vent their rage as well as facilitate escape. Either everyman was a potential beast, or blacks were inferior to whites. Either slavery was benign and every violent Nat Turner an aberration, or slavery was inhuman and Nat Turners were lurking behind every tree. To Elkins, and presumably to most traditional conservatives, all people were potentially exploitable to the point of infantilization; but while liberals seemed to sense the truth of this, they also wanted heroic role models like the radicals. And, unfortunately for such desires, Nat Turner was one of a kind, and only a minute number of slaves made any effort to rebel in any organized or violent way. The vital center could not hold on this issue.

Styron strongly felt that the slave experience and the Holocaust had much in common. Just as Elkins' *Slavery* made a decisive impression on him, so did Richard L. Rubenstein's *The Cunning of History* (1975). "If slavery was the great historical nightmare of the eighteenth and nineteenth centuries in the Western world, slavery's continuation in the horror we have come to call Auschwitz is the nightmare of our own century," Styron wrote in a review of the latter. And as with the experience of the blacks, that of the Jews had touched his life at a formative phase, although the gestation of that exposure took several decades. Writing it up in *Sophie's Choice* (1979) also provoked just as much controversy, and as much ethnic resentment about its portrayal of Jews and women, as *Nat Turner* had in its treatment of blacks; it was also equally illuminating about the dilemmas of liberalism during its years in the wilderness.

With his genius for finding trouble, Styron surely knew the risks. He recalled later that Jews warned him that no one should write about the Auschwitz experience, for even to try to put it into words somehow dignified it. If that argument lacked merit, the next was more pointed: no one had the right to write about it unless he were a survivor of the camp experience, for to do so was to usurp the emotions of the victims. A third warning recalled that of the black critics of *Nat Turner*: you have no right to write about it unless you are Jewish. Styron was no more Jewish than he was black; he was a Southern white Anglo-Saxon Protestant atheist who had a thing about the victims of total disaster. He was also that odd phenomenon, the liberal who experienced life and time vicariously, from safe desks in Connecticut and Massachusetts.

Structurally understood, *Sophie's Choice* was less a novel of victimization than a bildungsroman of an innocent young author as he encountered total evil in a New York boardinghouse. As Styron commented later, it was "not so much about the Holocaust but about discovering evil from uniquely American Innocent eyes." It gives every appearance of following the known outlines of Styron's life, beginning with him age twenty-two in 1947, with occasional flashbacks, through a brief apprenticeship as a publisher's assistant, the problems he faced in seeing an extensive novel in the material that led to *Lie Down in Darkness*, his structurally irrelevant efforts at sexual fulfillment, and his need to write about slavery, to his realization that the extremes of human behavior in his lifetime were simply beyond his understanding. As the use of the term *bildungsroman* indicates, much of the novel is traditional, nineteenth-century stuff; the bildung of a sensitive soul going back through Meredith and Dickens at least to Goethe.

But again, this liberal practitioner of a traditional form had absorbed modernism, here especially the works of Conrad and Faulkner. What Stingo, the narrator, discovered chronologically was that most of what he knew was what others had told him, and most of what they told him was not true. Sophie's Jewish lover, Nathan, fabricated a whiz-kid background for himself in scientific research, including Harvard training and Pfizer research toward a cure for cancer; he was really a drug addict of high native intelligence but little ability to cope with reality. All he had was a sinecure and a gift for deceiving himself and everyone else except his medically successful brother. Sophie lied even more prodigiously. A gentile anti-Semite, daughter of a pro-Nazi academic, she invented tales about her own views and those of her parents. She left out vital information about her lovers, husband, and children. She shaded the truth about the scale of her collaboration with the rulers at Auschwitz. Much came out by the final pages of the book, a double suicide that seemed inevitable for hundreds of pages, but nothing really explained all the lies and the irrational behavior. It seems clear, however, that Styron still has the same psychology on his brain that he borrowed from Stanley Elkins to use on Nat Turner: the psychology of victimization, of infantilization, of the ability of a malign system so to co-opt one's personality that its effects seem ineradicable. Styron, Stingo, and liberals generally couldn't stop thinking along these lines, nor could they ever find solutions. In a sense, the Jews who agreed with George Steiner that silence was the only possible response to Auschwitz were right. Words only seemed to make things worse. No government grant, no rational analysis, no democratic nurturing, no adjustment counseling could ever deal with the reality of slavery or the Holocaust.

XII

American culture entered the middle 1990s with an air of exhaustion, of ideas that had run their course. Radicals had felt defeated since 1968 and postmodernists since the late 1980s. Liberals had nothing new to offer after 1965, and although Bill Clinton seemed liberal during the 1992 elections, he offered nothing creative in a cultural sense, only a new face and a semblance of energy after two consecutive presidents who seemed managerially fatigued. In their turn, the conservatives were no better, having nothing substantive to offer beyond calls for experience and suggestions of an unpleasant nature about the character of their opponents. Countries always survive these low points, and new ideas were probably lurking in the nether reaches of the culture. The cosmopolitan nation needed them desperately, for the situation in employment, in medical care, in rebuilding the infrastructure of the nation, seemed close to desperate, even as the levels of decay in the cities and of violence everywhere seemed to rise inexorably with every day's news. Unfortunately, many of the other countries of the world were doing no better; few of the problems seemed specific to the United States. How the country dealt with them could have ramifications everywhere, however, for no nation on earth could equal the range of American communications. The films, the books, the music, and television reports went everywhere, and if new ideas were to develop, the rest of the world would be able to profit from them quickly. At a time when Christianity, capitalism, and democracy seemed to be taking root again even in Russia, that seemed of more than local interest.

Bibliographical Essay

The first edition of this book closed with an essay that paid obvious scholarly debts and recommended books that were especially appropriate for the collections of foreign university libraries. For this much-revised edition, the focus is more on those volumes which individual readers in the English-speaking world might wish to consult in the pursuit of more specialized concerns. This essay does not, however, aim at the professional historian. It does not, except in the most cursory fashion, take account of important scholarly disagreements, and does not make a fetish of either "coverage" or of being "up to date." Many professional concerns are of no interest outside the guild of history, and the sheer number of books and the length of many, especially biographies and political chronicles, can be more intimidating than illuminating. Things are also a bit out of control in matters of technical theology and in social history. It used to be a standard joke in graduate schools that students were turning out a book for every sermon and every puritan town; now they have one for every cow, and even the plants are getting attention. Enough is enough. The works below only scratch the surface, but will lead the devout to more arcane areas.

Part I: A Local Culture, 1630–1815

British puritanism has been an area of massive research in recent years, much of it political and demographic in ways that have little bearing on American developments. The three most useful books remain William Haller, *The Rise of Puritanism* (New York, 1957, c. 1938), Herschel Baker, *Wars of Truth* (Cambridge, 1953), and Patrick Collinson, *The Elizabethan Puritan Moment* (London, 1967).

Vast quantities of primary materials are available for puritan studies. Among the best for understanding intellectual life in the larger Boston area are James K. Hosmer, ed., *John Winthrop's Journal "History of New England"* (2 vols., New York, 1953, c. 1910); David D. Hall, ed., *The Antinomian Controversy, 1636–1638* (Middletown, 1968); Paul Boyer and Stephen Nissenbaum, eds., *The*

Salem Witchcraft Papers (3 vols., New York, 1977); and M. Halsey Thomas, ed., *The Diary of Samuel Sewall* (2 vols., New York, 1973). Two textbook collections cover the entire period: Perry G. E. Miller and Thomas H. Johnson, eds., *The Puritans* (New York, 1963, c. 1938), and Alan Heimert and Andrew Delbanco, eds., *The Puritans in America* (Cambridge, 1985). Two excellent more specialized collections are Edmund S. Morgan, ed., *Puritan Political Ideas, 1558–1794* (Indianapolis, 1965), and Perry Miller and Alan Heimert, eds., *The Great Awakening* (Indianapolis, 1967).

The study of Massachusetts Bay and its successor communities, as the population spread west through New England, has been very much a specialization of major East Coast graduate schools, chiefly Harvard and Yale, and their outposts such as Brown and Wesleyan. Both professors of English and of history made seminal contributions. Modern work essentially began with the labors of Perry G. E. Miller, with *Orthodoxy in Massachusetts, 1630–1650* (Cambridge, 1933), continued with the two volumes entitled *The New England Mind*, of which the second, *From Colony to Province* (Cambridge, 1953), is the more relevant here. An abbreviated version, "The Marrow of Puritan Divinity," has circulated widely both separately and as a chapter in *Errand into the Wilderness* (Cambridge, 1956). Edmund S. Morgan has been the most eminent contributor in the next generation, and all his many books remain a model of clarity for anyone baffled by theological or political detail. See especially *The Puritan Dilemma: The Story of John Winthrop* (Boston, 1958); *Roger Williams: The Church and the State* (New York, 1967); and *The Puritan Family* (New York, 1966, c. 1944). Key volumes from the third generation would include David D. Hall, *The Faithful Shepherd: A History of the New England Ministry in the Seventeenth Century* (Chapel Hill, 1972) and *Worlds of Wonder, Days of Judgment: Popular Religious Belief in Early New England* (New York, 1989), and T. H. Breen, *The Character of the Good Ruler: A Study of Puritan Political Ideas in New England, 1630–1730* (New Haven, 1970).

Many of the ideas in these works have been the subject of criticism by those both within and without the Miller–Morgan establishment. Stephen Foster reexamines many of the issues in a broad recent synthesis, *The Long Argument: English Puritanism and the Shaping of New England Culture, 1570–1700* (Chapel Hill, 1991), and Jon Butler questions several long-accepted views about religious behavior in *Awash in a Sea of Faith: Christianizing the American People* (Cambridge, 1990). Harry Stout has become the modern authority on homiletic writing, in *The New England Soul: Preaching and Religious Culture in Colonial New England* (New York, 1986). Darrett Rutman provided criticisms of many accepted views in his *Winthrop's Boston* (Chapel Hill, 1965), while Kai T. Erikson brought the insights of social psychology to his study of deviance, *Wayward Puritans* (New York, 1966). Literature continues to be a focus for the study of creativity in two works by Sacvan Bercovich, *The Puritan Origins of the*

American Self (New Haven, 1975) and *The American Jeremiad* (Madison, 1978), and in Andrew Delbanco, *The Puritan Ordeal* (Cambridge, 1989).

As the colony matured, the Mather family became central. Robert Middlekauff provided an overview of the clan in *The Mathers* (New York, 1971), while Michael G. Hall, *The Last American Puritan* (Middletown, 1988), provides a comprehensive view of Increase Mather, and Kenneth Silverman, *The Life and Times of Cotton Mather* (New York, 1984) does the same for his son. The Winthrops persisted into this era and remained important well into the next century, as Richard S. Dunn details in *Puritans and Yankees: The Winthrop Dynasty of New England, 1630–1717* (Princeton, 1962). Richard L. Bushman puts the generational shifts into perspective in *From Puritan to Yankee* (Cambridge, 1967).

Social history is not the focus of this book, and a vast range of new work has come out in this area. The most useful overview is the extremely detailed work of David H. Fischer, *Albion's Seed* (New York, 1989), which would be a good place for most beginners to start. Legal history is closer to cultural history. See especially David Grayson Allen, *In English Ways* (Chapel Hill, 1981); William E. Nelson, *Americanization of the Common Law: The Impact of Legal Change upon Massachusetts Society, 1760–1830* (Cambridge, 1975); Morton J. Horwitz, *The Transformation of American Law, 1780–1860* (Cambridge, 1977). Closely related is James H. Kettner, *The Development of American Citizenship, 1608–1870* (Chapel Hill, 1978).

Professors of literature have continued to be major contributors to cultural history since Perry Miller, although several disregard his sometimes esoteric emphases. Larzer Ziff has been the most industrious, as in *The Career of John Cotton* (Princeton, 1962) and *Puritanism in America* (New York, 1973). Jay Fliegelman carries the story into the revolutionary period in *Prodigals and Pilgrims: The American Revolution against Patriarchal Society, 1750–1800* (New York, 1982), as does Emory Elliott, *Revolutionary Writers: Literature and Authority in the New Republic, 1725–1810* (New York, 1982). For the application of controversial new theories of feminism and even deconstruction, see Cathy N. Davidson, *Revolution and the Word: The Rise of the Novel in America* (New York, 1986), and Jane Tompkins, *Sensational Designs* (New York, 1985).

On special problems from the late seventeenth to the late eighteenth centuries, see John Demos, *Entertaining Satan* (New York, 1982), a study of witchcraft from several different disciplines; Edwin S. Gaustad, *The Great Awakening in New England* (New York, 1957), the best brief study of an event with many chroniclers, even though Jon Butler doubts it ever existed; Norman Fiering, *Jonathan Edwards' Moral Thought and its British Context* (Chapel Hill, 1981), one of the most impressive achievements in intellectual history since Miller; and Richard Hofstadter's effort to see why America proved so resistent to real thought, by Edwards or anyone else, *Anti-Intellectualism in American Life* (New York, 1963).

Works have poured from the presses about the period between the Great Awakening and the Revolution, vigorously proposing the centrality of religion and just as vigorously questioning it. On the religious side, see especially Alan Heimert, *Religion and the American Mind: From the Great Awakening to the Revolution* (Cambridge, 1966); Carl Bridenbaugh, *Mitre and Sceptre* (New York, 1962); and Charles Akers, *Called Unto Liberty: A Life of Jonathan Mayhew, 1720–1766* (Cambridge, 1964). The most secular treatment is probably Arthur M. Schlesinger, Sr., *Colonial Merchants and the American Revolution, 1763–1776* (New York, 1918), still influential despite its publication date. The dominant view in recent years has been that of Bernard Bailyn, *Ideological Origins of the American Revolution* (Cambridge, 1967) and *The Origins of American Politics* (New York, 1968); and his student Gordon Wood, in *The Creation of the American Republic, 1776–1787* (Chapel Hill, 1969), and *The Radicalism of the American Revolution* (New York, 1992).

For Quakers and the Pennsylvania area, Rufus M. Jones, *Quakers in the American Colonies* (New York, 1911), remains a useful overview. Melvin B. Endy, *William Penn and Early Quakerism* (Princeton, 1973), deals clearly with religious matters, while Gary B. Nash, *Quakers and Politics: Pennsylvania, 1681–1726* (Princeton, 1968), handles political ones. For recent perspectives, see Richard S. Dunn and Mary M. Dunn, eds., *The World of William Penn* (Philadelphia, 1986). On more specialized issues, see Jack D. Marietta, *The Reformation of American Quakerism, 1748–1783* (Philadelphia, 1984); Jean R. Soderlund, *Quakers and Slavery* (Princeton, 1985); Frederick B. Tolles, *Quakers and the Atlantic Culture* (New York, 1960); and Barry Levy, *Quakers and the American Family* (New York, 1988). On secular considerations, Carl Van Doren, *Benjamin Franklin* (New York, 1938), remains an excellent beginning, while Raymond P. Stearns gives an encyclopedic overview of all science in *Science in the British Colonies of America* (Urbana, 1970). For Philadelphia during the crucial period, see Richard Ryerson, *"The Revolution is now begun": The Radical Committees of Philadelphia, 1765–1776* (Philadelphia, 1978).

Virginia and Maryland have received extraordinary attention lately, chiefly from Jack P. Greene and his students at Johns Hopkins University. In opposition to the New England emphasis of this volume and much of the previous literature cited above, they maintain that Chesapeake Bay, not Massachusetts Bay, was the more crucial for American culture. In terms of social and economic attitudes the view has some merit; it has far less in terms of culture conceived as creative achievement. The Greene view is given a central statement in *Pursuits of Happiness: The Social Development of Early Modern British Colonies and the Formation of American Culture* (Chapel Hill, 1988); see also Jack P. Greene and J. R. Pole, eds., *Colonial British America* (Baltimore, 1984); and Richard Beale Davis, *Intellectual Life in the Colonial South, 1585–1783* (3 vols., Knoxville, 1978). For a view that will be more influential in the long run, see Edmund S. Morgan, *American Slavery, American Freedom* (New York, 1975), and continue with Rhys Isaac, *The Transformation of Virginia* (Chapel Hill, 1982). Slavery, rather than cultural achievement, remains at the core of the Virginia problem. See especially David Brion Davis, *The Problem of Slavery in Western Culture* (New York, 1988, c. 1966), and *The Problem of Slavery in the Age of Revolution, 1770–1823* (Ithaca, 1975), and Winthrop Jordan, *White Over Black: American Attitudes Toward the Negro, 1550–1812* (New York, 1977, c. 1968).

Biographies have proliferated to meet the popular demand for hagiography, some running to six volumes, representing an industry that seems most un-Virginian. Most normal readers will be content with James T. Flexner, *Washington* (Boston, 1974); Merrill D. Peterson, *Thomas Jefferson and the New Nation* (New York, 1970); and Ralph L. Ketcham, *James Madison* (New York, 1971). The use of a biographical focus to illuminate an important cultural issue is another matter, as Drew McCoy has demonstrated in *The Elusive Republic: Political Economy in Jeffersonian America* (Chapel Hill, 1980), and *The Last of the Fathers: James Madison and the Republican Legacy* (New York, 1989), and Lance Banning in *The Jeffersonian Persuasion: Evolution of a Party Ideology* (Ithaca, 1978).

The most recent overview of the revolutionary era is Robert Middlekauff, *The Glorious Cause: The American Revolution, 1763–1789* (New York, 1982). Two volumes of the American Nation series remain useful: John C. Miller, *The Federalist Era, 1789–1801* (New York, 1960), and Richard B. Morris, *The Forging of the Union, 1781–1789* (New York, 1987). From the point of view of cultural history, the best synthesis remains Kenneth Silverman, *A Cultural History of the American Revolution* (New York, 1976). Of the many treatments of the Enlightenment, the most accessible is probably Henry May, *The Enlightenment in America* (New York, 1976).

Primary sources are plentiful for this period, often in multivolume sets. Among those that have appeared over the last generation that might be missed, see A. W. Plumstead, ed., *The Wall and the Garden: Selected Massachusetts Election Sermons, 1670–1775* (Minneapolis, 1968); Herbert J. Storing, ed., *The Complete Anti-Federalist* (7 vols., Chicago, 1981); and Charles S. Hyneman and Donald S. Lutz, eds., *American Political Writing during the Founding Era* (2 vols., Indianapolis, 1983).

On intellectually significant issues toward the end of the eighteenth century, see Willi Paul Adams, *The First American Constitutions: Republican Ideology and the Making of the State Constitutions in the Revolutionary Era* (Chapel Hill, 1980); J. G. A. Pocock, *The Machiavellian Moment: Florentine Political Thought and the Atlantic Republican Tradition* (Princeton, 1975); Jack Rakove,

The Beginnings of National Politics: An Interpretative History of the Continental Congress (New York, 1979); Forrest McDonald, *Novus Ordo Seclorum: The Intellectual Origins of the Constitution* (Lawrence, 1985); Patricia Bonomi, *Under the Cope of Heaven: Religion, Society, and Politics in Colonial America* (New York, 1986); Jackson T. Main, *The Antifederalists* (Chapel Hill, 1961); Joyce Appleby, *Capitalism and a New Social Order: The Republican Vision of the 1790s* (New York, 1984); Linda K. Kerber, *Women of the Republic: Intellect and Ideology in Revolutionary America* (Chapel Hill, 1980); and Mary Beth Norton, *Liberty's Daughters: The Revolutionary Experience of American Women, 1750–1800* (Boston, 1980).

On the history of the fine arts, Gilbert Chase, *America's Music* (Urbana, 1987), has the fullest coverage of colonial music. For painting, see Virgil Barker, *American Painting*, and the first two volumes of James T. Flexner's highly readable history, *First Flowers of Our Wilderness* (Boston, 1947) and *America's Old Masters* (New York, 1981, c. 1939).

The best survey of the colonial experience in a single volume remains Daniel Boorstin, *The Americans* (New York, 1958), the first and best of the three volumes sharing that title that examine all of American culture. Two figures who do not easily fall under my organizing rubrics are examined in John C. Miller, *Alexander Hamilton* (New York, 1959), and Eric Foner, *Tom Paine and Revolutionary America* (New York, 1976).

Part II: A Sectional Culture, 1815–1901

Phillips Bradley has edited the standard American edition of Alexis de Tocqueville, *Democracy in America* (2 vols., New York, 1965, c. 1945); Henry Commager edited a convenient abridged edition, (New York, 1946). I took most of my data from George W. Pierson's pioneering *Tocqueville and Beaumont in America* (New York, 1938). James T. Schleifer, *The Making of Tocqueville's 'Democracy in America'* (Chapel Hill, 1980), adds important new material.

Marvin Meyers has focused on the political culture in *The Jacksonian Persuasion* (Stanford, 1957). Dirk J. Struik, *Yankee Science in the Making* (Boston, 1948), is an exemplary regional study. For the economic background, Bray Hammond, *Banks and Politics in America from the Revolution to the Civil War* (Princeton, 1957), is essential, while Thomas P. Govan, *Nicholas Biddle* (Chicago, 1959), humanizes a man too often treated only as a symbol. Joseph L. Blau, ed., *Social Theories of Jacksonian Democracy* (New York, 1947), is a standard collection of primary sources. The most important contributors to Whig culture emerge most clearly in Samuel Flagg Bemis' two volumes, *John Quincy Adams and the Foundations of American Foreign Policy* (New York, 1949), and *John Quincy Adams and the Union* (New York, 1956); and Glyndon G. Van Deusen,

William Henry Seward (New York, 1967). The most recent sectional overview is Merrill D. Peterson, *The Great Triumvirate: Webster, Clay and Calhoun* (New York, 1987).

For the larger cultural history, Russel Nye is the leading authority, in *The Cultural Life of the New Nation, 1776–1830* (New York, 1960), and *Society and Culture in America, 1830–1860* (New York, 1974). In the arts, the first important work, William Dunlap's *History of the Rise and Progress of the Arts of Design* (New York, 1969, c. 1834) continues to be crucial; Dunlap was an important figure himself in several areas. Neil Harris, *The Artist in American Society: The Formative Years, 1790–1860* (New York, 1966), has long been the standard modern study. It should be supplemented by Lillian Miller, *Patrons and Patriotism: The Encouragement of the Fine Arts in the United States, 1790–1860* (Chicago, 1966); and James T. Flexner's final two volumes, *The Light of Distant Skies* (New York, 1954), and *That Wilder Image* (New York, 1962).

For many writers, the best place to begin is with Perry Miller's once-standard textbook, *Major Writers of America* (New York, 1962). The best place for students of the novel looking for more detail and context remains Alexander Cowie, *The Rise of the American Novel* (New York, 1948). Larzer Ziff, *Literary Democracy* (New York, 1981), offers a briefer, more generalized survey. The most influential thematic studies, have been Henry Nash Smith, *Virgin Land* (Cambridge, 1950); Richard W. B. Lewis, *The American Adam* (Chicago, 1955); Richard Chase, *The American Novel and Its Tradition* (London, 1958); and A. N. Kaul, *The American Vision* (New Haven, 1962). William Hedges, *Washington Irving* (Baltimore, 1965), studies Irving's career to 1832 and brings out important themes that earlier scholars passed over. Arthur Hobson Quinn began modern Poe studies with *Edgar Allan Poe* (New York, 1941); the best recent contextual study is Kenneth Silverman, *Edgar A. Poe* (New York, 1991).

Literary studies have gone through major changes during the past twenty-five years, as the final section of this volume indicates. One way to experience the changes would be to read Lawrence Buell, *New England Literary Culture from Revolution through Renaissance* (Cambridge, 1986); proceed to David S. Reynolds, *Beneath the American Renaissance: The Subversive Imagination in the Age of Emerson and Melville* (New York, 1988); examine Martha Banta, *Imaging American Women* (New York, 1987), and Mary Kelley, *Private Woman, Public Stage* (New York, 1984); then review two works cited earlier, Cathy N. Davidson, *Revolution and the Word*, and Jane Tompkins, *Sensational Designs*.

Religious revivalism has been the subject of a great many books and shorter studies. For most students the following three books will provide an adequate survey of this complex subject: Whitney R. Cross, *The Burned-Over District* (Ithaca, 1950); Bernard Weisberger, *They Gathered at the River* (Boston, 1958); and William McLoughlin, *Modern Revivalism* (New York, 1959). Robert Abzug has rethought the whole context of religion and politics in *Cosmos Crumbing:*

American Reform and the Religious Imagination (New York, 1994). On Harriet Beecher Stowe, Forrest Wilson, *Crusader in Crinoline* (Philadelphia, 1941), is far better than its title would lead one to expect; for the intellectual side, see Alice C. Crozier, *The Novels of Harriet Beecher Stowe* (New York, 1969). Kathryn Kish Sklar, *Catherine Beecher* (New Haven, 1973), has made Harriet's sister even better known among contemporary students. Thomas F. Gossett, *Uncle Tom's Cabin and American Culture* (Dallas, 1985), deserves to circulate far more widely than it has; it is a broad, major cultural study by a prize-winning student of race in America.

Abolitionism has received wide attention, and many of the books remain useful. Louis Filler, *The Crusade against Slavery, 1830–1860* (New York, 1960), is one standard survey. On specific individuals, see especially Jonathan C. Messerli, *Horace Mann* (New York, 1972); Robert H. Abzug, *Passionate Liberator: Theodore Dwight Weld and The Dilemma of Reform* (New York, 1980); and Bertram Wyatt-Brown, *Lewis Tappan and the Evangelical War against Slavery* (Cleveland, 1969).

The best collection of primary sources on Transcendentalism, with an excellent introductory essay, is Perry Miller, ed., *The Transcendentalists* (Cambridge, 1950). The best brief secondary source is Paul Boller, *American Transcendentalism, 1830–1860* (New York, 1974). Octavius Brooks Frothingham, *Transcendentalism in New England* (New York, 1959, c. 1876) was a pioneering study that remains important for European philosophical background. Also useful in this area are the more recent essays of René Wellek, collected in *Confrontations* (Princeton, 1965), and Arthur O. Lovejoy, included in *Reason, the Understanding and Time* (Baltimore, 1961). For the religious environment out of which most Transcendentalists emerged, see William R. Hutchison, *The Transcendentalist Ministers* (New Haven, 1959).

Scholars of Southern literature and culture often write as if their region were unjustly neglected. In fact, Southerners were neither original nor especially conscious culturally when compared to New Englanders; despite the major Southern writers who emerged during the twentieth century, circumstances have changed little among the general population even now. Nevertheless, the nagging irritation has led to some worthwhile scholarship, in efforts to recover whatever activity did take place. The three who have done the most are Jay B. Hubbell, *The South in American Literature, 1607–1900* (Durham, 1954); Richard Beale Davis, *Intellectual Life in the Colonial South, 1585–1783*, already mentioned, and *Intellectual Life in Jefferson's Virginia* (Chapel Hill, 1964); and Michael O'Brien, *Intellectual Life in Antebellum Charleston* (Knoxville, 1986), and *Rethinking the South* (Baltimore, 1988).

Other scholars have chosen court records or the diaries of slaveowners. Bertram Wyatt-Brown, *Southern Honor* (New York, 1982), is a major effort in this regard, but see also Drew Faust, *A Sacred Circle* (Baltimore, 1977), and

James Henry Hammond and the Old South (Baton Rouge, 1982); and Carol Bleser, *The Hammonds of Redcliffe* (New York, 1981), and *Secret and Sacred: The Diaries of James Henry Hammond* (New York, 1988). The most accessible study of the chief Southern leader is still Margaret Coit, *John C. Calhoun* (Boston, 1950).

As my own organization indicates, Audubon in many ways has been a more important if untypical Southerner. Francis H. Herrick, *Audubon the Naturalist* (2 vols., New York, 1968, c. 1938) is the definitive modern treatment, while Alexander B. Adams, *John James Audubon* (New York, 1966), is the best current introduction for most readers.

The coming of the Civil War, the fighting of it, and the long-term results of it have been growth areas for culture studies since the 1950s. Eric Foner is the most eminent modern student here, with *Free Soil, Free Labor, Free Men: The Ideology of the Republican Party before the Civil War* (New York, 1970), *Politics and Ideology in the Age of the Civil War* (New York, 1980), and *Reconstruction: America's Unfinished Revolution, 1863–1877* (New York, 1988). Daniel W. Howe, *The Political Culture of the American Whigs* (Chicago, 1979), restudies the conservatives. James M. McPherson, *Battle Cry of Freedom* (New York, 1988), is a best-selling retelling of the war itself. William S. McFeely, *Frederick Douglass* (New York, 1991), recovers the best-known black involved. The rather odd literary consequences of the war come through best in Edmund Wilson, *Patriotic Gore* (New York, 1982), and Daniel Aaron, *The Unwritten War* (New York, 1973). George Frederickson, *The Inner Civil War* (New York, 1965), and *The Black Image in the White Mind* (New York, 1971), are the works most like this one in terms of strategy and organization.

The best study of the West as an intellectual experience is William H. Goetzmann, *Exploration and Empire* (New York, 1966). Henry Nash Smith, *Virgin Land* (Boston, 1950), and Edwin Fussell, *Frontier* (Princeton, 1965), provide essential literary supplements. Richard W. Slotkin, *Regeneration through Violence: The Mythology of the American Frontier, 1600–1860* (Middletown, 1973), is a radical reading, the first of three volumes, with a clear application to the events of the 1960s. I have unjustly neglected specific work on the Far West; to fill in this gap, see Kevin Starr, *Americans and the California Dream* (New York, 1973), *Inventing the Dream: California Through the Progressive Era* (New York, 1985), and *Material Dreams: Southern California Through the 1920s* (New York, 1990).

On individual figures, see Robert W. Johannsen, *Stephen A. Douglas* (New York, 1973), and Stephen B. Oates, *With Malice Toward None: The Life of Abraham Lincoln* (New York, 1977), for politics. In literature, the best places to begin are still Randall Stewart, *Nathaniel Hawthorne* (New Haven, 1961); Lawrance Thompson, *Melville's Quarrel with God* (Princeton, 1952); and Justin Kaplan, *Mr. Clemens and Mark Twain* (New York, 1966).

Part III: The Northern Nation: From Religious to Capitalist Democracy, 1865–1917

Perry Miller edited what is still the best collection of primary sources for the years after the Civil War in *American Thought: Civil War to World War I* (New York, 1954). On Darwinism, R. Jackson Wilson, ed., *Darwinism and the American Intellectual* (Homewood, 1967), is central, as is F. O. Matthiessen, *The James Family* (New York, 1947).

One would normally assume that the climate of Darwinism was long gone from American culture, but it has instead not only had lingering consequences of itself, it has been a vital if sometimes straw-filled enemy for reformers ever since. The place to begin is Robert C. Bannister, *Social Darwinism: Science and Myth in Anglo-American Social Thought* (Philadelphia, 1979), with long-range consequences appearing in *Sociology and Scientism: The American Quest for Objectivity, 1880–1940* (Chapel Hill, 1987). The debate has in recent years become entangled with controversies concerning sociobiology and the nature/nurture squabbles of the Reagan years. Compare Dorothy Ross, *The Origins of American Social Science* (New York, 1991), with Carl N. Degler, *In Search of Human Nature: The Decline and Revival of Darwinism in American Social Thought* (New York, 1991).

Work on modern business history has also passed through several phases. Peter Collier and David Horowitz began as 1960s radicals and headed toward the right over the years. *The Rockefellers* (New York, 1976) and *The Fords* (New York, 1987) give them plenty of targets along the way; both books are exceedingly well-written. Joseph F. Wall, *Andrew Carnegie* (New York, 1970), is basically sympathetic, one of several lengthy volumes that have done much to rehabilitate capitalists as builders of society rather than destroyers. Ron Chernow, *The House of Morgan* (New York, 1990), is now the best introduction to the banking history of the period.

On pragmatism, Milton R. Konvitz and Gail Kennedy have edited a useful collection of primary sources, *The American Pragmatists* (New York, 1960). Studies of technical issues have proliferated, while biography suffered until recently. Philip P. Wiener, *Evolution and the Founders of Pragmatism* (Cambridge, 1949), was an early survey; Morton White, *Social Thought in America* (New York, 1976, c. 1949), is a bit more attentive to larger cultural concerns. Joseph L. Brent, *Charles Sanders Peirce* (Bloomington, 1992), is now the standard study of Peirce. Jacques Barzun has given us a much-needed book on William James, *A Stroll with William James* (New York, 1983), which is far clearer and more useful than most longer works. Neil Coughlan, *Young John Dewey* (Chicago, 1975), also has good material on George Herbert Mead. Robert Westbrook, *John Dewey and American Democracy* (Ithaca, 1991), is now standard for the entire life. I have sketches of both Dewey and Mead, among other progressives, in *Ministers of Reform: The Progressives' Achievement in American Civilization, 1889–1920* (New York, 1982). Two large-scale general examinations are Morton Keller, *Affairs of State* (Cambridge, 1977), and Alfred D. Chandler, *The Visible Hand* (Cambridge, 1977), on business behavior. R. Jackson Wilson, *In Quest of Community* (New York, 1968), is a brief look at several figures in terms of their long-range communal goals.

Several scholars have lately focused on particular universities or cities. Bruce Kuklick, *The Rise of American Philosophy* (New Haven, 1977) is actually a study of Harvard, exemplary except for its slighting of Chicago and especially Dewey. Darnell Rucker, *The Chicago Pragmatists* (Minneapolis, 1969), partially fills the gap. Thomas Bender, *New York Intellect* (New York, 1987), takes the mental life of that city into the early twentieth century.

Much of my material on early American modernism and its context is now documented in *American Salons: Encounters with European Modernism, 1885–1917* (New York, 1993). More specialized general works include Larzer Ziff's literary history *The American 1890s* (New York, 1966); Nathan G. Hale, Jr., *Freud and the Americans* (New York, 1971); and Henry May, *The End of American Innocence* (New York, 1959). David Perkins, *A History of Modern Poetry* (2 vols., Cambridge, 1976, 1987), is an invaluable set. I have published a collection of primary sources in *The Superfluous Men: Conservative Critics of American Culture, 1900–1945* (Austin, 1977).

Biographies abound of key figures in the arts. Stanley Weintraub, *Whistler* (New York, 1974), is a worthy study of the painter who set many of the precedents for modernists. James R. Mellow, *Charmed Circle* (New York, 1974), retells all the Gertrude Stein anecdotes. Hemingway seems to have an annual biographer; the shrewdest on most issues is Kenneth Lynn, *Hemingway* (New York, 1987). Humphrey Carpenter, *A Serious Character* (Boston, 1988), covers Pound in detail, whereas most other volumes devoted to Pound pursue special political or poetic agendas. Lyndall Gordon has examined T. S. Eliot in two tidy volumes, *Eliot's Early Years* (New York, 1977), and *Eliot's New Life* (New York, 1988).

Two large-scale volumes have redefined the nature of cultural studies in the black community. Lawrence W. Levine, *Black Culture and Black Consciousness* (New York, 1977), and Leon F. Litwack, *Been in the Storm So Long* (New York, 1979), are now the places to begin, supplemented by the briefer work of Robert Toll, *Blacking Up: The Minstrel Show in Nineteenth Century America* (New York, 1974). John Blassingame, *Black New Orleans, 1860–1880* (Chicago, 1973), was a crucial source. Louis R. Harlan, *Booker T. Washington* (New York, 1972, 1983), is the best recent biography of any black leader. C. Vann Woodward, *The Strange Career of Jim Crow* (New York, 1974, c. 1955), is a history of segregation.

Nat Henthoff and Nat Shapiro, eds., have collected a fine group of primary sources for the history of jazz in *Hear Me Talkin' to Ya* (New York, 1955). James Lincoln Collier, *The Making of Jazz* (Boston, 1978), will be the best place for most general readers to begin any study of jazz. Fanatics will want to continue on to Gunther Schuller, *Early Jazz* (New York, 1968), and *The Swing Era* (New York, 1989). There are now a great many "autobiographies" and oral histories of jazz available, most of them problematic in terms of useful historical information.

Part IV: A National Culture, 1901–1941

Many of the works cited in the preceding section are useful for this one as well.

For most students wishing a conventional political approach to the period, three volumes of the New American Nation series are central: George Mowry, *The Era of Theodore Roosevelt, 1900–1912* (New York, 1958); Arthur Link, *Woodrow Wilson and the Progressive Era, 1910–1917* (New York, 1954); and William E. Leuchtenberg, *Franklin D. Roosevelt and the New Deal, 1932–1940* (New York, 1963). To fill in the many gaps these works leave on cultural subjects, see my *Ministers of Reform* and Paul Boyer, *Urban Masses and Moral Order in America, 1820–1920* (Cambridge, 1978), for the early years; William E. Leuchtenberg, *The Perils of Prosperity, 1914–1932* (Chicago, 1958), for the twenties; and Richard H. Pells, *Radical Visions and American Dreams* (New York, 1973) for the 1930s.

Culturally speaking, this was the age of the great outburst of literary activity, with music and other arts not far behind. It also produced an astonishing number of autobiographies that remain useful and at least sporadically in print. For progressives, see especially Lincoln Steffens, *Autobiography* (New York, 1931), for a man who headed left, and Albert Jay Nock, *The Memoirs of a Superfluous Man* (New York, 1943), for one who headed right. Brand Whitlock, *Forty Years of It* (New York, 1914), expresses the current level of optimism, while Frederic C. Howe, *Confessions of a Reformer* (New York, 1925), expresses postwar gloom. Alice Hamilton left a tactful autobiography, *Exploring the Dangerous Trades* (Boston, 1985, c. 1943), but a better source for her ideas is Barbara Sicherman, *Alice Hamilton: A Life in Letters* (Cambridge, 1984). Jane Addams, *Twenty Years at Hull-House* (New York, 1910), may well be the best known of them all.

Those whose careers were most active during the 1920s were even more concerned with themselves. Malcolm Cowley, *Exile's Return* (New York, 1952, c. 1934), provides the best overview of the most people, with some effort at systematizing the experience. Kay Boyle and Robert McAlmon, *Being Geniuses Together* (New York, 1968), comes in second. For a view of Hemingway and Fitzgerald in their brief primes, Morley Callaghan, *That Summer in Paris* (New York, 1963), is the intelligent assessment of an underrated Canadian novelist. Among publishers, Gorham Munson, *The Awakening Twenties* (Baton Rouge, 1985), and Matthew Josephson, *Life among the Surrealists* (New York, 1962), collaborated and then feuded, not an unusual sequence. Van Wyck Brooks gathered three volumes together for *An Autobiography* (New York, 1965), a work more useful than his frequently vacuous literary histories. Samuel Putnam, *Paris Was Our Mistress* (New York, 1947), and John Glassco, *Memoirs of Montparnasse* (Toronto, 1970), have evocative sidelights. Gertrude Stein's *The Autobiography of Alice B. Toklas* (New York, 1933), is not to be trusted on any subject, starting with its title, but retains an ineffable charm.

The other arts contributed as well. Man Ray's *Self Portrait* (Boston, 1963), is one of the best by any standard, especially useful for painting and photography. George Antheil never grew up in several ways, as he seems to admit in the title of his *Bad Boy of Music* (New York, 1945); Virgil Thomson did, and *Virgil Thomson* (New York, 1967), also contributed material on Gertrude Stein. John Houseman, *Unfinished Business* (New York, 1989) condenses three long volumes into one, all useful for the drama, and especially the 1930s. Eileen Simpson, *Poets in Their Youth* (New York, 1982), covers the Berryman–Lowell–Tate–Gordon–Blackmur circle as it formed in the 1930s, and is one of the best literary memoirs ever.

Biography has subsequently flourished. Frank Freidel's *Franklin D. Roosevelt* (Boston, 1990) covers one politician throughout half of the century; Justin Kaplan's *Lincoln Steffens* (New York, 1974) covers leftist journalism for almost as long. Louis Sheaffer, *O'Neill* (2 vols., New York, 1988, 1990, c. 1968, 1973), is invaluable on drama. Ronald Steel, *Walter Lippmann and the American Century* (New York, 1980), covers the comparable figure in journalism. The coming fad seems to be for studies of Alfred Stieglitz and Georgia O'Keeffe: Benita Eisler covers them both in *O'Keeffe and Stieglitz* (New York, 1991); Roxana Robinson studies *Georgia O'Keeffe* (New York, 1989), and Sue Davidson Lowe *Stieglitz* (New York, 1983). William I. Homer offers more focused studies in *Alfred Stieglitz and the American Avant-Garde* (Boston, 1977) and *Alfred Stieglitz and the Photo-Secession* (Boston, 1983).

Among the best literary biographies are these: Kim Townsend, *Sherwood Anderson* (Boston, 1987); James Woodress, *Willa Cather* (Lincoln, 1987); Joan Richardson, *Wallace Stevens* (2 vols., New York, 1986, 1988); Richard S. Kennedy, *Dreams in the Mirror* (New York, 1980), on E. E. Cummings; Charles Molesworth, *Marianne Moore* (New York, 1990); Paul Mariani, *William Carlos Williams* (New York, 1981); John Unterecker, *Voyager* (New York, 1969), on Hart Crane; Virginia S. Carr, *Dos Passos* (New York, 1984); James Hoopes, *Van*

Wyck Brooks (Amherst, 1977). As the newer writers of the 1930s and 1940s develop, see Ian Hamilton, *Robert Lowell* (New York, 1982), and Virginia S. Carr, *The Lonely Hunter* (New York, 1975), on Carson McCullers.

In the other arts, see Edward Maisel, *Charles T. Griffes* (New York, 1984, c. 1943) on one of our most unjustly neglected composers; Frank Rossiter, *Charles Ives and His America* (New York, 1975), on our most original; Aaron Copland and Vivian Perlis, *Copland* (2 vols., New York, 1984, 1989), on one who went from obscurity to fame; and Charles Schwartz, *Gershwin* (Indianapolis, 1973), on the one whose works almost everyone can hum, however unknowingly. Neil Baldwin, *Man Ray* (New York, 1988), covers photography especially, while Martin Duberman, *Paul Robeson* (New York, 1989), covers the most important black in film, theater, and voice. Donald L. Miller, *Lewis Mumford* (New York, 1989), deals with the most important cultural critic.

The history of architecture has emerged into its own in recent years. William H. Jordy, in volumes three and four of the series *American Buildings and Their Architects* (New York, 1972), offers a useful overview; Alan Gowans, *Styles and Types of North American Architecture* (New York, 1992) takes a quite different approach. For conservative design at the start of the century, Paul R. Baker has an entertaining introduction in *Stanny* (New York, 1989), on Stanford White. H. Allen Brooks, *The Prairie School* (New York, 1972), looks at Frank Lloyd Wright and his contemporaries, while Robert C. Twombly, *Frank Lloyd Wright* (New York, 1975), remains the best-balanced of the many Wright biographies. Thomas S. Hines is now the most eminent of the new generation of students of the fine arts, as in *Richard Neutra and the Search for Modern Architecture* (New York, 1982). Linda D. Henderson conquers both physics and math in *The Fourth Dimension and Non-Euclidean Geometry in Modern Art* (Princeton, 1983), a lengthy study broader in scope than its title might suggest.

General literary histories have proliferated without replacing old standards. Alfred Kazin, *On Native Grounds* (New York, 1942), and Daniel Aaron, *Writers on the Left* (New York, 1961), remain useful, as does Jay Martin, *Harvests of Change* (Englewood Cliffs, 1967). Albert Gelpi, *A Coherent Splendor: The American Poetic Renaissance, 1910–1950* (New York, 1987), stands next to David Perkins' longer history of modernist poetry, already cited. Thomas Schatz, *The Genius of the System* (New York, 1988), is now the best way to enter the field of Hollywood film. I tried to cover progressives in the arts, especially Frank Lloyd Wright and Charles Ives, in *Ministers of Reform*, and modernists in *American Salons*, but those works do not cover the 1920s, and Frederick J. Hoffman, *The Twenties* (New York, 1962), remains useful.

On black cultural life, in addition to Duberman's *Robeson*, see David L. Lewis, *When Harlem Was in Vogue* (New York, 1981), the best of several studies of the Harlem Renaissance, and Arnold Rampersad, *The Life of Lang-ston Hughes* (2 vols., New York, 1986, 1988), for its most famous poet. James Lincoln Collier has covered those jazz musicians that the writers found dis-tressing in *Louis Armstrong* (New York, 1983), and *Duke Ellington* (New York, 1987).

O'Neill aside, work in theater history has lagged behind other areas, but see Joanne Bentley, *Hallie Flanagan* (New York, 1988), and Wendy Smith, *Real Life Drama: The Group Theater and America, 1931–1940* (New York, 1990).

General studies on women's issues are also becoming more common. Among the best are Eleanor Flexner, *Century of Struggle: The Women's Rights Move-ment in the United States* (New York, 1970, c. 1959); Anne Firor Scott, *The Southern Lady from Pedestal to Politics* (Chicago, 1970); Gwendolyn Wright, *Moralism and the Model Home* (Chicago, 1980); and Dolores Hayden, *The Grand Domestic Revolution: A History of Feminist Designs for American Homes, Neighborhoods, and Cities* (Cambridge, 1981).

William Faulkner is in a class by himself, for many reasons. Biographies of him have started appearing, several of extraordinary dullness. Many of the critical studies are unreadable to normal folk who just find him a great writer. Start with either David Minter, *William Faulkner* (Baltimore, 1980), or Michael Millgate, *The Achievement of William Faulkner* (New York, 1966), and then if puzzlement remains, consult the relevant chapters of Cleanth Brooks, *William Faulkner: The Yoknapatawpha Country* (New Haven, 1963), and *William Faulkner: Toward Yoknapatawpha and Beyond* (New Haven, 1978). Brooks always had a rather protective view of both Faulkner and the South, which skeptics can ignore while profiting from his immense learning and critical patience.

The subject of industrial design is becoming increasingly important as a subject in cultural history, bordering as it does on studies of business on the one hand and economic power in society on the other. Two books are especially sensitive in handling the complexities: Roland Marchand, *Advertising the Amer-ican Dream* (Berkeley, 1985), and Jeffrey Meikle, *Twentieth Century Limited: Industrial Design in America, 1925–1939* (Philadelphia, 1979).

Finally, the intellectual migration is slowly receiving the attention it also deserves. Bernard Bailyn and Donald Fleming edited one pioneering volume, *The Intellectual Migration* (Cambridge, 1969), which appeared almost simul-taneously with Laura Fermi, *Illustrious Immigrants* (Chicago, 1971, c. 1968). H. Stuart Hughes then contributed *The Sea Change: The Migration of Social Thought, 1930–1965* (New York, 1975). Lewis A. Coser brought a great deal of additional information together in *Refugee Scholars in America* (New Haven, 1984), and individual studies are slowly appearing. One of the best is Elizabeth Young-Bruehl, *Hannah Arendt* (New Haven, 1982).

Part V: A Cosmopolitan Culture, 1941–Present

For the history of the civil rights movement, the best place to begin is Richard Kluger, *Simple Justice* (New York, 1976). The role of Martin Luther King, Jr., is the focus of David J. Garrow, *Bearing the Cross: Martin Luther King, Jr., and the Southern Christian Leadership Conference* (New York, 1986), and Taylor Branch, *Parting the Waters: America in the King Years, 1954–1963* (New York, 1988), the first of two projected volumes. William Chafe, *Civilities and Civil Rights* (New York, 1980) is a rare example of successful contemporary history. Richard Gid Powers gives the background on J. Edgar Hoover and the FBI in *Secrecy and Power* (New York, 1987). Many primary sources are most conveniently available in Francis L. Broderick et al, eds., *Black Protest Thought in the Twentieth Century* (Indianapolis, 1965).

Largely because of controversy concerning the Cold War and Vietnam, the literature concerning post–World War II foreign policy is now as proliferated as nuclear weapons and loose rhetoric. A good overview is Stephen Ambrose, *Rise to Globalism* (New York, 1991, c. 1971), regularly revised. The two specialists I have found most reliable are John L. Gaddis, in *The United States and Origins of the Cold War, 1941–1947* (New York, 1972), *Russia, the Soviet Union and the United States* (New York, 1978), *Strategies of Containment* (New York, 1982), and *The Long Peace* (New York, 1987); and Lloyd C. Gardner, *Architects of Illusion: Men and Ideas in American Foreign Policy, 1941–1949* (Chicago, 1970), *A Covenant with Power: America and World Order from Wilson to Reagan* (New York, 1984), and *Approaching Vietnam, From World War II through Dienbienphu, 1941–1954* (New York, 1988).

The most illuminating memoirs in terms of foreign policy have been Dean Acheson, *Present at the Creation* (New York, 1969), George F. Kennan, *Memoirs* (2 vols., Boston, 1967, 1972), Henry Kissinger, *The White House Years* (Boston, 1979), and *Years of Upheaval* (Boston, 1982), Townsend Hoopes, *The Limits of Intervention* (New York, 1973), and George Ball, *The Past Has Another Pattern* (New York, 1982). On Asia, I found Michael Schaller, *The United States and China in the Twentieth Century* (New York, 1979), the best place to begin, but Theodore H. White and Annalee Jacoby, *Thunder out of China* (New York, 1946), and Ely J. Kahn, *The China Hands* (New York, 1975), are essential for details. David Halberstam, *The Best and the Brightest* (New York, 1972), and Walter Isaacson and Evan Thomas, *The Wise Men* (New York, 1986), cover the individuals who were in and out of the White House for an extraordinarily long run of influence. Isaacson then published *Kissinger* (New York, 1992), one of the more balanced treatments of a man who seems to invite unbalanced ones.

Other books that deserve mention are Jonathan Kwitny, *Endless Enemies* (New York, 1984); George C. Herring, *America's Longest War: The United*

States and Vietnam, 1950–1975 (New York, 1986, c. 1979); Walter La Feber, *Inevitable Revolutions: The United States in Central America* (New York, 1984); and Strobe Talbott, *Deadly Gambits: The Reagan Administration and the Stalemate in Nuclear Arms Control* (New York, 1984), and *The Master of the Game: Paul Nitze and the Nuclear Peace* (New York, 1988).

In an age when deconstruction has run through the academy like a plague of the mumps, sterilizing all but the healthiest of scholars, literary history has fallen on hard times. Few people seem to read many primary sources, fewer still have any interest in seeing them in context. Even works that purport to be historical frequently are not, substituting opinions about lists for actual criticism. Honorable exceptions would include Chester E. Eisinger, *Fiction of the Forties* (Chicago, 1963), Tony Tanner, *City of Words: American Fiction 1950–1970* (London, 1971), and Morris Dickstein, *Gates of Eden* (New York, 1977). Of the collaborative histories, the most useful is Daniel Hoffman, ed., *Harvard Guide to Contemporary American Writing* (Cambridge, 1979), although it is uneven. Frederick R. Karl has made a heroic effort to be comprehensive in *American Fictions 1940–1980* (New York, 1983). But, like many voyagers in American fiction, you have to light out for the territories on your own. One of the few to come back alive has been Brian Boyd, *Vladimir Nabokov* (2 vols., Princeton, 1990, 1991). Albert E. Stone has ranged even farther afield in *The Return of Nat Turner: History, Literature, and Cultural Politics in Sixties America* (Athens, 1992). A historian can only sigh and wish literature professors would return to doing this sort of work.

In the history of the fine arts, I have mapped the opening of the century in *American Salons: Encounters with European Modernism 1885–1917* (New York, 1993). Milton Brown has told *The Story of the Armory Show* (New York, 1963) and Dickran Tashjian coined the term *Skyscraper Primitives* to tell the story of *Dada and the American Avant-Garde* (Middletown, 1975); he followed it with *William Carlos Williams and the American Scene, 1920–1940* (New York, 1978), oddly titled since it concerns the artistic scene far more than Williams himself or his work. Adele Heller and Lois Rudnick have edited a remarkably useful collaborative volume, *1915: The Cultural Moment* (New Brunswick, 1991), which contains separate essays by well-known experts on a wide range of topics.

One of the best historical sources for the 1930s as well as later is now Steven Naifeh and Gregory W. Smith, *Jackson Pollock* (New York, 1989), a massive work. Erika Doss, *Benton, Pollock, and the Politics of Modernism* (Chicago, 1991), supplements it in places. David Revill, *Roaring Silence: John Cage* (London, 1992), fills in musical details. The essential institution outside New York is Black Mountain College; see Martin Duberman, *Black Mountain* (New York, 1972) for a traditional history, and Mary Emma Harris, *The Arts at Black Mountain College* (Cambridge, 1987), for pictures and many new details. As many of these figures head into post-modernism, the best critical guide is Marjorie Perloff, *The Poetics of Indeterminacy, Rimbaud to Cage* (Princeton, 1981). As they fall off the deep end, follow the arc in David Lehman, *Signs of the Times: Deconstruction and the Fall of Paul de Man* (New York, 1992, c. 1991).

For recent art history, see especially the three-volume work of Irving Sandler, *The Triumph of American Painting* (New York, 1970), *The New York School* (New York, 1978), and *American Art of the 1960s* (New York, 1988). Serge Guilbaut, *How New York Stole the Idea of Modern Art* (Chicago, 1983), takes politics more seriously than most art historians. Donald B. Kuspit, *Clement Greenberg* (Madison, 1979), studies a leading critic.

Calvin Tomkins is one of the most entertaining as well as perceptive writers on art. *The Bride and the Bachelors* (New York, 1968, c. 1965) goes back to Duchamp; the story continues in *Off the Wall: Robert Rauschenberg and the Art World of Our Time* (New York, 1980). *Post- to Neo-: The Art World of the 1980s* (New York, 1988) is unfortunately only fragmentary. Understandably, history gets thinner as it approaches the present, but see Corinne Robins, *The Pluralist Era: American Art 1968–1981* (New York, 1984), and Henry M. Sayre, *The Object of Performance: The American Avant-Garde since 1970* (Chicago, 1989).

New York intellectuals have always regarded themselves as the most important figures in American culture and left a vast trove of published primary sources to help epigones wishing to participate in such accumulations of wisdom. The best autobiographies are William Barrett, *The Truants* (New York, 1982), and Lionel Abel, *The Intellectual Follies* (New York, 1984). In chronological order, analyses include: James B. Gilbert, *Writers and Partisans* (New York, 1968); William L. O'Neill, *A Better World* (New York, 1982); Richard H. Pells, *The Liberal Mind in a Conservative Age* (New York, 1985); Alexander Bloom, *Prodigal Sons* (New York, 1986); Terry A. Cooney, *The Rise of the New York Intellectuals* (Madison, 1986); and Alan M. Wald, *The New York Intellectuals* (Chapel Hill, 1987). Many of these works are written from outspoken political positions and of course in several instances range rather far from the city itself, but the same names keep recurring and the long-term yield of original ideas nothing extraordinary.

The best autobiography to come out from an American liberal has been John Kenneth Galbraith, *A Life in Our Times* (London, 1981). David McCulloch, *Truman* (New York, 1992), is a popular rehabilitation of a president who needs all the help he can get. Thomas K. McCraw, *Prophets of Regulation* (Cambridge, 1984), is a superb survey of four varieties of reform, far more useful than abstract considerations of liberalism. Richard Fox, *Reinhold Niebuhr* (New York, 1985), is the best source for the leading theologian on the left. Alonzo Hamby, *Liberalism and its Challengers, F.D.R. to Reagan* (New York, 1985), is political in focus and generally defensive. Peter Collier and David Horowitz, *The Kennedys* (New York, 1984), is a cold-eyed view from the left. Robert A.

Caro, *The Power Broker: Robert Moses and the Fall of New York* (New York, 1974), explains like no other book the failures of urban liberalism in the most liberal of all urban areas. Caro then moved on to *The Years of Lyndon Johnson* (2 vols. of a projected 4; New York, 1982, 1990), a work of demolition on a grand scale. Robert Dallek is much more appreciative in *Lone Star Rising: Lyndon Johnson and his Times, 1908–1960* (New York, 1991).

American intellectuals have long scorned conservatism as a subject, as well as individual conservatives, unless they could claim a radical past. The years of Nixon, Reagan, and Bush helped to change this situation at least a little: some scholars became more sympathetic; others determined that they had to understand the enemy. Primary sources also became more available. A single publisher, for example, has made available a collection of articles long out of print by one grandfather of the modern right: Charles H. Hamilton, ed., *The State of the Union* (Indianapolis, 1991), the work of Albert Jay Nock; an anthology, *Modern Age: The First Twenty-Five Years* (Indianapolis, 1988), edited by George Panichas, bringing together a vast number of articles from the leading intellectual journal of the traditionalist right; and *New Individualist Review* (Indianapolis, 1981), a complete run of the chief outlet for libertarianism.

Secondary material remains thin but some titles stand out. John P. Diggins, *Up From Communism* (New York, 1975), tracks four major figures from the far left to the far right. George H. Nash studies *The Conservative Intellectual Movement in America, Since 1945* (New York, 1976), although he has a terrible time defining the word *conservative*. J. David Hoeveler, *Watch on the Right* (Madison, 1991), studies eight figures, chiefly journalists. The most eminent gets extended treatment in John B. Judis, *William F. Buckley, Jr.* (New York, 1988). A good many other works give the distinct impression that both authors and subjects spend most of their waking hours watching television, thus largely destroying any capacity to think or create.

It is also something of an open question if most Southern thought should be included under "Conservative" even when it thinks of itself as "liberal." See Daniel J. Singal, *The War Within: From Victorian to Modernist Thought in the South, 1919–1945* (Chapel Hill, 1982); Richard H. King, *A Southern Renaissance: The Cultural Awakening of the American South, 1930–1955* (New York, 1980), and Michael O'Brien, *The Idea of the American South, 1920–1941* (Baltimore, 1979).

The far left talks incessantly about popular culture and the media but at least a few of its members seem to survive the experience with a black sense of humor intact, as many novels over the past several decades bear witness. Judith C. Albert and Stewart E. Albert, eds., *The Sixties Papers* (New York, 1984), and Gerald Howard, ed., *The Sixties* (New York, 1991), provide primary sources. Laurence Veysey, *The Communal Experience: Anarchist and Mystical Communities in Twentieth Century America* (Chicago, 1978, c. 1973), is a very sober account of individuals not so sober in their perceptions of American culture. Vivian Gornick, *The Romance of American Communism* (New York, 1977), and Jessica Mitford, *A Fine Old Conflict* (New York, 1977), humanize leftists who seem stuffed in conventional accounts of the Communist party. Maurice Isserman, *If I Had a Hammer . . .* (New York, 1987), traces the connections between the old left and the new. Richard King, *The Party of Eros* (Chapel Hill, 1972), looks seriously at the sexual radicals. Todd Gitlin, *The Sixties* (New York, 1987), is a sympathetic combination of autobiography, history, and sociology and Allen J. Matusow, *The Unraveling of America* (New York, 1984), a major critique from the left.

The role of science in American culture never gets the attention it deserves, and this situation gets worse as each discipline gets yet more specialized and less able to communicate to a larger public. Daniel J. Kevles, *The Physicists* (New York, 1977) is a rare example of what could be done in terms of the history of the professions. But the most persistent humanizer of science in recent culture is N. Katherine Hayles, in *The Cosmic Web: Scientific Field Models and Literary Strategies in the Twentieth Century* (Ithaca, 1984), *Chaos Bound: Orderly Disorder in Contemporary Literature and Science* (Ithaca, 1990), and *Chaos and Order: Complex Dynamics in Literature and Science* (Chicago, 1991).

Finally, for those who simply wish an overview of recent history, Godfrey Hodgson, *America in Our Time* (New York, 1976), William Chafe, *The Unfinished Journey: America Since World War II* (New York, 1986), Peter N. Carroll, *It Seemed Like Nothing Happened: America in the 1970s* (New Brunswick, 1990, c. 1982), and Lou Cannon, *President Reagan: The Role of a Lifetime* (New York, 1991), are all competent journalism.

Index